POSITIVELY FOURTH
AND MERCER

Stanley Snadowsky and Allan Pepper.

POSITIVELY FOURTH AND MERCER

THE INSIDE STORY OF NEW YORK'S ICONIC MUSIC CLUB, THE BOTTOM LINE

BY ALLAN PEPPER AND BILLY ALTMAN

Backbeat Books
Bloomsbury Publishing Inc, 1359 Broadway, 12th floor, New York, NY 10018, USA
Bloomsbury Publishing Plc, 50 Bedford Square, London, WC1B 3DP, UK
Bloomsbury Publishing Ireland, 29 Earlsfort Terrace, Dublin 2, D02 AY28, Ireland
www.bloomsbury.com

Copyright © 2026 by Allan Pepper

Quotes from Bruce Springsteen interview. Copyright © Bruce Springsteen. Reprinted by permission. International copyright secured. All rights reserved.

Quotes from Jon Landau interview. Copyright © Jon Landau. Reprinted by permission. International copyright secured. All rights reserved.

Photos on pages 30 through 35 © Raymond Ross Archives/CTSIMAGES.

Insert photos by Peter Cunningham © Peter Cunningham Photography.

All rights reserved. No part of this publication may be: (i) reproduced or transmitted in any form, electronic or mechanical, including photocopying, recording or by means of any information storage or retrieval system without prior permission in writing from the publishers; or (ii) used or reproduced in any way for the training, development or operation of artificial intelligence (AI) technologies, including generative AI technologies. The rights holders expressly reserve this publication from the text and data mining exception as per Article 4(3) of the Digital Single Market Directive (EU) 2019/790.

British Library Cataloguing in Publication Information available.

Library of Congress Cataloging-in-Publication Data Available.

Names: Pepper, Allan author | Altman, Billy author
Title: Positively Fourth and Mercer : the inside story of New York's iconic music club, the Bottom Line / by Allan Pepper and Billy Altman.
Description: [1.]. | New York : Backbeat Books / Bloomsbury Publishing, 2025. | Includes index.
Identifiers: LCCN 2025018407 (print) | LCCN 2025018408 (ebook) | ISBN 9781493080144 hardback | ISBN 9781493080151 epub | ISBN 9798765161425 pdf
Subjects: LCSH: Bottom Line (Cabaret : New York, N.Y.) | Concerts–New York (State)–New York–History | Music-halls–New York (State)–New York–History | LCGFT: Oral histories
Classification: LCC ML3477.8.N48 P46 2025 (print) | LCC ML3477.8.N48 (ebook) | DDC 781.640978/7471–dc23/eng/20250721
LC record available at https://lccn.loc.gov/2025018407
LC ebook record available at https://lccn.loc.gov/2025018408

ISBN: HB: 978-1-4930-8014-4
ePDF: 979-8-7651-6142-5
eBook: 978-1-4930-8015-1

Typeset by Deanta Global Publishing Services, Chennai, India.
Printed and bound in the United States of America.

For product safety related questions contact productsafety@bloomsbury.com.

The paper used in this publication meets the minimum requirements of American National Standard for Information Sciences—Permanence of Paper for Printed Library Materials, ANSI/NISO Z39.48-1992.

For Eileen, who stole my heart.
—Allan

To Joyce, always my favorite + 1.
—Billy

"Bill Graham wanted to be Sol Hurok. I wanted to be Bill Graham."

—**ALLAN PEPPER**

"Everything is negotiable. If they tell you it's not, they're lying to you."

—**STANLEY SNADOWSKY**

CONTENTS

Introduction 1

1 A Devotion to Music, and a Devoted Friendship, Grows in Brooklyn 9

2 Two Hundred and Fifty Dollars, a Dream, and a Match Made in the College Library 15

3 Tastes of the Big Time, Bitter and Sweet 37

4 From a Red Garter to a Bottom Line: We Built It, and They Came 51

5 Hells Angels, a Jazz Devil, and New York Dolls 63

6 Born to Kill: The Boss Raises the Bar 75

7 A Punk Priestess, a Rock 'n' Roll Animal, a Country Darling—and a "Formula" for Success 91

8 Meat Loaf Burns, and No-Show Jones Finally Arrives 109

9 The Chairs Hold Firm: Doo-Woppers, Rock 'n' Roll Prisoners, and the Great French Fry Caper 121

10 I Got My Job Through the . . . Village Voice? Working at The Bottom Line 137

11 Leader of the Pack: A Village Smash, a Broadway Bust 153

12 Fast Folks: From the Cool, Cool, Cool to the Hot, Hot, Hot 177

13 From the Bluebird to the Big Apple: A Bunch of Songwriters Sittin' Around Singing 193

14 'Tis the Season: Caroling Carolers, Hallelujah Choruses, and New Year's Hi-Jinx 213

15 Stanley 235

16 The "Bottom Line" Sinks The Bottom Line 243

Epilogue 259
Acknowledgments 265

INTRODUCTION

"Passing through the doors of The Bottom Line could change your life."
—MELANIE MINTZ

From The Cotton Club to Studio 54, New York nightclubs have always been at the mercy of the whims of public taste in terms of both music and atmosphere. And yet The Bottom Line, a cabaret located at the corner of West Fourth and Mercer Streets, just east of Washington Square Park in Greenwich Village, was a notable exception to the city's scene-obsessed club culture. From its opening in February of 1974 until January of 2004, when a dispute with landlord New York University over an expiring lease led to the club's closing just weeks shy of its thirtieth anniversary, The Bottom Line was an oasis of purity for the serious music fan. That's because the 5,000-square-foot club and its 400-seat rectangular performance room—well known to regulars for its long, narrow tables, hardback chairs, and barely traversable aisles—was geared toward listening, a priority symbolized by its impeccable sound system. And throughout its memorable history, the club's co-owners, Allan Pepper and Stanley Snadowsky, steadfastly maintained a clear vision of what a club—a real music club—should be. Childhood friends and fellow Brooklynites who'd gone into business together in the late 1960s as a singularly complementary team—talent booker Pepper an unabashed music enthusiast, and lawyer Snadowsky an attention-to-detail, hard-bargaining deal maker—the two founded the club after several years of promoting acts at popular downtown nightspots like the Village Gate and Folk City. When the club first opened, it was the era of free-form FM radio in New York where, in just a matter of minutes, a listener could go from hearing folk to jazz to rock, and they wanted to do live what those disc jockeys were doing on the air.

That philosophy produced a club that could seamlessly veer from presenting glam punks the New York Dolls to glam country queen Dolly Parton, from bluegrass pioneer Bill Monroe to jazz master Bill Evans, from reserved guitar hero Richard Thompson to wildman rock and roller Little Richard. In so doing, the club's identity was its innate diversity and its adventurous spirit of openness—an openness that was complemented by the special relationships Pepper and Snadowsky developed with artists, managers, agents, radio and record industry executives, their own employees, and, at The Bottom Line, the well over three million patrons who, over the course of its three-decade existence, filled its seats night after night.

Whether on, behind, or in front of its famous stage, The Bottom Line meant many things to many people.

LOUDON WAINWRIGHT (Performer): When you walked into the club to the left, there was a long bar, and early on Allan and Stanley gave us [artists] the welcome to just drop by the club and hang out and see whoever we wanted to see. I don't remember ever being asked to pay for walking into the room. I remember not long after the club opened, leaning at that bar with [fellow singer-songwriter] Paul Siebel, and he said something like, "Well, we finally got a place of our own." For some of us, it really felt like a little clubhouse.

RICHARD BARONE (Performer): The Bottom Line was legendary because any evening that you walked by, there was a line around the block for whoever. And then there was the second show line, which was on the next block. So there was such a buzz about that venue. It was a thrill to play there because it felt like you were in a major concert venue, and other clubs didn't have anywhere near the production value of The Bottom Line. So I fell in love with it right away. But I had already been in love with it as a venue to see artists. And a big point, from a performing point of view, is that you could see the audience very clearly, and that could affect your performance, because you had that intimacy with the audience.

JOHN HIATT (Performer): There wasn't a bad seat, and you felt like when you showed up to play there and saw Allan, you felt like gold. Playing there was about the artistry and the music and the audience, and that's why we do it: To connect with the audience. There's not a lot of clubs over the years that I can think of that had that same vibe. The lighting was just right, because you had some lights on you and some low lights in the audience, so you could see all the way around and all the way back. You just had that feeling as a performer like an arched bridge, and you were trying to meet the audience halfway up in the air there. There was a sense in that place, more than in a lot of other clubs, that the stage was hallowed ground, and you knew that.

BETTY BUCKLEY (Performer): All my favorite artists who played at The Bottom Line, from singer-songwriters to rock and roll bands, besides wanting to be on Broadway, I wanted to be an artist like them, so that seemed to be the place for me to be. It was always anything goes at The Bottom Line. Allan wasn't a guy who had a bar and decided to put music in it. His first love was the music, and he wanted to present it to people. Allan was the antithesis of what I would think of in terms of most club owners that I've known over the years. Allan and Stanley weren't looking for a niche. It wasn't like Studio 54 or CBGB's, or anything in between. The Bottom Line was a place for music, and whatever music was there that night, that's what the club was about for that night. I felt like it was such an honor to be part of their roster. The music was always so eclectic. When you played there, you could think you could do anything you wanted.

SONNY ROLLINS (Performer): My producer was one of those old-time jazz buffs, and he said, "Sonny, why do you want to play at a place like that? You can play at the Village Vanguard or the Blue Note." But at The Bottom Line, because it wasn't a jazz club per se, there were always people coming to see me that I sensed maybe didn't know who I was, and I really liked that. At a jazz club, you'd see the same faces every time you were there, but when you went to The Bottom Line, almost anybody could be there.

BILL SCHEFT (Performer): To me as a comedian, it was always a destination for two reasons. A, because you got your name in the paper, because they ran their ads every week and always put the name of the opening act. Nobody else did that. And B, because of just how comfortable it was there. I don't know why, but I think that people in the audience understood what it meant for a comic to come out before some jazz artist, or some maybe avant-garde musician, or some other act with a solid following. They seemed to understand what that meant.

PAUL SHAFFER (Performer): After Richard Belzer passed away [in 2023], we spread his ashes in front of where The Bottom Line had been. George Carlin's daughter did that in front of several New York nightclubs Carlin had appeared in after he died [in 2008], and Richard's daughter Jessica said she wanted to do the same thing for Richard. Allan explained to me that it might not have been the most appropriate place for it, but it was a nice day, and it felt good to do it.

DAVID FINKLE (Performer): I always admired Allan and Stanley. What really worked for them was the way their strengths were blended. Stanley had great business sense, which I think was also displayed over the years in the way he played poker. Allan was one of the great visionaries in the business; he could sense the possibilities in artists. And The Bottom Line was just the right size. Intimate without being tiny, and no bad sightlines.

DAN DALEY (Performer): I remember when I stopped playing live in the 1980s, and on Bleecker Street there'd be four or five clubs with four or five bands playing every night, like an assembly line, with everyone's equipment outside on the sidewalk as they waited to go play. Allan always told me he'd rather be dark than do that. That was an operational guideline. You knew Allan's heroes were Bill Graham and Steve Paul. He wanted everything to be an event. It didn't have to be a big event, but an event. A Carl Perkins late show, with maybe twelve people in the audience, and Eric Clapton shows up. Even when it wasn't full, those kinds of things would happen.

JIMMY VIVINO (Performer): What struck me about it was that it was a rock club that was kind of like a jazz club in that you could sit down. There were tables and chairs, and so it was a different kind of experience and more of an adult experience. The Bottom Line was a place that you had to get to; you didn't just get in. You didn't just get booked for The Bottom Line. You could get a gig anywhere, but you had to get *to* The Bottom Line. And it was the stepping stone for the next stage, which could be Madison Square Garden or something that big. It really was a prestigious place to play.

MAX WEINBERG (Performer): What I really remember through the years about The Bottom Line was the hospitality of the owners, Allan and Stanley, particularly if you played there, and I'm sure they extended it to their patrons. To me, it must have been like the rock show biz equivalent of the Village Vanguard in its heyday when everybody who was anybody played there and people wanted to be seen there. They were in the mold of the classic impresarios, in that they were more than club owners. They were presenters, which really doesn't exist anymore. New York used to have that legitimate supper club world, places like the Latin Quarter or the Copacabana, in the 1940s, '50s, and early '60s. You look at all the great jazz artists that played The Bottom Line, and, of course, all the great rock bands; I mean, the list is just endless. It's where you wanted to play.

LENNY WHITE (Performer): New York is such a melting pot, and that's what The Bottom Line was as a club. There were the jazz clubs and rock clubs in the city, sure. But The Bottom Line took all kinds of music. There was CBGB's, the Village Vanguard, but they were genre-performing clubs, and The Bottom Line was a multi-genre club. We needed a venue that changed with the music scenes and times, and The Bottom Line was that.

AL KOOPER (Performer): I got along very well with Allan and Stanley, so I'd spend a lot of time down at the club in the afternoons, and if I wanted to see somebody play, I would say to them, "Why don't you book this person?" And they would listen to me! And as a result, a lot of people that I wouldn't have been able to see got booked in there—and they usually did well.

DAVID BROMBERG (Performer): For many years I played the club's anniversary, and they always gave me a gift, maybe a pin of a guitar with precious stones on it or something. It was a really nice thing to do. And when I got married, we had our reception at the club. At one point many years later I asked them if they would find a job for my son when he was out of high school. They did, but Allan and Stanley didn't give him *a* job. They gave him *every* job in the place, one after another, and Allan loved him, and he loved them both. So that was a great thing and was typical of the kind of relationship that we had; they would give my son a job.

DENNIS ELSAS (Radio Host): One of the things that I think Alan and Stanley did, to their credit, was that they were good bookers. You generally didn't go see just one group there. The evening had two, perhaps three, and they weren't all necessarily the same genre. They would mix jazz with rock. That was something special about The Bottom Line. That and also the creature comforts. You could actually use the bathroom there, and you could sit and have a drink or have something to eat—all that, to go along with all the great music.

RICHARD NEER (Radio Host): I remember seeing shows there and sitting in that center, at the little tables, and sitting next to me was Mick Jagger, and I didn't even know it. I just turned around, and there's Mick Jagger. Or it could be

Pete Townshend or Elton John. I mean, in the audience there were celebrities, and it was really the best venue in town to see anybody. And word got around that if you were an artist, and whether you were a veteran performer who was already successful or you were just trying to break through, that was the place to play, and record company people and talent and a & r guys—everybody frequented the place.

MEG GRIFFIN (Radio Host): It's like over all those years, nearly thirty years, how much music I wish I had written down, every show I ever went to there, because it was so many and it was so wide and varied, with every kind of music you could think of. There were a lot of moments when artists were recognized, and you knew they were about to go on to much bigger things, but so often it started in that very room. Allan really knew who he was, and he knew that his room was a listening room, and I always appreciated that he stayed consistent rather than following trends and becoming a prisoner of them. He created trends and didn't change the blueprint of what that room was just to follow what other people were doing.

Allan understood the importance of community, too. The community between, say, radio and records and a nightclub. He understood the importance of all those ingredients, and the audiences benefited because not only did you get turned on to so much good music, but so many relationships were made there. Friendships were made there that were lifelong. People who met there got married. I mean, it was its own world, and I was so happy to be part of it, and thankful for all the memories that we got from these places.

CLIVE DAVIS (Music Executive): To see an artist that's gifted in a setting like The Bottom Line was unique and special. Allan and Stanley were always more than gracious. From the day I met them when the club opened, they made me feel ultra comfortable, and that never changed the whole time the club existed. I always felt at home there. I cherished it. It was one of the high spots in the arc of that great era for music in New York.

WINSTON SIMONE (Talent Manager): Everything about The Bottom Line was a big deal. Even though it was, in finger quotes, "a club," there was nothing about it that wasn't of the most enormous importance in everybody's career.

RICK DOBBIS (Music Executive): What The Bottom Line represented was a unique positioning of open to everything, open to all music. It was the premier place to play for both professional people in the industry and music fans. I went many, many times to see artists that I had some professional connection to, but at the same time, so many of the memories that I have about shows and experiences at The Bottom Line were for events and artists with whom I had no professional connection. It was just a joyful place to see music, to hear music, and to experience music in what was to me a perfectly sized setting. And it had its act together. The waitresses really paid attention. The bartender made a decent drink. And it had great brownies. Never forget the brownies.

It was a rock and roll supper club, except on the nights that it was a folk supper club, or a jazz supper club, or a country supper club, or a classical supper club. And I use supper club as a compliment because it takes a lot of work and effort and care to operate that side of the business rather than just throw beers at people. I have nothing against beers being thrown at customers, but it's such a different level of care and concern for the customer that, in most clubs, is not only unexpected—it doesn't exist. The hospitality was always there. There was always a table. And the other thing is, unlike other clubs, you weren't hustled to buy drinks or buy this or buy that. I mean, they may have wanted you to do that, but for them, the music was more important. And I think that's how it came through, because, while it was an economic enterprise for Stanley and Allan, the music seemed to always be the priority.

SUSAN DECRENY (Club Waitress): I loved working at The Bottom Line. I had the best time. Allan and Stanley were wonderful. They were both very warm, and it was really like a family. It was always an interesting night. Every band was so different, and it was such a small club that we all knew each other, and we all got to really see the performers up close and personal and wait on them in the green room and the dressing rooms and stuff. Anytime anybody had an important album coming out and they were playing New York, they had to play there. If you didn't play there, something was wrong.

PATRICK CLIFFORD (Club Host): I showed up one day and asked for a job, and why I don't know, but they hired me on the spot. I worked my first show that very night, and I wound up working there for six months. I'd work every day and every night that I could because of the quality of the music and the opportunity to meet people. I loaded equipment; I was a host. The things I got to do, because Allan and Stanley trusted me. For years, after I left and went to work in the music business, whenever I came to see a show at the club, Allan would always introduce me to all the kids that worked there with such a sense of pride. "This guy figured it out," he'd say. "Look what this guy did with his career." I mean, if it wasn't for The Bottom Line, I wouldn't be standing.

MARC SILAG (Club Stage Manager): Allan and Stanley were extremely confident in what they were doing, and I was young and very impressionable, and I dug the fact that they'd created the venue. Nothing like it existed in the country at the time, and the caliber of artists who were coming in night after night was so high. They had a knack for locating enthusiastic personnel. I was there from May of 1975 to February of 1977, and to this day, there's an eighty percent chance that any artist from that era that comes up in conversation, I did something with them at The Bottom Line. It was wonderful; high school with beer. The connections I made in that very brief two-year period when I was in my early twenties are still active in my life. I got on an escalator for my career with Allan and Stanley, and I didn't get off until the mid-2000s. I didn't come in aiming to do this work as my career. There were opportunities that just presented themselves to me, and I said, "Sure, I think I can do that—and I get paid, too?"

TERRY GABIS (Staff): When I started doing sound at The Bottom Line in 1981, there was a five-man crew—a stage manager, front house sound, a lighting designer, and two stage hands—and keep in mind it's just a regular, non-union nightclub. That was pretty unheard of. I liked to pitch in on loading gear in and stuff like that, but it was always, "You're the sound man, you don't have to." And I'm like, "Well, I feel left out." There was always a family feel to the way the club was run, and I dug it, and over the years—and I was there on and off until the club closed—I'd do just about anything that was needed. I would come in on Saturday mornings and run the box office. I worked lights a couple of times, and I sometimes would just fill in for the stage manager, or do sound or run the monitor board. About the only thing I didn't do was work in the kitchen. Well, I didn't tend bar, either. Then again, I don't drink.

BOBBY SCORE (Patron): I have what my wife calls the fan's gene, and The Bottom Line was like my home away from home. It was nirvana to me, especially when I wanted to impress a girl. I was drawn to the clubs in Manhattan, and once I went to The Bottom Line, I thought this was the best place—ever. It was exciting to be there. The lights were always decent, the sound was perfect, and the variety of artists you could see was fantastic. You were there to see the act, not to drink or just hang out; you went to watch and listen. You felt like part of the music industry just going to shows there.

BUDD MISHKIN (Patron): I met my wife on a blind date on November 7, 1987, at a show with JD Souther and Karla Bonoff. When I finally got around to asking her to marry me, I called Allan and asked him if I could ask her on the stage of The Bottom Line during a dark day at the club when they didn't have a show. He said yes, so I stowed my guitar there the day before and got her down to the club on a Thursday afternoon. Allan invited us in. He had two seats and a table set up on stage, invited us on stage, then brought out my guitar from the wings, and I sat and played for my girlfriend for an hour before getting down on one knee and asking her. She said yes. We then continued playing music and singing for another hour, figuring, "When are we going to get a chance to be on stage at The Bottom Line again." Allan and Stanley brought out champagne. It was memorable. When word came that it was going to close in early 2004, we brought our baby girl to The Bottom Line, just to say that she had been inside the club.

Many of the factors alluded to above contributed to making The Bottom Line not just a revered performance space. It became as much a community center as a "cabaret-theater" (as it was christened on day one)—a center situated, fittingly, in the heart of Greenwich Village, home to some of New York's most vital creative energy throughout the twentieth century, and a center that bore witness to the numerous, often near sea-changing shifts in music, culture, fashion, society, technology, and the city itself.

Told through the reminiscences and reflections of many of its key players both on and off the stage, Positively Fourth and Mercer: The Inside Story of New York's Iconic Music Club, The Bottom Line, is a story about a time and a place. It is also a love story about friendship, romance, and following a dream: The story of its co-founder and artistic director Allan Pepper who, along with his best friend and business partner Stanley Snadowsky, and his adored wife and life partner Eileen, has led a lifelong journey as a passionate presenter and lover of music—of the people who make it, and of the people who find pleasure, and meaning, in hearing it.

1 A DEVOTION TO MUSIC, AND A DEVOTED FRIENDSHIP, GROWS IN BROOKLYN

ALLAN PEPPER: I was born in Newport, Rhode Island, on September 13, 1942. America had entered World War II, and my father George was working there in an ammunition plant. We stayed there until I was about two and a half, when we moved back to Brooklyn, which is where my parents were from, and we lived for a while with my maternal grandmother. After the war, my father was a salesman, and he could sell anything once he learned the language of whatever the job required. So he managed a men's clothing store for a while, and when I was four, we moved to Rego Park, Queens, where he opened a little stationery store that also sold records. There were booths where people could listen to 78s, and he'd bring records home, and my mother would later tell me that when I was little, I would sit cross-legged on the floor and listen to classical pieces and be able to recognize the music and tell who the composers were. I was just very taken with music very early.

My mother, Edna, worked in the store with my father, and they hired somebody to take care of me when I got home from school. I went to nursery school, kindergarten, first grade, and a portion of second grade in Queens. Then the store closed, and we again moved back to Brooklyn's Flatbush section. I had an aunt who had an apartment and we moved in, and then she went to live with my grandparents and we stayed. My father remained in sales. On our block on Avenue C, two blocks from Ocean Parkway, there were four big apartment houses. We were in 403 Avenue C; the next ones were 409, 415, and 420. I finished second grade and started third grade, and then we moved again, this time to Poughkeepsie, where my father had another job managing another men's clothing store, and we lived there for six months. During that time I had to teach myself how to write cursive because I could only print and all the kids there were already writing. I had to stay in at home after school and practice writing. I was a fish out of water. In that school system they'd start morning classes with a prayer, which I found really uncomfortable, and I didn't meet many Jewish kids like myself. I also sensed anti-Semitism for the first time. When we moved back to Brooklyn again, we were now in the 409 building and finally had our own apartment.

With his family finally settling into their Flatbush neighborhood for good, Pepper, like many kids growing up in Brooklyn in the late 1940s and early '50s, spent much of his afternoons and weekends hanging out on the street corners with friends. One of them was often outside with a relative who stood out, literally, because he was considerably bigger than most of the other neighborhood kids. He was Stanley Snadowsky, the son of Jacob and Florence Snadowsky, born just a few months before Pepper, on May 28, 1942.

Stanley had a cousin that I knew, Robert David, who lived in 420 Avenue C, the last apartment building on the block, and Stanley, who also lived nearby, would visit him several times a week. They were close, and that's how I became aware of Stanley. Stanley didn't have to say much to make an impression. He was large for his age, big-boned, and slightly overweight. He looked older than his ten years and was intimidating to a person of my size, but he was always kind of friendly. Very interested in sports. So we were kind of aware of each other. We went to the same school. Stanley lived two blocks from us on Ocean Parkway. When I went into fifth grade at local PS 149, Stanley and I wound up in the same class. I can't say we were immediate friends, but we gradually got to know each other, and we became pretty friendly. In those days, I was something of an instigator. There was a very attractive girl in our class, and I encouraged Stanley to write her love notes, which I then delivered, and we'd stand back and giggle in anticipation of her reaction. We went through that rite of passage when you first really notice girls. We'd tease them or wrestle with them in the schoolyard.

In sixth grade we were separated, and then we went on to Montauk Junior High School and started to go our separate ways a little. Stanley loved to go fishing in Sheepshead Bay and was an active member of the local Boy Scouts troop all through his teens, which I wasn't. He was seriously involved with sports—especially football—but that didn't interest me in the least. We were still friends, but I was never athletic or even interested in sports. What I was most into was music.

For anyone living in New York in those days, the AM radio dial was a source of seemingly endless possibilities. The more knob twisting you did, the more you could discover, and throughout the years after World War II and into the new decade, many young listeners, for whom the music of the swing and big band era that had soundtracked life in America from the mid-1930s throughout the war years held no great affinity, began searching for music they could call their own. What they increasingly began to be drawn to were small stations broadcasting the brash sounds of rhythm and blues—energetic, dance-oriented music that had sprung up from cities across the country such as New York, Chicago, Memphis, New Orleans, and Los Angeles—all urban centers with sizable African American populations. While radio stations playing r&b had started out relying heavily on a black listenership, by 1954 an emerging new generation of white listeners was now tuning in as well, resulting in a groundswell that, in just a few short years, would soon turn into the musical and cultural tidal wave known as rock and roll. And riding that tidal wave were the generation's pied pipers—the disc jockeys spinning the "latest and greatest" for their devoted followers.

In August of 1954, Alan Freed, the DJ who had famously recast rhythm and blues as (in his words) rock and roll and had risen to national status on Cleveland's WJZ, left Ohio to join the on-air staff of New York's struggling WINS. Banking on Freed's star power, WINS had signed him for $75,000 a year, plus a percentage of profits if he could help turn the station's fortunes around. The investment paid off almost immediately, as Freed helped the station zoom toward the top of the ratings, and in no time was promoting touring all-star revues at local movie theaters and even appearing in jukebox musical movies such as *Rock! Rock! Rock!* and *Mister Rock and Roll*.

Freed had been on the air in New York for about a month when Allan Pepper turned twelve in September of '54, and in no time, Pepper had joined the ranks of the faithful.

When I heard Alan Freed on the radio, my whole life changed. I found him when he first came to New York. He was on at night, from seven to nine. Even then, I was the kind of person that when I'm in, I'm totally in, so I was really getting into music and I'd start to find stations up the dial playing r&b music that my white friends didn't really know was there, and it was all very exciting to me. My day became come home, listen to Doctor Jive [Tommy Smalls] while doing my homework, have dinner with my family, then tune in to Alan Freed, and after him speed-talking Jocko [Douglas Henderson] and his *Rocket Ship Show* late at night. I had a few really good friends at that time, like Steve Rosenblum and Artie Butler, and we'd hang out on the street corners on Ocean Parkway and maybe sing and listen to other kids singing doo-wop, and talking about all our favorite new songs and performers.

ARTIE BUTLER: I think I met Allan in third grade. I lived on Ocean Parkway; he lived on Avenue C, a block over and a block up. Back then, Allan was a lot like Opie, the kid on *The Andy Griffith Show*. A little redheaded kid who rode a bike. You just wanted to pinch his cheeks. He was very friendly and smart, inquisitive, and curious. And funny. We became fast friends. If he was a chick, I would've probably dated him. He had all the qualities of someone I'd want to be friends with, so we rode bikes together and hung out in the neighborhood. I used to go over to his house all the time, and his mom would make us eggs and beans—scrambled eggs and Heinz baked beans.

STEVE ROSENBLUM: Allan and I go back to junior high school. We met in seventh grade at a school talent show. He was doing stand-up comedy. Even then, he had a certain talent to draw people to him to get groups together. There were a bunch of us friends who hung out together on Ocean Parkway, which was a big hangout street. We were all into doo-wop. Frankie Lymon was the big thing in 1956. Some of us tried to put a vocal group together. Nothing really came of it, but we had fun.

ALLAN PEPPER: After a while, Stanley and I were hanging out with different people. We were still friends and still talked and all, but we were moving in different circles. For one thing, Stanley got into Stuyvesant High School in Manhattan and started going there, and I was now at Erasmus in Brooklyn. Also, Stanley started working after school, and I didn't. His father, Jack, was traumatized by the Great Depression of 1929 and was forced to discontinue his education after the eighth grade. He wound up on the street corner, selling everything from shoe laces to apples for any change that would help his family survive. In later years, he found financial security working in retail, like my father, and he sold baby furniture and clothing at a store in Brooklyn. Jack never stopped stressing the value of money to both of his sons as they grew up. Stanley shared with me when we were adults that one time when he was young, he was walking home with his dad, and Jack saw that at one of the apartment buildings in the neighborhood some people had thrown out some fixtures or furnishings, and he started rooting around to see if there was anything they could use at their house. Stanley was just humiliated by it. For the Snadowskys, it was a major event if they went out to eat at a restaurant.

Now, the Peppers, we always were going out, for any occasion. While Jack clung to his money, George had a very romantic relationship with his credit card. My grandfather, Morris Pepper, was an auctioneer, and there were times when he came into a lot of money, and he was very expansive when he had money. So while money was very important to Stanley—he was always looking for ways to make money after school—it was not to me. Money was never an end-all. Meanwhile, I'm buying records all the time. I found a place on Coney Island Avenue that sold jukebox records, so I'm going there once or twice a month, spending all my extra money on records. Music was my passion.

By the late 1950s, I was getting bored by some of the things being played on the rock and roll radio stations, but it's not like I'm getting bored by music. I was still going to the Alan Freed shows. I remember one at the Palladium on 14th Street. The house band was Count Basie, and with the Cleftones, the Cadillacs, the choreography, everything, it was just terrific. My first real date was to one of those, and Stanley and I double-dated to some of them, at places like the Paramount and the Fox. I'd buy the programs and afterwards cut them up and hang the performers' pictures on my wall—especially the doo-wop groups, because they were always my favorites.

It was toward the end of his time in high school that Pepper's pal Artie Butler began playing him jazz records whenever he was at Butler's house. A precocious kid who as a youngster learned to play piano, clarinet, vibes, and drums, Butler's career in music began one day during lunch break at school when the fifteen-year-old went over to the Manhattan brownstone offices of King Records—he'd seen the album covers in the window—and, without an appointment, told the receptionist that he was "passing through" and thought the label might want to hear him sing and play, and let him make a record. Amused by the teenager's chutzpah, King executive Henry Glover sat Butler down at the piano in his office and was impressed enough to arrange for him to record. And while "Lock, Stock and Barrel," the Frankie Lymon soundalike single he recorded for King's Deluxe subsidiary in 1957, failed to click, Butler was driven enough to drop out of school, and before long was on his way to a lifetime in music as an in-demand session player, arranger, conductor, and composer. Over the years, he participated in classic recordings by the Drifters, the Shangri-Las, the Dixie Cups, Neil Diamond, Janis Ian, Dionne Warwick, Louis Armstrong, Peggy Lee, and numerous others—including, perhaps most notably, Joe Cocker's 1969 version of "Feelin' Alright," which features his memorable piano intro and solo.

Butler's influence on Pepper was noteworthy. Acknowledged by his Ocean Parkway peers as "the hippest guy in the neighborhood," it was Butler who turned his pal Allan on to jazz during the late 1950s.

ALLAN PEPPER: Once Artie turned me on to jazz, and as crazy as I was about rock and roll, that's how involved I now got with jazz. Miles Davis' *Sketches of Spain;* the Modern Jazz Quartet. I started selling off my 78s—four for a dollar—and took that money and started buying jazz albums by Miles, the MJQ, Freddie Hubbard, Art Blakey, Horace Silver. I also started going to Birdland, the great jazz club located at Broadway and 52nd Street in Manhattan. It cost $2.50 to get in. The club was very intimate and had a low stage with tables and chairs in front of the bandstand where you could sit and order food and drinks from waiters, with a $3.50 minimum. To the side of the stage, though, was an area they called "The Gallery," where you could sit with no minimum. Before long I was there once or sometimes twice a week, sometimes with a friend or a date, lots of times just by myself, seeing such great jazz artists as Dizzy Gillespie, Bill Evans, Miles, John Coltrane, Cannonball Adderley, Charles Lloyd. It was really fantastic.

By the time Pepper was finishing high school, he'd moved from obsessing over doo-wop and rhythm and blues to hard bop and cool jazz. He'd also continued to be a fan of live theater and cabaret, which he'd been introduced to as a youngster by Morris Pepper.

My grandfather was a very colorful guy. Family lore relates that he did everything from in the early days of prohibition making bathtub gin and selling liquor to his neighbors to losing his auctioneer's license at some point for taking the fall for some guy who was illegally selling something. For whatever reason he would always have the theatrical newspaper *Variety* in his house. As a kid when I'd go over to visit, I'd thumb through *Variety* because I was always looking for movies to go to and see how much the grosses were. Even at age eleven, twelve. And my family went to the theater a lot. So birthdays, anniversaries, all kinds of special occasions were usually celebrated with theater tickets. Through his business contacts, my grandfather had access to tickets to sold-out shows through brokers. In fact, the first Broadway show I ever saw, when I was about six or seven, he took me to see *Where's Charley*, and my earliest recollection of the theater is watching Ray Bolger dance across the stage singing "Once in Love with Amy."

Throughout high school, Stanley and I spent our summers quite differently. Stanley stayed in Brooklyn and worked in a variety of jobs, including a stint at Nathan's hot dog counter. Meanwhile, we spent our summers at a bungalow colony in South Fallsburg in the Catskills, and my grandfather had a business relationship with Jack Barksy, the owner of the Flagler Hotel. He and my grandmother would stay there, and on Saturday night they'd take our family to the casino to see the shows. I saw Marge and Gower Champion dance there, and comedians like Buddy Hackett, Myron Cohen, and Alan King. That was my first introduction to the world of the nightclub, but the theater remained a real constant for me growing up. I saw the original production of *West Side Story* three times.

When I was a teenager, I had a pretty strong resemblance to actor Robert Morse, whose stage career really took off in the late '50s when he was in several big Broadway shows like *The Matchmaker* and *Say, Darling*, and I was actually stopped for his autograph on more than one occasion. In 1959, my parents took me to see the hit show *Take Me Along*, which starred Jackie Gleason, Walter Pidgeon, and Morse, and when we left the theater, sure enough, someone stopped me for an autograph. I guess the playful side of me took over, and I said, "Look, I'm going to share something with you that I don't tell a lot of people. Robert Morse isn't my real name. I'll sign my real name." And I signed, "Best wishes, Allan Pepper."

2 TWO HUNDRED AND FIFTY DOLLARS, A DREAM, AND A MATCH MADE IN THE COLLEGE LIBRARY

The Sixties were fast-moving, turbulent times in the United States. The social structure of the country was in flux, as both the burgeoning civil rights movement and the rise of the art-driven counterculture sought to move the country left of center in terms of its attitudes and ambitions. Politically, while it began with the emergence of John F. Kennedy and his rise to the presidency after his defeat of Vice President Richard Nixon in the 1960 election, the promise inherent in JFK's youthful energy and liberal leanings toward the burgeoning civil rights movement would be quickly tempered by increasingly escalating tensions on the international front. Epitomized by 1961's failed Bay of Pigs attempt to overthrow Cuban dictator Fidel Castro and the ensuing missile crisis of 1962, America's Cold War with the Soviet Union was palpably threatening world peace. By the end of 1963, Kennedy had been assassinated in Dallas, Texas; often violent backlash against African Americans seeking equality and social justice was on the rise; and the country's involvement in the affairs of Vietnam was significantly deepening. In increasing numbers, young men described not as soldiers but rather "military advisors" were being dispatched to South Vietnam to aid in its ongoing battle against Red China-backed North Vietnam, and eventually a full-fledged commitment of US troops to the small Southeast Asian country was being ordered by Kennedy's successor, Lyndon Johnson.

For young Americans like Allan Pepper, the war began to edge closer to home throughout the first half of the decade, as thousands of eighteen- to twenty-six-year-old men were being drafted into the military and pressed into active service overseas. There were ways to avoid being conscripted, and one of them was through a student deferment, which allowed matriculating full-time college and graduate school students to continue their academic careers without fear of being called to active duty. As Pepper wouldn't reach the age of twenty-seven until the fall of 1969, these years carried with them a constant undercurrent of uneasiness regarding his future. Meanwhile, music—and jazz in particular—continued to be the greatest source of joy, and comfort, in Pepper's day-to-day life as he navigated his way from adolescence to adulthood.

ALLAN PEPPER: I never particularly liked school, and I was never a great test taker, and when I was finishing up high school, my grades weren't good enough to get into any four-year college. However, my mother, who was a school secretary, knew that you could go to a community college, which was open admission, and after two years you could transfer into a four-year college. So, in the fall of 1960 I enrolled in Staten Island Community College—I took a bus and a ferry to get there—and that was fine, but in the very first term, I came down with mononucleosis, so I had to stay home for six weeks and teach myself. Once I settled in there, though, I blossomed, because of the intimacy and at last feeling somewhat like an adult. And after two years, I was able to transfer into Brooklyn College. I didn't have any problems there, but, again, because of the enormity of the campus—I'd go into a lecture hall, and there'd be 50–75 people—I felt like just a number.

I wasn't really motivated, but my mother had emphasized to me that if I got a teacher's license and went into the New York school system, I'd never be without a job. So I'm going along with it, but I'm so much more obsessed with jazz and the Manhattan club scene, going to Birdland all the time, mostly by myself, and before long I'd flunked out. By now the conflict in Vietnam is starting to heat up, and I had a student deferment, but if I'm out of school, I lose it. So after I flunk out in June '63, I really need to get back in, and to do that I had to be fully matriculated, at least twelve credits. So I took two courses in the summer, and now that I'm motivated again, I ace both of them, and when the fall 1963 term comes, I'm back taking enough courses at night and doing well enough to get back in fully matriculated for the spring term.

One of the courses I really liked was a sociology class taught by a young, charismatic guy named Chuck Nanry, who, besides teaching at Brooklyn College, was a PhD student at Rutgers' Newark campus. We were pretty close in age and started to become friends, and I turned him on to jazz the same way Artie Butler had done for me, and we started going together to Birdland a lot. Now jazz was never Stanley's thing. He was really into folk music; he really liked Peter, Paul and Mary, and also Simon and Garfunkel, though he had an extra special reason for liking them. Stanley was living on his own at a pretty early age in his family's apartment after his mother died and both his father and brother moved away, and he had a friendship with a young woman in our neighborhood who used to go over to his place every now and then. She was an incessant talker, and he'd give her about fifteen minutes, and then he'd put on S&G's *Sounds of Silence* album, and always got lucky. We also listened to music differently. He liked to listen to songs over and over again, while I was always looking for something new and different. So I'd be home, listening to the jazz stations and reading *Metronome* and *Down Beat*, and when I started dating, none of the girls I was going out with were into jazz.

One day in June 1964, I'm in the library at Brooklyn College with a friend, just horsing around, when I see this girl with a long ponytail sitting alone at one of the desks, and there's something very hip about the way she looks. My friend Ira and I go over, and I try to engage her, and one thing leads to another, and I say, "You look all dressed up, like you're going out later," and she says, "Yeah, I'm going out with my boyfriend; we're going to Birdland to see Miles Davis." I am stunned. I mean, be still my beating heart. I'm looking at someone who's not only attractive but speaks a language I haven't been able to speak to any girl up to that point. Before I know it, though, she's gone. The next day, at the same time, I happened to be walking toward the library, and suddenly from the opposite direction, I see her coming toward the library too. Only now she's in jeans. I looked at her, and the first thing I said to her was "How was Miles?" and she says, "Miles was great, but I really loved the opening act, [vibes player] Terry Gibbs," and she starts talking about how great he and his band sounded. I'm looking at her again, and now I'm thinking, "This can't be real," so I ask her if she wants to go get coffee.

She says yes, so we go to the *Sugar Bowl* coffee shop right across the street from campus, and we take a booth with a tabletop juke box—they had some jazz records—and right after we sit down, she says, "I'll be right back. I have to make a phone call." Now, the thing is, I actually don't even know her name yet, so while she's gone, I grab one of her books and turn it around, and when she comes back, I mischievously say, "So, your name is Eileen, right?" and she says, "Yes. How did you know?" and I confess that I looked at her book to find out. Then I extended my hand and said, "I'm Allan," and we shook hands—and there was an instant connection. Needless to say, I pursued her relentlessly, and before long she ditched the boyfriend—who she later said she was going to break up with anyway—and our first date later that summer was going to, where else, Birdland, to see the John Coltrane Quintet with Eric Dolphy. She was beautiful, smart, and sexy, and I could share how I felt about music with her, and she'd understand. I felt like I'd won the lottery.

My last year in high school, I had written a show with Artie Butler that I called The Story of Jazz. I had always flirted with the idea of performing. I always felt comfortable telling jokes and stories like that. What started to happen is that while performing appealed to me, I started to get into putting shows together. Artie organized a five-piece band that we called the Jazz Representatives—a nod to Art Blakey's Jazz Messengers—and I was able to start booking it into school auditoriums and social halls in New York. The first part was a pretty simplistic overview of jazz, with me narrating, tracing its roots from New Orleans brass bands through swing and up to "modern" jazz, and we'd explain melody and improvisation with the band. Then for the second part, I'd come back out and do a little stand-up comedy for about ten minutes, and then I'd bring the band back on and they'd play popular things like "A Night in Tunisia," "Moanin'," stuff like that. I was learning how to stage a production, get bookings. At one point, I even added some interpretive dancers to the show. I did one every three months or so, for a couple of years.

ARTIE BUTLER: For the show, Allan was calling himself Red Pepper, after Red Buttons. How was Allan as a stand-up? I don't know. Was he great? No. But he was as good as we were. Was he Buddy Hackett? No. But he was fine.

In 1965, Allan Pepper made a phone call that would prove to be a pivotal moment in his life. The recipient was Rev. John Gensel, known around New York as "The Jazz Minister." Born Juan Garcia in 1917 into a Roman Catholic family in Puerto Rico, he was sent to the United States at age six to be raised in Pennsylvania by his Aunt Fina and her husband Charles Gensel, who legally adopted him. Following a calling to his faith as a teenager, John Gensel achieved his divinity degree at a Gettysburg seminary and, after being ordained, served in the US Navy during World War II as a chaplain in Guam. From the late 1940s into the '50s, Gensel became a traveling minister, at one time working out of a trailer near a nuclear power plant in Piketon, Ohio, which led to him being dubbed "The Atomic Pastor" in a feature story about him in Life *magazine.*

Gensel moved to Harlem in 1956 to become pastor of the Advent Lutheran Church. An avid jazz fan, he began frequenting many of the city's jazz nightspots, where he and his collar no doubt stood out at clubs like Birdland and the Village Vanguard. Befriended by the musicians whose work he admired, and understanding that the late Saturday night hours they kept while plying their trade precluded them from joining him in plying his on Sunday mornings, Gensel came up with the idea of creating a special Sunday afternoon service for them. Almost immediately, his "Jazz Vespers" became its own attraction in both the religious and jazz scenes in New York, and in 1965 he was officially recognized by the Lutheran Church as full-time minister to the jazz community at St. Peter's Church in midtown Manhattan, known to this day as the "Jazz Church." (Gensel, who retired in 1994 and passed away four years later at age eighty, presided over the funerals of John Coltrane, Duke Ellington, Thelonious Monk, Miles Davis, and other jazz giants, and himself was the recipient of many musical tributes—most notably from Ellington, who composed "The Shepherd (Who Watches Over the Night Flock)" in his honor. Asked once if he was concerned that his association with jazzsters might bring some tarnished ones to his services, Gensel replied, "That's the kind we want in church. The good ones can stay home. A church is a congregation of sinners, not an assembly of saints.")

ALLAN PEPPER: I'd first met John Gensel, New York's "Jazz Minister," back when I started doing The Story of Jazz. He came to a performance at New Utrecht High School in early 1960, and we talked a bit after the show, and I guess he was taken by my earnestness and my enthusiasm, because that started a lifelong friendship. We'd kept in touch a little over the years, and in 1965 I called to tell him that I had something I wanted to do that maybe he could help me with. At that point in my life, I was back at Brooklyn College full-time, but I didn't really feel like I belonged. I had friends, but I was missing purpose. I wanted and needed to create. And I came up with an idea. I was always hearing about how jazz musicians felt they were getting ripped off: The type of clubs they had to perform in, and the bad record and publishing deals they had to accept. I was really innocent and very idealistic. It was real for me.

Feeling as I did about jazz being America's original art form, I wanted to help make people understand that. And I'm thinking, "I go to concerts. I have a lot of records. There have to be a lot of people around like me, and we have buying power. We can make a difference." So I started to think about how I could unite fans maybe across the country and, with our economic power, make working conditions for jazz musicians better. I talked to some other jazz fans, and they thought it was something that maybe we could try if we could figure out a way to do it.

The way it started to become a reality was that someone told me that there was a lawyer who might be able to help named Dudley Gaffan, a law partner of New York Congressman Ted Weiss. I made an appointment, but this was stepping into a legal place that I wasn't familiar with, so I called Stanley and told him about it, hoping he'd come with me. Now right at this time, Stanley had his plate full, working at a title insurance company and going to Hunter College at the same time, but I convinced him to accompany me. Gaffan was a really nice guy, and a supporter of the arts. I explain what I wanted to do, maybe come up with some sort of jazz lobbying group of fans, and he says, "There is a way. You could start a nonprofit, a membership-accepting organization that has cultural goals. Like a club, people would join and pay a yearly dues-like fee, and you'd accept their money and use it to provide services—music, news, etc.—but your stated goal is for the betterment of jazz. You could even figure out different levels of membership. And to give it some heft, if you can assemble a board of directors who are known in the field, that would help a lot." In order to do that, he advised I start a nonprofit corporation and said he could help with filing the papers to set it all up; the cost would be two hundred and fifty dollars.

Now you have to understand, I was still living at home with my parents and still in school at Brooklyn College, and I had no money; I had an allowance to get through the week. And Stanley was the only person my age I knew who worked and had a bank account. So we leave the office and I start to tell Stanley how excited I am. He's letting me talk, and I say, "Stanley, I need two hundred and fifty dollars, and I just don't have access to that kind of money. But you do. You could put up the money." The look on his face said, "Allan, what the fuck is wrong with you?" You have to understand that, along with food, money was really sustenance to Stanley. At the time, he was breaking his ass working, going to school, and making extra money at card games and the stock market. I said, "Look. This is a great opportunity for us to get into the music business. We'll make money, and it'll be fabulous."

It was like I was speaking a foreign language. "I don't want to be in the music business," Stanley said. So finally I said, "How about you put up the money, and it'll be a loan to the corporation. I'll be the executive director and you can be the treasurer, so you can keep track of the money." I wore him down, and he agreed to put up the two hundred and fifty dollars, and knowing how much money meant to Stanley, it showed how important our friendship was to him. So we gave Gaffan the money and now, to make it a reality, I had to put together a board, so I called John Gensel again, explained what I was doing and asked him to be on the board. He immediately agreed, and when I asked if he could help find other people, he said, "Let me think about it, and see what I can do."

Within a short period of time, Gensel was able to help Pepper put together a board of directors. Bringing his girlfriend Eileen Herman with him, Pepper met with longtime Count Basie Band trumpeter Joe Newman, who enthusiastically agreed to join and help recruit as well. Before long, the board had expanded to include saxophonist and woodwind player Jerome Richardson, saxophonist Jay Cameron, critic Rudi Blesh, jazz film collector Ernie Smith, jazz fan and United Nations executive Donald Hanson, as well as Stanley, Eileen, and Pepper's sociology professor and jazz club running mate Chuck Nanry. From there, an advisory board took shape as well, headed up by Birdland house pianist and "I Wish I Knew How It Would Feel to Be Free" composer Billy Taylor and nationally known critic and author Nat Hentoff. The first board meeting was held at Rev. Gensel's Harlem apartment where, in addition to Pepper being named Executive Director and Snadowsky Treasurer, Nanry was elected President, Newman Vice President, Herman Membership Chairperson, and Bob Menges, a psychology student and jazz fan who was a member of Gensel's congregation, was elected Secretary. A name was needed, and, drawing on his sociology creds, Nanry came up with the title: Jazz Interactions. Now what they needed were some events to get the organization out in the public eye, and ear.

ALLAN PEPPER: We decided to start presenting weekly concerts made up of three fifty-minute sets from five to nine on Sundays. Joe [Newman] found us a place, a bar called Embers West inside the Edison Hotel in midtown, and he went to the musicians' union and got us a deal for the groups: $25 for each player and $38 for the leader, and he led the first session. We would have anyone who bought a ticket fill out a questionnaire and offered them memberships. The money at the door each week would go to the musicians' fee, and everything left over went into the treasury. Chuck and I put together our press releases, and jazz disc jockeys like Billy Taylor and Alan Grant started talking it up on their shows. The third week at the Edison, we present Roland Kirk, and we've got a good crowd. Kirk is on a roll, and it's coming up on nine o'clock when we're supposed to finish up. The deal we made with the Edison was we'd get the door and they'd get the booze and food. Well, the bar manager wants us out of there, so all of a sudden he puts the jukebox on—while Kirk is still playing! This was exactly the type of thing we were trying to cure; jazz artists getting no respect. We decided not to continue at the Edison, and so I went down to the small jazz club the Five Spot on St. Mark's Place in the East Village and got the owners, the Termini Brothers, to give us a home. We stayed there about a year, and things really took off during that time.

Meanwhile, at one of our early meetings, Jay Cameron had suggested we set up a jazz phone line that people could call at any time of the day and find out when and where people were playing. So we did, with one of our members, Gaitha Martinez, as the voice on the announcements, changing the taped recording several times a week. I went back to the jazz DJs, and they started promoting the jazz line as well as our Sunday shows, so we're getting all this publicity and promotion, and all for free. My phone at home is ringing off the hook. I'd come home and my mother would say, "You got a call from a guy; I wrote down his name: Freddie Hubbard." So now I'm booking heroes of mine, all out of my folks' apartment. I was astounded that this was really happening.

STEVE ROSENBLUM: Allan and I met in seventh grade. He always had a certain talent to draw people to him, to get groups together. I remember a talent show where he did stand-up comedy. When it was time for high school in our neighborhood, I went to New Utrecht and he went to Erasmus, but we stayed friends. And after we each started college, when Allan met somebody he thought was appropriate for me, he'd try and put us together. That's how I met my wife Sarah. Allan met her at Staten Island Community, and they'd become friends and he arranged for a blind date, and we clicked. Later, when Eileen's parents split up and she needed a place to live, we had a house on Ocean Parkway with a finished basement, and she stayed with us for about a year until they got married.

When he was doing The Story of Jazz, Allan brought a lot of people into his home—and from very diverse backgrounds, black and white. It spoke very well for him and his family. They opened the doors to everyone. One time Allan asked me to ask my folks if people could rehearse at our home, and they said ok. As long as they had the talent and the desire to play, Allan was for them.

Within two years, Jazz Interactions established itself as a small but high-profile presence in New York's jazz scene. By the spring of 1967, the nonprofit claimed some 300 members, and had gained enough traction to warrant a feature story in The New

York Times, *authored by arts reporter and critic John S. Wilson, centered around the nonprofit's anniversary party at the Five Spot—a jam session that drew such jazz luminaries as Coleman Hawkins, Howard McGhee, Herbie Mann, and Clark Terry. As Wilson noted in his article, the audience for the weekly Sunday sessions was* "a mix of anonymous jazz enthusiasts and such well-known jazzmen as Charles Mingus, Gil Evans, Booker Ervin, Ornette Coleman, Milt Jackson—all of them listening, learning and exchanging views. 'This,' declares Marion Brown, an alto saxophonist who is one of the leaders of avant-garde jazz—'is the best place for any musician to be on a Sunday afternoon.'"

The article ended with quotes from Nanry and Snadowsky regarding the organization's hopes of securing additional funding to help it achieve its goals, and the publicity generated by Wilson's piece helps Jazz Interactions receive a $10,000 grant from the New York State Council on the Arts for school assembly programs where jazz musicians lectured and performed. Additionally, Jazz Interactions began an annual excursion to the Newport Jazz Festival, and started a "Battle of the Bands" styled workshop program at a studio on the Upper West Side where, before a panel of professional jazzmen, young combos competed for the winning prize of performing at one of the Sunday sessions at the Village Gate.

As the summer of 1967 approached, both Pepper and Snadowsky's lives and careers were moving into high gear. Snadowsky, having finished his studies at Brooklyn Law School, was awaiting the results of the bar exam, which in those days were printed in the local New York daily newspapers. In a reversal of roles from when a nervous Pepper had asked Snadowsky for support by accompanying him to the meeting with attorney Dudley Gaffan that had gotten Jazz Interactions off the ground, it was now an uncharacteristically nervous Stanley who asked Allan to accompany him to their neighborhood candy store to find out if he'd passed the bar exam and could now begin his own law practice. Snadowsky picked up a copy of the Daily News and rifled his way to the exam results, where he found his name among the successful test-takers—leading to, in perfect Brooklyn fashion, a celebratory round of egg creams and pretzels at the store's soda fountain. And in late June at a ceremony at his parents' home in front of forty friends and family members, and with Snadowsky and Chuck Nanry holding up two of the four poles of the chuppah under which vows are exchanged in traditional Jewish weddings, Allan and Eileen were married by her family's rabbi, Joel Schmilchensky, with additional blessings from the couple's other, unofficial clergyman—John Gensel.

Not long after the wedding, the Five Spot announced it was closing, leading to brief stays at a variety of places in Greenwich Village, including the Andy Warhol/Factory nitespot The Dom (later the Electric Circus), the Village Gate, and The Red Garter, as well as wunderkind promoter Steve Paul's The Scene in the Hell's Kitchen section of midtown. During its 1964–70 existence, The Scene was one of New York's hippest hangouts—the clientele ranged from Tennessee Williams and Allen Ginsberg to Richard Pryor and Jimi Hendrix—before Paul left to focus on managing Johnny and his brother Edgar Winter and then running his Blue Sky record label. Known for his almost offhanded adventurousness, Paul regularly used the then little-known ukulele-strumming Tiny Tim as an opening act, and once famously paired Hendrix with classical harpsichordist Arnold Valenti for a concert at Philharmonic (now David Geffen) Hall.

ALLAN PEPPER: The Scene was a club I was really interested in. We just showed up one night to pitch Steve, who came to the door on roller skates. That's the kind of fun place he had. We quickly told him who we were—I'm not sure he even knew who we were beforehand—and we told him we'd just take the door for our Sunday afternoon sessions, and he immediately said ok, so we were there until The Scene closed. We became friends, and I really liked his approach to booking acts. Cabarets and clubs like The Bitter End and Folk City often booked acts for successive weeks, and if you booked an act without a big following, if you had a good one, there were so many newspapers in town that if you could get critics to come the first week, and you got good reviews, then hopefully the second week you'd do good business. And usually you weren't paying the acts a lot of money, so it paid off. Steve looked at it a little differently. He realized he could pick up nationally touring acts a few days after they played at the Fillmore, and that was gold. Plus, Steve knew to mix audiences and how to get a buzz going. And he got tastemakers in by picking up tabs. Of course, Bill Graham at the Fillmore was for me the whole deal. Taste, the booking combinations, the care about production and sound, and how things looked. These were both very creative guys who could look ahead to what might be, prescient in their own ways.

By the fall of 1967, we were already really doing a lot. We had the Jazz Line, the programs in schools, and the Sunday sessions. We also successfully lobbied City Hall to set aside a day featuring special events honoring jazz, and on October 7, Mayor John Lindsay officially proclaimed "Jazz Day in New York." To commemorate it, we commissioned Oliver Nelson to write an original piece called "The Jazzhattan Suite," and we got BMI to underwrite the fee. We debuted it in the afternoon with a free concert in Central Park attended by a crowd of some 4,000, and a second one in the evening for an invited audience at the Metropolitan Museum of Art's Grace Rainey Rogers Auditorium. A month later, Verve Records recorded the work in their New York Studios, with Joe Newman conducting a group that included Zoot Sims, Phil Woods, Ron Carter, Ed Shaughnessy, and Bobby Rosengarden, and it came out in early 1968, with the liner notes written by Chuck [Nanry], who later became the founding administrator of Rutgers' Institute of Jazz Studies.

By that time, I was in the doctoral program in sociology at NYU, but it wasn't something I really wanted to do; I was doing it because I didn't want to get drafted and get shipped off to Vietnam. I'd called the draft board sometime in 1967 to check on my student deferment, and I get this woman on the phone who's really irritated that all these college kids are getting deferments, and then she gleefully tells me that beyond college, there aren't deferments anymore for graduate school, only for teaching or other lines of work that they called "occupational" deferments, which meant work that was in the interest of the nation. So I called Stanley and I said, "Stanley, we're both fucked." Now thanks to my mom, I had taken some education classes as an undergraduate, so I made some inquiries and found out that if you went to New York's Board of Education, they really needed teachers in some of the inner city schools, and if you had enough credits you could take what they called an emergency exam, and if you passed you could get assigned to a school right away. John Gensel knew the principal of a school in Ocean Hill, Brownsville that had just opened, and called him on my behalf and he said he'd take me if I passed the test. So in January 1968, after I passed the exam, I started at Intermediate School 55, just a few blocks from where Eileen was teaching elementary school at PS 144.

Meanwhile, Stanley, since he had no education credits, did the equivalent of what I'd done at Brooklyn College. During the spring of '67, he loaded up on education credits, taking courses at night while he was still working on getting his law degree. So Stanley got his emergency license, too, and he got assigned to Berriman Junior High in East New York. Of course, Stanley being Stanley, he doesn't want to do lesson plans, so he makes a deal with the principal there. He says, "Look, if I don't have to do lesson plans, and I can punch out early, I'll take your worst students for the whole day and I'll deal with them." And the principal went for it. So he had this group of incorrigible kids, and he taught them about math and logic, and life, mostly by playing poker with them. When he first walked into the classroom, I think he said something like, "Don't fuck around with me—I've just gotten out of prison, and nothing you can do will upset me." And the kids went for it. And even better, it was where he met his future wife, Michelle Galpern, who was also teaching there.

Now for myself, it wasn't that easy. The kids at my school were hellacious. I wasn't assigned a particular class right away. The first day I went in as a sub to administer a test. I'm in a sports jacket, looking formal. And understand when I was a kid, if you got caught chewing gum you might wind up in the principal's office. So I'm standing at the front of the classroom, trying to explain the test, and a kid takes the test, folds it up to make a paper plane and throws it and it lands at my feet. I tell him to come and pick it up, and he does that, and then he crumples up the paper, puts it in his mouth and chews it up.

Even though we were still involved with Jazz Interactions, by 1968, Stanley and I are trying to branch out on our own. In March, we formed our own company, ALSTAN Productions, and we were looking for money to help us promote our own shows. Through a mutual friend, Steve Rosenblum knew a guy named Sonny

Weissen, a young discount store executive, who was very full of himself. We arrange to meet with him, and Stanley's pretty skeptical, and the first thing he says is, "Weissen's my name, cash flow is my game," and Stanley smiled slightly and his body language immediately changed. We started pitching him—me about the music and Stanley about the business—and we got him to put up money for one of our shows. We rented the Loew's King's Theater on Flatbush Avenue, and put together a show I titled "Sounds in Motion."

At that time, FM radio stations like WNEW were playing all kinds of music. You could listen for a half hour and hear, rock, jazz, blues, folk, all in a row; there wasn't any predetermined playlist. It was why they called it at the time "free form" radio. And I wanted to do something like that with concerts. So we booked jazz flute player Herbie Mann, blues harmonica ace James Cotton, jazz-rock saxophonist Steve Marcus, and the psychedelic rock group Autosalvage. And we got John Zacherley—the "cool ghoul" DJ and horror picture TV host—to emcee. We were very excited about the show, but the day it took place that June, it wound up raining all day, and it poured right up until when the show started at eight o'clock. The theater held over 2,500, and we were lucky if we had 250. Autosalvage didn't even show up. And we lost all of Sonny's money.

LARRY GOOBERMAN: It was a nightmare. My wife and I stood outside in the rain, on the verge of tears. We were all losing our money, but we felt for Allan and Stanley.

Several months later, in September 1968, ALSTAN rented out Town Hall for a show they called "Contemporary Expressions," with saxophonist Roland Kirk headlining, along with drummer Elvin Jones and his trio and the Dave Liebman Group, featuring Randy Brecker. This time they gathered up the money to produce the show from friends and colleagues at their respective schools.

ALLAN PEPPER: I had come up with an idea: At both schools where we're teaching, it's a mixture of older people and young people like us who were basically there to avoid the draft. And I see them as a source of money and potential investors. Well, we start pitching our colleagues and, lo and behold, we actually raise enough money to put on some shows.

LARRY GOOBERMAN: I first met Allan during senior year at Brooklyn College, and then we were in grad school together. We recognized each other early on because we were different. Both of us were older than most of the other students. He used to call me his doppelganger. We weren't going to join fraternities or go out for a sports team. We were different. I was working as a cab driver and a billiard hall attendant, and Allan was putting together concerts. Neither one of us really wanted to go to college. Our mothers, both of whom were school secretaries, applied for us. We both dropped out of college after two years. We both didn't want to get drafted, so we went back to school. We both married our college sweethearts. We both had no money, but we were ambitious and thought we'd rule the world. I put up money for some of his and Stanley's shows. I enjoyed it, hoped they'd be successful.

Allan had great energy. I think of him in those days as a little guy running around, with papers always falling out of every pocket. Notes. Callback numbers. Very busy. If you went over to his apartment, there'd be records lying around everywhere. The record companies would send him albums, and he'd always be offering me some. I thought, "He's important enough that people would send him stuff." I knew he was for real. I knew that with his energy and connections, for a very young guy, I knew he'd make it. We were what, twenty-four, twenty-five?

I'd go to the Jazz Interactions shows and hang out, and it was clear Allan really enjoyed the atmosphere. The Village was evolving, and in those times, the crowds were so interesting at the jazz clubs. Interracial, and not really hippie-ish. Hitter clothes. Women at the bar, with red lipstick, smoking.

The Contemporary Expressions show did well in terms of ticket sales, but the day after the concert, when Pepper and Snadowsky went to settle up with Town Hall, they found an extra charge from the venue that all but wiped out any profits. Puzzled, Stanley asked what it was for. As it turned out, he and Pepper had left the venue after the audience had left and the stage had been broken down. What they didn't know was that Roland Kirk, his band and assorted well-wishers had stayed in their dressing room and thrown an impromptu party, which required Town Hall personnel to stay on the clock—and on overtime no less—for a good hour and a half. [As Pepper would note years later, "We learned from that night to always be the last ones out the door at any of our own shows."]

In March of 1969, ALSTAN presented another all-jazz show at Town Hall, this time headlined by one of Pepper's jazz heroes, saxophonist Sonny Rollins, with opening acts pianist Jaki Byard and his quartet and Lenny White's group, the Jazz Samaritans. Pepper had negotiated directly with Rollins, settling on a $1,000 fee for his performance. Three weeks before the concert, however, Rollins told Pepper that there'd been a misunderstanding. The $1,000 fee, he explained, was the price for him, but money for his accompanying musicians was separate. Pepper said ok, thinking Rollins intended to have three, maybe four people playing with him, but Rollins told him that for this show, he'd arranged to be accompanied by The New York Bass Choir, a troupe containing no less than seven bassists and a rhythm section that had been founded and led by the bracing Bill Lee (better known in his later years as the father of filmmaker Spike Lee). With healthy ticket sales and his investors' already spent money at risk, Pepper reluctantly agreed.

As headliner, Rollins was contracted for a one-hour set, and the night of the show, he played for forty-five minutes, then he and the Bass Choir left the stage. Pepper quickly intercepted him and began to ask if he'd play more, and Rollins, without a word, simply turned back, returned to the spotlight, and improvised an additional unaccompanied solo before exiting again. Pepper attempted to get him to return for an additional encore, but Rollins, again without saying a word, simply put out his right hand and extended his palm, saying, in effect, "If you want more music, it'll cost you more money." Since there was none to give, Pepper shook his head no, and Rollins calmly turned and headed backstage. With that, the house lights came on, and the concert ended—leaving Pepper and Snadowsky to learn another valuable life lesson about the separation of show and business and presenting one's heroes in that business.

ALLAN PEPPER: During this time period, we did jazz shows downstairs at the Village Gate on Bleecker Street. We had already done some Jazz Interactions sessions at the Top of the Gate for owner Art D'Lugoff, and moving downstairs was a big deal for us. Art was, for me, another role model. Like me, he was a little guy, a bundle of energy, all over the place. One of the things I really admired about him was that he was a visionary in terms of who he presented. He was very drawn to theater as well as music—*"Jacques Brel Is Alive and Well and Living in Paris"* played for years there—and he presented Billie Holiday at Carnegie Hall. Art was mainly a businessman who was moved by the arts. He was not above walking around and bussing tables, cleaning up. He just couldn't sit still. His mind was chock-full of stuff, and politically he was pretty left. Those three—Bill Graham, Steve Paul, and Art D'Lugoff—were all big influences on me in terms of what I aspired to do.

Among the young players who performed at the Jazz Interactions sessions and went on to significant careers in jazz was a group of players that included drummer Billy Cobham, guitarist Larry Coryell, trumpeter Randy Brecker, pianists George Cables and Weldon Irvene, bassist Clint Houston, and saxophonists Steve Grossman and Dave Liebman. Another was Lenny White, a teenaged drummer from Queens who, at the tender age of nineteen in 1969, would be part of the extraordinary team of musicians that helped Miles Davis record his groundbreaking album, Bitches Brew, and who would, as of 2025, still be active as a recording artist and jazz educator in New York City.

LENNY WHITE: That time period when Allan and Stanley had Jazz Interactions was a great time in New York for young musicians. I don't know if their actual intention was to get the young jazz community acquainted, but that's what they did by having those competitions. And that was *real*. I mean it's New York City, not Oshkosh. In order for you to be a young jazz musician in New York, you had to be on your game, because most of the top musicians lived and worked here. And if they didn't, then they moved here. So you could show how good you were. For me coming up, if I was gonna play a gig in New York City, I had to be good enough so that people like Art Blakey and Max Roach would think I had it. I was in a group and learning about the competition that Jazz Interactions had, and if you won, you got a gig at the Village Gate. I was like, "WHAT?" I mean, you couldn't get *into* the Village Gate. So here was an opportunity to do that.

The first band I was in was called the Contemporary Jazz Quartet. We had a flute player who later became an actor, Justin Lord, and the pianist was Danny Nixon, who married [singer] Betty Carter. Then there was saxophonist Steve Grossman, who had a group, and guitarist Larry Coryell, and saxophonist Jim Pepper, who had the Free Spirits, one of the first jazz-rock bands. Also, the Jazz Samaritans, with bassist Clint Houston, pianist George Cables, and Billy Cobham. And that group won. They got the chance to play at the Village Gate, but Horace Silver called Cobham to join his group, and the Samaritans needed a drummer, so I joined them. And the thing is, many of these musicians became good friends of mine for my whole musical life.

Sometimes people who are heads of associations, you might not want to be around them, or only enough to get what they can give you. But Allan and Stanley were much better than that. They were "unjerkified," if you know what I mean. And they were young like us. The synergy was great, the time period, the music, the age we were. There was so much going on at the time, in music, in art, in movies, in culture, and everything was influencing everything. When you had artists Pablo Picasso and Jackson Pollock alive and still doing things, their work was helping shape how musicians made music. And the music was shaping how artists were painting and poets were writing. Plus there was the tension about Black people recognizing they didn't want to be called "Negroes" anymore. I knew my presence should be accepted—and the art helped shape that.

How I was growing up had a lot to do with the city, and with Greenwich Village. I lived in Queens, but I was in the city [Manhattan] all the time. I went to Art & Design and then the New York Institute of Technology. I had to take a bus and two trains to get to school. So I'd go to school, come home, have something to eat, and get back on the bus and the two trains to go back to Manhattan to do things. One night I went to see John Coltrane play at Philharmonic Hall, and I was starstruck—not just by him, but by his music, by the whole *Ascension* band, what they were doing. I went by myself, and after the concert, I was just walking on air. It was such an experience. Everything was turning into a wave of new things, and the music many of us were playing was morphing. As a drummer, I was certainly influenced by the "Magnificent Seven," the architects of modern jazz drumming: Kenny Clarke, Max Roach, Art Blakey, Philly Joe Jones, Elvin Jones, Roy Haynes, and Tony Williams. But I wasn't just listening to jazz. I was listening to James Brown, and Jimi Hendrix, and Clyde Stubblefield, and a lot of Latin music, like Eddie Palmieri. And most of the young jazz musicians I knew were all doing that, too. And Jazz Interactions helped us all connect to each other, and to the generation before us. The support meant so much, it was so special for young artists. That's how you develop and find your way.

ALLAN PEPPER: We put on very eclectic shows at the Gate. One week, Sun Ra, the next Howard McGhee, the next Pharoah Sanders, and then Larry Coryell and his jazz-rock fusion. We wanted to be true to our vision, opening jazz up, all stripes, all elements, not just Dixieland and beboppers. A lot of people thought free jazz was all noise, but I booked a lot of ESP artists. It was a way to build up membership; trying to turn people on so they'd become members. And I can't say enough about John Gensel. When we were doing Jazz Interactions, John was doing his prayer vespers at 5 p.m. at St. Peter's, and many times right after the service he'd bring forty to fifty people from Midtown down to our shows, and often youth groups he was working with. And getting people to come allowed me to book people who maybe weren't so well known, because it helped ensure a paying audience. It was just a great learning experience for me.

When we were at the Gate with Jazz Interactions, Eileen and Stanley would be at the door. Eileen would sign people up, and Stanley would take the money. One night we're there and Eileen gets up to go to the restroom, and this guy comes by and starts looking around, sizing the place up, and he sits down in Eileen's seat next to Stanley, looks at him and says, "Give me the money." Stanley says no, and the guy opens his jacket and he's got a gun, and Stanley doesn't say anything, just stares him down, and the guy finally gets up and walks out. When Stanley told me about it later, I couldn't believe it. I said, "Why didn't you give him the money?" And Stanley said, "I couldn't. The guy just pissed me off."

Board of Directors outside the Five Spot (First Row: Reverend John Gensel, Allan Pepper, Eileen Herman, Gaitha Martinez, Joe Newman; Back Row: Eric Steinbock, Chuck Nanry, Stanley Snadowsky, Bob Menges).

Howard McGhee introducing musicians ready to help celebrate Jazz Interaction's First Anniversary (Starting stage left: Artie Simmons, George Cables, Jay Cameron, Joe Farrell, Billy Taylor at the piano, Howard McGhee at the mic, Chris White, unidentified trombone player, Billy Cobham at the drums).

Jazz Interactions Board Meeting (Left to Right: Stanley Snadowsky, Gaitha Martinez, Joe Newman, Allan Pepper, Reverend John Gensel, and Chuck Nanry).

Coleman Hawkins is getting ready to play at the Five Spot Celebration.

Allan and Freddie Hubbard are in deep conversation at a Jazz Interactions Sunday Session.

Eileen and Art Farmer were in conversation at a table that Eileen was using to sign up new members at a Sunday session.

Front view of Loews marquee advertising Allan and Stanley's ill-fated "Sounds in Motion" concert featuring Herbie Mann.

Sonny Rollins on stage at Town Hall with The Bass Violin Choir.

Randy Brecker performed at an outdoor summer concert organized by Jazz Interactions.

Allan and Eileen tie the knot.

3 TASTES OF THE BIG TIME, BITTER AND SWEET

On the night of August 5, 1969, Stanley Snadowsky and his wife Michelle were coming home from a celebratory dinner on their one-year anniversary when they passed the Brooklyn home of Pepper's parents, George and Edna. As it happened, George Pepper was sitting on his porch, and the Snadowskys stopped to say hello before heading to their apartment only a few blocks away. Just a few hours later, in the early morning hours of August 6, George Pepper, just fifty-one, suffered a fatal heart attack. The impact on his son Allan was understandably enormous.

ALLAN PEPPER: About a month after my dad died, I turned twenty-seven, and Stanley had recently turned twenty-seven as well. We both weren't eligible for the draft anymore, and especially since my father had died at such an early age, I thought, "Life is too short. I gotta do what I really want to do." And teaching just wasn't it. Stanley was eager to stop teaching as well, so we both decided to quit our jobs in the fall of '69 and start to try and really make a go of it as promoters. Stanley was doing ok with his solo law practice, and here, Rev. Gensel was again so important in our lives. He brought Stanley business by recommending him to many of the jazz musicians he knew who needed legal help for one thing or another—marital issues, drug busts, bad recording contracts—and it gave him invaluable experience. As for myself, though, I didn't have any other job, so it was Eileen who was going to have to support us, at least in the short term. We talked, and I promised her that if I wasn't making a living in music by age thirty, I'd try something else. And for the time being at least, that was ok with her.

By the start of 1970, Pepper and Snadowsky had both resigned from Jazz Interactions and began to concentrate on booking shows, primarily jazz concerts, in Manhattan, where they presented the likes of Elvin Jones, Freddie Hubbard, Sun Ra, and McCoy Tyner, to mixed results. [After one sparsely attended concert by the Keith Jarrett Trio, Jarrett's manager George Avakian saw Pepper and Snadowsky cleaning up the auditorium and joked, "You big-time jazz promoters—always ripping off the artists."] Additionally, that summer, as an outgrowth of their Jazz Interactions sessions at the Top of The [Village] Gate, the two began booking acts downstairs at the basement part of the club for owner Art D'Lugoff.

ALLAN PEPPER: Art was used to booking jazz, comedy, and folk at his club. But as the 1970s started, free-form progressive radio stations like WNEW and WPLJ were playing a great mix of rock, blues, and singer-songwriters, and Art didn't listen to FM stations. He mostly listened to jazz, and so he started to lose touch with the marketplace and who the up-and-coming acts were, and we were two young guys who seemed to know what was going on. One day he said to us that, right after the Jacques Brel show was finished for the night, he wanted to do something new afterwards. He let us book who we wanted, but he gave us a very low amount of money to spend on talent to guarantee the acts, and just a token amount of money as a weekly fee for our production company. And if we wanted to spend anything over a thousand dollars, we had to get his approval. He just didn't know the value of the acts he was being pitched by agents, and you couldn't take an agent's word for it, that's for sure. So we started to book the place, and I tried to make it eclectic. Stuff we were hearing on FM radio that would work in a club: Rock groups like NRBQ, Seatrain, Elephant's Memory, Mandrill, Todd Rundgren's Runt, Billy Joel's band Attila, folk acts like David Bromberg and Carolyn Hester, and naturally, jazz acts we already had relationships with, like Billy Cobham and brothers Randy and Michael Brecker's group, Dreams.

Dreams was a band that had some of its roots in Jazz Interactions, as trumpeter Randy Brecker first heard of it from his early bandleader, saxophonist Dave Liebman. Among the most prolific and eclectic jazz artists of his generation, Brecker, like Lenny White, was able to navigate the line between the bop-grounded generation before him and the increasingly wide-angled newer one he was a part of, all without a trace of self-consciousness or "place" in the overall jazz world of the era. The path of his early career, which would blossom in the 1970s with the Brecker Brothers Band, reflected the boundary-stretching promise of jazz and rock in the mid-to-late 1960s.

RANDY BRECKER: I had been born in Philly, but I actually came to New York from there after three and a half years at Indiana University. In February of 1966, after our jazz ensemble had won the 1965 Notre Dame Jazz Festival, we were sent on a four-month US State Department tour of the Middle East and Asia. After that tour, there was another band competition in Vienna that we'd read about in Downbeat, so I went there and won a second prize on trumpet. A Swiss-Italian guy named Franco Ambrosetti, who I'm still very close with, beat me by a tenth of a point. But this laid the essentials of my career. The judges on this thing were Art Farmer, Cannonball Adderley, JJ Johnson, Joe Zawinul, Ron Carter, and Mel Lewis.

I stayed in Europe until September of '66 when I decided to switch schools, enrolled at NYU, and moved to New York. Not long after that, I met [saxophonist] Dave Liebman and we started playing together in a quintet along with Lenny White and a guy named Mike Garson, who ended up with David Bowie for many years. I think the first time I played for Allan was at a Jazz Interactions date with Dave at The Red Garter, where The Bottom Line later got built. While I was playing with Dave, Mel Lewis asked me to join the Thad Jones–Mel Lewis Jazz Orchestra. So I was in the right place at the right time.

The guys in Thad and Mel's band were really open to new ideas and having younger guys in the band. It was looked upon as a way to learn new things and try to get in on some of the other things that were happening, which at the time had to do with what was known as jazz rock or fusion. The hippie generation was just getting going, and we were dressing the style; anti-suit and tie and letting our hair grow. And for whatever reason back then, the next thing you know, a lot of the jazz musicians, especially in Thad and Mel's band, switched from suits and ties to dashikis and Nehru jackets and let their hair grow. I thought they all looked kind of funny at the time. They looked better when they had the suits and ties; it was more natural.

But it was an exciting time in New York. There was so much going on in every direction. I remember seeing a double bill that had Charles Lloyd with Keith Jarrett and Cecil McBee, and then Miles Davis with Wayne Shorter and Tony Williams. There were sessions, and the main thing was there were all these lofts in the city where people got together and played. I went over to Liebman's loft quite a bit, and we played all different styles, a lot of free jazz. It was crazy. Five horns blaring away at the same time. And there were more structured kind of jam sessions under the Williamsburg Bridge, kind of Miles-influenced stuff. So those were two of the great meeting places.

For a while I had a regular side gig playing with a soul band at the Metropole [Café in midtown Manhattan], which had these go-go dancers wearing bikinis. It was an interesting sideline. What helped me was that when I was at Indiana U., Booker T. Jones of Booker T. and the MGs was studying music composition there, and he had a band of local cats from the school, and we played at sororities and fraternities on weekends. I learned all the Stax and soul stuff firsthand from him. At the time, there was also a big jazz band at Juilliard, and although I wasn't going to Juilliard, if they needed somebody, which they quite often did, I'd sit in and play. Blood, Sweat and Tears had just started, and they'd already hired Jerry Weiss, who was the lead trumpet player in the Juilliard band, and someone else who was a high school band teacher, but he decided he didn't want to take chances losing his gig, so he dropped out, and I got called and asked to join. I stayed in that band for close to a year and did the first record, *Child Is Father to the Man*, with really good charts by [saxophonist] Freddy Lipsius. I had no trouble playing that style of music, although I didn't get to solo that much. That was the only problem for me with Blood, Sweat and Tears; I would only play maybe one or two solos.

I left Blood, Sweat and Tears to join Horace Silver. He came beckoning for me, and he was one of my idols, so to play with him in a real jazz group was just too much to turn down. I stayed with him for two years until he broke up the band in California, and then [drummer] Billy Cobham and I trudged back to New York, where I ran into my brother [saxophonist Michael Brecker], who had just moved to New York and had met a wonderful trombone player by the name of Barry Rogers. Rogers had met two singer songwriters, [keyboardist] Jeff Kent and [former Doors studio bassist] Doug Lubahn, and they were looking for a trumpet player and a drummer, so me and Billy got the gig, and that's how Dreams started. Dreams became kind of the house band at the Village Gate. We would play there quite often, especially on weekends, opening for comics, and good ones. Richard Pryor was on his way up, and we'd open for him quite a bit, which was really great. I became familiar with his whole show. He'd packed the place, and we'd open, play for an hour, and then watch him, and he was hysterical.

Like many nightclubs at the time, the Gate did not have Monday events, so Pepper and Snadowsky asked Art D'Lugoff if they could produce their own Monday shows, taking responsibility for the talent and the promotion. This led to an infamous booking of Sun Ra and his Intergalactic Arkestra. Well before Parliament-Funkadelic, the inscrutable bandleader Ra—born Henry Blount and raised in Alabama, though he spent most of his life claiming a celestial identity—would outfit his musicians in outrageous costumes, with a near-army of accompanying dancers, singers, and assorted percussionists spilling off the stage and out into the audience.

One Monday, as often happened in New York clubs at the time, musicians union representative Norman Posner showed up to make sure that the group had a proper contract for the gig and that all the members were up to date on their dues to New York's Local 802. As Snadowsky stalled for time with the middle-aged, straight-laced rep, Pepper went downstairs to the dressing rooms to let Ra know that he needed to show the union man a signed contract. "Nothing to worry about," replied Ra. "Just tell him this stuff doesn't apply to us. We're from Saturn. They don't have a local there." "You really want me to tell him that?" asked Pepper. "Yes, because it's true," said Ra matter-of-factly and closed the door to his dressing room. Pepper went back to the union rep and told him verbatim what Ra had said. The incredulous Posner looked to Snadowsky, who just nodded back with a straight face, in blind trust of whatever his pal Pepper was up to. And with that, the befuddled union rep turned around and left, repeating loudly as he slunk out the door: "They come from Saturn. They come from Saturn! The office has no idea what I'm dealing with!"

ALLAN PEPPER: What happened when we started booking for Art at the Gate was that it was right at the time when the record companies, from a promotional standpoint, had started doing press parties, and they were making t-shirts, belt buckles, and other promo items and sending out invites to press and disc jockeys because they were trying to break acts in what was emerging as a new marketplace, ranging from small and medium-sized clubs to theaters and the big arena shows.

And there were new magazines and local papers being published where they could get great feature and review coverage—national magazines like *Rolling Stone, Creem, Crawdaddy, Circus, Rock Scene,* and *Hit Parader,* and local weeklies like *Good Times, The Aquarian,* and, of course, *The Village Voice.*

The record companies were picking up tabs for drinks and even food for writers, and I was told by more than one journalist that in those early days the companies supplied some of their wardrobe and maybe even a good meal. It also allowed many of them who were freelancing opportunities to network. Many of these writers were just starting out and learning the trade, how to write about and cover the music scene, and I was paying my dues booking these acts, and we got to know them. There were always nice surprises, too: We did a press party for United Artists with the Nitty Gritty Dirt Band from LA, and they brought their own opening act—a young comedian/musician named Steve Martin. A whole new thing was opening, and Art wasn't in contact with that, but we were, and it opened up the Gate to a whole new scene. To a point, though. For example, we had the opportunity to book a new band from Macon, Georgia called the Allman Brothers, available at what we assured Art was a great price of $1,500 for five nights. But that was too rich for his blood.

In the spring of 1971, as Pepper and Snadowsky worked on their club bookings and the occasional concert show, they also began thinking about other areas to explore, and to that end, Pepper convinced his partner to try their hand at some theatrical ventures.

Stanley wasn't a real theatergoer, but I saw there was a course at The New School on theater and how to produce a show, and I thought we should take it. I told Stanley about it, and once again, he just went along with me for the ride. At that time there was an arts program at City College where Black and Latin students had put together a version of the *Three Penny Opera* that took place in Harlem. Stanley met the director, and we started producing a little show called *There's a Shadow Over This Land* at a club in midtown, so we had had some vague experience in producing. And we were already doing concerts, so we had a knack for putting shows together. The guy at The New School who taught the class was Leo Kerz. He'd had a long career on Broadway, mostly as a set and lighting designer, and in the early 1960s he'd produced Ionesco's play *Rhinoceros* with Zero Mostel and Eli Wallach on Broadway. Leo was one crazy character. Very dramatic. He said, "The public is too fickle. They let the critics decide what's good for them," so he wouldn't print any reviews in ads for his shows, even though it could help ticket sales. There's a story that when *Rhinoceros* opened and got great reviews, he wouldn't print any of them in his ads, so Zero put a sign on his dressing room at the theater that said, "All are welcome—except Leo Kerz." So that's who we took the course with.

One of the assignments for the class was to produce something, so since we were already doing the *Shadow Over This Land* show, we invited Leo and the class to come and see it. We were very far ahead of everyone else, and Stanley was very cogent with questions about how to put together a budget for a production, and one day Leo says he wants to have a separate meeting with us, and he says, "How would you boys like to co-produce a show with me on Broadway?" We were completely flabbergasted. What was going on was that Leo had designed a set for a show that was being staged at the prestigious Arena Stage theater in Washington—a revival of Strindberg's *The Dance of Death* starring Rip Torn, Viveca Lindfors, and Michael Strong. The production, directed by Alfred Ryder, had gotten great reviews and everyone wanted to try and move the show to Broadway. In fact, the actors were so enthused that they all agreed to work for scale. In addition, Leo informed us that Gregory Peck, an old friend of Ryder, had already committed to put up one-third of the budget if he could get it on track to get to Broadway. Of course, we didn't learn until later that the one thing Leo had neglected to tell us going in was that Ryder, the director, was a raging alcoholic, and the entire production budget was severely undercapitalized, making the entire transition even more challenging.

Anyway, after explaining what he wanted to do, Leo asked if we wanted to co-produce, which meant that we'd help raise the rest of the money he said was needed to capitalize the show, which came to about $30,000. Well, we jumped at it. We weren't teaching anymore, so why not try? And we were able to raise the money, again from colleagues and friends. Stanley goes and negotiates with Rip's agent, and knowing that Torn has already agreed to work for scale, Stanley keeps saying no to all the agent's demands. He comes back to Leo, says that we got everything we wanted. Leo says, "Oh, how wonderful," and Stanley says, "I did give them one thing. I let them have a dresser." Stanley thought it was a physical dresser—a chest of drawers. Leo says, "Stanley, a dresser is a person, it's another salary!" Stanley immediately cancelled the dresser.

Rip and Viveca were on their best behavior until the production went into rehearsals in New York, and then Leo started to lose control of the show. The two stars became very disrespectful to Paul Avilia Mayer, the adapter of the revival. Viveca was Swedish, and Rip also had some Swedish lineage, and Viveca started reading the original in Swedish to Mayer and changing his dialogue. The poor guy would sometimes leave the theater screaming, and he kept threatening to quit. One day during the rehearsals, the writer, Mayer, brought his agent, Ad Schulberg—she was [author] Budd Schulberg's mother—to see how things were going, and in anticipation of Paul having a meltdown and running out of the theater, Leo locked the exit doors. The first act goes by and since Leo had threatened Rip and Viveca with their lives, there were very few errors, and Paul starts to relax, but the two of them would not leave well enough alone, and the second act comes and they start changing lines again. Paul had a fit, jumped up, and tried to leave, but when he yanked on the door and it wouldn't open, he yelled out, "They're kidnapping me!" and ran upstairs to the office. Ultimately, we calmed him down, but he was so pissed he said he was going to take his name off the production.

Leo hired a company manager to run the day-to-day details of the production, and he didn't exactly have it together. The day the scenery was coming in, we got to the Ritz Theater very early, and all the big burly stagehands were just hanging around outside, drinking coffee. Meanwhile, this big truck is sitting there parked right by the stage door, and nobody's moving. Now Stanley and I, we really don't know what we're doing, so Stanley goes over and says to one of the stagehands, "Excuse me, that's the truck with all the stuff for the show, yeah?" They nod yes. Stanley says, "Shouldn't you guys be moving it off the truck?" "Oh no," one of the guy says. "We don't do that. You have to hire teamsters to take it off the truck and over to the stage door. We move it in from there." We couldn't get any teamsters until nine o'clock—we'd been there since seven—and finally, these two scrawny guys show up and and take it off the truck and carry it from the curb to the stage door. And then while we were approaching previews, because of the lack of a decent budget, the company manager hired just one guy to clean the theater. And he treated him so disrespectfully that one day during previews, the poor guy just up and quit. So guess who's gonna clean the theater? Every morning at eight, I had to open the place up, clean out the orchestra from the night before. At 11:30 or 12, Stanley would come uptown from court, dressed in a suit, and he cleaned out the balcony.

All told, we had about a half dozen previews, and as we got near opening night, things got so bad that Paul, rather than just quitting, decided instead to send out letters to all the critics expressing how badly he'd been treated, and that what they were going to see was not his version. Not that we needed another nail in the coffin, but when the show finally opened on April 28, 1971, it received pretty bad reviews, and *Dance of Death* danced its way into the grave on May 1, closing after all of five performances. But Stanley and I could now honestly say that we'd produced a show on Broadway.

Between their downtown activities with Jazz Interactions and their experiences booking for the Gate, Pepper and Snadowsky got to know most of the club owners in the Village, and after the Dance of Death experience, they transitioned from booking acts for D'Lugoff over to Gerde's Folk City on Third Street near Sixth Avenue. The owner was Mike Porco, who had started out running a bar/restaurant called Gerde's right on West Fourth Street near Mercer. In 1960, with all the young musicians who were then hanging around nearby Washington Square Park and looking for venues to play, he added the name "Folk City" and began presenting live acts. Throughout the folk boom days in the first half of the 1960s, Folk City was the live music epicenter of the Greenwich folk scene, especially after Bob Dylan's 1961 performance there drew the rave review in The New York Times *by critic Robert Shelton that helped him get signed to Columbia Records. By the time Porco moved the club to the other side of the park on Third Street in 1970, however, Folk City had lost much of its cache—Porco was still leaning heavily toward solo performers and all-acoustic instruments—and as the music scene was changing, with competition from more eclectic clubs such as The Bitter End on Bleecker, the Gaslight on Macdougal, and Max's Kansas City on Park Avenue just north of Union Square, Porco was struggling to attract acts. And so, like D'Lugoff, he hired Pepper and Snadowsky to help out with bookings.*

ALLAN PEPPER: Working with Mike was a challenge. He was a wonderful guy, but very old school. He was really a restaurant/bar owner, and the music had come to him. When we booked rock acts, and they'd bring in their gear, Mike would come over to me and say, "Don't they know this is a club? It's not Madison Square Garden!" He didn't like spending money, but we actually got him to upgrade the sound system during our time with him. His wife and brother-in-law worked there, and they'd walk through the club shouting at the top of their lungs, asking people if they wanted water, right in front of the stage as people were playing. It drove us crazy. Mike would say, "A good performer won't be affected by noise." And he never wanted to tune the piano. I'd say, "You need to do it. It's really out of tune," and he'd say, "Look. Here's what you do. You don't tune it, but you tell them you did. Most of them won't even know. And if they do complain, the ones who say 'Well, you should fire the piano tuner. He's robbing you,' those are the ones you should get the piano tuned for." That was his mindset.

Most nights at Folk City, Pepper and Snadowsky could be found outside the club, standing around the parking meter at the curb that after a while functioned almost as an impromptu office where they'd talk to artists, agents, managers, and writers who'd come for shows. One of them was critic Ira Mayer, who was covering the music scene for The Village Voice, and who would go on to become a close friend of the two promoters.

IRA MAYER: The first time I ever encountered them was at the very end of the 1960s. I was in the city with a group of friends. We went to the Village Gate to hear Richie Havens. It was in December, and it was a very cold, snowy, slushy night, and the second show was running about two hours late, so everybody was standing on line out on Bleecker Street, and the two of them were outside talking to customers to keep things calm. Eventually, we got in, and I was there with like six or eight of my friends, and we got our pitcher of coke or whatever the minimum was, and when it came to our table, which was behind a pillar in the basement of the club, there was a roach in the pitcher. Now we had just been standing out in the cold for two hours, and my friends had all but had it, and now there's a roach in the pitcher at our bad table. So I called the waitress over, showed her the pitcher, and said we wanted our money back, and she said, "Well, go see him," and she pointed to Stanley. I went over and told him what happened, and he calmly took out a roll of cash, asked how many people were at our table, gave me our money back, and said, "Ok, have a good time." It wasn't until years later that I realized that it had been Stanley.

When they were running Folk City, I was writing for the Voice already, and I loved to make the rounds to the different clubs and see what was going on, and if somebody caught my eye or ear I stayed, and if they didn't I just kind of wandered out. Eventually, I had to stop doing that because managers started calling and saying, "What did you mean walking out on my act?" And sometimes the acts called me about that, too. At any rate, Allan and Stanley were there, and Mike Porco introduced us, and we started schmoozing regularly. They were always hanging out at the parking meter in front of the club, and as soon as the show started, I'd go in. They would always be my last stop for the night. Stanley would ask me what was doing at the other clubs, and he always wanted to know how many people were at the shows, and Allan would always want to know about the performers and what good music I'd seen. And that was them, in a nutshell.

While booking Folk City, Pepper and Snadowsky also began managing several acts who played there. One of them was a quartet from Queens called Revival. They were led by their chief songwriter, singer/guitarist Dan Daley, who later in his career would compose the Vietnam War veteran's tune "Still in Saigon," a hit for the Charlie Daniels Band, and their bassist was Paul Guzzone, who would go on to play with, among others, Tom Rush and the Bacon Brothers Band.

PAUL GUZZONE: We formed Revival in our senior year in high school in Middle Village. It was Dan, [singer/keyboardist] Michelle Conway, and me, and our drummer Mike Malfesi was a former Christ the King student who was thrown out of school because his hair was too long. We considered ourselves a folk rock band, hence the name Revival. A couple of acoustic guitars, bass, drums, and four-part harmony. We'd go into the Village, and every Monday was a hoot at Folk City, and Tuesday it was the Gaslight on MacDougal. We eventually landed a regular gig at Folk City and played there and college coffeehouses. One night Allan came in and saw us. He was booking for Art D'Lugoff at the Village Gate, and he was just roaming around the Village looking at acts and he came in and heard us, and after our set he talked with us and said he wanted his partner to come in and see us. So he sent Stanley over on some other night to see us. He wasn't as excited about us as Allan was, but Allan prevailed, and they signed us to a management deal.

We were all kids and a little nervous. We knew what we were doing was pretty good. There were other people coming to hear us besides friends and family. Allan was a nice guy and not a manager type, you know cigar-chomping business type. He and Stanley, from the beginning, were like big brothers, to me at least. They were only ten years older than us. So we didn't know anything about the business, and these guys didn't look like business types.

ALLAN PEPPER: Revival was folk rock, with an element of country. Great harmonies, and Dan was a great songwriter, with a great ear for melodies. Because we were booking at the clubs, we were now knowing people at record companies, and we got Neil Bogart, the head of Buddha Records, to come down to a showcase for Revival, and we got them signed to their Kama Sutra subsidiary.

PAUL GUZZONE: They were our college course on the music biz, and right from the get-go. Stanley especially wound up being a huge supporter. He sat us down and explained what the management contract was all about, and when we got our record deal, he did the same thing. He explained what every paragraph meant, what we should expect from the contract, and how it all worked. And they did this at one of their apartments, not in an office. They were not going to take advantage of us, and looking back on it now, and some of the people I've dealt with over the years, that was remarkable. They were really open to us. We didn't even think of taking the contract to another attorney to look at. It was very fair. Part of the deal was controlling the publishing, and at some point, there was a guy who was interested in some of my songs outside of the band, and they picked up the phone and negotiated an advance of 500 bucks and gave me half, which was very cool. Our publishing was Sunshine Rabbit, nicknames for their wives. We made one album. We were a great live band, but the producer didn't know what he was doing, so it wasn't a good mix of personalities. Still, we sold a couple of thousand copies, and played some festivals. We were hot shit in Queens and around New York City, and our labelmates were NRBQ and Buzzy Lindhart, which was cool. And Allan and Stanley stayed supportive, especially Stanley, even after they stopped managing us.

During this period, in 1971 and '72, Pepper and Snadowsky weren't really making enough money from their production company to live on, though Snadowsky was making money in his law practice, which found him involved with a variety of aspects of the music business, and business in general. Meanwhile, it was Eileen's teaching salary that was pretty much paying the bills at the Pepper house. Things became more complicated when each of their wives gave birth to their first children—Leslie Snadowsky in September of '71 and Gordon Pepper a month later.

DAN DALEY: From the time Allan and Stanley came to my parents' house to talk to them about managing us, we knew they were good people. My affinity was always for Allan, who was the real music fan of the two, but Stanley fascinated me. I had a car—neither of them did—and for a little while I was picking up extra money driving Stanley around to various courthouses. After the Fillmore East closed at the end of 1971, the promoter John Scher acquired the Capitol Theater in Passaic, New Jersey, and he started to present shows there. With the theater apparently came a fairly flourishing Sunday night porno film business, and that same year the Supreme Court made the ruling that said that localities could determine pornography standards. They were giving John a hard time about that, so I took Stanley to the courthouse in Passaic a bunch of times on behalf of Scher, and in the process I'd learn about the law from Stanley. I also learned about negotiations and business. He told me, in every negotiation, always make one outrageous demand, because you never know. And you know what? I found out it was true. He was a front seat guy, not a back seat guy.

Another musician who Pepper and Snadowsky began managing during this time was Carolyn Hester. Unlike Revival, Hester was a seasoned performer whose career dated back to the late 1950s. A Waco, Texas native, her interest in folk music as a teenager led to her making her first recordings at producer Norman Petty's fabled Clovis, New Mexico studio, where she met and was befriended by Petty's best-known artist, Buddy Holly. Holly, who assisted on several of Hester's earliest tracks, would remain a friend until his untimely death in a plane crash death at age twenty-two while on tour in the Midwest in early 1959. By that time, Hester had relocated to New York and become a part of the budding folk scene centered around Washington Square Park. At the time he passed, Holly had been living in a loft just blocks from the park, and Hester, who saw him just before he left on the fateful tour, used to end her shows with one of her favorite Holly songs, "Lonesome Tears." One night in 1961, she was approached after a set by a young musician who had recently moved to the city and, excited that she knew Holly, wanted to hear more about him. Not long afterward, Hester brought the baby-faced newcomer along to accompany her on harmonica when she made her first album for Columbia Records that fall—and it was there that Bob Dylan first came under the eye of legendary producer John Hammond, who soon signed him to the label as well, setting in motion the start of Dylan's extraordinary recording career.

Hester, who was briefly married in the early '60s to singer-songwriter and author Richard Farina, also had the distinction of being the very first performer to play Gerdes when it was re-christened Folk City in 1960, and she continued to perform there through the years. After being booked at the club by, and getting to know, Pepper and Snadowsky, she and her second husband, pianist-songwriter David Blume (co-author of the 1966 hit by the Cyrkle, "Turn Down Day"), approached the two about taking on management duties for her.

CAROLYN HESTER: I was looking for people I could trust, and there were Allan and Stanley. What was not to like? They were very positive people. Allan was the music guy and Stanley was the financial guy and a lawyer. That appealed to me because my dad was a lawyer and my brother was a lawyer. I felt they would always be fair, no matter what. And they worked hard for their clients. We moved to LA in 1972, and David was connected to RCA, so I did a record for them. It was Allan who called the A&R guy at the label, and we went to the offices and made the deal with them. That 1973 album had a song I'd written about my sister Donna, who had Down syndrome. I was twenty and my brother was fifteen when she was born. I had written the liner notes explaining each song, and I wrote that one of the reasons I composed the song was that I had seen the reports that Geraldo Rivera had done about that horrible institution Willowbrook, and I thought it was important to talk about it. I'll be damned if someone who was a friend of Rivera's didn't show him my album and that I'd mentioned him, and Geraldo was tickled. He got in touch with me and we talked, and in 1974, after The Bottom Line opened, Allan and Stanley had me come back to play, and Rivera came to the club and asked if he could tape me for his show, and that's what they did. Because of Down syndrome in my family, I'd been fearful about having children at an older age—fortunately, I was able to have my two daughters—and I got to talk about amniocentesis and Down syndrome to his TV audience. Folk music is where you could discuss things like that, and Allan and Stanley were so cool about it.

While Pepper and Snadowsky continued booking Folk City and were producing occasional shows on their own (they returned to Town Hall in the spring of 1972 for a folk program featuring Carolyn Hester, singer/songwriter Jim Dawson, and guitarist/singer David Bromberg), Pepper continued to lament the fact that they didn't have a space they could call their own. Having seen what worked and what didn't at the Village Gate and Folk City, they knew that if they had their own venue, they could control their costs for performers and employees, and finally present music the way they had always envisioned it, they could probably make it work, and work well. But where would that place be? And, if and when they found it, how would they raise the money to get it off the ground? In early 1973, the answers to both questions came to them.

ALLAN PEPPER: When we were doing Jazz Interactions and bouncing around presenting our weekly jam sessions, one of the places we used was The Red Garter, right at the corner of Fourth Street and Mercer. It was run by a guy named Chuck DeLorme. We got friendly with Chuck, and we'd often go right across the street to Folk City and hang out, which is how we first got to know Mike Porco, and then started booking for him when he moved over to Third Street. The Red Garter was what they used to call a beer and banjo joint. The music was mainly turn-of-the-century Dixieland jazz through standards from the Roaring Twenties, and everyone working at the place was in straw hats, striped shirts, and armbands. The waiters, all guys, would sing and clap along. And if you can believe it, the stage where the band played was a big red flatbed truck that was made up to look like a fire engine. They had sawdust on the floor, barrels of peanuts, with peanut shells everywhere, and mugs of draft beer that they turned out like there was no tomorrow. Chuck made deals with bus tour companies to bring in the tourists. They'd pull up and people would stream out, file into the club, spend some time and money, and then head off to the next destination.

By the start of 1973, though, with the changing times, The Red Garter had turned into a relic, and one day Chuck told Stanley, who had been doing some legal work for him over the years, that he was going to abandon the joint, which he'd been renting from the landlords, New York University. Since we knew the space and the neighborhood well, Stanley and I talked about it and thought that while we might have to basically tear down the whole club and rebuild it to make it what we wanted it to be—a good, comfortable place for people to come see and hear great shows, be it music, theater, or cabaret—this seemed like the right time and the right place. Since I'd started promoting, I had always felt that controlling two things would help make you successful: Controlling the cost of the talent and controlling the real estate. And here was a chance not only for us to get our own place, but be able to build it to our own specifications. The only thing missing was the money to do it.

Eileen had an uncle, Marvin Bernstein, who was a very successful businessman in the garment industry in New York, specifically in the area of sportswear. He had a company called Variety Knit, and this was the way he made his money: When the TV show *Laugh-In* went on the air and became a huge hit in 1967, they had those two big catchphrases that everybody used—"Sock It to Me" and "Here Comes the Judge"—and in those days, people weren't paying a lot of attention to licensing or marketing. Marvin had a hunch that if you put those slogans on T-shirts, they'd sell, and he was right. The shirts were flying out the door, to such an extent that they had to keep their production going twenty-four hours a day to keep up with the demand—and Marvin really cashed in. He then got into other investments and made even more money. He was a street-smart guy who understood numbers and business in a very savvy way. Plus, he was a real character, kind of like a cross between Mel Brooks and someone out of Damon Runyon's *Guys and Dolls*.

At some point when Stanley and I were starting out, Eileen had mentioned that if we needed some financial backing, maybe she could talk to Marvin about it, as he was always open to lending a hand to anyone in the family. Still, he was a tough businessman, and it took five years until I could convince him to put any money into anything we were doing. But once we found the space we wanted, we knew that if anyone could help us with the kind of money we'd need to build it, it'd be Marvin. We'd had meetings with him over the years about trying to set up our own place, and he'd listen and ask questions, but getting a real commitment from him seemed impossible. So many people in the family approached Marvin about investing in some kind of idea for a business that he would say, "I put my hand in my pocket a lot, but I only take it out once in a while." A big plus for us, though, was that Marvin had a great rapport with Stanley. Marvin knew all about numbers and, like Stanley, he had played high school football, and liked to play the market, as did Stanley. When they were talking, it was a language I couldn't comprehend.

With The Red Garter out of business, we knew we had to move, and move fast, and finally Marvin was ready to come on board. Because we had inside info, about a week after Chuck closed his club, we went to NYU before it went on the market and negotiated a new lease. We tried to close the deal as quickly as possible. At that point in time, NYU was not in good shape financially. They had divested themselves of uptown property in the Bronx, putting all their marbles in the Village, and we were able to make a good deal. Our first rent was I think $1,250 or $1,500 a month. Stanley said to me, "We're going to do ok because we'll be able to cover the rent on a good night just from the back bar." We didn't say anything to anyone, and we actually ran into The Bitter End owner Paul Colby on the street a day or two later, and he was very chipper, talking about how he was going to acquire The Red Garter as well. Needless to say, we said nothing to him and just wished him well, and couldn't help chuckling once we were clear of him. Why ruin his day?

Now we were feeling pretty good, and we knew we had to come up with a name. Stanley and I had an agreement that whatever we called the club, both of us had to like it. I started thinking, with a tip of the hat to all the great music places from the 1940s, how about the Roxy or the Paramount? Stanley called me, and I told him, and he didn't think much of it and said, "I don't know. How about Al and Stan's place?" I told him I didn't think much of that one, either. Soon after we'd acquired the space, Stanley took his family off on a vacation to Puerto Rico, and one night I went out to dinner at Emilio's in the Village with Michael Rosa, who had played drums with the Quinn Ames group that we'd booked at the Gate and Folk City. He was now working as an a&r guy at Elektra Records, and he'd just come back from a company retreat in Las Vegas. I asked him if he'd had a good time, and he said, "Yeah, we were having a great time until the bottom line boys got there."

Somehow, when I heard that phrase, it just resonated with me. I called Stanley in Puerto Rico and said, "I think I have the name, and I really like this one." I said, "What's the one expression that people in our business use more than any other one?" And without missing a beat, he said, "The bottom line." I said, "That's the name." I held my breath, and Stanley started repeating it like he was tasting a fine wine. "The Bottom Line. The BOTTOM Line. The Bottom LINE," and he said, "I think I like it." And that was it. The name really appealed to us both. It appealed to Stanley because of the business connotation, and it appealed to me because it meant the essence of what I wanted to do—present the best music available in any genre at any time. It was who we were, and our club was going to be called The Bottom Line.

4 FROM A RED GARTER TO A BOTTOM LINE

WE BUILT IT, AND THEY CAME

In the spring of 1973, when Pepper and Snadowsky took over the lease for the 5,000 square-foot space that had been The Red Garter, the corner of West Fourth and Mercer Streets was not exactly a hotbed of activity—or at least much aboveboard activity. Situated two blocks east of the southeast corner of Washington Square Park, it was a location that during the day mainly consisted of students and people connected with New York University making their way around the maze of buildings connected with the college's main locations to the south and west of the park on Fourth Street. And while that might have implied plenty of youthful energy circulating through the immediate neighborhood, most of that energy, especially after dark, was usually spent several blocks away where the real action was—either heading north on University Place or, better yet, south to ever-bustling Bleecker Street, where strings of longstanding bars, cafes, restaurants, and clubs had been operating for decades.

Meanwhile, one block to the east of Fourth and Mercer was lower Broadway, along a stretch of mostly deserted after dark industrial buildings whose sidewalks catered on most nights to sex workers and drug dealers off-ramping from evenings plying their trades in the park itself. As with most of the country at the time, New York's economy was also in a downturn, and with hard times came the always accompanying rise in crime, both on the litter-filled streets and down in the dank, badly lit subway system. If you had a car and parked it at night in most dicey neighborhoods for any length of time, you stood a good chance of returning to your vehicle only to find it broken into, with a gaping hole in the dashboard where the car radio had been. People in those strange days often resorted to portable players that could be disconnected and stored in the trunk, and then sticking handwritten "NO RADIO" signs inside the car's side windows to ward off potential thieves.

Still, for Pepper and Snadowsky, the guiding word was optimism, and an "If you build it, they will come" belief that would quickly extend to the small group of dedicated people who came on board to help transform the dead Red Garter into what would be The Bottom Line. Some were people who the two promoters had worked with at the clubs they'd been booking over the last few years, some were specialists recommended by others, and some just kind of showed up at the door and began pitching in, without defined roles, yet game for whatever was needed at any given moment. Among them were: Jack of all trades Alan Luzinski, known to all simply as Riley, who would go on to work at the club off and on for many years; Bob Iozzia, who would become The Bottom Line's first day manager; and, perhaps most importantly, contractor Bruce DeForeest, whose contributions helped provide the club with not only a state-of-the-art sound system, but a physical design ensuring that customers in every seat of the club could comfortably see and hear everything transpiring on stage.

RILEY: In high school, I was a gigantic rock fan, and while I went to a lot of big shows, in the late '60s I really got into folk music and started going to folk clubs to see artists like Eric Andersen and David Blue. In 1970 I went to see Carolyn Hester at Folk City, and I was there every night for her three-night stand. The last night, I went alone, and I was having one last beer before hitting the subway to go back to Park Slope, where I was living with my parents. Carolyn always brought her own set of speakers when she played, and the person who was supposed to be there for her on the road to pack up her stuff didn't show up, and I overheard a conversation between her husband David [Blume] and Mike Porco about loading up. David had tennis elbow and couldn't do much lifting, so I shyly went over and said, "Do you need a hand?" and they said, "We sure could." So I loaded out their stuff, and Carolyn thanked me and asked if I minded coming back to their place and unloading, and I was like, "Holy shit!" and I went back with them. They offered to send me home in a cab, and I wound up talking with them for hours until four in the morning. At some point, Carolyn said, "Listen, I took two years off, and I'm just restarting my career. Are you free to do car trips to load and unload every once in a while in the tri-state area?" And I said, "Sure." I was working somewhere during the day, but if I gave them notice, I was able to take time off, and I started doing that. Allan and Stanley hadn't started managing her yet, but cut to a few years later: Carolyn had moved out to LA to record an album, and I went with them to witness the recording.

I hated LA, so I came back after two months, and in May 1973 when the album came out and Carolyn started doing a promotional tour, she did a week at Folk City. By that point she'd signed with Allan and Stanley, and I had met them just before she left for LA, but in May 1973, the last night she played was Saturday, May 5, and Allan and Stanley had just gotten the keys to The Red Garter. They told Carolyn, "We want you to see what we've gotten ourselves into," and she asked if I could come along, so we got in a cab and went over. We walked in the door, and it was this cavernous dark place, all black, and what wasn't black was covered in this horrible red and gold wallpaper. And with a fire truck sitting in the middle of it all!

Carolyn had been staying at Allan's place in Brooklyn, and I was still living with my parents, so the four of us got in a cab at two or three in the morning, and they were about to drop me off, and before I got out of the cab, apparently Carolyn had pow-wowed with them in the back seat—I was in the front seat—and she said to them, "Why don't you hire him to help you get the club together?" And the next Monday I showed up at The Red Garter to start helping them demolish the place, and well, I just never left.

BOB IOZZIA: In the early 1970s I was a music reviewer for *Variety*. Allan and Stanley were managing the young pop rock folk country group Revival, and one day they cold-called me at the *Variety* office and asked if I would come down to Folk City and review them, which I did. We struck up a friendship—they were wonderful guys—and after I left *Variety* I'd continue to go to Folk City as a patron, and one day as we were talking they asked me if I wanted to work the front door at the club. While some people would have thought that would have been a step down, working the door and stocking the bar, I loved it. It was a change of pace, a chance for me to still be around music. The only thing I didn't like about it was that I didn't like working nights and weekends, and also I had aspirations of being a rock musician—clearly I wasn't on the right path for that lifestyle—so I did that for a while, and one day Allan and Stanley said that they wanted to talk to me about something. We went out for a cup of coffee, and they laid out the plan for the club, and they asked if I wanted to join them, and I said yeah. They said, "Think of what you'd like to do," and I said, "How about day manager?" They said, "Day manager?" I said "Yeah, prepare the club for the evening. Ordering everything you'd need from day to day, making sure the place was cleaned up from the night before, etc." So I became an actual Bottom Line employee very early. At first I was cleaning up peanut shells from The Red Garter and chipping away concrete, and it evolved into a very cool job. It was great to be on the ground floor of something that became what it became.

RILEY: I know there was some kind of plan, but it seemed to just develop as it was being built. For me, at the beginning, Bob was the knowledgeable older guy who knew a little bit about how to tear things apart, and I liked him a lot, so the first six weeks or so, the only humans inside were me, Bob, and Allan. Then finally a phone was put in behind the bar so Allan could start making calls and lining up bookings for when we'd finally open. We left the bar that ran against the side wall to the left of where you came in, but we had to destroy all the booths and everything, so when we ate lunch or had a coffee break, there were only two places to sit down—an old bar stool that Bob hammered back together for Allan to sit on while he was on the phone, and the other was the VIP booth all the way in the far corner. That was the only thing we didn't demolish and the only thing comfortable to sit on. Allan used to call it "The Veranda." For a while, we'd get these quote "professionals" coming in, telling us what they would do. Like a lighting guy would say, "Well, I just finished a Stones tour, or I'm about to go out with Bowie." They were all name-dropping, and then in June, Bruce DeForeest came in, and I didn't know he'd been part of the production crew that put Woodstock together until maybe six months later. He didn't need to name-drop.

ALLAN PEPPER: People like Art D'Lugoff, Mike Porco, and Paul Colby all kind of fell into being music club owners. But we didn't. We had a vision, and we knew what we wanted. Conceptually, we wanted to build a club whose main purpose was to present music, and Bruce was the one who physically figured it all out. We knew him from the Village Gate and Folk City, when he'd worked as a soundman and a road manager for David Bromberg, who we'd booked there. We weren't using a general contractor. Our architect Larry Segretti was the son of the guy we hired to build the formica-top tables. He was a young architect starting out, and then we brought Bruce in to work on all the important sound and stage logistics—and he ran with it.

Tall and slim, with long blonde hair that he often wore in a braid, Bruce DeForeest was, as Bob Iozzia put it, "the personification of a proverbial strong silent type whose presence commanded whatever room he entered. You may not have met him before, but you knew he was a force. He was the most professional and expert tech I ever met." Once he came and assessed what building the 400-plus-seat venue envisioned by Pepper and Snadowsky would entail, DeForeest, who had been part of the construction crew that miraculously transformed part of Max Yasgur's farm in Bethel, New York into the immense live music space of the Woodstock Festival, reached out to people he'd worked with over recent years, John Geier and Tom Battiste, who, like him, had been part of the new breed of music-grounded stage-and-sound-design carpentry and sound design professionals who'd changed the face of live concerts during the late 1960s and early '70s. Seeking to maximize the acoustics of the rectangular-shaped room, Bruce turned for help to John Chester, who'd built the sound system for Bill Graham at the Fillmore East. Recognizing that with different acts coming in virtually every day of the week, often with their own sound engineers, they designed a high-end but, most importantly, functional and easy-to-use soundboard. Chester also consulted on the construction of the walls, which were treated with materials to help uniformly absorb and distribute sound, and it was determined that, while harder to keep clean, carpeting would be installed on the floor of the club to help absorb noise from the audience.

Since sound quality and sight lines were the main focal point around which all other layout considerations were based, DeForeest determined it would make the most sense to hang the PA speakers above the stage, rather than to the sides. A catwalk above the audience at the back wall of the venue was built for the sound mixer, with stage and spotlights built to operate from the same location, thus freeing up as much of the floor space as possible for tables and chairs. When all was said and done, the club could accommodate a little under 440 patrons. Once the height of the stage area was determined, it was DeForeest who came up with the novel idea of "grading" the seating area and creating several tiers, which would enable nearly everyone in the audience to see over the heads of the people in front of them and have an unobstructed view of the stage. As for the two dressing rooms, which would be located directly behind the stage, each had its own bathroom—and here again, DeForeest's acute understanding of musicians' habits came into play.

ALLAN PEPPER: The most amazing thing about Bruce was how he could anticipate problems. When they were building the dressing rooms, Stanley and I walked in one day and Bruce had just gotten finished. For the walls for the bathrooms, he'd used a certain very hard material, and for a good reason. He told us he was doing this because after a show, if some pissed-off drunken musician who hated how his set had gone—and then he paused for a minute and with all his might he kicked the wall—it stayed in place. Which certainly played out over the years. One night, ex-Eagle Randy Meisner headlined, with Rosanne Cash opening; it was her first time at the club, and after his set, he came backstage and did just that. Bruce also came up with the idea of an overhanging sound wall built over the bar area to hold in conversations there.

Meanwhile, from our own experiences at clubs, we decided to have bell-less cash registers, which just slid open, and Stanley got the telephone company to give us phones that lit up instead of ringing. We even used heavy duty paper plates and plastic utensils to eliminate noise while serving food during performances. Building the club, the bar stayed where it was, but it had been much longer; it veered around to the back, and that's where the dressing rooms were built. We left the kitchen in the same place, and the two huge coolers in the back by the dressing rooms where The Red Garter used to keep things cold, that stayed, too. It did result in the dressing rooms being a little smaller than we would have liked, but we thought it was important that the dressing rooms be backstage, so that acts would be able to just come out of the dressing rooms right through the curtains and onto the stage. We worked in clubs where performers had to make their way through the customers' tables to get to the stage, and we didn't want anything like that. I always felt it killed the magic.

RILEY: As the club was being built, I know that Allan and Stanley were borrowing more and more money from Uncle Marvin, because Bruce would say, "If you wanna do it right, it's gonna cost this much," and they really wanted to do it right. And through it all, Allan was very confident and upbeat. Bob [Iozzia] would be very serious while Allan would be joking, and Bob would almost sneer at him. And I'd laugh at Bob and so I'd get in trouble with the guy I was taking orders from. Meanwhile, Stanley was always lawyering like crazy. He'd come in a suit with his briefcase, and I don't think I had an actual conversation with him for maybe six months, but he was very friendly and amiable. He was very imposing from the start, but he had a screaming sense of humor. He also had a heart that was as large as his girth and personality. The first time I wanted to move out of my parents' house and into an apartment in the village, not only did Stanley take time to look over my lease before I signed it, but he and Allan lent me the money for the security deposit, and they immediately gave me a pay raise.

BOB IOZZIA: There were many admirable attributes of Allan and Stanley, singly and as a team. Stanley was a lawyer and a savvy financial investor. He was detail-oriented and a brilliant thinker on his feet. Allan's genius was in the creative side of presenting acts, including putting together a bill of two acts nobody else would have thought of. Their combined strength made them a formidable team, and when required, each could assume the "good cop" to the other's "bad cop"role, and often trade roles depending on the circumstances.

During the nine-plus months that The Bottom Line was being built, Pepper and Snadowsky—neither of whom ever learned how to drive—decided to hire a driver to get them from Brooklyn to the club and back, and to run errands for them as well. His name was Richie Shulberg, an out-of-the-box singer and fiddler known professionally as Citizen Kafka, leader of the aptly named Wretched Refuse String Band. One day during construction, Snadowsky sent Shulberg to a nearby Nathan's restaurant to get him lunch—which for Stanley usually meant enough hot dogs, burgers, roast beef sandwiches, and french fries to feed a small army—and to then also stop at the Orange Julius stand on 8th Street and Sixth Avenue to pick up plenty of their signature drinks to wash it all down. After more than an hour, Shulberg still hadn't returned, and then the phone rang, and it was Richie. "Where are you?" asked an annoyed Snadowsky. "I'm starving." "I'm sorry I'm not back yet," said Shulman. "I'm at the police station."

What had happened was that, just as he was leaving Orange Julius, a robbery was in progress at the jewelry shop next door. Running out of the store, the robber ran past Shulberg and, brandishing a gun, commandeered a taxi. Terrified, the cabbie accidentally put the car in reverse and slammed it into a store window across the street, just as a swarm of police cars arrived. Guns drawn, the cops pulled the suspect out of the backseat of the taxi, and when one of them asked if anyone had seen what had happened, Shulberg instinctively waved his hand to signal yes. "So I'm at the station now," he told Snadowsky, "I'm waiting to give my statement, and they said I could make a call." "Ok," said Snadowsky, "I understand. But do you still have my lunch?" "Yes," said Shulberg, "It's right here next to me." To which Snadowsky responded, "Good. If there's a sergeant nearby, can you put him on the phone?" After Shulberg handed the phone to the cop, Snadowsky shifted into his businessman's voice: "Hello. My name is Stanley Snadowsky. I am the co-owner of a new nightclub that is currently under construction at 15 West Fourth Street. Over an hour ago, I sent one of my employees, Mr. Shulberg, to pick up lunch for my construction team. Since the food is an hour late, they've stopped working and are now just milling around and nothing is getting done. And that's costing me a lot of money. Obviously, Mr. Shulberg needs to stay there as long as you need him, but I was wondering if you could help me out and bring the food here so my crew can eat and get back to work." A few minutes later, a police car pulled up at the club and, remarkably, two of New York's finest from Manhattan's 6th Precinct got out and delivered Stanley his lunch—proving yet again that when it came to getting things he wanted, Counselor Snadowsky could be very persuasive.

* * * *

Construction on The Bottom Line finally finished near the end of 1973, at a cost that went far past the initially projected $75,000 to something more in the neighborhood of $125,000. While Marvin Bernstein wasn't thrilled with the amount that had been spent, he had given his word to be there for Pepper and Snadowsky, and stayed true to it. And as the two partners deliberated on how they envisioned the club would operate, they came up with "house rules" that would basically remain intact throughout The Bottom Line's entire existence.

ALLAN PEPPER: One thing that Stanley impressed on me when I began to undertake booking acts for us to present at the club was that, for us to succeed as a business, we needed performers to very clearly understand that we *were* a business as we developed our relationships with them. He said, "Allan, do you want us to be loved, or do you want us to be respected? To be loved is easy. All we need to do is give the bands free drinks, don't put limits on their guest lists, pick up a lot of important people's tabs, and everyone will want to work here. Every night will be a party, but we won't be able to pay our bills. On the other hand, if we establish basic house rules, which are the same for the headliner and the opening act, and stick to them, we won't be loved but we might be respected, and we will still have a business." This led to two of our boilerplate rules for performers at the club: When it came to guest lists, besides the performers, each person connected to the band—roadies, tech people, etc.—would be allowed two guests per show; and all acts would get a 30 percent discount on any food or drinks delivered to the dressing rooms, and a 50 percent discount on anything they ordered themselves from the front bar. [*There would be exceptions over the years, as a particularly rewarding engagement might result in artists' tabs getting ripped up. But mostly this rule stuck and worked.*]

We also decided that, since this was now our club, we wouldn't negotiate for "options," which nearly all the other club owners did in those days. Options in contracts gave clubs exclusive rights to an artist for future performances, and usually, you got one or two for a fixed rate, and that would hold even if, say, an up-and-coming performer became a full-fledged concert star before their next appearance. We just figured if someone liked playing the club and was treated well, they'd want to come back, and we'd be willing to pay them more because they'd likely draw more. And when it came to customers, we knew the sound was going to be great, and we knew they were coming first and foremost to hear music. Those nights I spent at Birdland had always stayed with me, especially knowing that I could pay my money to get in, and if I wanted a drink or some food, I could get something, but if I didn't want anything, I wasn't forced to. So we decided to have only an admission fee and never a minimum. Even though it would cost us money, I felt very strongly about it.

The chef, we got from the Village Gate—a wonderful guy named John Hargrove, who everybody called "John the Chef." He was an amazing short-order cook; this guy could get out hamburgers and fries like a one-man army. The rest of the kitchen staff was a prep person and a dishwasher. The first house manager we hired was Al Lewis, a guy from the Mercer Arts Center, which Art [D'Lugoff] had also operated. His background was as a restaurateur and theater person. He always wore a jacket and tie, and he did look pretty out of place. And the person we hired for security was Tony DiGiovanni, who to most people seemed like he stepped out of a Martin Scorsese movie, but was also a great guy—if you got to know him.

BOB IOZZIA: Al was the epitome of old-school, from his slicked-back Al Jolson hair to his many years in the restaurant/bar/nightclub industry. He was by far the oldest among us, maybe three times older than some of us, and at least twice as old as Allan and Stanley. His wardrobe of choice, a gray suit with a necktie never loosened, contrasted sharply with the staff's typical look of long hair, wrinkled shirts, and faded jeans with honest rips and holes. Al also insisted on being called *Mr. Lewis*. I guess he thought his status as boss would be undermined if he wasn't addressed formally, at least while we all were "on the floor." One day, probably when we were not "on the floor," I said to him, "Al, no matter what you're called, everyone will still know you're the boss. You're the only one here with a real haircut and neatly pressed clothing." Tony, while not as young and casually dressed as the rest of us, still bristled at addressing him as *Mr. Lewis*. His response to one of Al's *Call Me Mr. Lewis* lectures was, "Ok, Al, I got it," before walking away.

ALLAN PEPPER: We built small offices for ourselves up a circular flight of stairs from the main club, and on a recommendation from our accountant, we hired a bookkeeper, Rose Singer, who was a modern Orthodox Jew. So it was a pretty diverse crew of people, to say the least. We also brought on music publicist Carol Strauss to help get the word out as we were getting close to opening night, and ad agent Jude Lyons to handle all our advertising.

CAROL [STRAUSS] KLENFNER: It was Ira Mayer who put me together with Allan and Stanley. He told me he had these friends who were opening a club and would I talk to them about publicizing it, so we arranged for a meeting. They were still in the construction phase when I first met them, and nothing much was there, but I had an idea about how to publicize it. It was going to be the only venue of that size in New York, and it came to me that it would be welcomed by the music community and also by the journalists who covered music in the city. So I came up with an idea to make them feel like they were a part of it, and that was to do a few small receptions—do a walk through, giving people all the details about the care that was being put into the sound system, the lighting, all the technical stuff, and how comfortable it was going to be and what a great place it would be for listening to music. And we got some stories in advance. And what happened was it really became that. It was logical to me that that was the way to go, so people could feel like they were a part of making it succeed. That was my little stroke of genius. We sent out a press kit in advance of the opening, explaining just how carefully the club was being put together, and it included pre-printed Rolodex cards with the address and Allan and Stanley's names and phone numbers on them. *[Once the club opened, a Bottom Line press kit was also sent to acts in advance of their appearances. It included pictures of the club, diagrams of the stage with technical specifications, information about the house soundboard and monitors, the house rules about guest lists, food, and drinks and, last but not least, an explanation of New York State drug laws.]*

JUDE LYONS: I first got to know Allan and Stanley when I was working at Buddha Records and they had Revival signed to the label. I was in the production department, booking studio time, working on album covers, dealing with pressing plants, and in general getting records ready for release. I then moved over to marketing, and from there got involved with the ad agency that handled Buddha product. That led me to start getting clients who were local promoters, and when I heard about The Bottom Line opening, right away I got what they were trying to do. I took them out to dinner at Joe's Pier 52, the big seafood restaurant—Oh, god, the way to Stanley's heart was through his stomach, wasn't it?—and we had quite the feast, and by the end of the night, they were coming with me and I was going to be their agency. At that time, the advertising business was in a state of flux when it came to record companies and rock and roll. Promoters really didn't do radio spots, and you were lucky if newspapers let you place an ad COD. At the *[New York] Times*, forget it; you had to pay when you ordered the ad, and they wouldn't give you credit. The big agencies weren't into it; they didn't think rock and roll was going to be big, but because of my Buddha connections, I was able to get credit and that was a big thing. After Allan and Stanley signed on with me, I had a young woman named Olga working as an art director, and she designed the Bottom Line logo, which was in the ads and went on the club's marquee. Like the theater illustrator Al Hirschfeld, who used to work his daughter Nina's name into all his drawings, Olga snuck her name in the Bottom Line logo, in the last loop of the last "e." We also came up with the "tombstone" design for the club's print ads, though we had to flatten out the top very quickly after Stanley found out that it was a $350 pop for the extra room the top took up in the ads for the Times.

While Pepper and Snadowsky were hoping to open The Bottom Line right at the beginning of 1974, a snag in getting the liquor license approved delayed the scheduled opening until the middle of February. Adding to the general anxiety of getting things ready for the grand opening was the fact that Eileen Pepper had been expecting the birth of another child sometime around the first week of March. Nature, however, had other plans.

IRA MAYER: I was living on the Upper West Side, and I often went to Brooklyn for little parties that Allan and Eileen would throw at their house. On January 22, 1974, I went there for one of them. Eileen was practicing her breathing exercises from her Lamaze classes for the upcoming birth, and all of a sudden she said, "Put your hand on my thigh and squeeze as hard as you can. I want to simulate a contraction." I got a little skittish. I was twenty, and I didn't really want to see a baby being born, but I did it, and after a little while, I went home. That very night, Eileen's water broke, and they took her to the hospital, and the next day Allan called to tell me she'd given birth. "Mazel tov," I said, and Allan said, "Say it twice, Ira. She had twins." It was five weeks before her due date.

Just as Bonnie and Stacey Pepper had a twin debut, after some final preparations (the sound system was tested out with a run-through set by Revival, thus giving them the distinction of being the first act to ever perform on the club's stage), The Bottom Line had double opening nights as well: On February 11, a "soft" opening was held for family, friends, and others who'd assisted in some way in making the club a reality. Entertainment the first night was provided by Labelle, who later in the year would explode into major stardom with their frisky hit, "Lady Marmalade." The next night, February 12, came the "official" opening—a dazzling affair featuring as opener the British folk/blues singer Gary Farr and headlined by Dr. John, the bon temps roulezing New Orleans singer/pianist, who was joined by surprise guests Johnny Winter and Stevie Wonder for a rollicking impromptu jam session. The audience this time included scores of music industry insiders, members of the music and entertainment press, and a host of celebrities including Mick Jagger, Carly Simon, Bette Midler, Charles Mingus, Billy Cobham, Don Kirshner, and actors Rip Torn and Geraldine Page. For those on the inside, the grand opening was an especially magical and memorable night.

SAM MCKEITH (Booking agent): In 1973, I had to go down to Washington, DC, to cover an appearance by Cheech and Chong, who I represented at the time for my agency, William Morris. While I was there, I met Carol Strauss, who was working as their publicist for Gibson and Stromberg and, as fate would have it, we ended up on the same flight back to New York. So we began talking about our jobs, what she did, what I did, we exchanged business cards, and when we landed, she went her way, and I went my way. A few months later, I received a call from Carol out of the blue telling me there was a new club that was going to open and if I was interested, I should give these guys a call—and that happened to be Allan and Stanley. So I called them, and we got together in the Village and chatted, though at that time, it wasn't my booking territory. I had New England, Philadelphia, Delaware, and Ohio. Another guy was handling New York, but right around that time he'd become one of the department heads at the agency and really wasn't doing much booking himself, so New York was open to me as an agent. Allan and Stanley told me about the club and what they were trying to do, more like a small theater, where people could come, have something decent to eat, and see good music, tasteful music, in a really good environment. I still remember the address—15 West Fourth Street. When they were looking around for an act for opening night, I had Dr. John, who'd had that hit "In the Right Place" not too long before that, and I was able to convince his people that it would be great exposure to make inroads in the New York market, and they went for it, and we did the deal. Not much money, but a great deal of publicity.

I was also working with Stevie Wonder at the time. Stevie had just moved to New York, staying at the Fifth Avenue Hotel, and I told him about this new club opening and Dr. John playing. I said, "You should come," and he said, "Get a table, I'll show up." I was married at the time to actress Sheila Frazier, who was the female lead in the *Superfly* movies, and we had a good table, and then Stevie showed up; we got him in and seated, and now all kinds of people are coming by the table to say hello. Out of the blue, there's Mick Jagger. He sits down, starts talking to Stevie, I try to interject something, he just keeps going, talking about *Goat's Head Soup* and "Angie." Anyway, that's how Stevie got there. And in those days, the custom was if someone big showed up, they jammed. And that's what happened. You don't see that much these days, 'cause now everybody would want to get paid. In those days, you didn't think about getting paid. You just got up and played.

IRA MAYER: I know Allan and Stanley originally wanted the space to the right side of the stage for dancing. I danced with Eileen that night—and I don't dance. I think they may have been a little disappointed at the time that they couldn't get a bigger name than Dr. John, but musically they were thrilled to get him. They were hoping for something to make a big splash. But it established a hipness factor, and that certainly proved to be very important for the club.

BOB IOZZIA: Everybody had a sense that because it was unique—a 400-seat nightclub that was really going to fill a void in the local music scene. The industry took notice that they were building a first-class facility, and musicians, record company executives, managers, booking agents, everybody was aware of the club coming, and it created a buzz. Sure, there was some trepidation, but even on opening night, there was a real spirit inside the club. We felt it couldn't fail.

PAUL GUZZONE: My girlfriend at the time was a hippie type—she later went off to join the Peace Corps—and she was very outspoken and not impressed by celebrities. Opening night, it was fairly star-studded, and there was a rumor that Mick Jagger was going to show up, and sure enough he did. We were at the first one, and we'd had some drinks, and after it emptied out, there was a limousine idling across the street from the club. It was during the time of the gas shortage, and my girlfriend walked over to the limo, knocked on the driver's window, and started screaming at him to shut off the engine. "You're wasting gas and polluting the planet!" she yelled. And then Jagger came out and guess where he headed—right to that limo. I don't recall him saying anything. He just got in, and the car pulled away, thank goodness.

For Stanley Snadowsky and Allan Pepper, it was a triumphant moment which, like all good things, had come to two who'd waited. Eight years after he'd put up the $250 to start Jazz Interactions, Stanley's belief in his best friend was paying dividends clearly beyond anything he could have envisioned. And not far past the deadline for the pledge Allan had made to Eileen that he'd make something concrete happen with his career by the time he turned thirty or look for something else to do, he now had his very own club to own and operate. Pepper and Snadowsky had built it—and people came. And beginning with opening night, what was soon transpiring inside The Bottom Line's front doors on a regular basis were moments and events that would significantly affect not only the musical landscape of New York City and the overall music industry, but the very lives of people on both sides of its welcoming stage.

5 HELLS ANGELS, A JAZZ DEVIL, AND NEW YORK DOLLS

The Bottom Line had been open for only a few months in 1974 when Pepper and Snadowsky welcomed Grateful Dead guitarist Jerry Garcia to the club for his side project with Bay Area keyboardist Merle Saunders. As an outgrowth of early 1970s impromptu jam sessions at San Francisco's club the Matrix that teamed the ever-adventurous Garcia with soulful jazz/r&b organist Saunders, the duo were looking for an intimate venue to make their band's New York debut. To that end, Pepper and Snadowsky had been contacted by John Scher, the promoter best known at the time for running Passaic's Capitol Theatre and his association with the Dead, for whom he'd been coordinating East Coast appearances since the '71 closing of Bill Graham's Fillmore East. A deal was quickly struck, and the band was booked to play for three nights just prior to the Fourth of July.

ALLAN PEPPER: Two hours leading up to the first show, we already had a line around the block just for standing room, and John took us backstage to meet Garcia. We went to the dressing room, and Jerry could not have been nicer; he even thanked us for letting him do the gig at the club. We were feeling great, but as we left the dressing room, we heard this enormous roar outside. We went out to the door to take a look, and as far as the eye could see, there were Hells Angels coming up the block on their bikes. We just froze. Coming back inside, we learned that Garcia [long a friend of San Francisco's Hells Angels motorcycle club] had placed on the guest list members of the New York chapter, whose clubhouse was just blocks away on East Third Street. We go back to the dressing room to see Jerry, and in walks Sandy Alexander, who was the president of the Angels' New York chapter. Jerry introduces us, and we shake hands and engage in some small talk, and as we left the dressing room, I pulled Stanley aside and said, "Look, I think we gotta do something, and quick, because if not, we might have a real problem."

We talked a little bit, and Stanley came up with a few ideas. Then we found Sandy and said, "Can we talk to you outside for a minute?" He said, "Sure. What about?" We said, "Look, you guys are welcome here, but we need to establish some ground rules." He said, "Like what?" We were feeling pretty nervous, because we didn't know how he might respond. I mean, he was the leader of New York's Hells Angels. So Stanley said, "Well, there's three things," and for each thing Stanley asked for, we just held our breath. He said, "One, you guys can come any time you want, and we won't charge you admission, but since the seats at the club are for the paying customers, you must hang out only at the bar, and pay for your drinks and any food you order." Sandy said ok. "Second," Stanley said, "under no circumstances can we have you guys intimidating the bartenders or any of the staff to get anything for free." He said ok. "And third, the most important, if there is any kind of problem, you have to take it outside. There can never be an altercation, or fight, or disturbance inside the club." And Sandy said ok to that, too. He gave us his hand, we shook on it, and then he gave me his home phone number and said if there was ever a problem to let him know.

The Garcia/Saunders shows went off without a hitch, and from then on, the Angels came and went to The Bottom Line mostly without incident. (It was agreed that it would be best for everyone if they didn't have to stand in line to get in, figuring something was bound to happen if they did, so when they showed up for a show, they'd be ushered in through the front door, go straight to the bar, and stay there.) There was one show in early 1975, however, where the "house rules" were tested.

ALLAN PEPPER: We had (singer-songwriter) Phoebe Snow headlining. Her song "Poetry Man" from her debut album had become a big hit, and the club was packed; we had celebrities in the audience like Paul Simon and Caroline Kennedy. Dick Feller opened, and part of his act was being self-deprecating. Two of the Angels were at the bar, and they thought reacting to him would be part of the show and started yelling things at him. I could sense that some of the audience was getting uncomfortable, so I went over and said, "Hey, guys, that's not cool. You think you could stop?" And one of them looked at me and said, "Get the fuck out of my face," so I went to the front office and called Sandy. I was nervous and, frankly, I was scared, and I said, "Sandy, I hate to bother you, but I have a potential problem here, and I need your help." I told him what had just happened, and he said, "Ok, I'll be right over." He came over in a few minutes, walked into the club, and gestured to the two guys with his finger to follow him to the end of the bar. I don't know what he said, but after a minute he came over and told me, "You won't have a problem," and left.

At the end of the night, I'm standing in front of the office, and the two Angels come walking over to me and say, "Are you the owner of this place?" I said, "Yeah," and they said, "What's your name?" I said, "Allan Pepper," and I'm thinking to myself, "Oh my god, I'm gonna get hit." I'm standing against the door of my office, with my hand behind me feeling for the doorknob, and this really big guy towering over me—I think his name was Filthy Phil—suddenly his whole tone shifts and he says, "Hey, man, why did you have to call the chief? You just should have told us who you were. The chief was not happy." And I said, "Ok, guys, next time it'll be different." Once Sandy had talked to him, all the bravado and menace he'd shown me before turned into a childlike whimper.

Sandy Alexander was a hell of a guy. He was very articulate, and very charismatic. Not a very big guy physically, but he was a former Golden Gloves boxer and an ex-Marine. He was originally from California, and he actually came to New York looking to try and study at the Actor's Studio and maybe make it as an actor before he became the founder of the Angels chapter here. He started hanging out at the club a bit, and he was pretty easy to like; we became friends. One time he was there during the day, and we were just talking, and I happened to mention that my wedding anniversary was coming up, and he asked when it was. I said, "June 24," and he said, "Shit, that's my anniversary, too. Why don't we go out together and celebrate?" As soon as he said it, I started going through the mental Rolodex in my mind of what polite excuse I could make, and I guess he saw the look on my face because he leaned over and hugged me, and with a smile, he whispered, "It's Ok, I won't wear my colors." I knew he liked theater, so I told him, "I have an idea. Let's all go out and see *A Chorus Line*. I'll pay for the tickets, and you can pick up dinner afterwards." And that's what we did. Eileen and I and Sandy and his wife, Collette, celebrated our anniversaries watching *A Chorus Line* and then a late dinner afterwards at Joe's Pier 52.

We figured that'd be the night, but when we finished dinner, Sandy said, "Hey, you guys ever go on a hansom cab ride around Central Park?" We said we hadn't, and he said, "Neither have I, and I've always wanted to. Let's do it." So we're in the cab, riding through the park, and Sandy starts talking to the driver. He made it sound like we were tourists, and says to the guy, "I'm just curious. You guys get robbed much?" We wind up at the Plaza Hotel, where Sandy had booked a room for the night, and first he asked if we wanted him to book us a room, too. We said no, but then he wants us to come up and at least see his suite. We get to the room, and there's a chandelier, and soon Colette is standing on a chair seeing if she can take some pieces of cut glass for a souvenir. All in all, it was quite a night.

***

ALLAN PEPPER: The day after opening night in February, Stanley and I woke up in our apartments in Brooklyn, and we were really flying high. But as for any notion of "Be careful what you wish for because you might get it," that didn't enter the picture for us. The glow of getting the club off the ground certainly stayed with us, but it was really hard work. In the beginning, the shows were at 8:30 and 11:30 during the week, and nine and twelve on the weekend. So if we did a weeknight late show at 11:30, we were getting out at 3:30, maybe even 4 a.m., heading home to Brooklyn, and coming right back to the club at 10:30 in the morning.

When we first opened, we had an alarm system because we had equipment on the stage, liquor behind the bar, and that alarm would go off on its own sometimes because of a car horn on the street or a mouse. So we'd be home sleeping, and the phone would ring telling us, "Attention. Attention: Robbery in progress on West Fourth Street." Stanley and I would call each other, get dressed, grab a cab, and go in. We'd quietly open the door and find nothing. So after it happened the fifth or sixth time, we said, "Fuck it," and made a deal with the janitor to stay over all night so we'd always have somebody on premises.

New and exciting things were also going on at home for both Bottom Line owners. Between the newly arrived twins Stacey and Bonnie and their two-and-a-half-year-old son Gordon, the Peppers now had three very young children at home. Meanwhile, Snadowsky's daughter Leslie was also just two and a half, making sure that things were fairly hectic in both owners' personal and professional lives. Still, once the club opened, their focus on work remained true.

ALLAN PEPPER: We had opened the club, and it was a dream come true because we had a very specific vision of what we wanted this place to be. And it was: Very quickly, just a couple of weeks in, the opening Dr. John shows had done really well, and soon we were selling out our shows and working virtually every single night.

In planning strategies regarding contracting talent to perform at The Bottom Line, Pepper was spiritually guided by three important behind-the-scenes musical figures from recent times: Art D'Lugoff, whose Village Gate had featured greats from the fields of both jazz and comedy—two genres dear to Pepper since his teen years; Steve Paul, the onetime wunderkind promoter whose midtown Manhattan nitespot The Scene had been one of the hippest clubs for live music during its 1964–70 run; and Bill Graham, the towering showman of late '60s rock music presentation and his many legendary shows at the Fillmore East before its closing in 1971. (As Pepper would often say: "Bill Graham said he wanted to be Sol Hurock," referring to New York's iconic classical music impresario. "I wanted to be Bill Graham.")

ALLAN PEPPER: Like Steve had done at the Scene, I started looking at what acts would be scheduled to be in the area and started booking whichever were the best acts that were available, in any genre. From the get-go, we wanted the music we presented at the club to be very eclectic, so after Dr. John's shows were finished, we had [bluegrass band] the Dillards and then [singer-songwriter and "City of New Orleans" composer] Steve Goodman and [acoustic blues artist] John Hammond. We were open to anything, and as the weeks and months progressed, we looked and saw what was and what wasn't working and started fine-tuning things because a number of things were theoretical until we opened.

The certificate of occupancy was for 450, including standing room at the bar. Originally, we had space for 435 people, but very quickly we learned the space between the tables was too tight for the waitresses to squeeze through, so we took some tables and thirty-five seats out, and that made a difference. It was helpful that we had a long bar, which could seat about a dozen more. We also realized that we had to do something about the menu. We had pretty lofty ideas about what we wanted to serve, but then we saw the reality. We simply could not get the food out fast enough, mostly because the menu was too broad. On the original menu, we actually had things like different kinds of omelets, French toast, filet mignon with mushroom caps au jus, sliced steak, and Chinese spare ribs with duck sauce. We got rid of all of them and finally narrowed it down to standard club food: Burgers, fried chicken, pizza, french fries, and brownies. And when it came to the talent, we weren't offering performers anything they weren't paying for, and an agent named Sandy Foster said, "Look, you gotta put *something* in the dressing rooms," so we came up with a fruit basket along with candy and Oreo cookies with a note that said, "Welcome to The Bottom Line." We took a lot of ribbing for it, but we thought it was cool. I remember one of the opening acts was told by the stage manager the house rules and said, "Look, they're treating everyone, even the headliners, with the same disrespect, so you can't be pissed, ok?"

Almost from the very start, word got out around New York about The Bottom Line's excellent sound system, the tight but mostly comfortable seating arrangements, and, most importantly, the professionalism with which Pepper and Snadowsky were going about their business. And as the club settled into its place in the city's live entertainment landscape, the sheer range of acts appearing there helped quickly build its reputation as arguably New York's premier showcase venue, for both rising artists as well as established ones. In just the first eighteen months of the club's existence, The Bottom Line presented stars from all points of the musical compass. From the world of folk were the likes of Pete Seeger, Eric Andersen, Buffy Sainte-Marie, Doc Watson, Tom Rush, David Bromberg, Loudon Wainwright, Carolyn Hester, the New Lost City Ramblers, Dave Van Ronk, Mary Travers, Taj Mahal, and Janis Ian; from the blues, Mike Bloomfield, Elvin Bishop, James Cotton, Bonnie Raitt, Freddie King, Buddy Guy, and Junior Wells; from jazz, Mose Allison, Larry Coryell, Gato Barbieri, George Benson, Weather Report, Gary Burton, the Brecker Brothers, Roy Haynes, Bill Evans, and Charles Mingus; from rock, the Hollies, Eric Burdon, Orleans, Flo & Eddie, and Patti Smith; from country, Emmylou Harris, the Nitty Gritty Dirt Band, Jerry Reed, Asleep at the Wheel, John Hartford, and Waylon Jennings; and from r&b, Labelle, Betty Davis, Grover Washington Jr., and the Pointer Sisters.

Very quickly, record companies began to utilize The Bottom Line to promote emerging artists. In April, just weeks after the club's opening, Epic Records bought out the club for a press party for one of their country acts that they were trying to cross over to the pop charts: Tanya Tucker, who'd recently been featured on the cover of Rolling Stone and had just achieved her third straight chart-topping country single with the provocative "Would You Lay with Me (In a Field of Stone)"—a record made all the more provocative because Tucker had yet to reach her sixteenth birthday.

ALLAN PEPPER: Because of Tanya's age, we consulted our liquor lawyer, and he said, "You probably should close the bar for her performance." So we did, and the poor promo man who'd brought down [influential WNEW-FM personality] Scott Muni got so uptight he snuck in a bottle for Scott, and Stanley and I kind of flipped out over it, because after all the thought we'd put into it, and now this happens. But keep in mind, until the [country-leaning downtown venue] Lone Star Café showed up [in 1976], there really weren't good places for country music to showcase in New York.

Tucker's show didn't result in any major movement for her over to the pop charts, even though her record company tried to present her in a "different" light than what the conservative country establishment in Nashville was accustomed to. As the irrepressible rock critic R. Meltzer loudly observed from his ringside seat, the teen starlet didn't quite fit the part of country sex kitten; one could plainly see the panty lines beneath her skin-tight orange leather jumpsuit.

In April 1974, Pepper booked his first straightforward rock and roll show—a glam-rock themed affair with the Detroit-by-way-of-England pioneering female singer/bassist Suzi Quatro headlining and local glam-rockers New York Dolls opening. With their gender-bending image and snotty attitude, the upstart Dolls were ahead of the curve as influencers on the nascent punk scene that was beginning to develop in the city, and their lone appearance at The Bottom Line was a memorable one for lead singer David Johansen and his band—albeit mostly for what went on offstage rather than on. Before the early show even started, there was a bomb scare, and the club needed to be immediately cleared while the police were called in and the club was searched. While thankfully no bomb was found, there was damage done to the club, and the Dolls were the culprits—specifically their bass player, Arthur "Killer" Kane.

DAVID JOHANSEN: While everyone was out, Arthur went around the room and started drinking everything left on the tables. And then we got into an argument backstage, which at the time wasn't really anything new for us. Whenever we had any kind of disagreement, within a few sentences, it'd usually turn into a fistfight with several of us rolling around on the floor. Anyway, Arthur threw a bottle at me, and I ducked, and it broke the dressing room mirror.

ALLAN PEPPER: Our stage manager had heard a crash backstage and came and got me. I rushed into the dressing room, and I was horrified by what I saw. There was glass everywhere and the whole room was a mess. They were the first act that literally showed no respect for the club.

DAVID JOHANSEN: Allan was yelling at me, saying they were going to deduct the cost of the mirror from our pay, and he swore I'd never play the club again. I guess because I was the lead singer, he thought I was the band leader.

As it happened, after the Dolls' demise in 1975, David Johansen did begin returning to The Bottom Line as a solo performer starting in 1978.

ALLAN PEPPER: After the Dolls debacle, I booked David the first time out of respect for, and my friendship with, Steve [Paul], who was by then managing him. Over time, though, David and I became friends as well, and had a lot of laughs over that first encounter. In fact, over the years, David exhibited every one of his musical personalities at The Bottom Line, from the Dolls to his own early solo work to his partying "Hot Hot Hot" Buster Poindexter persona to fronting his Americana roots group the Harry Smiths.

DAVID JOHANSEN: I give Allan credit for giving me a forum for a lot of things I've done. Poindexter started out as a lark, but Allan let me do a residency once a week for several months. Then we did one of the anniversary shows, and he said, "Do anything you want; if there's an idea you've been toying with, try it out," and that's how the Harry Smith thing got going, which took me back to bluesy '30s stuff I used to sing before the Dolls even got started.

That November, The Bottom Line hosted jazz icon Miles Davis. The mercurial trumpeter, long known for his unpredictable performances, didn't fail to live up to his reputation.

ALLAN PEPPER: I was very excited that he wanted to play the club because, since I came from a jazz background, Miles meant a lot to me. Not to mention the fact that the very first time I met Eileen, she was going to see Miles at Birdland, and that really blew me away. Anyway, he wanted each show to be two sets; he would play forty-five minutes, take a break, and then play another forty-five. A little tricky, given we had two shows each night, but we said ok. Well, comes the late show the first night, and Miles comes out, plays twenty-five minutes, and then I guess he decided that was enough, and he just walks off and doesn't come back; he's finished for the night.

SAM ELLIS (Stage manager): I thought something might have gone wrong, so I went backstage. I asked if Miles was coming back out, and his road manager Jim Rose says no. I said, "That can't be it. He only played twenty-five minutes!" And without missing a beat, he said, "Yeah, but wasn't it a solid twenty-five?"

ALLAN PEPPER: Stanley and I were pretty much dumbfounded by what was happening, so we quickly conferred about how to handle it. Now keep in mind that when we opened the club it was very important for us to be consistent and very professional. We charged a higher ticket price for Miles, and we just didn't think it was right to take that money from the audience and then for them to get only twenty-five minutes, so we announced over the PA that, since Davis had to end his set prematurely, anyone who wanted their money back could turn in their ticket stub at the box office on their way out and get a refund. A lot of people were upset, obviously, and did just that. But there were also folks who said to us, "Why are you doing this? You don't have to give us our money back. That's Miles." It was like it was almost hipper to be stiffed than to ask for a refund; part of the Miles mystique. The fans were more forgiving than we were. He still had a second night to play, so Stanley called Miles' manager and renegotiated the price. He told him we weren't going to pay for that second show. But the next night he gave two great, long performances.

Miles played a few more times at the club, and let's just say that you never knew what would happen with him. He usually was on time for his performances, but one night it's getting to be thirty-five, almost forty minutes past his start time for the second half of his early show, and we've got a long line already outside, and we need to get things moving. So I decide to go backstage and I'm about to go into his dressing room when Jim Rose steps in front of me and says, "Listen, you can't go in right now," and I say, "Why not?" and he says, "'Cause he's getting head. He'll be out soon." Apparently, they'd brought a hooker in to service him before the show. That was Miles.

November of 1974 also saw Tom Waits, the gravel-voiced singer-songwriter who'd recently come into some commercial good fortune when the Eagles featured his song "Ol' 55" on their hit On the Border album, make his Bottom Line debut opening for pop-rockers Orleans, of "Still the One" fame. The notoriously eccentric hipster pianist proved to be just that during his time at the club.

ALLAN PEPPER: When Tom Waits came through for the first time, he showed up in the afternoon and Steve Rosenblum (the club's general manager) thought he was just a bum who had wandered over from the Bowery. Steve took his arm and started, gently, to walk him out of the club, and Waits was trying to tell him who he was, but the way he looked, Steve just didn't believe him. They get to the lobby by the front door, and there's a promo picture of Waits, and Tom points to it and says, "Hey man, I keep telling you, that's me. *I'm* Tom Waits." And Steve turned him around and brought him back in.

SAM ELLIS: We'd just gotten a brand new baby grand, and during his set, Waits left a lit cigarette on the piano and singed it; we never replaced it.

RILEY: After the shows were over, especially on weeknights when we finished up earlier than on the weekends, a bunch of us would go bar-hopping and usually wind up at Phebe's on the east side, where we'd drink 'til four and then throw money at the bartender. We were headed there pretty late the night that Waits had played. He was the opening act and had left after his second set. Well, we get to the corner of Bleecker and University and there's Waits, really drunk and literally hanging onto a lamppost. We were concerned, but a friend of his came over and said, "Don't worry, we got him."

On February 12, 1975, exactly one year after The Bottom Line's opening, folk-blues guitarist/singer David Bromberg played The Bottom Line's first anniversary show—a date that came about, in somewhat of a roundabout fashion, because of Bob Dylan.

ALLAN PEPPER: Stanley and I were approached by (Columbia Records executive) Don DeVito. Dylan had already come down to see Buffy Sainte-Marie, and Don said that Dylan had talked about doing something at the club. Our mouths dropped open at the thought. Then Don said that, given the size of The Bottom Line, Dylan certainly wouldn't want it advertised. So we got to talking, and we said, suppose we got a band together, or somebody he'd be really comfortable with, and say we advertise them, and then if at the last minute he wanted to play, he'd perform with them. DeVito agreed that it was a good idea, so we said, how about Bromberg? And that's how that first anniversary show came about. David was actually a placeholder for Dylan.

The ever-elusive Dylan didn't wind up playing that night, but Bromberg's Bottom Line anniversary appearance started a tradition that would continue for the entire existence of the club. Indeed, he'd long been booked to play on February 12, 2004, when, just weeks before, the club closed for good.

ALLAN PEPPER: Those anniversary shows were some of the happiest moments for me at the club. When Bromberg was hot and got going, he was equally as charismatic as Springsteen in terms of what he could do with an audience. When he was inspired, he was like a puppeteer, and it was unbelievable what he could get an audience to do as a body in terms of responding to him.

DAVID BROMBERG: The first time I recall meeting Allan and Stanley was when they were booking Folk City. Their office was the parking meter. I saw The Bottom Line as they were getting it built, and I actually persuaded them to put toilets in each dressing room. At first they were just going to have the bathrooms at the side of the club for everyone, but I told them they really needed to have separate ones for the performers; it's embarrassing to be taking a leak and having to shake hands with people. And they did. They had very strict business rules, which I understood. When you played there, you got a bread basket—well, not quite a bread basket—with some fruit, cookies, and candy. That was the entire hospitality. And you had to pay for every drink. But if I came there not to perform, but just to hear somebody, my money wasn't any good; they just wouldn't take it. And that was very sweet. I remember taking the subway home after gigs, and once I could afford to take a cab home, I felt I'd made it. In 1979, when I got married, my wife Nancy and I had our reception at the club. That was an event: There were people there who I still don't know or how they got there. I know John Goodman was there; he came with Richie Shulberg. Goodman wasn't famous then. [*Shulberg at the time had a radio show on WBAI that featured improvisational comedy by the then-struggling actor.*]

Allan and Stanley booked me for The Bottom Line for the first time on the anniversary of the club opening, and while I didn't play there on the second anniversary in 1976—I found out later that they were so crazed running the place they actually forgot it was the club's anniversary that year—they did bring me back for the next one, and then they kept booking me for that date, and I never wanted to say no. They always gave me a gift when I played the date, and it was a very nice thing for them to do. One thing I always remember about those shows: We always sold out, and seats were hard to get, but there was always somebody at one of the tables right in front of the stage who would fall asleep after they got too drunk. That was funny.

While Dylan didn't make that initial anniversary show, he did make an unannounced onstage appearance several months later, when blues legend Muddy Waters came in for a three-day engagement and Dylan showed up the first night. (He was possibly drawn to the show because Waters had as a special guest the great '20s vocalist Victoria Spivey, who in March 1962 had given then twenty-one-year-old Dylan one of his earliest opportunities to record; he appeared as a sideman on several tracks alongside Big Joe Williams, Roosevelt Sykes, and Lonnie Johnson on the Three Kings and the Queen album released on Spivey's eponymous independent label.)

MARC SILAG (Stage manager): Allan brought Dylan backstage and introduced Bob to me and said, "Just tell Marc what you want to do." Dylan says to me, "I got two harmonicas—I think they were C and G—so tell Muddy I'll do anything he wants to do, but it'll need to be in those keys." I waited until the next song ended, and I got onstage and whispered in Muddy's ear, "Bob Dylan is here and he'd love to sit in with you and play harmonica, as long as it's in these keys 'cause those are the harps he's brought." Muddy says, "Ok, tell him I'll bring him up after the next song." I go backstage, tell Dylan that Muddy's going to bring him out after the next song ends. Sure enough, the song ends, and Muddy says, "Ladies and gentlemen, we've got a friend who's gonna come up and sit in with us. Give him a big hand—*Bob Denver!*" Dylan looked at me, I looked at him, and he just shrugged his shoulders and went out and played with Muddy.

In the spring of '75, Pepper and Snadowsky negotiated to bring singer-songwriter Neil Sedaka to The Bottom Line for a weekend engagement in early May. Sedaka's hit-making career had started when Connie Francis scored with his (and co-writer Howard Greenfield)'s "Stupid Cupid" in 1958 (the two also composed the theme for the 1961 film, "Where the Boys Are," which Francis starred in and would become her signature song), and throughout the late '50s and early '60s, Sedaka himself registered six Top Ten hits, including 1962s chart-topper, "Breaking Up Is Hard to Do." A casualty of the coming of the Beatles and the British Invasion, Sedaka's star had been reduced to a bare glimmer when fan Elton John signed him to his Rocket label in 1973, and the association led to a surprising comeback. In early 1975, Sedaka's recording of "Laughter in the Rain" reached Number One, as would the cover of his song "Love Will Keep Us Together" by the duo The Captain and Tennille. For the Brooklyn native, the Bottom Line shows were to be a fitting homecoming. The contract talks for his appearance, however, took an interesting turn when Sedaka's manager asked Pepper and Snadowsky for a favor that would have ramifications at the club for the remainder of its history.

ALLAN PEPPER: We'd booked Neil Sedaka for three days, but then we got a call from his manager, Elliot Abbott, who said, "You know Neil's playing there for much less than he could get in other places, and it looks like we can get a date in Connecticut. Could you let us out of Sunday night?" We'd only been open for a little over a year, and we'd already sold a lot of tickets for both Friday and Saturday. He said, "Look, I'll do anything you want, within reason, to get out of this date." We kept saying no to anything he proposed, and finally, as a joke, he said, "Hey, I'll even take you to any restaurant you want in Manhattan." Now at that point, Stanley and I had always been curious about the Palm [*a well-known Manhattan steak and lobster restaurant*]. So Stanley says, "Would that include the Palm?" So Elliot for the first time now realizes he has an opening, and says he'll take us anywhere we want to go. So Stanley says, "Hold on for a minute," and gets back on the phone with the contract in front of him. "Ok," Stanley says, "But for the rider, I want you to include that talent agrees to take presenter to the Palm before the engagement," and Elliot agrees to put it in. Later, Sedaka's agent calls us and says, "What are you doing? You can't put in the contract that Neil Sedaka will take you out to dinner!" And Stanley says, "I don't see why not. You guys always ask us to provide catering. Every once in a while I think it would be nice for the talent to provide the catering. Just ask Elliot Abbott if he wants me to take it out." So the agent calls Abbott, calls us back, and it goes in the contract. So now we go to the Palm. We're having lobster, and Stanley is enjoying all this a lot. After the main courses, Elliot says to us, "You guys need to try the cheesecake." We do, and Stanley loves it, and he immediately says to me, "You know, Allan, we gotta put this cheesecake on our menu." So, if you ever enjoyed the cheesecake at The Bottom Line, you have Elliot Abbott to thank.

[*A footnote—and a large one at that—to Neil Sedaka's appearance at the club came on his Friday night show, when a small contingent of Hells Angels visiting from California showed up, brought by local Angel Vinnie, who was serving as their tour leader. Looking to impress his party, the gargantuan-sized biker approached Pepper with a request.]*

ALLAN PEPPER: Vinnie was as prototypical a biker as there ever was. He was so big he couldn't even close his vest. He comes over and tells me he wants to meet Neil, and I say, "Ok, I'll see if he can come out." I go backstage and tell Sedaka this Hells Angel named Vinnie is a fan and wants to meet him, and if he could just say hello, I'd appreciate it. From the look on his face, I'm not sure he really believed me, but he comes out from his dressing room and sees this monster in front of him, and he just freezes. Then he puts his hand out, and in that high voice of his, five-foot-five Neil Sedaka says to him, "Hello, Mr. Vinnie. Nice to meet you." It was quite a sight.

6 BORN TO KILL

THE BOSS RAISES THE BAR

On Wednesday, August 13, 1975, Bruce Springsteen began a five-night stand at The Bottom Line that would forever go down in both his and the club's history. The ten-performance engagement, timed to coincide with the imminent late August release of his third album, Born to Run, *turned out to be the star-making event of the singer-songwriter's career. Even as it happened, Springsteen was aware that the whole dynamic of his live act had changed with the success of the shows. "The band cruised through those shows like the finest machine there was," Springsteen told writer John Rockwell in an article for Rolling Stone soon afterward. "There's nothin'–nothin'–in the world to get you playing better than a gig like that. The band walked out of The Bottom Line twice as good as when they walked in." Decades later, in his Born to Run autobiography, he still regarded those performances as game-changers. "The Bottom Line was the gig that finally put us on the map as big-time contenders," he wrote. "For five nights, two shows a night, we left everything we had on the tiny stage at 15 West Fourth Street. For us, they were groundbreaking appearances . . . leaving that burn in the air of something happening . . . inside the band and on the street, you could feel the whole thing taking off . . . We got born again there . . . As Born to Run had defined us on record, these shows defined us as a live act intent on shaking you by the collar, waking you up, and all-or-nothing performances." He wasn't exaggerating, either: The shows became the stuff of legend almost as they occurred. Rave reviews poured in from every critic that covered the appearance, which helped spur increased radio airplay for the album and, with it, the record's notable commercial success: Two weeks after its release,* Born to Run *reached* Billboard's *Top Ten and soon became a gold record—and the buzz remained so high that within two months, both* Time *and* Newsweek *magazines placed Springsteen on their covers, anointing him as "Rock's New Sensation."*

Springsteen's marathon-like three-hour Bottom Line shows, which found him dancing not only on the grand piano onstage but out on the tables in the audience as well, would leave lifelong impressions on everyone who was there, from the feverish audiences that packed the club each night to The Bottom Line's own staff as well. And for Pepper, who had presented Bruce Springsteen only thirteen months before for a three-night appearance at the club that came and went with little fanfare either before or after, it was an absolute revelation.

ALLAN PEPPER: I think that first time—the summer of 1974—while a lot of his songs were getting played on the radio, you might not have been able to get it. I always joke that his first time at the club, if you wanted to come with a hundred of your friends I could have gotten you good seats. I think on the Saturday we might have done good business, but on the other two nights there were a lot of empty seats. His shows were already very long, and there was an opening act [*singer-songwriter Jeffrey Commonor*], and Columbia Records was still under something of a cloud [*the label was still reeling from a company scandal that had cost president Clive Davis his job in 1973*], so there wasn't all that much support for him. Bruce came out in an undershirt with sunglasses, kind of evoking that Marlon Brando/James Dean look from the 1950s, that *Wild One, Rebel Without a Cause* image. Meanwhile, the band was taking long solos on some of the numbers; there was a lot of improvisation all around. If you were paying attention, you could tell there was something going on in his head; it was almost like a rough draft of what ultimately happened a year later. But to be honest, those 1974 dates to me were, as a businessman, well, interminable. Each night during the early set, I was muttering to myself, "C'mon, Bruce—finish it up. We've got a second show to do."

BRUCE SPRINGSTEEN: We did a lot of club playing to stay alive at the time, like The Main Point in Philadelphia, and I guess we played The Bottom Line, too. Basically these were gigs to keep us in cornflakes, so they did what they could, and we did a lot of shows like that. At one point, we played Fat City on Long Island, and all the top echelon of the record company came in to see the opening act and then left when we came on. And [*then Springsteen manager*] Mike Appel stood at the front door taking their names as they walked out. So that was the atmosphere that we were dealing with at that time. I went down south to a radio station, and they didn't even know I had two albums out. They told me that a guy had come down from Columbia and told them to take my record off. My own record company! So I lose my airplay—my songs are too long—and I think they were more interested in pushing Billy Joel at the time. So these are the things that were happening.

It was Jon Landau who, in 1974 in Boston's alt-weekly The Real Paper, *had written perhaps the most-quoted line in the history of pop music criticism: "I have seen rock and roll's future, and its name is Bruce Springsteen." By the time of the Bottom Line shows, Landau had become not only a trusted friend and advisor but the coproducer of the pivotal Born to Run album. (He would also soon replace Appel as Springsteen's manager, a position he holds to this day.)*

JON LANDAU: Clive did a big campaign on the first album. So now the second album comes out, Clive is gone, and some of the key people are gone who had been supportive of Bruce, and they had done the big campaign and it flopped. So the general attitude at the label went from being very excited the first time out to being very cold the second time. And I mean, the album, which is a great album, never had a chance. So now it was even down to where Mike Appel told me, after I met him, that Columbia had been thinking of dropping him. And somewhere in this, two things happened. The successor to Clive Davis was Irwin Segelstein, and Irwin was from the television department. He was meant to be an interim person just to manage the company, and presumably they would have a search going on and at some point bring in somebody more specialized in music. Meanwhile, the second album is a complete flop, and Bruce is out there touring and just playing for whoever comes to the shows. And I guess that's when I saw him for the first time in Boston. And so two really important things eventually happened. One is that I wrote this article which, because of my so-called stature at that point, had some influence, and it shook things up over there.

The second thing that happened was that Irwin, I believe, lived on Long Island, and there was a theater there, the Westbury Music Fair. So Bruce plays there [in February of 1975], and as I recall the story, Bruce does his great show. At that time, he had that great version of the Dylan song, "I Want You," and he had the violinist in the group, Suki Lahav, and she was doing great stuff. And Irwin's teenage son goes to the show and he tells his father, "I don't know, Dad, but this guy's phenomenal. Why isn't this record selling?" Now CBS would have these big meetings once a week that Irwin would chair, and he comes into the meeting, I was told anecdotally at the time, and he holds up Bruce's second album cover. And he said, "My son went to see this man last Sunday night, and I have a question. Why isn't he a star?" And he just changed the direction of the company's attitude toward Bruce. The combination of that incident and the review, and what Columbia did pre-*Born to Run* was in this sort of middle period after the second album had flopped. Bruce had been getting the cold shoulder, and all of a sudden, they're taking out full-page ads in *Rolling Stone* and other relevant magazines and papers like *The Village Voice* with my quote, and they did a whole late campaign.

So now we're making *Born to Run*, and I have connected with Bruce, and so we're making the album, and I knew one thing—we were going to get a great album. I didn't have a doubt about it, but it was a very painful, taxing process. Lots of angst and just youthful intensity. And so we finished the album, and because we kept postponing it, Bruce had no money. So Mike, looking at the schedule, had set up a bunch of shows to go into immediately as soon as we finished the album, which means we would be doing shows before the album even came out. And what happens is, delay upon delay, and we're still recording. Finally we finished the sax solo on "Jungleland," and we finished mixing it, and that's the end of the album, and the guys all take the minibuses or little vans that they were using up to, I think it was Rhode Island, where Mike had booked shows.

Mike and I had a good relationship at that time. We have a good relationship today. And obviously there was a very negative period, but we would talk, and he was in the studio and he was an asset in the studio. He was a bulldog. He had energy. He could be a little, well, he had his strengths and weaknesses, as we all do. I don't remember how The Bottom Line comes up, but I think it was Mike's idea; maybe it was me talking with Mike. But the idea of five nights, whoever came up with it, Mike must have talked to Bruce about it, and I think Bruce thought it was a great idea, too. He had the confidence.

Mike Appel, Springsteen's first manager, had himself gotten a taste of musical success during the late 1960s as guitarist and singer for a primarily studio group called The Balloon Farm, which achieved one-hit wonder status with their 1968 Top Forty psychedelic rocker, "A Question of Temperature." As Springsteen's manager, Appel gained a quick reputation for two things: His unshakable belief in Bruce's talent and promise, and his often overly aggressive, at times hostile, ways of advocating for his client. Not only did Appel, as Springsteen recalled, take names when Columbia executives walked out on one of Bruce's shows, but during the winter holiday season of 1974, to underline his anger at the label's neglect in promoting Springsteen, he sent the company's top brass identical gifts—Christmas stockings stuffed with lumps of coal.

By the time Born to Run *was being completed, Appel put the band on the road for some money-making dates in the Northeast, and the Bottom Line shows were quickly lined up.*

BRUCE SPRINGSTEEN: There were a lot of expectations for the *Born to Run* album. Also, it was my last record with Columbia on the three-record deal. If it didn't go, they could have dropped me and I'd have been back in Asbury Park, millions of dollars in debt. So we had a hot thing going on around us, and a lot of it was due to the live show, of course, and the expectations for *Born to Run*. So we went into The Bottom Line.

MIKE APPEL: The booking agent, Sam McKeith, was conjuring up, "What am I going to do? What date do I want to pull here? What moves do we make?" Etcetera, etcetera. And all of a sudden, Bruce just called me. He says, "Mike, why don't we play The Bottom Line?" I said, "Well, you're not going to be able to do your full-length show. I mean, because they have to turn the audience on twice to make it profitable." He said, "Ok, I'll cut my shows, but I want to play it." I said, "Ok, I'll set it up." And I did. And that's how it started. But it came from him. It wasn't like it came from me. Let's do that. No, no, no. It came right out of his mouth.

ALLAN PEPPER: It's 10 in the morning, and I'm still in bed in Brooklyn. The phone rings. It's Sam McKeith. He says, "Springsteen at the club five nights. Columbia is supporting it big time." I say, "Ok." As it turned out, the label had a game plan; there was real strategy involved. They'd come to the conclusion that everybody by that time had—that seeing Bruce was so different from listening to him on record. Now at that time, there were a lot of people who thought the whole thing about Springsteen was just a lot of hype. So they bought up 50 percent of the house for the whole run. They wanted the other 50 percent of the house to be put up front; they wanted the press and the rest of the industry to see how the "real" people responded to him. They knew he could deliver the goods.

Sam McKeith, the William Morris agent who secured both the 1974 and '75 dates for Springsteen, had been working with Pepper and Snadowsky since the very beginnings of The Bottom Line, when he'd booked Dr. John for opening night. Like many of the serendipitous connections that went into helping the club get off the ground and succeed, it was that 1973 plane ride when he'd met Carol Strauss that began the chain of events that would ultimately lead to Springsteen's appearances at The Bottom Line.

SAM MCKEITH: I'd say that from the club's opening night, I was thinking to myself, "This is the kind of place where Bruce has to perform." I had him working New England early on, but I was looking for a place for him to really score in New York, and thus far there really hadn't been any place. Once The Bottom Line opened, I got him a three-night gig in the summer of 1974. His second album [*The Wild, the Innocent & the E Street Shuffle*] was out, and "Rosalita" was the standout track that people really responded to. Despite his live performances, Bruce was having a tough time coming up with a commercial album, but you knew Columbia was behind him. We did the 1974 shows, Friday through Sunday, and he did ok, but not great. Still, it was a place that people could really look at him and see what he was all about. From that period on, I knew I could get him back in there. And the next summer, the *Born to Run* album was going to be released in late August. Everything was lined up, and finally we were ready to go, to get him in there just as the album was coming out, and Mike Appel, his manager, called me up early in the morning and said, "Ok let's book it—and I mean *now*." I knew I had to move fast before the dates weren't open anymore, and I was told to wake him up, so I did. I got to the office early, and I called Allan at home, and I could tell when he answered the phone that I'd woken him up. Soon as he picked up, I said, "Allan, it's Sam McKeith. It's ok. Nothing's wrong. Bruce Springsteen is free. I'll call you later. Go back to sleep."

As soon as we made the booking, everything went into motion: Columbia bought out half the seats for the five nights, and all of a sudden, the publicists are involved, the newspapers are involved, everybody. The first shows were really good, but the early show on Friday was just a monster, and that one got broadcast live on WNEW, which was the hottest station in New York. I'd seen him a lot, and this one was just the best I'd ever seen, and it laid the foundation for everything that followed.

Leading up to the five-day stand, there were some tense moments behind the scenes—most of them attributable to the strong-armed tactics of manager Appel. Looking to put an "I'm in charge" thumbprint on everything, Appel had already had a brush with the club's staff during Springsteen's 1974 appearance, when he sabotaged a live radio broadcast of one of the shows scheduled to air on the WNYU college radio station.

DAVID VANDERHEYDEN (Radio concert engineer): My college radio station at NYU made a deal with The Bottom Line to record shows for the station, which had just become FM. And the irony was the equipment we used was stuff we acquired from a benefit concert by David Bromberg at Town Hall that NYU had sponsored. I had just graduated but continued to do some work for the station. At The Bottom Line, we set up a small system above one of the dressing rooms on the side of the stage near the kitchen. We had a small board and a Teac quarter-inch recorder, and we split all the microphones at the source so we did our own IDS, independent of the PA. The very first show I did at the club was Ry Cooder with Leon Redbone opening, and Neil Young showed up and did a surprise set at the end of the broadcast. So whoa! that's how I fell into remote engineering.

The first time Springsteen played the club in 1974, Appel showed up and angrily claimed the club didn't have the right to broadcast the show, and even after being told that Columbia had set it up, he was still annoyed. He said to me, "Well, look, bring the tape deck down and put it on the stage, and I'll take care of it." I said no. I mean, he was a *manager. He* was going to mix it? Ultimately, the show never got recorded.

Before the first of the 1975 shows, Appel again made his presence felt.

MARC SILAG: They had a 48-foot semi-truck filled with sound equipment out on Fourth Street, which of course we couldn't let them bring into the club, and when they ran stuff through our system, we blew a diaphragm in the PA and had to replace it, which we thankfully could before the first show. Then Appel came in and chased me around backstage and said, "We want to bring in our sound system and they told me you won't let them." I said, "Look, it's not me, it's the club. You just can't do it. You'll have to work with our in-house PA." The next thing I know, he's grabbed me by the collar and lifted me about 12 inches off the floor, and he goes, "We got a problem here. What are you gonna do about it?"

Silag, who would go on to a long career working with a variety of jazz and pop artists—most notably an eighteen-year association with Paul Simon—says the moment wound up being a pivotal one for him professionally.

MARC SILAG: In that instance I realized I probably had a future in the music business, because I was able to deal with the situation by just thinking quickly and clearly. I told Appel, "There's not much I can do while you're holding me like this." And he released his hold and let me down. We got everything squared away, as I knew we would. We had a working engine at The Bottom Line. Looking back, that incident gave me a lot of confidence.

With half the tickets already gone by the time the box office opened, there were enough Springsteen fans in the area for the shows to sell out, and that they quickly did. And, even before the first show, Pepper got a taste of what was to come.

ALLAN PEPPER: The very first night, there was a huge line down the street. I was out there to let the initial group of people in—Stanley and I were very hands-on back then; I would let people in the back door and he would do the front door, so we could get everyone in as quickly as possible, but tonight we decided to let everybody in through the front door. As it happened, the very first folks on line were two people who'd driven up from Philadelphia. We were just kibbitzing, and they said to me, "Bruce has ruined live music for us. Ever since we've seen him, all live music pales by comparison—with the exception of the Kinks." Now keep in mind I had not seen the new version of Springsteen. I thought to myself, "What sick puppies these people are."

We let everybody in and then the show started—and holy shit! He hit the stage and he had it all together and it was unbelievable. He had the audience from the minute he came out, and I was simply astounded. It was magic, and in that moment I totally understood what these people had said to me. Eileen had come to the show and we were sitting there, and at one point she said, "Look around. You've got guys who came in with women, and it's the guys who start standing up, and they're pumping their fists in the air and playing air guitar and singing along. I've never seen such male identification with any artist that's been on the stage."

MIKE APPEL: Bruce normally was used to doing four-hour shows. But he cut it up for The Bottom Line, and it was the greatest thing that could have happened, because sometimes less is more. In that particular case with Bruce, he was giving you less, but he was murder. He was giving you the very, very essence of the best songs that he had to give. And boy, was he blowing your head off. And when you get an artist that's that good, that professional, that knowledgeable about where he is in his career, even though if you asked him, he would say, "I don't know what to tell you. I don't know where I am. This is all new to me." And he'd be telling you the truth. But the fact is, somehow when you're with the right guy at the right moment, it just happens, and he knows it, and the whole world knows it.

BRUCE SPRINGSTEEN: I don't remember feeling extra nervous about it or anything. We just went in and it was a gig. The Bottom Line was then *the* place to play in New York City, and it was a gig we took to the limit, which was just kind of what we normally did. And it just took off. It changed our entire way of proceeding. It was a real game changer. It solidified our reputation as one of the great live acts.

Springsteen's triumph at The Bottom Line was especially rewarding for music executive Clive Davis. As president of Columbia Records in 1971, Davis signed Springsteen to his first recording contract after getting the recommendation of John Hammond, the legendary a&r man who back in the early '60s had persuaded Columbia to take a chance on Bob Dylan, and it was Davis who championed young Springsteen before losing his job at Columbia in the summer of 1973. Two years later, while no longer at the label, he was still rooting for the young performer he'd helped nurture to become a star.

CLIVE DAVIS: I had just formed Arista when The Bottom Line opened, and I loved the idea, the look, the feel. I loved everything about it. At the beginning and over the years, I had a number of memorable evenings there. I know early on that we engaged the club twice for Barry Manilow. The first time was before he really made it, before "Mandy" came out. He did nicely, but the show did not sell out, and then after "Mandy" became a hit and went to Number One, it was the hottest ticket and sold out instantly. With 400 seats, it was the perfect place to show that Barry was a very gifted live performer, and it was very exciting.

But certainly the most vivid memory of The Bottom Line for me was Bruce. In 1971, while I was head of Columbia, Bill Graham closed the Fillmore East and West, and *The New York Times* had an article that asked, "Is Rock Dying?" I felt compelled to do something, so I took over the Ahmanson Theatre in Los Angeles for seven or eight nights. I mixed and matched artists from our label: Santana, the New Riders, Dr. Hook, Loudon Wainwright, Miles Davis, Herbie Hancock—and Bruce. I remember going to the rehearsal when Bruce was playing, and keep in mind, I had only seen him in small Max's Kansas City-style places, and he was very stationary and just sang his songs. It had never before occurred to me to discuss his performance style with him, but here it was a stage comparable to Radio City Music Hall, and it seemed he was dwarfed by the size and the whole setting. After the rehearsal, I went to talk to him and said, "Bruce, when you play an environment like this, I think it's dwarfing you as an individual. Would you consider, on the appropriate song, maybe moving to one side of the stage or the other to sing it?" Fast forward to my founding Arista. Three years had passed, and before *Born to Run* came out, Jon Landau called me and said, "Bruce is playing The Bottom Line, and he'd love for you to come and see him perform." Other than that, no details, but I said, "I miss him, I love him, of course I'll come."

I went with Lou Reed. We sat there and I could not believe the Bruce Springsteen who performed that night, with his band, jumping on every table. He was the most vibrant, captivating, incredible live performer, and not remotely related to the folk artist he'd been before. It was the most astonishing change in a performer I'd ever seen. After the show ended and things calmed down, I said to Lou, "Give me a moment, I really have to go backstage." I go backstage and I look into the dressing room, and there, sitting all by himself was Bruce. I walked in, and he jumped up to greet me, and he said, "Clive, did I move around enough for you tonight?" It was forever etched in my memory; what a punchline.

MIKE APPEL: I went over to talk to Clive Davis and he was sitting with Lou Reed, and he said, "Well, Mike" he said, "you did it." And he slapped me on my knee, and I said, "No. Bruce did it." I mean, he was the one we were all betting on. He was a good bet, obviously looking back and retroactively, in any case, and Clive says, "Mike, he's the real deal." So Lou Reed enters the conversation. It's not like, I mean, I know of Lou Reed, but I'm not familiar with everything he does. I don't know all of his records with the Velvet Underground and all that kind of stuff. So he says, "No, he's not." I said to myself, "What is his problem? Why is he being so antagonistic?" I'm not in the mood for him to be antagonistic. But Clive is great. He says, "Lou, I'm telling you, he's the real thing." And Lou says, "I don't see it. I just don't see it that way." And then I got called away, thank God, so I didn't have to enter that little thing there and make it get to a conflagration to where everybody got thrown out of the club. So that was my real first interaction with Lou Reed live—and, thankfully, I never had another one. I just looked at him, and I said to myself, "I'm a guy that knows talent when I see it, when I'm in the presence of it," and I didn't think much of Lou Reed's talent at the time. I thought he was very lucky with the little flaky things that he did and became successful. And here he is having a lot to say about Bruce Springsteen, who could mop the floor with him.

For Springsteen's E Street Band's drummer Max Weinberg, the Bottom Line shows were especially memorable, both as an event as well as a life lesson experience.

MAX WEINBERG: In the summer of 1974 I'd been playing in a band from Rockland County, New York, while also going to Seton Hall University and playing on the Broadway show *Godspell*. The keyboard player from that band had shown me this ad that was in *The Village Voice* for a rock band looking for a keyboard player and a drummer. [*The ad famously said, "No Ginger Bakers."*] He had auditioned for the keyboard position, and he knew several people who worked at Studio 914 in Rockland where Bruce had recorded his first two records, and one of the other guys in the band had gone to see Bruce earlier that summer and came back raving about him and the performance of Clarence and everything. The group I was in was playing a lot of progressive rock, Jethro Tull and Yes type stuff, what they were calling progressive rock in those days. It wasn't my cup of tea because I liked straight-ahead rock and roll, and when I met Bruce and auditioned, he was delivering the goods in that respect, so it was like fingers fitting into a glove.

Roy Bittan [*the keyboardist who also answered the* Voice *ad and likewise got the gig*] joined the band that August, and every time we played, it felt like an event. You could clearly tell something was happening. We were playing colleges, small theaters, large clubs, and the response was phenomenal to Bruce and the band, and by the time we played The Bottom Line—and I'd been to the club a few times, seeing fusion bands like Weather Report and Return to Forever—well, there was a lot of talk about us. *The New York Times* did a big story, and it wasn't terribly flattering. But that stretch of shows turned out to be much more than it seemed like going in. Because we were there for five nights and doing two shows a night, it was like a residency. And of course it was just a small stage at the club, and Bruce utilized every area of that stage, and radiated out, literally dancing on the tables, and the reaction to him and the band far surpassed the doubters who were writing stories at the time because the reaction was so universally positive. It was the first time that I had experienced lines of people waiting around the block to get in, and the record, *Born to Run*, wasn't even out yet. And they were going to broadcast one of the shows on the radio, so for us it was really the debut—an incredibly auspicious debut in an amazingly prestigious place.

The Friday night show we played there, which was the third night, the second show was broadcast live. During "Rosalita," there was a section where we would vamp on this particular riff, as we call it, and Bruce would do these very impromptu cues to stop. I'd only been in the band about a year, and something distracted me, and I missed the cue to stop. And it really shook me up. It was sort of, I mean, are there mistakes in music? Not really, but this was, in my view, a terrible mistake. But Bruce, being Bruce, worked it into the act, pretended to grab my sticks. So how old was I? I was twenty-four. And the wild thing is, I mean, it was a very memorable night for me. I actually went to Bruce afterwards and said, "Sorry, I missed the cue. I was distracted or something." And all he said was, "You got to watch out for the curves." He was only twenty-five, I was twenty-four, and it was such a wise statement because it applies to life, not just playing at The Bottom Line. And onstage, I've never taken my eyes off him ever since. It's like that connection between pitchers and catchers. And when I grew into that role, I mean the drummer's role, whether it's me or anybody else, and any band, the drummer has to really lead the band. And the drummers that I admire were the drummers that took command in that way. I had to learn how to do that. I had a lot of potential, and I'm still playing, so I think I achieved my potential. But the odd thing is, about ten years ago, somebody took a picture and sent it to my management of the moment where that mistake happened in "Rosalita." I have it in my office, and it reminds me. It's incredible because my face looks like Emmett Kelly, the clown, and Bruce is obviously facing me. I can't see his face, but I do remember his face irritated, to say the least. And Steve Van Zandt is kind of suppressing a laugh in the picture. But I have it in my office where I see it every day. It's a reminder to watch out for the curves. You just never know. I've been watching out for the curveballs ever since. The hardest things in a rock band to get are three things: A great singer, a great front man, and great songs. So we check off all those boxes. That's by far the hardest thing. I auditioned against fifty, sixty drummers, and Bruce saw something in me, and after fifty years, here we are. We are still doing it.

As Springsteen's longtime pal, and then new member of the E Street Band, guitarist Stevie Van Zandt would recall in his book Unrequited Infatuations, "A funny thing happened on the way to the hype. We lived up to it." He also noted another reason the Bottom Line shows always remained special to him: It was there that he first met his future wife, Maureen, whom he described at their first meeting as "A New Jersey Brigitte Bardot."

STEVIE VAN ZANDT: It was a big moment, for several reasons. I had just left the [Asbury] Jukes, and Bruce only had like seven gigs booked, and I believe the Bottom Line shows were the end of that run. So, for me, I wasn't even sure if it was a temporary thing or a permanent thing or just what it was. All I knew was I wanted to get out of town, and Bruce decided to try and front the band, and that turned out to be a huge transformation that began right there, at The Bottom Line. He had a tough time with his first two records getting across to audiences, so he was like, "Let me try this," and growing up with him as I did, seeing that transformation was quite remarkable. Because he was really a very shy person. He didn't talk much; he wasn't really a show business kind of guy at all. Like the beginning of grunge, those guys staring down at the floor with their long hair covering their faces? That was Bruce ten years before. But suddenly, I watched my very shy, introverted friend turn into this unbelievable performer. One night he was just there playing, and then at The Bottom Line, he's walking on the tables, man, he became this other creature. And I talk about it in my book about how every singer is an actor whether they know it or not, and Bruce at that point just became this other character, and he really embodied it in his mind—that "Born to Run" character, a guy from across the tracks, looking with envy across the river at the big city, that innocence, that street kid, and he became that at The Bottom Line. It was a very important point in his career, and to witness that was something. And I just had the joy to be the guitar player at that point. He soon would miss it [*playing lead*], and by *Darkness [at the Edge of Town]*, he was back to being the guitar player, but in those very early moments, at the Roxy [in LA], at [London's] Hammersmith Odeon, he really became a front man.

We definitely broke from that Bottom Line gig. People came to that show basically to put us down. That's why it was so crowded. We didn't have any real following. This was after the Jon Landau "Future of rock and roll" thing, but it was a bit of a joke, because who was this Bruce Springsteen? Was it just hype? And hype was the dirtiest word you could use back then. It ended Moby Grape's career before it started. People were coming in, you know, "Future of rock and roll? Never heard of this guy." People came in not knowing us, but we'd been playing for ten years. We'd been making a living, and that's what gave us the edge over all the other new bands. We'd been through the origins of being a bar band, a club band. I'm not exaggerating; we'd been playing since 1965. We knew how to kill people live. And at The Bottom Line, that's exactly what we did.

JON LANDAU: The shows were not the length that we had become accustomed to, but I seem to remember that they approached between an hour and a half and two hours. So he's doing that twice a night. What happened during the shows was certain bits, certain bits of business he invented there or refined there. And one of the greatest moments when you were at the club was what he did with the story he'd tell as a prelude to performing "E Street Shuffle." The story was this incredible tale he creates about the night he met Clarence Clemons. The stage is very dark. And we had a great lighting director then, Mark Brickman, who went on to do great things with us, and later worked with Pink Floyd and Paul McCartney. So, anyway, Bruce tells this tale, dramatized with humor, while the stage is really dark. He's doing a very slowed-down version of the song, and if I remember right, on the very last line, he says some line that sort of brings him right to the song, and he touches Clarence's hand as he's saying that line, and this light that had the feel of a bare lightbulb on the darkened stage, just when they touched, from that little light, the big lights came on.

And that performance, that routine, the story that he told, turned everybody into a character. So he wasn't talking about Clarence. He was talking about a guy, a character called The Big Man, and Bruce, he was very thin at the time; he hadn't started working out the way he did later on. He was a little almost waif-like, and the contrast between him and Clarence physically, which he used one way or another, he used that forever. When I saw that bit, it was being invented. I don't know if he had tried it out of town or some version of it, but you felt like he's creating this in front of your eyes. It was just one of the memories for me.

And then there's the walking on the tables, of course. It was almost like breaking through the fourth wall, and that's what Bruce wants to do, always, is to create devices that break through the fourth wall. And he's a master of it. And this was the beginning . . . he'd already been doing it, I'm sure, at points where I hadn't yet seen him. But it was one of the things that really came out of the Bottom Line shows.

BRUCE SPRINGSTEEN: I always believed in breaking down that fourth wall. We played in the rain the other night [*on his summer 2024 European tour*]—and I mean the pouring rain—and it's very simple what to do. You have to walk out on stage, you have to walk down, and you have to get soaked with the crowd. And then anything goes. Once you've broken that wall and put yourself in their shoes, the rest of the night flies. And so The Bottom Line was a place where I just did what I was used to doing, which was going into the crowd, breaking that wall, and creating some excitement. The Bottom Line was tricky to do because they had those skinny little tables. I just decided, "Hell, I'll just go out on those." You're young, you've got your balance, everything is fine. And I just had a hell of a time dancing around on those tables, knocking some drinks over, and letting people have fun.

MIKE APPEL: Bruce was, I don't know, maybe fifteen minutes into one of the sets at The Bottom Line, and I'm sitting with my wife across from Peter Wolf from the J. Geils Band and his wife, [actress] Faye Dunaway. So Bruce Springsteen decides to stop whatever song he is doing . . . well, actually, what he does is he dances on those little long cocktail tables. I don't know how he didn't spill and break glasses and knock over drinks onto people. I have no idea how he scooted up about 15, 20 feet of tables, cause they're loose. They're not all locked together so that they don't fall over. If one of them falls over, each one of them could fall over. That's the problem. And I'm looking at this and I'm thinking, "This is just going to end in a disaster." But it doesn't. He dances right up next to me, and then he drops himself right onto my lap with his guitar in his hands, and he says, "Hey, this is my manager, Mike!" And he starts talking to the audience, and the next thing I know is he gets up and he dances all the way back to the stage. And he again didn't knock anything over, not one ashtray, not one glass. It's still a miracle that he actually did that. But the final thing was, all of a sudden I said to myself, "Why am I feeling all soaking wet on my jeans right now? I'm wearing jeans and he's wearing jeans, and he's been up there only like fifteen minutes, and his jeans are already drenched. They went through his jeans and into my jeans, so now my jeans were soaking wet. It looked like I peed my pants. Oh, god. And I'll never forget that, because it was the most visceral thing that I could have felt, literally, to know the kind of show that this guy puts on. When you're together with him, the whole audience are like prisoners of Zen. There's no way of getting out. You're going to have to go past this guy and he's going to pummel you, right?

SUSAN HASKINS-DOLOFF (Waitress): When I walked in the first night of Springsteen's *Born to Run* gig in 1975, I saw his picture at the front of the club and asked the bartender, "Who is this guy?" And he said, "Springsteen. He's the new Bob Dylan." After Bruce started to perform "Tenth Avenue Freeze Out," I immediately went to the waitressing sign-up board, and before that song was over, I had signed up for every available slot for the rest of his run. All it took was one song to get me hooked—and on a performer I'd never even heard of before. I remember standing on one of those back tables while Springsteen was singing "Rosalita" at the end of the show. Everyone was just going crazy. The best musical performer I ever saw was that young Bruce Springsteen.

RICHARD NEER (WNEW-FM radio host): I emceed the Friday night early show that we broadcast. I don't know where we got the idea, but we treated it like a sporting event. We were backstage, and like before a boxing match, I was going,

"Here's Bruce . . . He's coming out the dressing room with the E Street Band . . . Hey, Bruce, how are you feeling? What are you thinking?" And he goes, "Yeah, I'm ready to play tonight! I'm psyched!" He did the whole thing like Muhammad Ali before he got in the ring for a title fight. It was great, so after that we'd try and arrange in advance that we'd speak to the performers before their shows.

During Bruce's set, I actually went out of the club for a little bit and went to my car parked on the street and turned the radio on to see how it sounded on the air. David Vanderheyden did a great job and it sounded fine, except the weird thing was that for people who heard it, there were these weird scratchy noises that showed up every now and then on the broadcast. We don't know exactly how that happened, but we always suspected that Appel, who was so possessive of everything about Bruce's career, had figured out a way to do that so the show wouldn't be bootlegged. Anyway, I was there on Friday night, and I came back on Saturday and Sunday as well. We had one of the center tables, and seeing him from just 15 feet away was just incredible. When people ask me what were the best rock and roll concerts you ever saw, it was Bruce Springsteen at The Bottom Line.

ALLAN PEPPER: As the week went on, things just got crazier and crazier. We were just about pushing people through the doors. The last night we let in more people than we could possibly comfortably accommodate. There were people sitting on the floor, sitting everywhere; we weren't even selling booze at the front bar because there were people sitting on it. Stanley and I went out on the street for some air, and a woman who must have been in her 30s came over, and she said, "You've got to get me in. Please." And we said, "Sorry, but we can't squeeze in even one more person." And she said, "I have to be in there." Then she started to cry, and this wasn't a young girl; she was an adult woman. She said, "I know history is being made in that room the same way it was at Folk City when Bob Dylan performed." Now keep in mind that there we were, standing outside, right across the street from the original site of Folk City, where Dylan had played the very gig she was talking about back in 1962. The moment wasn't lost on us. Stanley and I looked at each other, and she was so earnest, we said to her, "Well, you're going to hear much more than you can see," and we opened the door and literally shoved her in, like it was a sardine can.

JON LANDAU: I remember on the last night, my dear friend [*J. Geils Band lead singer*] Peter Wolf came and Peter, his whole thing was about live performance. And I sat with him the second set on Sunday night, and he was gone. I remember him coming backstage, and Bruce would come off these shows and it was hot in there, and he would come off and he would be drained, and he needed a few minutes before he could talk to people. Peter just goes bashing in there and gives Bruce such a hug that I think that it was like they fell down. He tackled Bruce. And then of course Scorsese was there. And, of course, there is the famous story because *Taxi Driver* had not come out. And Bruce, he had this bit where he turned his back on the audience and he somehow would cue applause, and the clapping would keep building, and he would just throw his eye back over his shoulder, right over his shoulder, and go, "You talkin' to ME? Are YOU talking to Me?" And so the movie comes out not too long afterwards, and there's [Robert] De Niro saying that line.

The Bottom Line, from my point of view, was this incredibly creative event for Bruce. He took those ten sets and they became the norm for him. He didn't do the same set twice. I mean, he varied everything, and he just made the most of it. And it became a legend. It became a little Woodstock, where there were 25 million people there. If everyone who says they were there actually was there . . . well, let's just say it'd be a lot more people who saw it than were actually there.

BOBBY SCORE (Patron): I was in college at the time, and I guess I saw the ad for Bruce at The Bottom Line in the *Village Voice*. I went to the club and stood outside for like twelve hours and got in with a standing-room ticket. And that show with the E Street Band just blew my mind completely. I was over by the kitchen. They were doing "Jungleland"—a phenomenal song in itself—and there's the line where Bruce says, "From the churches to the jails," and when he said the word "churches," there was a light cue, and Danny Federici hit a major chord on the Hammond B3, and those three things—the lights, the lyrics, the organ—together in my mind it was just perfection. It was barely a few seconds, but I turned to the person next to me, and I think I said, "Why am I going to school?" I wanted to go backstage and say, "Can I carry something, anything, for you?" For me, it was an "I saw God" moment.

One afternoon a few years later, Score was standing at the bar with his musician friend Suzzy Roche during a sound check before a Roche Sisters appearance and was looking at the row of pictures from Bottom Line shows that adorned the wall in front of the bar.

BOBBY SCORE: There was one of Bruce with his newsboy's hat from that 1975 show, and he's holding his hat, and he has a look of pure joy on his face, and Allan was there, and I said, "Would it be possible to get in touch with the photographer? I really love that photograph." And Allan said, "Hold on, let me see." And he got on the phone and called the guy [house photographer Peter Cunningham] right there—he didn't even know my name—he just said, "Peter, there's a guy here who wants to buy the Springsteen picture, what do you want for it?" So I got it, framed, right off the wall, for 35 bucks.

A Bottom Line regular who would go on to a long career as a lighting director at New York's Lincoln Center and then as secretary of the New York chapter of the International Stagehands Union (IATSE), Score still has the picture on the wall in his home.

BOBBY SCORE: A while back I reframed it with my ticket stubs from the show, and below that stubs from three shows consecutive at Madison Square Garden for the *Darkness at the Edge of Town* tour. My Bottom Line ticket was 5 bucks, and for the Garden it was 8.50. For one of them, I went big: 9.00.

ALLAN PEPPER: Over the years I've talked to a lot of people [about the 1975 Springsteen shows] and over time, yes, it's been magnified by hype. But it really was every bit as magical as people say it was. For months it stayed with me. Everything Bruce had been working on had finally come together. We had a live radio broadcast [on WNEW-FM] and then within weeks he'd made the cover of *Time* and *Newsweek*—simultaneously—and all of that kind of came out of the club. We had plenty of acts who would come in and their record companies would buy tickets and advertising support for them, but after Bruce's shows at the club, they couldn't live up to the hype. Springsteen had the goods, and I saw the evolution and how it took shape between one engagement and then the other.

SAM MCKEITH: Things just exploded out of the Bottom Line shows. My counterpart in the LA office set up shows at the Roxy for after the New York dates. I went out there, and it was the equivalent—and then the next thing you knew, Bruce was on the cover of both *Time* and *Newsweek*. Now everyone knew his manager Mike Appel was very aggressive, and he made that happen. What he did was he got calls from both magazines, and he wanted the covers, and *Newsweek* said, "Well, if he's on the cover of *Time*, we can't give him the cover of our magazine." So he said, "Look, why don't you guys grow up? Do something you've never done before. Both of you put him on the cover. Let's see how you do it and how they do it." And they did different kinds of stories, and he got both of them. When it happened, I know there was a lot of jealousy from other performers who were a lot better known and been around longer than Bruce. But you have to give Appel a lot of credit. He got it done.

BRUCE SPRINGSTEEN: From there in that tour, you had to choose sides. People chose sides. Is this the greatest thing we've ever seen? Is this a record company hype? And people chose different sides at different times in different cities. And as a young twenty-five-year-old kid, that was a little disturbing, but I eventually developed a thicker skin, and that's the way it went. And we just went on and played as great as we could every night in every city. But The Bottom Line was the game changer. It increased expectations and it was living proof, enormously. It changed our lives. Those shows changed our lives. After that, we were looked at differently and had different expectations of ourselves, which we were glad to have because it was all about live performing, which we loved to do.

ALLAN PEPPER: At those *Born to Run* shows, Bruce really set the bar for the club as to what could be accomplished. Interestingly, in the next few weeks, while we were presenting a lot of terrific people, his spirit and energy were still in the air, and other acts just paled in comparison. It made me really understand emotionally what that couple from Philadelphia standing on line that first night had meant.

7 A PUNK PRIESTESS, A ROCK 'N' ROLL ANIMAL, A COUNTRY DARLING— AND A "FORMULA" FOR SUCCESS

As the 1970s progressed, The Bottom Line increasingly expanded its aesthetic purview to include under its widening tent everything from punk to politics. While CBGB, the former dive bar on the Bowery which owner Hilly Kristal had reopened as a music club just two months before The Bottom Line in late 1973, was rightfully recognized as the New York/US/World birthplace and official home of the three-chords (maybe)-and-a-prayer garage-rock-based movement that noisily tried to shake up the musical establishment, the path for most of the groups who first took their sneaker-shod baby steps in its grungy environs toward any real semblance of a "career" inevitably was tied to getting a record deal. And if a recording contract was indeed secured, the logical place for the bands, and their labels, to herald their "advancement" would be to perform at least once at an industry-friendly space in the city—and as Springsteen's triumphant stand in August 1975 had shown, no club-sized venue could provide as instantly recognized a symbol of showcase-able validation as The Bottom Line.

Less than four months after Springsteen's shows, Patti Smith and her band came to The Bottom Line for a series of dates coinciding with her late December birthday (a tradition she's kept going nearly every year to this day at various venues). Smith, who'd come to Clive Davis' attention the previous March during a two-month weekend residency at CB's, released her John Cale-produced debut album Horses on Davis' Arista label in November. And while her three-night December 1975 appearance at The Bottom Line—which included the club's first-ever three-show night (the last one began at 2 a.m.)—was not quite the game-changing stepping stone it'd been for Springsteen, it nonetheless effectively showcased, in abundance, the woman who'd soon be dubbed The High Priestess of Punk's talents—and attitude.

MARK SILAG: One show Patti did a tap dance on top of the grand piano; that got me very upset. And then the next show she took a guitar and stuck the neck through one of our stage monitors, and that got me really pissed. I took it personally. After the show, I picked up the monitor, carried it backstage, and said to her, "What am I going to do with this tomorrow night?" and the band just pushed me out of the dressing room. She was a handful back then.

SUSAN HASKINS-DOLOFF: Patti wanted to put an amp on one of the front tables. The roadie kept pushing it, telling Stanley that Patti needed to do this, and Stanley tried to patiently explain that this meant taking out some seats that were already purchased, but Patti's rep wouldn't take no for an answer. So finally Stanley said, in his own calm, practical way, "Look, I am a very rich man and I could take an ad out in the *[Village] Voice* saying, 'Patti Smith canceled. Come and get your refunds.' It wouldn't affect me in the slightest." So there was no amplifier on a table.

Even though stage manager Silag, and Pepper and Snadowsky themselves, had a difficult time with Smith and her bandmates on those initial dates, it didn't stop them from bringing Smith and her group back to The Bottom Line the following November for what would ultimately be one of the longest single consecutive night residencies by one artist in the club's entire history—a seven-night, fourteen-show stay in late November that included guest appearances by both John Cale and Bruce Springsteen himself. (Backstage after he appeared, New Jersey native Smith told Springsteen about another Garden State product, her college friend and photographer Frank Stefanko. Bruce then got in touch with Stefanko, leading to him shooting the iconic album covers for Springsteen's Darkness at the Edge of Town *and* The River *albums, as well as his best-selling autobiography,* Born to Run.*)*

LENNY KAYE (guitarist, Patti Smith Group): I remember one of those nights running through the audience on the tabletops with Patti chasing me during a particularly manic version of "Radio Ethiopia." They were pretty sturdy if the people held on to your ankles. It was always good sound, and I also liked the way they spread the guests out and put the fans up front. You could pretty much make eye contact with the audience, so you really felt one-on-one with the people you were playing for. You were literally one step away from them. There was room for the grand gesture. The room never seemed cramped because of the high ceilings, so it felt spacious. The dressing rooms were extremely cramped, so you were happy to get onstage and just fling your arms out to full extent. And I always liked the two shows a night thing; the second one you can always loosen the bonds.

ALLAN PEPPER: I loved Patti Smith. She was hard to get along with, but I loved her. She was an example of someone you present and they can make your life hell, but you forgive them, or tolerate them, because of their art and their talent. When she first came to the club, Jane Friedman was managing her, and we were still new. It was very important for Stanley and me to run the club in a certain way, and people got to know our house rules that we used to charge the acts for everything, but then we would discount it, and lots of times we'd eliminate coffee and tea, but everything had to be written on a tab and accounted for for inventory purposes. Patti could never understand why she and her band had to pay for stuff, and not only did that become a point of contention, but any of our house rules became a point of contention. So she'd make us crazy and be fighting. At the time, life was hectic for her, but I would stand there and watch her perform with real admiration for her talent. She'd come out all alone to start her show and just kind of riff before the band came out. It was like Sonny Rollins coming out and doing an opening, unaccompanied solo; she'd riff off of what was in the newspaper, what was on her mind that day, what have you, and I was aghast at her talent.

Years later, there were only a very few things I ever looked back on and felt sad and badly about, and if I had an opportunity to do it again, I'd have done it differently. And one of them one was Patti Smith. There was a time when we called Patti and Jane up to the office after an engagement—now keep in mind, they got a very good percentage; they were making money—but we called them up, told them how great the show was, but we still charged them for their tabs. And years later, I thought to myself that she'd done a great show, and to show our appreciation we should have ripped up the tabs or given them a bottle of champagne or something like that, but we didn't. We really didn't handle it properly. So I called Jane out of the clear blue sky and said I wanted to take her out to lunch. We sat at the restaurant, and I said, "I just wanted to apologize," and she just looked at me, and I had to remind her of what had happened. That did make me feel a little better.

For one Patti Smith fan, a particular Bottom Line performance stood out as a life-changing event. Yolanda Cuomo, later to become a highly successful art director and book designer, was just a teenager when she ventured into the city one night from her parents' home in New Jersey to see her idol in action—and wound up part of the action herself in a spontaneous moment that would have truly unexpected repercussions.

YOLANDA CUOMO (Customer): It was the day after Thanksgiving, 1976, and I went to The Bottom Line to see Patti Smith. Patti really changed my life. I used to follow her, go to every show, and it was like she catapulted me into New York. I said, "I got to get out of New Jersey. I got to move to New York," really because of her. So I go to the city to see her at The Bottom Line, and I'm there with a friend of mine who is not my boyfriend; he's just my buddy, and he's from the neighborhood where we grew up. The show starts and Patti is out there by herself, and she's really stoned or drunk, and she was just talking shit. And I was just so disappointed. So I decided to leave and went to the coat check to get my coat, and there was another guy there who I kind of recognized from my town in Jersey, and I looked at him and I said, "She really sucks. I'm leaving." And he goes, "Yeah, me too."

So then all of a sudden the band comes out and they start to rock. And so I look at him and I go, "Hey, I'm going back." So I went back and sat down, and she took out a guitar and she started playing, and then I guess it was her assistant who came out and Patti gave them a guitar. I was really pissed off because she wasn't playing great. So I yelled out, "Hey, if you have another guitar, I'll play too." And she gave me an evil eye, and she pointed and said, "You wanna play? The piano's empty"—I guess the piano player was sick that night—and she says, "If you want to play piano, come on up." So I jump up, walk across the tables onto the stage, and I start playing piano for [the Who's] "My Generation." But I don't play piano. So I'm there banging away and the guys in the band are glaring at me, she's giving me the evil eye again, and I see the people in the audience are, too. Anyway, after the song I go back and sit down, and then at the end of the show, Joe, the guy that I saw at the coat check, follows me home. He lived in North Bergen, and he went to school with my older sister. Like I said, I knew who he was. He used to run track and eat lasagna at my parents' deli on the way to practice. So he follows me home and he goes, "You want to come out and play?" And he had a football in his hand. And pretty quickly it was, like, "Whoa, I love this guy." And he was like, "Whoa, I love this girl." And that was it; we wound up getting married.

Many years later, I designed a whole Diane Arbus show for an exhibition and her book, *Revelations*. I work a lot with the Arbus Foundation, and we designed a show around the book that traveled the world, and it was in London at the V and A museum. And the curator from the Robert Miller Gallery was there because that was Arbus' gallery in New York at that time. Now the Robert Miller Gallery was also representing Patti Smith, so I tell him the story of how I met Joe and he's like blown away. He says, "You know, Patti is one of our artists. Do you want to meet her?" And I was like, "Sure, I'd love to." He says, "You got to tell her that story." So a couple of months passed, and there was a Lee Krasner show at Robert Miller, and the guy called me and said, "I know Patti's going to be there, so come and I'll introduce you to her." So we're meandering around the gallery, and there she is, so we go over. He goes, "Patti, this is Yo Cuomo. And she has a story to tell you." So I said, "Y'know back in 1976, I played piano for you at The Bottom Line. And as it turned out, though we weren't together, my future husband was in the audience that night, and we fell in love." And Patti looks at me and she goes, "Are you still together?" And I said, "Yeah. We have two kids. They're like teens now." And she goes, "Huh. I got a lot of power."

In May of '76, Queens, NY's arch punks Joey, Johnny, Dee Dee, and Tommy—aka the Ramones—played their one and only gig at The Bottom Line. It was a show remembered best by Pepper and his staff for the lead-up rather than the show itself. The Ramones were doing their sound check in the afternoon, and Pepper recalled that it was one of the rare times when the people in offices upstairs from the club actually came down and complained about the noise. Like Spinal Tap, the Ramones' amps were turned up to eleven, even at sound check—and they were not going to turn them down. As David Vanderheyden recalled, "The look on Johnny's face said it all: "These amps are here to intimidate you." And the sound guy said, "I think this is a point where art and engineering have met an impasse." Still, their show itself went off without a hitch—or any additional noise complaints.

Several weeks before the Ramones' show, The Bottom Line hosted Indian sitar virtuoso Ravi Shankar, who a decade earlier had been the key figure in turning the Western world on to the exotic majesty of the instrument through his friendship and tutoring of Beatle George Harrison. Playing the oversized instrument required a musician to play while sitting cross-legged on the floor, and thus also required that, for Shankar's appearance at the club, a riser would be needed so that the audience could see him while he performed. As The Bottom Line had no risers on the premises, it posed a problem that stage manager Mark Silag handled in a way that immediately went down in Bottom Line lore.

MARK SILAG: Allan and Stanley were so tight-fisted when it came to contracts. The rider for Shankar's appearance said he needed a stage riser, and I asked Stanley, "What do you want me to do?" and Stanley said, "I want you to figure it out." I was walking through the club one afternoon not long before his scheduled show, and two guys were coming in with hand trucks loaded with cases of Heineken. There was a whole line of them lined up against the backstage entrance, near where the coolers were. I said to them, "What are you doing with that beer? How many cases are you bringing in?" I'm not sure how the idea hit me, but I went in the back and got a tape measure and started measuring them. The delivery guy said, "What are you doing?" I said, "Never mind." I knew I had some sheets of plywood in the sub-basement of the club, and I got out a piece of paper and made some quick calculations. The day of the show, I got there early, stacked the cases of beer, put the plywood over it, and very quickly just wrapped black velveteen around all of it, so all people saw when they walked in was just a black cube. As they usually did, I guess, Shankar's people brought a carpet, and Ravi played sitting on top of it. And the really funny thing was, as per his contract, while the club served drinks before and after he played, they didn't serve any while he was actually playing. His tour manager would have gone crazy if he knew that Ravi Shankar had performed at The Bottom Line in New York while perched atop a mountain of Heinekens.

Bottom Line stage managers, it should be noted, were no strangers to handling unexpected problems with MacGyver-like feats of ingenuity. A year before, in February 1975, The Bottom Line hosted a two-night engagement by Eric Burdon, the feisty former lead singer of the Animals. It featured a guest appearance by pianist

John Mayall, who, as bandleader of England's revered Blues Breakers, mentored, in succession, guitarists Eric Clapton, Peter Green, and Mick Taylor on their respective paths to stardom. As Burdon and Mayall giddily jammed, manager Sam Ellis found himself confronted with the prospect of imminent disaster, and sprang into action.

SAM ELLIS: Eric Burdon was the headliner, and John Mayall showed up to sit in. I was standing backstage, and suddenly I notice that the piano is bouncing on the stage. I thought, "What's going on?" and I walked from backstage all the way around to the right where the piano was, and there's the two of them, pushing the piano into the audience. I grabbed one of the legs and was just holding on to it for dear life until some of the other crew guys ran over to help. So before the next night, I figured I better protect everyone in the club, including Burdon and Mayall from themselves, so I lashed the piano to the column with airplane cable and tied it to the deck. And I told the wait staff, "No bottles over there, just plastic cups." So, in effect, I childproofed the stage.

* * *

In July of 1976, coinciding with the United States's Bicentennial, the Democratic National Convention that culminated with Jimmy Carter receiving the party's nomination to run for President took place at Madison Square Garden. The event was commemorated at The Bottom Line by its first original theatrical presentation: From July 9th through the 17th, the club hosted "The Convention," a spoof of the political activities of the day put together by an improvisational troupe organized by the husband-and-wife performing duo of David Dozier and Janet Coleman.

JANET COLEMAN (Theater performer, WBAI radio host): I knew The Bottom Line building from when it was Square East and housed the Second City comedy group when they came downtown after their run on Broadway. They had Severin Darden, Barbara Harris, Andy Duncan, Alan Arkin, and Paul Sand, all the way through Sand's last show with Robert Klein, David Steinberg, and Fred Willard, and all of them were in it. So I knew the place and its history. So before The Red Garter, it had been a hip room. Once it became The Bottom Line, of course, it became something different. From the start, it had an atmosphere of welcome. At the time NYU was pretty ragged. The club helped a Village revival, and it was so grown-up! A comfortable place to hang out and listen to music.

My husband David [Dozier] and I were doing improvisational theater and comedy, and we wanted to put on a sort of themed show about the 1976 Democratic Party's National Convention, which was in New York. We had an agent, Ron Bernstein, to whom we brought the idea that we wanted to mimic and satirize conventions. Everybody would have a table representing each state. In the spring, we went to visit Allan and Stanley, and they were sitting in their office, with Stanley counting money as usual, and they were amenable to doing it. They didn't even want to see a script. They knew we were going to improvise, and it was all ok with them. Their sense of adventure was great, and we set it up. Our group was called The Convention, and we assembled a lot of good people. We wanted to use a lot of sound effects in the show, and we got David Rapkin, WBAI's sound designer, to help out. We used special guest stars from Off-Broadway plays, like [Drama Desk and Obie Award winning actor] Kevin O'Connor, who knew how to work their audience. Our delegates were people like him, [veteran actor and *Electric Company* creator] Paul Dooley, Bob Balaban's wife Lynn Grossman [seen in *You've Got Mail*], and the duo of songwriters [Bill] Weeden and [David] Finkle, who came up with a song that named all the fifty states in about a minute.

Unfortunately for us, there was no backroom politics leading up to Carter's nomination that year. We were surprised that we didn't have that much to satirize, but there was an influx of hookers at MSG for all the visitors to the city, so we had that to work with. I was friends with Charles Mingus, who lived nearby, and he said he wanted to be involved, but we didn't have it that together, so I couldn't ask him to do it. To get people in, they booked us with musicians, folkie enough to have a political bent, people like Tom Paxton and Mary Travers, as well as Kenny Rankin. There was some hullabaloo about Rankin; I think he asked for his money while he was performing. But all in all, it was great fun, and Allan and Stanley were supportive of the whole endeavor. *[Indeed, singer/guitarist Rankin had an infamous drug-related onstage meltdown during his Convention-related show that summer. At one point, he demanded to see the guest list for the show and proceeded to read the names of every person on it, decrying their getting in for free at his expense. In truth, Pepper and especially Snadowsky were so precise about tracking the club's admissions day in and day out that virtually all seats for every show were always accounted for monetarily. While he and Pepper eventually made up, Rankin would not return to The Bottom Line as a performer for well over a decade after the incident.]*

* * *

ALLAN PEPPER: When we opened the club we did a lot of business with record companies, and there were a lot of press parties we had on our books the first couple of months, maybe $100,000 in receivables, but it could take ninety days to get paid by the labels, and we had bills to pay. So there we were, fronting big parties and the companies were buying tickets and running up big tabs, but we weren't getting the money. The club was hot and doing a lot of business, but there wasn't a big cash flow coming in based on what we were doing. The audiences were coming in and buying tickets, and we had food and drink sales, but compared to the bills we had to pay we were behind.

Uncle Marvin was a very street-smart guy who really understood numbers and business in a very savvy way. He was our third partner, and his bank was where our account was, and early on he went to his account executive and said, "I never want their checks returned." So there were times we may have been behind forty grand, and he guaranteed it for us. For a young business not to have to worry about paying its bills when money was tight really relieved a lot of stress, and that was a real gift and a blessing.

The other thing Marvin did—and he did a lot of stuff besides putting up all the money when we started—was help us come up with what Stanley and I called "The Formula." Once we opened the club, Marvin came in and wanted to know what all our fixed costs were. We didn't totally know, so we sat down, and we'd been open for several weeks and had bills and stuff, so we sat down with a yellow pad and made a list of every conceivable cost in terms of running the business day to day, and we added it all up to see, as Marvin put it, what did it cost to turn the key in the lock, so we could amortize our fixed costs over a year. When we added everything up, it came to like $1,500 a day just to turn the key in the lock, plus the cost of talent on top of that, because that was a variable. You could calculate some things, but the cost of talent was a variable every single show.

Figuring out our daily fixed costs became a crucial part of negotiating with the talent agents we dealt with. At the time we opened in 1974, when a club owner called an agent about an act's fee, the agent usually responded by quoting a fee for the engagement (a guarantee) versus a percentage of ticket sales, whichever was higher. Sometimes the percentage the agent asked for could be as high as 70 or 80 percent. The first thing Stanley said was, "We're not giving away more than 50 percent of the ticket sales, and that's only after our fixed costs for the evening have been covered." Stanley realized that by not giving up any portion of the box office until all costs were covered, it was possible, on a good night, to have the ticket sales pay for all our expenses, thus allowing food and booze to be pure profit. And that realization led to a method we would use to determine at what point the act would share in the box office receipts. And that's what we called "The Formula." Simply stated, the point where an act would be entitled to a percentage of the box office sales was arrived at by adding the act's fee to the fixed cost for the night. By reframing the negotiation to approach the concept of a percentage of box office sales, as a bonus, for doing good business instead of something they were entitled to as part of their guarantee, Stanley reversed the dynamics in the negotiation in our favor—and that maneuver saved us a lot of money.

No sooner did we get the agents used to accepting the formula as part of the negotiation than our accountant informed us that we were responsible for paying the sales tax on ticket sales, and that led Stanley to retweak the formula. Stanley now told the agents that sales tax was our responsibility on the guarantee, but that once an act went into percentage it should be our mutual obligation. He reasoned that once an act reached percentage, we were 50 percent partners on the door, so it wouldn't be fair for us to pay 100 percent of the sales tax. The formula was now amended to deduct 100 percent of the sales tax on the additional amount of money an act was entitled to as a result of going into percentage. Also, once a deal with the agent was finalized, you were usually expected to send the agent 50 percent of the negotiated fee as a deposit to seal the deal. Here again, Stanley said, "Uh Uh. We're not giving any deposits. We'll have the money for you the night of the show; you can pick it up from us once the show is done." And because of that, we didn't tie up a lot of money in deposits and had full use of the money until the night of the show.

Everyone used to bitch about the way we did business, but we made it work because everybody had to follow the same rules, no matter how famous they were. As Stanley had said months before we opened, "If we ran a tight ship, as long as we treated everyone the same way, we wouldn't be loved—but we would be respected." Take our house rules, which were dictated by business considerations. Talent contracts invariably came with riders that demanded all kinds of catering, including cases of free beer as well as the club having to provide meals for acts and their crew. Some of the riders, depending on the act, also required that we would provide the equipment they needed to perform. Well, Stanley took joy in savaging the riders; he'd just cross out everything. If a band needed extra amps for the show we'd rent it for them, but then the cost of that rental would be deducted from the act's fee at the end of the show. And as far as elaborate catering or free beer or a free bottle of scotch, that was a nonstarter. Acts were told that if they wanted a case of beer in their dressing room, they'd get a discount of 30 percent, but it would still have to be paid for. We would repeatedly explain to an agent or a road manager that if we were audited by the IRS, they would be looking for the sales tax that should have been collected on the amount of sales on the beer we were ordering—and the IRS didn't want to hear that the tax wasn't collected because we gave the beer away to the acts.

Since almost immediately everyone wanted to play the club, we were in a strong bargaining position. I was very much the passionate, it's-all-about-the-music guy. I loved putting shows together. Stanley's creativity was all about making the deal—and he was a great negotiator. He would often say, "Everything's negotiable. And if they say it's not, they're lying to you." We were doing things that I'm sure no other club at the time was doing, and these were the kinds of things that allowed us to be successful.

Neither Stanley nor I took big salaries when the club opened. I think all we took was either $75 or $100 a week. After we'd been opened for about six months, we gave ourselves a raise and increased our salaries to $125. Although we had a lot of money coming in and going out, it wasn't a free ride, because keep in mind we still had to pay Marvin back. And every penny we saved helped do that. I had a sign on the wall opposite my desk, something I found in a Chinese restaurant fortune cookie, that said, "It is better to shun the bait than to struggle on the hook." When I was negotiating with an agent, I'd look up and read it.

One more very important thing was that Marvin never charged us any interest. He just came in as a third partner, and that was the deal. When the money was finally paid back to him, we got a call that he wanted to see us in his office. We walked in, and he was there with his lawyer. We sat down; we had no idea why he'd called for us, and he looks at the lawyer, and the lawyer says "The reason Marvin has called this meeting is he's turning back his interest in the club to you guys." We look at him, like why? And Marvin said, "I did all this for my niece, for Eileen, and you guys work very hard and long hours, and I don't need this money." And, he said, "You deserve it." We told him, We can't accept the offer, even though it took us so long to get you to the table; you were there when no one else was, and if not for you, this wouldn't have happened. Like it or not, you're in, and you'll stay in." Years later, when a Bottom Line opened in Japan in 1989, we got a lot of money, maybe $125 grand, for a signing bonus. I called him from an airport in Tokyo, and he got on, and we told him he was going to get a check for like $40,000, and he said, "What are you talking about?" We told him that the money was going to be split three ways, and he was just flabbergasted. But that's what Stanley and I were about, period.

There was a period after a while where we hit a bad spot. We took off like a bat out of hell, successful from our opening night all the way to the late '70s, but one day Stanley said to me, "Marvin's been great to us, but we need to establish our own relationship with our own bank." So we moved our account down to the branch on 8th Street, and Stanley formed a relationship with an account executive there, and we took out a loan, and from that point on, we never went to Marvin when we needed money.

Stanley and I never let Marvin's birthday pass without giving him a gift. So every July we faced the same question: What do you get the man who has everything? One year we reached out to Al Hirschfeld, the famous caricaturist whose celebrity sketches were often featured on the front page of the Sunday *New York Times'* Arts and Leisure section. After all, finding yourself the subject of a "Hirschfeld" was a big deal; it meant you were an important person. After providing a photo, Hirschfeld created a sketch of the three of us, and we proudly presented it to Marvin on his birthday. We both liked it, but when we gave it to him, Marvin didn't really react; he seemed bewildered, and just stared at it. Not what we were expecting. We tried explaining the significance of a Hirschfeld drawing, and that caricatures weren't meant to be exact reproductions of what someone looked like, but Marvin remained unenthusiastic. He thanked us politely, and that was that. Stanley and I always figured he didn't like the way he'd been drawn, but many years later, after Marvin died, I found out from his sister-in-law Andrea the real reason he disliked the sketch. Apparently, it reminded Marvin of someone who got the better of him on a business deal early in his career—and every time he looked at it, all he could think of was the guy who'd screwed him out of money.

* * *

For a period in the late 1970s, self-proclaimed Rock and Roll Animal Lou Reed appeared regularly at The Bottom Line. The former leader of groundbreaking art-rockers The Velvet Underground had spent much of the first half of the decade brushing with commercial success during rock's Glam period, when his friendship with David Bowie brought him the lone hit single of his career—1972's "Walk on the Wild Side," which was featured on his highest-charting album, the Bowie-produced Transformer. *By '76, between his near-parodying bleached-blonde rock star phase and Reed's middle finger to both the recording industry and his fans with the all-instrumental, all ear-shattering double album* Metal Machine Music, *Reed's self-inflicted wounds began to, if not heal, then at least scar over, and his new skin found him venturing into almost theatrical territory as a live performer. The Bottom Line seemed a good fit for Reed at this juncture, and he clearly reveled in the intimate, heckle-filled, "I dare you to make eye contact" atmosphere offered by the club—so much so that in 1978 he recorded a series of edgy "Evening with" shows that were edited and released as the appropriately titled* Take No Prisoners *album, and he would continue to do such shows into the early 1980s.*

ALLAN PEPPER: I loved having Lou at the club, but depending on his mood, he could be very difficult to deal with. But the level of talent was so great, you accepted it. Artists like Patti and Lou gave you a hard time, but they were brilliant. I remember one time we had Lou for a midnight show, and he would not go on until two in the morning because he felt we were disrespectful to one of his band members, and the place was packed; he just wouldn't go on. Another time he was appearing, and at the end of the stage, he kicked a glass that I guess had liquor in it into the audience. I don't know if it was an accident or he meant it, but it splashed on two guys who got very offended and wanted to go backstage and confront him, and my guys stopped them. They were riled up, and it got physical, and we pushed them out the door, and then they started kicking at the door. We called the police, and they came, and this guy was so wound up he punched one of them, which of course got him cuffed and hauled off to the precinct. If you listen to *Take No Prisoners*, you never knew what to expect, but sometimes he could be very gentle. You just never knew what you were going to get.

LENNY KAYE: The Bottom Line gave Lou a chance to spar with the audience in a way he couldn't in a larger place.

JACK LEITENBERG (Host): I remember Lou Reed telling Allan and Stanley that his band would not go on because they did not "respect" his band—and when asked what they could do to show their respect, Lou suggested a bottle of Jack Daniel's.

DONNA DIKEN (Waitress): Every time Lou played the club, there were fights.

MIMI LIEBER (Waitress): When Lou Reed played, I had a rowdy crowd; guys who wanted to sit up front, and they were loaded in every direction; I mean ups and downs. And I brought my first drink order out on one of those big trays we used that had maybe seventy drinks on it. I was inching my way down between the lanes, which, if you recall, the chairs were always back to back with the other tables, so it was always, excuse me, excuse me, excuse me. I've got the tray over my head, and some guy, who from the very start looked to me like he was going to be trouble, bit my breast—or, in the parlance of the day, he bit my tit. And it was bad. It was a big bite. And of course, I don't think we were wearing bras. I was probably wearing something like a leotard, which was just our uniforms. And he bit me. I think I made a pretty bad sound, and I swung the tray down and asked if people minded if I just put this on the table, and where did I get this mentality? Everyone all my life thought I was a New Yorker, and there's no reason—my people are from Cleveland and LA—but I put the tray down calmly, picked up a Heineken and I said, "I think this is yours," and I poured it over him, and people cheered. People fucking went crazy. He had a look on his face, of kind of an "I gotcha." But this guy was loaded. I mean, I suppose it might have been Quaaludes then, but it also may have been heroin, their preferences for lifestyle at that moment in time; lots of torn T-shirts and crazy hair and eye makeup for guys. Anyway, I left the table. I asked everyone to please be patient for a second and made my way back out from between those seats.

I walked over to Jay, one of the bouncers, who was over at the door. He had his sort of one foot up on the wall, leaning on the wall, with that cowboy hat of his slightly down. He was literally a Black Marlboro man, only about six seven, and God knows what he weighed. I told him what happened, and you could see blood come to his eyes and he went, "You show me where that fucker is." I led him over to the table and I pointed, and you could see the guy was terrified; his face was filled with fear. And Jay went over and just leaned over and picked the guy's chair up with him in it, held it high, and walked him through the club to the front door. Somebody, probably [*club host*] Russell Wolinsky, opened the front door, and Jay hurled the guy from the chair out into the snow; just jettisoned him with enough thrust that the guy landed right in the middle of Fourth Street. And I mean, now they're going crazy in the club seeing all this. I went back to my station and served the drinks, like, "Nobody fucks with me." About a week later, there was an article in God knows which paper, it had to be the *Voice*, and it was a picture of this scrawny little asshole fronting a band, and we recognized that he was that guy, and the band was Jesus Christ and the Fucking Shits. That was the name of the band, and he was their lead singer. Perfect, right?

MARTY FOGEL (saxophonist with Lou Reed, 1975–79): How I got to play with Lou is a very serendipitous story, I guess. In 1975, I was in a jazz-rock group called the Everyman Band, which included violinist Larry Packer and bassist Bruce Yaw. We were a local band that played around Syracuse and Ithaca, and we were actually breaking up when Packer heard from a guitarist friend who was looking to put a band together for Lou Reed for a tour of Europe, and he got us to come down to New York to meet with Lou. We were living in a pretty rural area upstate, and the day before we went, Bruce and I were in his woods cutting firewood, and then the next day we're in Manhattan meeting Lou Reed, who was wearing, well, I don't remember what he was wearing, but he had a clear plastic suit, jacket and pants, over his regular clothes. And Bruce and I are in flannel shirts with hair down to the middle of our backs. Anyway, he hires us, we rehearse, and now we're going to go to Europe with him. I have to say that I didn't even know who Lou Reed was before I got the call to go play with him. In fact, I said to my wife, who was my girlfriend at the time, "I don't know if I want to do this. I don't know, just really not my thing." And she says, "What? Are you crazy? You're going to Europe, you're getting paid. You've got to go."

Anyway, the day we're leaving for Europe, I didn't witness this, but I later heard that as the cars are ready to pull away, he says to the guitar player who hooked us up to begin with, "You're not going." And then about a week or two into the tour, he fired Larry. I guess you just had to be a certain way to accept that you were part of Lou's circle. You're one of Lou's subjects, let's put it that way. The thing about Lou, and I've always described him this way, is both devil and angel. Though I was never particularly close with him, I always got along with him. If you're in the band, you hung out with Lou—if he wanted to hang out with you. And he was fun. He was great. But I saw him be really nasty, really just condescending to people. At the Roxy Club in Los Angeles one time, I saw him take John Belushi apart verbally. I mean, he just destroyed him right in front of everybody. It was incredible to see because Belushi was being really obnoxious. But at any rate, so that's how I came to be with Lou. I was with him for four and a half plus years. I played on *Rock and Roll Heart*, *Take No Prisoners*, *Street Hassle*, and *The Bells*.

When we were doing European or even American tours, we weren't playing stadiums, but we did do plenty of concert halls with a few thousand people. But playing at The Bottom Line, for me, that was a pretty big deal. I mean, it's The Bottom Line, and the bottom line was if you played at The Bottom Line, you were pretty happening. I know that we did some performances at The Bottom Line that musically were way better than what ended up on the *Take No Prisoners* album. And the reason I say that is because Lou just decided to keep in all his bantering with the audience going on and on and on, and on and on. Lou really was talking a lot at those shows. Knowing my own nature, I might've been up there going, "Can we move this along? Can I actually play something? I'm here to play." But we were certainly aware that it was different. He always, or let's put it this way, not necessarily always, but it was not unusual for him to go on these little rants with an audience, even in theaters as well, just whatever was on his mind. I think he was one of the original rappers. So that was not unusual. The amount of time that he spent doing it, though, that to me was unusual.

I described our band as a beast, and we put some incredible stuff together because everybody in the band was so attuned to his presence on stage, and even just the lift of a shoulder or just a certain kind of body movement. I remember the band changing its dynamic on a dime. We weren't just like a blazing, roaring out-of-tune rock and roll band. We were real musicians who could adapt and were tuned into our star. We were criticized for being too jazzy, which we were in a way, because we were coming from a place where we weren't only playing pop and rock; we were certainly playing jazz, like we were in the Everyman band before we joined Lou. And so some people didn't really like what we were bringing to him, but I've read that he considered us to be one of the best bands ever.

Having [jazz trumpeter] Don Cherry with us for a while with Lou was really special. Before I got to know Don personally, I was living on St. Mark's Place in the early '70s, and I rented a basement space nearby because I couldn't really practice during the day at my place because people would complain. The space I rented was next to Don Cherry's wife's art studio, so I'd see him on the street and I might say hello, but I never really interacted with him. But in 1976, when I was already with Lou, we had just landed at the LA airport, and I was waiting for our transportation near the exit door, and Lou was already in a limo outside the doors. I'm standing near the front doors at a telephone booth, and out of nowhere Don Cherry walks right up to the telephone booth next to me. I started talking to him, introduced myself, I don't exactly remember the conversation, but I told him I was there with Lou Reed and that I loved his work and so forth. And then he begins to walk away, and I run out to Lou's car and say, "Hey, I just saw Don Cherry," and Lou goes, "Don Cherry! Go get him." So I ran back inside and I grabbed Don and brought him to the limo and introduced them to each other. Lou invited Don to come play with us at the Roxy Theater where we were playing, and he came and sat in with us. Don came to my hotel room before the gig, and I said, "This is just rock and roll." And he said to me, "Man, it's all music." And so Don wound up playing and recording with us. Later on, Lou told me that when he was a student at Syracuse University, he had a radio show on the school station, and his opening theme was [Ornette Coleman and Don Cherry's] "Lonely Woman." I mean, that really took me back. I think my respect for him really was boosted.

It's funny, I wrote the music for the song "The Bells" that was the title track for Lou's album, and recently I listened to it for the first time in a long time, and I was really amazed that that was on a Lou Reed album, with what Don and I were doing. We're mixed way in the back, but we're just going out. We're out. Don's not only playing the line, but he's just playing some other stuff. I remember when we did it, I looked at him, and he said, "Whenever you have a chance to take it out, take it out." So we did.

After I left Lou at the end of the 70s, I was fortunate enough to play with Don in different settings for close to twenty years. I remember after one of the shows we played, some people came backstage. We happened to be standing there, and Don had his little pocket trumpet, and a couple came up to him and said, "What do you call that trumpet?" And he goes, "I call it my trumpet."

* * *

Following Lou Reed's first three-night stand appearance in 1977, The Bottom Line hosted a matching three-night stay by none other than Dolly Parton, whose career at that moment was truly at a turning point. Just three months prior, Parton had released her eighteenth solo album, the prophetically titled New Harvest . . . First Gathering. *Her first self-produced collection, the work signaled a clear shift in the singer-songwriter's musical direction in that she was not so much moving away from the folk-leaning country that had made her one of Nashville's brightest stars as she was stretching out to expand her musical horizons to see if a sequined pop shoe might also fit. And that it certainly did, as it became her first solo LP to crack Billboard's* Top 100 *album charts and set the stage for what was to come for the pride of Tennessee's Smoky Mountains region.*

Remarkably, while she'd made a few appearances in New York State over the previous decade during her long tenure with mentor and duet partner Porter Wagoner (her bittersweet split from him in 1974 provided the backstory to Parton's "I Will Always Love You," later to become a massive hit for Whitney Houston), Dolly Parton had never once performed as a solo artist in New York City before her May 12–14, 1977 engagement at The Bottom Line. Anticipation for her appearance was great, and her record company RCA pulled out all the stops, to the point of hosting an extravagant post-show party for her at the Windows on the World restaurant at the top of the World Trade Center in lower Manhattan. Parton's combination of over-the-top glitz and don't-get-above-your-raisin' lack of conceit charmed all who witnessed her, from the cheering customers (including pixilated celebrities like Springsteen and Jagger) to the entire Bottom Line staff.

ALLAN PEPPER: I think the date that Dolly did was very important. She was one of the classiest performers I have ever dealt with. Dick Feller *[a singer-songwriter best known for penning country novelty hits like "(I'm Just a) Redneck in a Rock and Roll Bar"]* was opening for her, and he was doing ok with the audience. I was hanging around in the lobby because I knew she was coming and wanted to personally bring her in. She showed up during Feller's last number, and the place was completely packed and I said to her, "Do you want to come in? I'll take you backstage," and she said "no." I said "why" and she pointed out something to me that I should have realized. She said, "If I go in right now, I'll get everyone's attention and shift everything he's been doing away from him. I'll stay here in the lobby until he's finished." And that's what she did. It was a classy thing to do, and that's what she was like from the moment she showed up until the end of her three nights at the club.

RUSSELL WOLINSKY (Host): The best show I ever saw, and I saw a couple of thousand shows in my years working at the club, was Dolly Parton when she was just breaking. The backstage area was very narrow, and the first night she was there, I'm carrying two cases of beer to the cooler near the dressing rooms, one on each shoulder, and I turn around and bang, I go right into Dolly's chest—and she just smiled at me. THE nicest performer, ever. After the shows, the record company threw a party at Windows on the World and the tour manager invited the whole staff. He said, "I have to invite people I can talk to . . . I can't stand these assholes from RCA any longer."

MATILDA PARENTE (Waitress): I worked at the Dolly Parton show, and Mick Jagger came to every show. He loved her act and he literally came to every show. And Jagger, he doesn't sit still, doesn't stay still. And so we had this little area that led directly to the kitchen, and it was sort of blocked off from the main room, that Allan kind of used as their VIP area. And Mick Jagger was there and just dancing. It was near the restrooms too, so there was a little bit of traffic there. But that little alleyway, that little hallway kind of was only for us. That was only in or out of the kitchen. And you just got out of somebody's way. If they were coming at you with a big tray, usually loaded with beers and things like that, they were heavy. And I'm coming out of the kitchen and I have one of those big trays with a bottle of champagne in the middle, surrounded by beers and glasses. And there I am trying to balance this thing and get out there and get these drinks served, ASAP. And there's Jagger just wildly dancing along to the music. And I'm yelling, "Move out of my way, move" and yelling, but not so loud that they would hear it in the room, and he's not moving. I'm trying to get his attention. And finally, I just cursed at him. I just said, "Get the fuck out of my way, Mick!" And he heard the "fuck," because he turned around and he got out of my way. I was trying everything, trying to be polite. I knew who he was, of course, but I couldn't get too close to him because he was such a wild man and not paying attention that I was afraid he was going to bang into me and knock over this tremendous tray. But until I told him to get the fuck out of the way and called him by his name, he didn't move. But he sure loved that act.

MIMI LIEBER (Waitress): When Dolly Parton came to the club, of course we were all cynical and far too hip to put up with this country girl with the giant boobs and the giant hair. She was the antithesis of everything going on in that moment. And there she was blowing our minds, playing with those fingernails on her banjo or singing. I mostly can recall the big famous song, "Coat of Many Colors." Because of the picking, the extraordinary playing, our esteem for her got zoomed up to the top and never left. It was wonderful too, to have your head turned around at twenty years old, twenty-one years old. She must have been a little scared, knowing that crowd. And it was really something, I mean, all of us were like, Dolly Parton? And then from the instant she came out, came out in a shirt tied under the boobs or at the waist and a red bandana, a triangle in her hair tied just dramatically so. Oh my God. It was so fantastic. And to do that in the face of that cynicism and turn it upside down, that was just wonderful.

JUDY JACKSINA (Broadway theater publicist): Thursday, May 12. Allan called me, I'm a workaholic so I'm always in the office. So he calls me up, and says, "You want to come down to the late show for Dolly Parton?" And I said, "I'll start getting ready now." I wasn't such a workaholic. Fuck Broadway. I'm going to see Dolly Parton! Now, correct me if I'm wrong, I think this was the first time she played New York. So I get down there. This is not for me. What, Judy, can you stand at the bar? Well, I guess so. No one is getting in to see this. Oh, I mean, someone should slap me upside the head. So I'm like standing at the bar thinking I can't stand at the bar. Ok, well, she comes out on stage. Well, first of all, the audience looked like a who's who—of everywhere. It was obviously the late show because we're all late people. So, well, me and The Stones are there, and I remember the *Saturday Night Live* cast came in, so it wasn't Saturday. I think I saw the second show on Friday, and they were there. But I think the show I was at Saturday night, I think it was Mick and Keith, and I think Charlie Watts, oh, I don't remember. Maybe it was all, ok, let's face it, no one sees anyone, but I think some other band people were there, but I think they were down there with their plus everybody was like, no, plus ones. Ok, so she's now never played Manhattan before. I would've been nervous because, wow. So I'm looking at this audience. It's like, seriously, who's who? I mean, really, entertainment royalty is in this. I mean, there's heads of record companies. So she comes out on stage, ha ha ha. And she starts, "My name is Dolly Parton," and it's like, "Yay, everybody." So she starts playing the first song.

Now I'm a theater baby; we're manipulators. So she starts, goes on, and she looks like Dolly Parton. And you can't believe she actually looks like her photos. She says, "I'm going to do my first song." So she starts her first song with her little tiny guitar, and she goes, "Oh, for goodness sake." And she stops now. Now this is a train coming, but ok, she stops. So now we're all into it. And she says, "Oh, my nail blew off. Well, goodness sake, you know what? I learned to play the G with my nails on, but ok." So she says, "Alright, hold on." And so she starts the song again, and she says, "I just can't do it like this. So hold on." So, right in front of all of us, she takes off the other nine nails. And everyone goes crazy. Ok, so that's it! She's the best! She wins all the awards! She's won us over, and we're addicted to her after two minutes. We're love slaves to Dolly Parton. We'll never buy another CD, album, whatever it's called again, just Dolly Parton's. And that's it. And she drove us crazy, and it was thunderous applause all the way through. Bunch of hard noses, aren't we? She was it. Knew how to play an audience. She didn't care who was out there. It was genius. Now I'm sure she did that every night. You are looking at someone who manipulates people so that we can figure out how to sell tickets. I said, ok, this woman is theatrically brilliant. Look who she was playing to because I was at the bar. So I could see everybody across the room, and I'm telling you, everyone in those 400 seats was leaning forward. And I'm thinking, "She knows how to work the room. My nail. Oh my goodness. I learned to play the guitar with these nails. No, you didn't. But I believed her. You learned to play the guitar in some holler in Tennessee with nails on? No, you didn't." But it was genius. It was theatrically astute. And everyone was leaning forward the whole show. And by the time she got to "Jolene," I mean, come on!

8 MEAT LOAF BURNS, AND NO-SHOW JONES FINALLY ARRIVES

Marvin Lee Aday had spent close to a decade kicking around the entertainment industry as a singer and actor before he catapulted to "overnight" stardom in late 1977 at age thirty under the nickname he'd been saddled with since he was a 5'2", 240 lb. middle-schooler in his hometown of Dallas, Texas: Meat Loaf. Meat had already recorded a barely heard album for Motown, appeared in both the American stage and film versions of the Rocky Horror Picture Show, *and had sung lead (though barely credited) on several songs on hard rocker Ted Nugent's multi-platinum 1976 album,* Free for All, *before he literally exploded into stardom with the surprise mega-hit* Bat Out of Hell. *The brainchild of composer/pianist Jim Steinman, who found in Meat Loaf the perfect outsized performer for his over-the-top, melodramatic music,* Bat Out of Hell *was released just a month before Loaf, Steinman, and their Neverland band descended on The Bottom Line at the end of the 1977 Thanksgiving holiday weekend for a two-night stand. The engagement proved pivotal to the success of the album, as the theatricality of the show played perfectly on the Bottom Line stage. With a heavy assist from a live broadcast of the show on WNEW that was distributed to radio stations across the country,* Bat Out of Hell *took off like its title—and would eventually become one of the twentieth century's all-time biggest LPs, to the tune of better than 40 million copies sold worldwide.*

While they hadn't performed on the album, two key members of the touring band that appeared with Meat Loaf at the Bottom Line shows were drummer Joe Stefko and featured vocalist Karla DeVito.

KARLA DEVITO: I had been in a band out of Boston called Orchestra Luna, and we performed in a production staged at the Kennedy Center in Washington of a show called *Neverland*. It was written by Jim Steinman and featured some of the songs that wound up on *Bat Out of Hell*. In June of 1977, we did a gig in New York at Alice Tully Hall, and Jim and Meat came to see us, and shortly thereafter, I got a call from Steinman saying, "Hey, we're putting together a band to go on the road. Will you move to New York and join us?" And it was one of these things where we had done that gig thinking we were going to be doing a showcase for a&r reps from all the labels, but in point of fact—and I probably wouldn't have left the band if I had known about it at the time—the guy who set up the showcase never sent out any invitations. He was really just using it as an audition so Jim could see me and the Orchestra Luna guitarist. Now we had just turned down Sire Records' Seymour Stein, who wanted us and actually was going to sign us instead of Talking Heads, which would have been a terrible mistake on his part. But as much as I did love my band, Seymour only offered us $15,000 for a signing fee, and there were eight of us, and we needed the money for amplifiers and all sorts of things it wouldn't even cover. Anyway, Jim wanted me, and since no record company made us another offer, when he called, I accepted.

Joe Stefko's route to the Meat Loaf band was more circuitous. Stefko had spent two years on the road with John Cale, founding member of the Velvet Underground, and had left the group after a notorious incident in England in which Cale, unbeknownst to the rest of the band, came out for his encore wearing a butcher's smock and, wielding a cleaver, decapitated a live chicken onstage while singing Elvis Presley's "Heartbreak Hotel" ("You'll be so lonesome, you could die"). Stefko—and not only because he was a vegetarian—was so horrified he immediately quit the band and was staying in London when a call to his folks led him to return home to Long Island, and a life-changing turn of events.

JOE STEFKO (Drummer): I call my parents to say I was ok, and my father says, "Your friend from Epic called. Something about a meat loaf." I said, "Dad, I just walked off the stage because of a chicken. I'm not coming home to a fucking meat loaf." And he says, "Well, he wants you to call him." So I called my friend and he tells me to get home because I might have another gig. I was friends with the Long Island band The Good Rats, and their manager was David Sonenberg, who managed Meat Loaf, and my friend at Epic knew this. Meanwhile, I was doing all these interviews about what had happened with Cale, including one for *Rolling Stone*. So I get home and now I'm in their gossip column, Random Notes, right under an item on John Lennon and Yoko Ono. I'd been given this number to call to get an audition for this Meat Loaf thing, so I call it and say I'm calling about this Meat Loaf thing; I'm a drummer." The guy on the other end says, "Nah, I'm Meat Loaf. I heard 500 musicians. I'm done." I said, "You're not done. You haven't heard me." He said, "Who the hell are you?" I said, "I'm Joe Stefko." Like it really meant something. And he said, "Hey, I just read about you in *Rolling Stone*. Ok, get down here." So I go, and it was just me and Meat and Jim, and maybe there was a bass player there, and Meat played me "Bat Out of Hell." I told them I never heard anything like it, and that it was incredible. He says, "Yeah, I know, it's my new record." I said, "Let's play it." At first they don't want to, but Jim gets on the piano,

I click it off and we play some of it, and I was lucky that I had balls because I guess I played well, and I walked out with the gig.

We put the band together, and were going to start from ground zero, playing clubs, but a guy from the booking agency says he can get us as an opening act for Cheap Trick in Chicago. And we thought, well, that sounds pretty good. So we're rehearsing, and Jim had us doing all kinds of things before we even did a song: There were speeches and instrumentals, and I mean, it was a big production, but [guitarist] Bob Kulick and I were trying to say, listen, you're making these people wait like fifteen minutes before you even give them *Bat Out of Hell*. This is going to be a tough sell. We really ought to just go with the songs. And he says, don't tell me what to do. So we opened up for Cheap Trick, and keep in mind, they're from the Chicago area; this is home turf for them. So we start playing all this intro stuff, and well, let's just say it didn't go well.

SAM ELLIS (Road manager): Meat walked out on stage while Jim was hammering out the long *Bat Out of Hell* "Bolero" intro with the band, and pretty soon the first three rows stood up and started screaming, "Get off the stage, you fat fuck." And it did not stop. We somehow got through the show, but it was a complete disaster, and afterwards there was a lot of soul searching and a lot of rethinking.

KARLA DEVITO: No one had heard of our record there. So we come onstage with Meat in the tuxedo, and it was a very theatrical presentation; that's what made it special. But these kids were not willing to listen to that, and it was pretty devastating to Meat Loaf. I mean, the rest of us were like, whoa. But to me, because that guy, he's Mr. Talent, he's never had people throwing things at him onstage and basically booing him off. But that was great in a way, because that was like Sam going, ok, and the record company going, ok, let's go back to the drawing board.

SAM ELLIS: We realized at that point that an opening act was not in Meat Loaf's cards. So in essence, we never opened for anybody again. We came back to New York and started putting the tour together with the idea that we would start in the clubs and then expand from there depending upon the markets. And the Northeast club circuit at that time was My Father's Place on Long Island, Toad's Place in New Haven, The Paradise Club in Boston, and the crème de la crème, The Bottom Line in New York. Of course, I'm a little biased about The Bottom Line because I'd worked there, so it was old home week for me. But those shows just turned out great, and everything just kind of exploded from there.

KARLA DEVITO: Yeah, I'm sure after Chicago, Meat probably lost his incredible confidence for a while. But the second we got out there in New York, it all worked. I had studied improv at Second City, and it was like musical improv in some ways because when we were rehearsing at what we called the Meat Loft, I said to Jim, "So, Jim, what do I do when I get out there?" And he goes, "You'll know when you're there." So that was my direction. But with Luna, when I was with them, it was very theatrical. We called ourselves a theatrical rock, jazz, and vaudeville band. So I came from that world. And with Meat, I just kind of created this character, "The Girl in White" is what they called it. But it just happened, and it wasn't like Meat and I talked about it. Nobody talked about anything. But it really led to the band feeling that same feeling, that theatricality. It was just different. We were creating something, kind of from scratch.

The album was so tremendous, but nobody was going to listen to it unless they saw what could be delivered. And The Bottom Line was a great place to do that. And it was just unbelievable. The audience was electrified, and there was Meat sweating eight tables deep in on them and just knocking people's socks off because we delivered. Look, it came out of the brain and the genius of Jim Steinman, who wrote every note and every word, but without all those pieces—without Meat Loaf, without that band, without me, whatever—without the theatricality of what that was, I don't know if it would have worked.

JOE STEFKO: Before those Bottom Line shows, Meat was really scared. As a matter of fact, he didn't want to come and do it. I mean, he was the last one to show up at the club. The manager had to go to the apartment and talk him into it, you know, come on, get out of the tub and get your clothes on. You've got two shows tonight at The Bottom Line, you got to do it. We're live on the radio. Meat was freaked out, but he did it. They built the stage out because it was small. It wasn't a tiny stage, but we built it out because it was a big thing, a big band. And we did it. I know that we were scared for him more than any of us. I felt like, "Hey, I'm at The Bottom Line!" To me, that was big because I used to go there and see pretty big bands. Not only that, we're live on WNEW. This was just ridiculous.

SAM ELLIS: In one of the early shows that we did, Meat came off and collapsed, and because he had a history of asthma and trouble breathing sometimes, we had a tank of oxygen, and we gave him the oxygen, and it revitalized him. So we had the oxygen protocol in place everywhere we went because we knew that when Meat came off stage, he would indeed often collapse and need it. Whether it was psychological or not, I can't tell you, but Meat was a very dramatic person, so we gave him the oxygen. He went back on stage, and it was great. Anyone else may have gone off stage, been tired, sat down, had a glass of water, and then gone back out. But Meat had a way of taking the dramatic as far as it could go, and it was pretty funny at The Bottom Line because the backstage was not necessarily that luxurious, and so it was quite a sight. I remember the DJ Richard Neer, who was hosting the NEW broadcast, was standing up over Dressing Room B, and Meat came off after the show and collapsed at the bottom of the stairs there. And Neer was going, "He's down, he's up," and someone on our crew lifted Meat up, and then he collapsed again, and Neer was broadcasting it like it was a prize fight, like a title fight. "He's up! He's down! This is unbelievable, ladies and gentlemen." And finally,

Meat got up and went back out on stage, and we did an encore or two and then came back off.

KARLA DEVITO: Look, that guy was so nimble. As much as he weighed, when we were on bigger stages, he's doing somersaults all the way across the stage. By the time he did it, it was sort of like when James Brown would go down and they would throw the cape on him, like, "I can't do any more." And if he needed the oxygen, who cared? If it was a little bit of an artifice, so what?

SAM ELLIS: When we came back out for our encore, we had worked out a few non-*Bat Out of Hell* numbers, including "River Deep, Mountain High," as a duet with Meat and Karla. And sometimes we did "Hammer Down," which was one of the songs that Meat had sung with Ted Nugent. Steinman was adamantly opposed to doing it, but we didn't have another encore, and we needed it. So Jim would very deliberately put on hockey gloves and just beat the piano to show his violent opposition to doing that song.

JOE STEFKO: I do remember that we had a guy come in that we were trying to get to take us on the road to oversee things, and he was sitting out there, and at first he thought, "What the hell is this? I'm not going out with this." Then he realized that the whole crowd was singing along, and he later told me that's what swayed him to do it because he didn't even know the record, and yet everybody at the club did, and they were singing the words. So this is something that had already ripped the hearts of a certain number of people—and it was only going to keep going. And boy, did it.

* * *

The fall of 1977 also saw the first of what would be several "non-appearances" by country music legend George Jones. Recognized by all as one of the greatest vocalists in country music history, Jones had his demons: During the 1960s and '70s, he earned the nickname "No Show Jones" for regularly getting so wasted on drugs and/or alcohol that he simply missed concerts, usually on little or no notice. (Forbes reported that at one point Jones had some 200 lawsuits pending against him for failing to perform.) Still, the prospect of George Jones coming to The Bottom Line created enough of a buzz that his record company, Epic, decided to throw a promotional Southern-style barbecue in his honor in the backyard of an East Village restaurant a few hours before his scheduled September 3 show. His band The Jones Boys had ventured north on their tour bus and cheerfully greeted the media and industry execs invited for the pre-concert dinner. The only problem was, as the clock crept up toward the time everyone needed to make their way over to The Bottom Line for the show, Jones was nowhere to be seen. Word started to circulate that the limo driver who was to deliver him to NYC had called to report that somewhere along the way, Jones had asked him to make a rest stop, and that he apparently escaped through a bathroom window and flat-out disappeared.

While the concert was officially canceled, and the club made it known that whoever wanted a refund could get one, The Jones Boys, who regularly played a warm-up set prior to George's own, graciously offered to try and make the best of things by saying that they'd still perform for whoever wanted to stay. Upon hearing this, several journalists from the ever-irreverent Creem *magazine who were on hand (including, full disclosure, the co-author of this book) conferred and hatched an impromptu plan to try and further salvage the evening. They'd brought to the dinner their vocalist friend Michael Simmons, known informally at the time as the king of country punk as leader of his band Slewfoot. Since Simmons was a great George Jones fan, they proposed, maybe The Jones Boys would let him sit in with them?*

MICHAEL SIMMONS: Looking back, I think that one of the reasons I went along with it was that it wasn't my idea. One of you guys got the cockamamie idea to get me to fill in for him. And when we got to the club, you went to Allan Pepper and said, "We got this kid here who knows every George Jones song, and he plays at the Lone Star Cafe and the Bells of Hell and blah, blah, blah." And so they brought me onto The Jones Boys' bus, and one of the guys in the band handed me an acoustic guitar and they said, "Ok, let's hear you sing." And I did "Window Up Above" and I think "White Lightning" and another of George Jones' classics. And they said, "Ok, you got the job." And I just did it. They played a set and then they got me up and I did, I think, four songs. My mind was totally blown. I mean, I was sentient as I recall. And I think I pulled it off, as I recall.

The postscript to all this is that about a month later, my band was playing in Nashville during Fanfare week. And after we played at the Exit Inn, I went over to Possum Holler, which was the club in town George Jones owned. I couldn't get in because it was Fanfare and the place was sold out; they weren't letting anyone else in. So I turned around to go back to the hotel when I saw The Jones Boys' bus parked outside near the club. I figured, what the hell, so I went and knocked on the door, and the bus driver opened it. I said, "Can I talk to the band? I'm a friend of theirs from New York." The bass player came out and greeted me and said, "Simmons, how you doing, man? What are you doin' here?" And I told him I'd just played at the Exit Inn, but I couldn't get into the Holler because it was sold out. And he said, "Oh, don't worry about it. We'll get you in." So they walked me to the door and said to the bouncer, "He's with us." And then they walked me to the bar and said to the bartender, "Give this guy whatever he wants. He's drinking on The Jones Boys' tab." I'll never forget that. I was greeted like a returning champ. It was so cool. They were really nice guys.

It would take another no-show and one more booking to finally get George Jones on The Bottom Line stage. And, naturally, it turned out to be worth the wait.

ALLAN PEPPER: I booked him a second time, we agreed on a date, signed a contract, and then again they had to cancel the gig. I would be more upset, but here's the interesting thing: We would announce there was a cancellation and the fans would come up to the box office window and ask us, "What is it this time? He got sick? He got into an accident?" They were prepared for this. They knew he was No-Show Jones. But I didn't give up. And the third time, in 1980, finally was the charm.

Not only did Jones at last appear and give a spectacular concert that August, but Linda Ronstadt and Bonnie Raitt—who had been in the audience—joined him onstage to sing backup vocals during his encore, as did another surprise guest, Johnny Paycheck, who once had been a member of Jones' tour band.

BONNIE RAITT: I had done a show in Central Park and Linda [Ronstadt] was starring in *The Pirates of Penzance* on Broadway, and we hooked up afterward at The Bottom Line to see George Jones and ended up sitting. It certainly was a memorable summer evening in New York.

May of 1978 brought a rare club three-night performance by singer-songwriter Carly Simon, coinciding with the release of her Boys in the Trees *album, which featured her hit single duet with then-husband James Taylor and their rendition of the Everly Brothers classic, "Devoted to You." Unbeknownst to most fans, Simon spent much of her career suffering from severe stage fright—which was witnessed up close throughout the engagement by most of The Bottom Line staff.*

PATRICK CLIFFORD (Host): I'm there the first night she appeared and someone gives me a little trash bucket, like from an elementary school. They tell me to take it to the dressing room for Carly Simon. I go and knock on the door and say, "Ms. Simon, they asked for me to bring this to you." And you know the dressing rooms were small, like closets there. So all of a sudden she takes it out of my hand and throws up into it right in front of me. It was like Linda Blair in *The Exorcist*. To which all I could say was, "Are you ok? Can I get you anything?" She goes, no, no, hands me the bucket back and closes the door. And then she and James Taylor played the show. And it was as joyous as anything I've ever seen in my life.

ALLAN PEPPER: Her manager, Arlyne Rothberg, came down to the club and sat in the office with Stanley and myself and she was demanding all kinds of stuff for Carly. We were very at ease refusing things, so she sat there and said "I need that and I need this," and we just kept saying no. She finally looked at us and said, "I could have had a couple of common laborers put this show on rather than dealing with you two." We just smiled. But then we saw that Carly was very nervous backstage. She had an assortment of people trying to make her feel comfortable, and James, who sat in with her, was just pacing back and forth, and finally he said, "For Christ's sake, Carly, let's just do this." And she did, and she was great.

Years later, their daughter Sally Taylor played the club and Carly came to see her perform. And at the end of the show, Carly went and stood in the little coat closet where performers sold their merchandise, selling her daughter's CDs. In the end, she's a mom, and that's what always stayed with me.

The fall of '78 saw another rare club date with the appearance of guitarist Carlos Santana and his band. The booking had special meaning to Pepper, as it came about because Santana was then being managed by one of Pepper's early heroes and now friends—Bill Graham.

ALLAN PEPPER: The first time Bill ever came to the club was with an agent, Johnny Podell, who's the one who had offered us the Allman Brothers years before at the Gate. Podell brought Bill down. The next time I knew he was coming, I was in the lobby and he walked in and he takes out his wallet and I said, "Don't take his money," and I said to Bill, "You can never pay in this place—ever." He looked at me and said, "Then I'm not going to come in." And I knew he meant it. I didn't want to disrespect him. The way I made it up to him was with a gesture I thought he'd easily accept. Across the street from us was Swenson's ice cream parlor, and I knew Bill loved ice cream. So every time I knew he was coming to the club, I'd send someone out to get a batch of different flavors, and I'd take them to the kitchen and we put them in bowls and brought him about half a dozen, and he loved it.

Bill got Santana to play the club, and he asked if he could introduce them. For me, to have Bill Graham emcee those shows on our stage was the equivalent of when Stanley and I first met him up at Columbia Records. I can't recall exactly why we were there that day, but we stepped off an elevator and literally bumped into Graham, and we started talking, and he told us that the Bottom Line stage had become what the Fillmore stage had been. And then, to see your idol select one of his acts to perform at the club and then come out on your stage and introduce them, well, it meant the world to me.

Graham also came down when another of his clients, Van Morrison, played his own rare club show at The Bottom Line. The mercurial singer-songwriter had quite the reputation for being a difficult performer—stories about him almost deliberately picking fights with audiences in the middle of shows were legion in the 1960s and '70s—and he proved to be just as prone to making things hard backstage.

RICHARD NEER: Van Morrison played The Bottom Line when his *Wavelength* album came out. We were going to broadcast the show live on NEW. Bill Graham was managing him, and at the last minute, Van said, "I'm not doing a radio show. If you're going to put this on the radio, I'm not going out there," and Graham just grabbed him by the lapels and shoved him against the wall of the dressing room. "Listen, you little Irish mother, you're going on," Bill yelled, "And if you don't, you're going to be missing some teeth." And Van went on, did the show, and it was great. Then, three days later, he played the Palladium on 14th Street, and I wasn't there, but from what I heard, he walked out in the middle of the show, and that was the end of the tour. He canceled the rest of the dates.

ALLAN PEPPER: In the 1980s Bill did some tours with the Stones, but he lost the next tour to a Canadian promoter, and he was very depressed. One night he came to the club, and I could see he wasn't himself; he sat down, and I knew he was sad. I sat down with him and asked him how he was doing, and he kind of just shook his head. I said, "I heard about the Stones," and he just nodded, and I said, "Listen. You're fucking Bill Graham. They're just another rock and roll band." And he gave me the biggest smile you could imagine. That's the respect and admiration I had for him.

* * *

Throughout the late 1970s, The Bottom Line continued to do brisk business with its now signature eclectic mix of artists and musical styles booked by Pepper. For example, during just one stretch, from June 1 to mid-September in '78, the club presented jazzsters Yusef Lateef, Gary Burton, Lonnie Liston Smith, and Spyro Gyra; bluesmen B. B. King, James Cotton, Johnny Winter, John Hammond Jr., Son Seals and Clarence "Gatemouth" Brown; rockers Lou Reed, Cheap Trick, Mink DeVille, and The Flamin' Groovies; punk/new wavers David Johansen, Tom Robinson, Television, and The Shirts; guitar giants Chet Atkins, Les Paul, Doc Watson, and Bert Jansch; singer-songwriters John Prine, Laura Nyro, Ralph McTell, and Jesse Winchester; country artists Carlene Carter, John Hartford, Asleep at the Wheel, and Tracy Nelson; roots rockers NRBQ; popsters Dion, Flo & Eddie (of the Turtles), and Bonnie Tyler; downtown alt-folk faves The Roches; and the ever-uncategorizable Leon Redbone.

Through it all, when it came to running the business end of the club, Stanley Snadowsky continued to demonstrate both his business acumen and his often wicked sense of humor.

ALLAN PEPPER: As a general rule, we allowed industry people to run house tabs, but they had to pay within thirty days. Ed Goodgold managed Sha Na Na, and we knew him from before the club even opened, and Ed had run up a big tab. Once a month, Stanley would sit down and look at who owed us money, and one month he's going through accounts receivable and he sees that Ed owes us a lot of money, and it's been about sixty days. Our secretary, Lorraine Rebidas, says she's called him a lot, but he doesn't return the calls, and she just can't get him on the phone. So Stanley tells Lorraine, "Ok, here's what I want you to do. Call his number on one line, and after you've done that, call the same number on another of our lines, but do not dial the last digit until I tell you, and then look at me and I'll tell you what to say." So she dials, and as it's ringing, she dials the same number on the second line but stops at the last digit. Stanley gets on the first line and the secretary there says hello and Stanley says, "Hi, is Ed there?" She says, "May I ask who's calling?" and he says, "It's Stanley Snadowsky," and she puts him on hold. After a minute, she comes back on and says, "Oh I'm so sorry, but he's not in right now. Can I take a message?" And Stanley says, "Sure. Can you hold for a sec? I have to pick up another call. I'll be right back." And he tells Lorraine, "Ok, hit the last digit—and when they answer, say Clive Davis is calling for Ed." So he gets back on with the secretary and says, "Yes, can you tell Ed that Stanley Snadowsky wants to . . . and the secretary says, "Can you hold again for a minute?" He says sure, and she gets on the line that Lorraine is on and she says, "Hi, it's Clive Davis' office calling for Ed," and the secretary says, "Hold on, I'll see if he's in. Can you hold?" and Ed jumps on the phone and says, "Hi, Clive," and Stanley says, "Hey, Ed, how're you doing? It's Stan Snadowsky at The Bottom Line." And he hears Ed on the phone utter, "Oh shit."

Another time we were making a deal with Sam McKeith, the agent, and he was looking for a co-bill with one of his lesser acts, the folk duo Batdorf and Rodney. I offer them $300, and he says he wants $500 for a co-bill. We're going back and forth and Stanley's listening to me trying to negotiate with Sam, and he decides to pick up. "So, Sam," Stanley says, "Allan tells me you want this group Batdorf and Robinson to play the club," and Sam says, "It's Batdorf and Rodney, Stanley." And Stanley says, "Oh I'm so sorry. I know you've told Allan that Batdorf and Robinson are getting a lot of radio play." Sam stops him and says, "Stanley, again, it's Batdorf and Rodney." Stanley says "Yeah, but Allan feels that Batdorf and Robins . . . I'm sorry, Sam, but that's my problem. I'm in the business and I don't know who they are. Nobody knows who they are. And even if they do, they think it's Batdorf and Robinson." And Sam finally says, "Ok, Stanley, you win. $300."

* * *

Comedy acts began to appear with regularity at The Bottom Line in the late 1970s. Richard Belzer opened for a number of acts, including Meat Loaf (he was responsible for nicknaming Meat Loaf's band "The Hamburger Helpers") and Mark Knopfler and Dire Straits, whose manager threatened that the group would walk if Belzer was allowed to open for them with a band behind him. Pepper and Snadowsky called the bluff, and Belzer did his set—including an uproarious bit in which he envisioned the then thirty-eight-year-old Bob Dylan decades into the future and now an elderly senior with a heavy Jewish accent, singing "Like a Rolling (Gall) Stone": "Vunce upon a time/You dthressed so fine/You tchrew de bums a dime/In your pchrime—didn' you?" . . . Now you don't talk so loud, mister big shot."

During 1977, a then struggling Larry David appeared four times, receiving mostly blank responses from The Bottom Line audiences.

ALLAN PEPPER: Larry David was one of those guys who thought funny. He was on stage one night and toward the end, he looked at his watch and said, "Oh, I gotta end this. It's very important that I get home in time because tomorrow is the start of a very important Jewish holiday, which is Shekukis. It celebrates the founding of the Kirsch beverage company." Our longtime staff member Jack [Leitenberg] would later say to me, "I'll be in late tomorrow, Allan. It's the start of Shekukis." It took on a whole new meaning at the club. Larry was one of those comics that bands often found funnier than the audience did.

RUSSELL WOLINKSY: David never really went over with the crowd, but the staff loved him. Him and Belzer. I remember running into him on the street near the comedy club The Improv one afternoon. I yelled out, "Hey, Larry David!" and he looked absolutely terrified that someone was calling his name out loud on the street.

In late October 1978, British new wave stars Nick Lowe and Dave Edmunds brought their side supergroup Rockpile to the club, and word got out that Stones guitarist Keith Richards was going to show up. Given that Richards was, like Edmunds, a huge Chuck Berry devotee, it seemed logical that he might sit in for a few Berry-flavored tunes. And that he did—though his cameo during their set proved more notorious than noteworthy.

RUSSELL WOLINSKY: I remember Keith coming in before Rockpile's show, and he walked in fine and sounded lucid. In the middle of the set, Dave Edmunds announces him, and the group goes into Chuck Berry's "Promised Land," and all you heard coming out of his guitar was feedback. He was kind of slouched around the back of the stage, and he's got the Keith look, but he's not really playing, the guitar is just hanging from his neck feeding back, and every once in a while he'd play half a riff. They get through the song, go into the next one—not a Berry song—and Keith is still playing his Chuck Berry riffs, and suddenly you saw a pair of hands come out and grab him from behind and get him through the curtains and off the stage.

Four days after Richards' aborted guest appearance, rockabilly legend Carl Perkins played the club. Sometime during the early show, a yellow cab pulled up at the curb by the awning. Its passenger jumped out, made straight for the box office, and asked if Perkins had gone on yet. Finding out that he had, he briskly headed in, where he was quickly recognized and steered to the backstage area. Late in Perkins' set, the creator of "Blue Suede Shoes," "Matchbox," "Honey Don't," and other '50s rock and roll classics brought out his surprise guest. A rapt audience got to see one guitar hero, Eric Clapton, accompanying one of his guitar heroes, Carl Perkins—and yet another magical evening at The Bottom Line was in the books.

Bruce Springsteen, Born to Run Tour, August 1975.

Allan and Stanley pay Marvin a visit at Variety Knit, 1975. (Back: Richie Schulberg)

Stanley, 1975.

View of the stage from the coveted VIP round tables; Bruce Springsteen famously danced on the long tables in front of the stage.

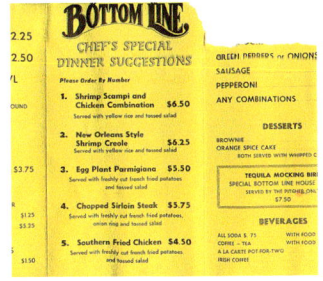

Menu from August 1975.

(Back, L-R): Peter Neptune, Charlie Pistone, Chrissie Faith, Jon Fiore, Jimmy Vivino, Bobby Jay; (2nd row, L-R): Annie Golden, Ula Hedwig; Center: Ellie Greenwich; Bottom, L-R: Pattie Darcy and Darlene Love.) *Leader of the Pack*, second production, April 27 through May 27, 1983.

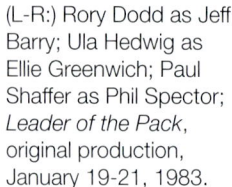

(L-R:) Rory Dodd as Jeff Barry; Ula Hedwig as Ellie Greenwich; Paul Shaffer as Phil Spector; *Leader of the Pack*, original production, January 19-21, 1983.

The 1980 Bottom Line Christmas card opened to reveal Allan and Stanley in drag, selling tickets for ten cents a dance, while the cover of the card mischievously proclaimed, "We always wanted to open a dance club."

Karla DeVito, *Leader of the Pack* original production.

Darlene Love, *Leader of the Pack* original production.

George Jones and Linda Ronstadt, August 18, 1980.

Paul Simon, 1974.

(L-R): Bill Graham greets Al Bunetta, 1974.

(L-R): Leon Redbone, Neil Young, John Hammond, May 16, 1974.

Tom Waits and Bette Midler, backstage April 11, 1975.

Grace Slick catches Allan Pepper by surprise, 1974.

(L-R): Maggie Roche, Suzzy Roache, Linda Ronstadt, and Terre Roche (backstage).

Tom Waits, April 1975.

Bruce Springsteen and Stevie Van Zandt, August 1975.

Flo & Eddie, January 1975.

Roger McGuinn, November 1974.

Carly Simon and James Taylor, May 1978.

Sonny Rollins.

Rita Coolidge, Kris Kristofferson, and Billy Swan, January 1979.

Rosanne Cash, March 1981.

(L-R): Clarence Clemmons and Bruce Springsteen, July 1974.

David Johansen, performing with the New York Dolls, April 21, 1974.

Karla DeVito and Meatloaf, November 1977.

Muddy Waters, 1974.

Loudon Wainwright.

David Bromberg, 1976.

Tony Bennett, May 5, 1981.

John Hiatt, July 1979.

Harry Chapin celebrates his two thousandth live performance, 1981.

Laura Nyro, July 1978.

Tanya Tucker, April 3, 1974.

Patti Smith, November 1976.

9 THE CHAIRS HOLD FIRM

DOO-WOPPERS, ROCK 'N' ROLL PRISONERS, AND THE GREAT FRENCH FRY CAPER

While it has always enjoyed a vibrant and varied club scene, the late 1970s and early '80s was a particularly exciting time for live music and entertainment in New York City. The Bottom Line had spent its first half-decade of existence as the city's dominant showcase venue for virtually any act coming to town, but the fact that New York had helped generate no less than three major movements over the course of that time—punk/new wave, disco, and hip-hop—led to a preponderance of new or repurposed clubs and concert spaces springing up from downtown to midtown to offer a great variety of options for music fans of every stripe. Punks and new wavers had the longstanding home base CBGB, as well as Max's Kansas City, and the Mudd Club. The dance crowd had the disco capital of the world, Studio 54 (which closed in 1980), the LGBTQ-friendly Paradise Garage, and the Latin/world music-flavored S.O.B.s, as well as the rock-oriented Hurrah, Danceteria, and the Peppermint Lounge. Blues buffs had Tramps and Trax, and country fans had The Lone Star Café. Mid-sized venues such as The Palladium/Academy of Music stage presented sit-down concerts, while both Irving Plaza and the cavernous Ritz enabled rock and pop-leaning visitors to stand or sit, as was their want. Not to mention the many small jazz clubs always sprinkled throughout Manhattan, such as the Village Vanguard, Sweet Basil, and the new Blue Note. There were cabaret clubs such as Reno Sweeney, comedy joints such as The Improv and Catch a Rising Star, and those longstanding catch-all clubs Folk City, Kenny's Castaways, and The Bitter End.

The Bottom Line ended the 1970s holding fast to Pepper and Snadowsky's original vision of a customer-friendly venue featuring performers from all points of the entertainment compass. However, while their always professional and upfront operating methods continued to afford them the respect of artists, managers, agents, and record companies alike, the sheer volume of competition and the changing nature of live music presentation in New York now began to take a perceptible toll on the club's business.

ALLAN PEPPER: '78, '79 started to be a turning point for me. On the one hand, you had Studio 54, the *Saturday Night Fever* craze, and all these disco hits flooding the market, and people going to disco clubs to dance. Then on the other, all these new English bands were coming here, and they weren't used to playing sit-down places, and because of that I was being told more and more by agents that I was going to lose a lot of the British bands. [Agent] Wayne Forte wanted to do The Clash with us when they did their first American tour, but they wanted the tables and chairs taken out. It wasn't about the money, but I said I wouldn't do it. It just wasn't who we were.

WAYNE FORTE: Early on at my agency, CMA, I worked all our clients' club shows at The Bottom Line, and I developed a great relationship with Allan and Stanley. I booked acts like Leo Sayer, Hall & Oates, Tom Petty and the Heartbreakers, Rory Gallagher. And we did a lot of these things where I'd say to Allan, "Hey, what about this?" And he'd go, "Oh, I don't know if that's strong enough." I'd go, "Ok, let's put a package together," so we'd do something like Canned Heat and Kansas. And The Bottom Line became really like a concert club. A manager would call me to book dates and tell me what they wanted, like, it's got to be this deal. And I'd say, "The Bottom Line? They're not going to do it." He'd be like, "Well, they have to do it." And I'd again say, "If you want a date there, they're not going to do it." I knew they wouldn't. I knew all about the "Formula." Like backstage, you got, I think, a pitcher of water and maybe a pitcher of Coke. I can't remember what else; maybe some nuts. That was it, and no catering. I remember the acts or managers would be like, "This is ridiculous. I can't even get catering?" And if they did order food, they had to pay for it. But that was the deal.

The interesting thing is, as an agent, you're always pushing to try to get better things for your client, and when you have a territorial issue, it's kind of worse because it's not just you talking to your client or manager and saying, "Ok, this is how it is." They're dealing with other people and saying, "Well, we can get this over here, and we get this over there, and you got to get this for this gig," and I would say, "Listen, they're not going to do it. They've got their formula." The nice part about it was I absolutely knew Alan and Stanley wouldn't bend, and that was helpful because the one thing you don't want to do is say, you're not going to get it. And then they turn around and they get it. Then they say, "You said you weren't going to get it, but we got it." So I wish I could have gotten it for some of them, but at least I knew they weren't going to bend. It wasn't going to make me look like a schmuck.

Forte was British punkers The Clash's American agent when they readied to do their first dates in the United States in the winter of 1979, and his first call went to Pepper. The deal sounded good, except for one caveat: For a club date, the band wanted an open floor. When Pepper said that they weren't amenable to taking the tables and chairs out for them, or really, any act, Forte knew there were going to be repercussions. And the seating situation was only part of it.

WAYNE FORTE: Not just with The Clash, but in general, when the alternative scene really started to happen in the late 1970s, a lot of the British acts just didn't do two shows in one day, which The Bottom Line always insisted on. So when it came to the alternative acts, they definitely weren't going to do it. They didn't care. I had a bunch of these acts starting in the late 1970s, and that's when I started doing less and less business with Allan and Stanley at the club, because these acts' scene really wasn't the sit-down scene. Their scene was those other clubs, whether it was Hurrah's or then The Ritz, open places where people could be hanging out and maybe even dance or whatever, right? But Allan and Stanley had their rules, they had their formula, and that's what they wanted to do.

ALLAN PEPPER: So at the end of the 1970s we were getting pressure to take the tables out, and we started to lose acts, especially British ones who wanted a stand-up crowd. And then once [promoter] John Scher took over The Ritz, which wasn't too far away from us on 11th Street, that was a whole other thing. I knew people enjoyed the vibe there, and of all the promoters and club owners out there, I also knew he was the one who could give me a run for the money, because he approached it like I did.

JOHN SCHER: I first met Allan and Stanley when I was in college at LIU in Brooklyn, and I had my eyes set on getting into the music business. I got on a concert committee and booked a show, it must have been in the fall of 1969. And so I started, and after a while I started working with a local bar band, and working with them, I struck up a relationship with Allan and Stanley starting at the Village Gate. When they moved to Folk City, they'd always be outside the club by the parking meter. In those days, a lot of agents and managers hung out in the village, and most nights pretty much everybody eventually ended up at Folk City, and since there wasn't a lot of room inside the club where you could schmooze, you'd eventually wind up at that parking meter. People of course would go in and watch the show or their client, but sort of the who's who of the younger generation of the 1970s all seemed to congregate at that one parking meter. It should probably be gold plated with a sign next to it. And for me, being about twenty years old, it was like an ongoing master class. Most of these people were only ten years older than me, if that, but they were the beginning of the modern concert business.

I can't remember who recommended Stanley, but early on he became my lawyer, and we hit it off right away. When I first began presenting shows at the Capitol Theater in Passaic late in 1971, they were showing X-rated films there, and on days where they weren't we were doing two, maybe three music shows a week. Now the box office was open seven days a week, and I had a couple of friends working there because people would still come up and want to buy tickets for the upcoming shows we were doing. I wasn't there when it happened, but one day the guys there got busted. There were some really backward-thinking politicians and officials in Passaic who were convinced that the Capitol was a den of iniquity, as we used to say, and I guess they thought they'd raid the place and find all kinds of drugs, etc. Well, there were no drugs. Luckily the X-rated film crowd and the concertgoers didn't overlap too much. My two friends who were working there each may have had a joint or two on them, but they were their personal joints; we sure weren't selling drugs out of the Capitol. Anyway, they both got busted, and when I got home, I found out that there was a warrant out for my arrest. I called Stanley, and I told him the story, and he said, "Let me check this out," and he called back and said, "Ok, I promised them that tomorrow you'd hand yourself in, and I'll meet you at the police station." Now you have to understand that I am the straightest human being you've ever met. I've never smoked a single joint. I've never taken really any drugs. So for me, it was absurd. So I went there, and they fingerprinted me and took my picture, and Stanley got me released on my own recognizance. After that, I don't even remember what exactly happened, but Stanley got it completely dismissed. A thing like that happens; it makes you bond, and we became pretty close.

By decade's end, Scher had established himself as New Jersey's biggest concert promoter and was presenting shows at increasingly bigger facilities including, by the dawn of the 1980s, the new Brendan Byrne Arena at the Meadowlands sports complex which also housed a football stadium and a racetrack. Before that arena's summer 1981 opening, though, Scher got into a bitter rivalry with prominent New York City music promoter Ron Delsener. While the territorial nature of the business at the time was such that Scher deliberately stayed out of New York, Delsener, sensing his business would be further cut down by the new venue close to the city, attempted to muscle Scher into a "partnership" at the new facility. A turf war quickly ensued—one that would have a serious impact on The Bottom Line as well.

JOHN SCHER: Delsener takes me to lunch and says to me, "Jersey"—he always called me "Jersey"—"We'll be partners on the shows at the new place, ok?" I thought he was kidding, but he wasn't. I said no, and Ron basically gave me this ultimatum, that I either do what he wanted or he was going to put me out of business. I got pretty mad—I'd spent ten years toiling away without ever setting foot in the city business wise—so I decided the best thing for me to do was to come into New York, and I did. What happened was there was a club owner named Jerry Brandt who—how shall I say this?—was way more important in the history of the music business, especially in New York, than anybody gives him credit for. I only knew him a little bit. But he first opened up the Electric Circus, which to this day was the coolest sort of open-floor psychedelic club I'd ever been in, and then he opened up The Ritz, an even bigger place, as sort of a straighter, not quite psychedelic open-floor club.

Once I decided that because of Ron's threats, I was going to go into New York, I got a phone call from somebody who knew Jerry who said he was going to sell

The Ritz. I said, "That's interesting, but isn't the place really successful?" "Well, yes," they said, "He's got the books to prove it, but he wants out. I don't know why." So Brandt sells it to two guys, and they're not music industry people, and they don't know what the fuck they're doing, and after about six months we got into a negotiation and I bought half of it, and we'd be in charge. We started booking it and putting back the kinds of things that these guys didn't know from, like how to try your best to keep the bartenders from stealing from you, and it was a roaring success. It became *the* place to play downtown, and we did some amazing shows there for a number of years.

But before I signed the deal, I called Allan. I told him the whole story, and I said, "Look. This place is really successful, but it's much bigger than The Bottom Line. You don't compete for it at all. And I promise you that if you call me and say you're trying to get the same act we are, I'll back away." But Allan was furious, absolutely furious with me, and told me I shouldn't do it. "I thought we were friends," he said, and I said, "Allan, somebody's going to run The Ritz. You need to understand you're not competing for the same acts, and again, I promise you, if you're trying to go after the same act, I'll back away." But Allan didn't want to hear about it. And from being very good friends, Allan didn't talk to me for, I don't know, it could have been close to a year. But it was clear they were two different kinds of venues. When Allan and Stanley first started at Folk City and the Village Gate, and in the beginnings of The Bottom Line, there weren't any rooms like a Ritz coming in. The Bottom Line was a sit-down music room, a place where people were there just for the music, not for a specific scene or for hanging out. And things now had changed. I really don't remember how we made up, but we did, and we've been good friends ever since.

ALLAN PEPPER: I would never book an act just to keep the doors open, so I preferred to keep the club dark rather than just put on a show just to put one on. Call it the economics of creativity. You have to work within an economy that'll let you survive. So now I had to start being more than a booker. I had to really start to be a producer and come up with shows that people would want to pay for. Bill Graham once told me that the name of the game is putting bodies in the seats. He said the public is not interested in the staff that didn't come in, or that you're running out of such and such in the kitchen. They want to come for what you're promising to give them. So I'm thinking we never wanted the place to be one kind of music, but now I had to really look around and see what kinds of things I could do.

Meanwhile, during this time, a lot was going on with both my personal life and Stanley's. In 1978, we both moved out of Brooklyn. Stanley got a place on Mercer Street just blocks from the club, and Eileen and I and our kids settled into a house we bought in Tenafly, New Jersey. Our families grew then, too. My youngest daughter Jessie and Stanley and Michele's daughter Daria were both born in 1979. But another major thing also happened: Eileen was starting to have a series of health issues that took a while to properly understand. First, she had some vision problems, so they sent her to an eye doctor. Then she had neurological problems where she had a numbness, so they sent her to a neurologist. It wasn't until 1980, when one doctor said she needed a spinal tap, that they finally diagnosed her with multiple sclerosis. So now we have Eileen's health, and our young kids, and the club is not doing exactly what it had been business-wise a few years earlier, and we were both worried. I remember one night coming home from the club, and as I walked up the path from the curb to go into my house, I was so upset I just remember saying to myself that I didn't really want to do this if she wasn't part of it.

I fell in love with Eileen for many reasons, but I was initially attracted to her by her warmth and accessability; we could talk about anything. She's always had an inner glow that radiates kindheartedness, and part of that sparkle is her positivity; she always looks at the cup not as half empty, but half full. So while I was thrown and frightened by the MS diagnosis, she believed we would get through this and be able to lead, with some adjustments, a normal life. And I knew instinctively that the best way to support her was to stay positive and try and carry on as normally as possible—and that meant clearing my head and realizing that, with the exception of adjusting our life to the issues associated with MS that we would now have to deal with, nothing else really needed to change. We still had four children to raise, and she and I could continue to live the life we set out to share.

When I began to return my focus back to the club, I realized I needed to start to produce some unique kinds of shows for us to present. Now, how was I going to find the content? One of the things that I did was I started to think back on how I started. I always came at things from what I was interested in and thought others would be, too, and I always had interest in the theater. At the beginning, when we built the club, Stanley and I had thought of it as a cabaret theater, like Art D'Lugoff had done at the Gate, and I thought maybe we could exploit that. So I was thinking of doing readings of new plays, and also matinees and evenings for certain types of shows on the weekend. And I started to think of some conceptual bookings. I put together a festival of big bands, with Mel Lewis, Lionel Hampton, Art Blakey, Panama Francis, and the Glenn Miller Orchestra. I did a weekend mini-folk festival, with no one act that might sell out the place, but three or four acts that each had a following, so together they would do well. We had Odetta, Tom Paxton, Dave Van Rock, Mimi Farina, Bob Gibson, and Josh White, Jr. But the reality was cash flow started to not be the same as it had been. I still had a lot of good acts, but it was not back to how it was when we were rocking in the 1970s.

Now Birdland had been very important to me as a young man, so in 1981 I concocted The Birdland Series. It was basically a salute to the nightclub. I tried, and at first the market wasn't there, but if I headlined certain groups that were admired by jazz people, it wouldn't do maybe the best business, but it was the same as the folk festival idea. I booked acts that had played Birdland back in the day, along with onstage interviews about what the club was like. Three bands, a low ticket price. It ran from March through May, and we presented people like Pepper Adams, Roy Haynes, Kenny Barron, David "Fathead" Newman, Cornell Dupree, Jimmy McGriff, and Slide Hampton. Tony Bennett also played the club during that stretch, which was a great thrill for me.

I also booked my first dates with the great drummer Buddy Rich, whose career went back to the Swing Era in the 1940s. Buddy was quite a character. He had an intimidating and mercurial personality and a biting wit; if so inclined, he could verbally cut you to bits in seconds. At the same time, he could be really warm and charming. As a player, few equaled him, and when he appeared at the club, musicians of all ages would come to sit in awe watching him play. Louie Bellson, another all-star drummer from the Big Band era, was also a friend of Buddy's. In '81, Louie played the club just a few days before Buddy was scheduled to appear. At the end of the gig, as Louie was getting ready to leave, he said, "I see Buddy Rich is coming in next week. Would you give him a message for me?" And with an impish smile on his face, he said, "Tell Buddy I said, 'Don't bother to unpack, I've played it all.'" We both laughed, and he left.

I thought about it for exactly five seconds and decided I was too young to die. That would be a message that not even in jest would ever see the light of day. When Buddy arrived for sound check four days later, he was in a great mood. His tour, I'd heard, was doing great. I was also in a good mood. There were lots of fans, but also a lot of his contemporaries as well coming down to see him. Now Buddy never remembered my name. Instead, he always called me "Boss." When he saw me that day, he greeted me warmly, the usual way. "Hey Boss, how are we gonna do tonight?" "Great, Buddy," I said. "Phones are ringing off the hook." "How's business been last couple of weeks, Boss?" "Pretty good," I said. "In fact, Louie Bellson was here last week," and before I could stop myself, I told him that Bellson had left him a message. Buddy stopped and the big smile on his face suddenly turned to something I couldn't really describe. "What was the message, Boss?" My heart stopped. All I could think of was to smile weakly and say, "He said, 'Don't bother to unpack, Buddy. I've played it all.'" And without missing a beat, Buddy shot back, "Yeah, but now you're gonna see it played right!"

MAX WEINBERG: I had a thing where every spring, Buddy Rich and his big band played The Bottom Line, and I'd go, and the first time I met him was there. He was, of course, my great drum hero. So one time Allan asked me if I wanted to meet him, and I think I said, "I'm not sure you want to meet your heroes." But I did, and that meeting turned into a friendship that lasted for the rest of his life. Every time I saw him at the club, the audience was generally composed of several hundred drummers and their wives or girlfriends. And because of those mirrors at The Bottom Line, when Buddy was playing, you not only saw him from the front, but the way the mirrors captured him you could see his technique from behind the kit. So that was always very, very interesting.

ALLAN PEPPER: Before I took Max backstage to see Buddy, I realized that Buddy might not even know who Bruce Springsteen was, let alone Max, and I didn't want to embarrass Buddy so I told him, "Buddy, Max Weinberg is here. He plays drums with Bruce Springsteen, really a very famous rock star, and he's a huge fan of yours and he'd love to meet you." Buddy said, "Sure, send him back." So Max comes back and Buddy smiles, shakes his hand, and says, "Max, how you doing? How's Bruce doing?" And I thought to myself, "Given that Buddy never remembers anybody's name, this was one time it would've been great if Buddy had asked him how the 'Boss' was doing."

***

ALLAN PEPPER: That same year, 1981, I started to do an evening of doo-wop series, because that was an audience not being served at the clubs, and it had been such a big part of my youth and teen years. I got DJ Bobby Jay involved to help me out on it, and it became a real success for us.

Called An Evening of Doo Wop, the series was a veritable primer on New York vocal groups from the "Golden Era" of rock and roll. Among the groups that appeared over the course of the series' 1981–83 run were the Cadillacs, the Cleftones, the Channels, the Five Satins, the Jive Five, the Del-Vikings, the Flamingos, the Teenagers, the Skyliners, the Chantels, the Impalas, the Clovers, the Elegants, the Capris, and Lee Andrews and the Hearts. A longtime New York disc jockey—and part-time harmony group vocalist himself—Bobby Jay at the time was in the midst of his fifteen-year (1970–1985) stint at r&b station WWRL and would go on to spend the next twenty years (1985–2005) at oldies station WCBS-FM. Jay helped book the acts and hosted the popular series from beginning to end.

BOBBY JAY: I started out in 1955 as a singer, and my voice hadn't changed yet. I was a first tenor. But then in 1956, from a group out of Washington Heights that I later spent close to thirty years with, Frankie Lymon and the Teenagers, I heard Sherman Garnes sing that intro from "Why Do Fools Fall in Love," and well, that was it. I knew from that moment on, I was going to be a bass singer. And that year my voice was at that crucial part of a young man's life where it doesn't know where it's going, and I started smoking cigarettes. So along with the cigarettes, and "You got a nickel, I got a dime, let's get together and buy some wine," and drinking wine, and going into what's now called Marcus Garvey Park, but when I was growing up in Harlem, it was Morris Park . . . I was going into the park, and I would just yell and scream and just did not know that I could have truly damaged my vocal cords, but I wanted my voice to drop because I wanted to be Sherman Garnes.

And that year, my voice did begin to change. So the following year, in 1957, when I joined the Laddins, I was then officially a bass singer, and I've been singing bass ever since.

Allan Pepper knew that before I was on the radio I was a singer, and I can't really remember how the conversation came about—maybe we're talking about the success that [promoter] Richard Nader had with his '50s revival shows—but at the time I was at WWRL and I was doing a show on Saturdays called The Doo Wop Corner, and one day Allan said to me, "Why don't we do some doo-wop shows here at The Bottom Line?" So I said, "Yeah, that sounds good." I helped line up the talent and hosted the shows, and it became very successful, so successful that I think we were doing it like every six weeks. And the club was always packed anyway because so many great acts played there, but somehow with the doo-wop shows, it became totally standing room only. And not only did the audiences love it, but I had so many of my friends, performers from the era, and they would come and they would be in the audience and they would be jivin' me from the audience, and it was so much fun. We all just loved it.

Many of the acts that were on the shows would have their friends come, and the performing community knew that we were doing it, and the word got out. I mean, what a reputation The Bottom Line had, so the venue helped play into the success of those shows. Plus, we had great musicians like [keyboardist/arranger] Ronnie Lawson leading the musicians behind us. I had so much fun hosting, and of course my original group, the Laddins, performed there too. I remember the great songwriter Doc Pomus [composer of, among other classic hits, "Save the Last Dance for Me" and "This Magic Moment"] used to come to so many shows at The Bottom Line, and his table was stage left, the little round table that he always used to sit at, and he just had a wonderful time at our shows. I mean, what a guy, such a talented guy. It's almost indescribable, the people I came in contact with that I met as a result of doing those shows at The Bottom Line.

ALLAN PEPPER: Toward the end of 1981, I also started thinking about some very clever commercials I was hearing on the radio, and I thought, if I'm into it so much, I bet there are others who would be, too. I went to Paul Dooley, who I met when we did The Convention in 1976. Paul made a lot of money not only as an actor but also as the co-creator of PBS' The Electric Company. I told him I wanted to do something with commercials, and he said we needed a visual element. So I made a deal with the people who did the Clios, the advertising industry's equivalent of the Oscars, to be able to use national and international commercials in a theatrical format. Dooley wrote some sketches between the ads, and he brought in some people who did voiceovers for them. We staged it in early 1982, and it was a real produced theatrical show, with lighting cues, visuals, multimedia, and Bob Balaban and Lynne Lipton doing sketch comedy. The show sold out, so I brought it back and it sold out again; we'd hit a home run. We were going to take it off-Broadway. We met with two producers, Liz McCann and Nelle Nugent, who'd produced hits like *Amadeus*, *Dracula*, and *Nicholas Nickleby*, and they came down and saw it and thought it might work. It wound up not happening, but it did establish a relationship with them for later productions.

That same year I started the Prisoners of Rock and Roll series in conjunction with WNEW, whose DJs Meg Griffin and Vin Scelsa were playing a lot of indie releases by local bands. We did it twice a month for almost a year, and groups like the Dbs, The Bongos, The Smithereens, and The Hooters all subsequently got record deals.

MEG GRIFFIN: The New York Dolls [in 1974] was my first show. I was not yet a DJ. By 1975, I was working at a small station only about thirty minutes north of New York City, WRNW in Briarcliff Manor. One of my fellow DJs there, Bob Maroney, said to me one day, "Do you want to go see Springsteen at the Bottom Line tonight?" I looked at him, and I was like, "Are you kidding?" And he said, "No, really." Because in those days, the record labels worked with the radio stations and the clubs, and Bruce was still new to a lot of people, even though it was the *Born to Run* album. So the labels or the club would give you a place on the guest list and a plus one. And so Bob let me be his plus one. And that was a life changer.

I think about one of the shows that I went to that really showed this great kind of symbiotic relationship between radio and the club, which Allan was very smart about utilizing, was when I went to see, for the first time that I'd ever seen them, Graham Parker and the Rumour. Their first booking at the club was pretty sparsely attended in 1976, when that great album *Howlin' Wind* came out. And so I'm there with about maybe twenty or thirty other people because people just didn't know who Graham was. And the show hadn't really sold, but I noticed that all of us who were there were singing along. We knew every word; we were totally into this new band. And because of radio play at stations like mine and also on WNEW-FM in New York with DJs like Vin Scelsa, the next time they came back to play the club the place was packed, and that to me was a reflection of not only the power of radio, but Allan's wisdom to work with people at radio stations, either by simply inviting them to shows and putting them on his guest list, or often enough with the live broadcasts that we would do from the club.

One night I was there, they weren't new for me and my group because we knew about them, but they were new to the world, and that was The Police. A lot of artists would play say Max's and CBGB's, and those were the sort of cool underground things. But by the time you were showcased at The Bottom Line, things were getting serious, and when the Police played there, and at this point, I'm already working at WNEW, and I just remember it so well: Our biggest DJ, Scott Muni, was maybe just slightly wary of the whole punk/new wave thing, which Vin and I were really into, but the station could see that there was a buzz about this band, so a broadcast was arranged for the Police on NEW-FM at The Bottom Line. Vin and I were hosting, and after we bring the band on, we go back to our table and we're sitting there with Scott, and I just never forget him leaning over to me, nudging me with his elbow and going, "Ah, that kid Sting, he's going to be a star." There were moments like that that happened a lot in that club where artists were recognized and they were about to go on to much bigger things. But so often it started in that room, which was like a living room for us, listening to so much great music.

In the late '70s into the '80s, and especially when punk and new wave were happening, a lot of people were going out to dance, and Hurrah's was one of the places where I was one of the DJs, and that dancing thing was a big deal. But I remember talking to Allan about it then, and then years later, why he never decided to take out the tables and chairs. Allan really knew who he was, and he knew that his room was a listening room. Now that didn't mean that you couldn't go nuts. I mean, there were times when we were in the aisles just dancing our heads off depending on who was playing. But I always appreciated that he stayed consistent rather than following trends and becoming a prisoner of them for quite a few years. He created trends and he didn't change the blueprint of what that room was just to follow what other people were doing. And I always respected that about him.

In 1982 I started to do a radio show on WNEW on Sunday nights where, for about an hour, everything I played was either cheaply pressed DIY [Do It Yourself] vinyl singles or homemade cassette tape demos of bands that were in the area that were seeking airplay and attention, trying to further their path. We would solicit it on the air, and they'd send things in, and I'd choose some and play them. We got a ton of mail and it was a lot of work, but it was always really fun, and eventually Allan, with some help from me, we'd choose some of them that we felt were the best to showcase at the club twice a month. Allan, in his wisdom, would say to each one of them, because these were kids that were hungry to play at The Bottom Line, "Look, if you want this booking, you have to do your best to get as many friends and family members to show up and buy tickets." And that would help fill the room. And I think that also goes back to that power of the relationship between the club and radio, because there was this show that I was doing where I'm giving these bands exposure, and then some of them are lucky enough to do a show in there. And one of the reasons it was a lot of fun was because it was very human, and not really a big part of the business machinery of music. It was kids that were excited to have a Fender guitar in their hands and go nuts on stage at The Bottom Line.

* * *

ALLAN PEPPER: In 1983, I came up with the idea of doing something related to the Academy Awards the week before the ceremonies aired called, "And the Winner Is . . . " It would be a show made up of great songs that were nominated for an Oscar but didn't win. I was thinking about using a host and a small stringed orchestra for it, with a conductor; I was going to ask David Amram. So I called Eileen up in the afternoon to run it by her, but the kids had just gotten home from school, so she was distracted. I called her later, but that was also no good. So I waited until I got home from the club around 3 a.m. I got undressed, got in bed, and since Eileen would usually hear me come in and wake up a bit, I tell her I really want to tell her about this idea I had. She says ok, and when I'm finished she says "So who are the singers?" I said, "What singers?" and she leans over, gives me a kiss, and says, "You're going to do a big production with all these great songs and not have any singers? You're going to lose your shirt." And with that, she turns away from me—and takes the covers with her. That middle-of-the-night conversation got me to hire [Broadway stage veteran and star of *Evita*] Patti LuPone, Ken Page [from the original New York production of *Cats*], and musician Robert Kraft. We put it on in April of 1983 with film historian Stuart Samuels hosting, and, thanks to Eileen, it too was a success.

* * *

Also beginning his three-decade-plus association with The Bottom Line during this period was comedian Floyd Vivino, aka Uncle Floyd, a local legend on metro New York TV. First broadcast on those pre-cable days of the 1970s on UHF's Channels 60 and 68 out of Newark, New Jersey, The Uncle Floyd Show appeared on the surface to be a standard weekday afterschool kids' program, complete with Vivino's hand puppet sidekicks Oogie and Bones Boy. In reality, though, it was more of a sketch comedy, music-sprinkled variety show straight out of old-time vaudeville. The program featured a stable of offbeat regulars such as Shakespeare-trained actor and improviser Scott Gordon, crumpled black-hatted, giant bow-tied "Looney" Skip Rooney, and song parodist Craig "Mugsy" Calan, who would appear as Neil Yukk or Bruce Stringbeen. (Mugsy once famously saluted Newark to the tune of Sinatra's "New York, New York" with the immortal line, "I want to wake up, in a city that doesn't reek.") Presided over by the porkpie hat-topped, loud plaid jacketed, piano-thumping combination host/ringmaster Vivino, The Uncle Floyd Show was discovered by young hipsters on both sides of the Hudson in the mid 1970s, and in its heyday, the program gathered a sizable cult following, leading to guest appearances by local punk and popster Floyd fans ranging from the Ramones and Cyndi Lauper to Bon Jovi and Paul Simon.

FLOYD VIVINO: I first worked that space when it was the banjo parlor The Red Garter. Armbands. Straw hats. We used to call them tourist traps. They liked the way I played piano because I had that stride left hand. I'd worked at Sammy's Bowery Follies, which was the same thing, in 1969. They closed. I learned a lot of the old style. So I worked The Red Garter, but I didn't get into The Bottom Line until December of 1979, with the gang from my TV show. And I was there up until June of 2002. I was there a lot also with folks like Soupy Dales, Dr. Demento, Vince Giordano, Tiny Tim, and I also did round-robin joke shows with other comedians.

The way I first appeared there was someone called me at the TV station and said, "Allan Pepper wants to book you," and I was like, "I'm busy. I'll call back," and everyone on the show was like, "Are you nuts? Everybody is dying to appear there." So we put a deal together right away on the phone.

SCOTT GORDON: Floyd did all the booking himself. We really had no specific booking agent or anything, but this is what Floyd did. He was a go-getter. He was an old-school entertainer, and he got us booked in the place. We were all kind of skeptical at first, but he got his brothers [musicians Jimmy and Jerry Vivino] involved, and we put together a little band and everything else, and we went and did a show. We basically did what we were doing on TV, but roughened it up a little bit, made it a bit more adult-oriented. Basically, what we were doing was old vaudeville and burlesque. That was our thing. We all loved that kind of show, and that's what we were doing.

UNCLE FLOYD: In January 1981, really out of nowhere for us, David Bowie came in to see us. That became quite a story. Supposedly 50,000 people were there that one night. He was sitting out front right by the piano.

SCOTT GORDON: We heard about it when we got there because the club was notified before we were that he was going to be there. And that's one of those things you don't let get around because of the fact of what his fan base would've done with it if they knew. And we were like, "David Bowie's here? Why is David Bowie here?" We couldn't figure out why he was coming to see us. We really didn't understand. And I have a great photograph of him that one of the fans took of him sitting there with a smile on his face wearing an *Uncle Floyd Show* button. Before the show, Floyd told us, "Look, don't acknowledge him. Don't stare at him. He's here to watch the show. Let him watch the show. The people are going to be bad enough with him when they notice him." That was Floyd's attitude.

UNCLE FLOYD: I told my cast, "Don't look at him. Don't make a fuss. Leave him alone, and let him enjoy the show." That was another thing about the vibe in the club. the audience was show business literate. They respected David Bowie's privacy that night. And then Bowie came backstage after the show. The whole company of my show were all shocked that he would come back to say hello.

SCOTT GORDON: Bowie had started watching the show with John Lennon the previous summer when he came to New York to get ready to appear in *The Elephant Man* on Broadway, and then he watched it at the theater that fall while he was in makeup before the show. And then he came to see us in January of 1981. We asked him how he knew about the show, and he told us that John Lennon had turned him onto it, and these were Bowie's words. He said, "In fact, I'm here tonight because John and I were supposed to come together, and I'm here as a tribute to him." From Bowie's lips, right to my ears. So we came that close to meeting John Lennon.

UNCLE FLOYD: I said, "How did you find out about me?" and Bowie said, "John Lennon turned me on to your show." Don't forget this wasn't long after Lennon got killed. You could hear a pin drop. The difference between us was extreme. We were at opposite ends of the show business ladder. I said, "What do you see in me?" He said, "I see in you the old British Music Hall performer. Look at you. You wear a costume. You're recognized because of that. Nobody does that anymore. Plus you play a musical instrument in your comedy act, which they do in variety halls and music halls in Great Britain."

Over twenty years later, on his 2002 album Heathen, Bowie paid tribute to Floyd and his puppet pals Oogie and Bones Boy with the wistful "Slip Away": "Once upon a time they nearly might have been/Bones and Oogie on a silver screen/No one knew what they could do/Except for me and you/Don't forget to keep your head warm/Twinkle Twinkle Uncle Floyd/Watching all the world and war-torn/How I wonder where you are."

UNCLE FLOYD: Out of nowhere, Bowie sent me a check for $6,000 when that album came out, and then he sent me another one for $5,000 for using my image projected on a back screen in his stage show when he performed the song. He sent me a Christmas card every year until 2016, and then he passed away about three weeks later, and I knew why I hadn't gotten one.

Then, of course, there was the great french fry caper. Somebody said to us that my crowd was ordering a lot of french fries, probably because it was the cheapest thing on the menu. So on my next show I said, "You know, we might have the french fry eating record at The Bottom Line." I don't know any other entertainer who wanted that footnote, but I was proud of it. Then I did the late-night *Tomorrow Show* with Tom Snyder on NBC, and I bragged about it.

For those who watched it from 1973 through '83 before David Letterman took over the NBC network's 12:30 a.m. time slot, Tom Snyder's Tomorrow Show was must-see TV in the way people liked seeing train wrecks as they happened. Veteran anchorman Snyder had joined NBC's Channel 4 station after many years in Los Angeles, and with an ego as big as all outdoors—it was once written about him that "Tom Snyder thinks news happens only so he can tell you about it"—his program saw him going one-on-one with all manner of newsmakers, film and TV stars, and pop culture figures, with often hilariously unintended results. The ever-bristly Snyder seemed mystified by Floyd's success on UHF and dubiously grilled him on how he made his little show work. Vivino responded as only an ex-vaudeville comic could. "What kind of sponsors do you get?" Snyder asked. "All kinds," he answered. "Magic shops. Jersey amusement parks. And we have a tattoo parlor. Their theme is "I've Got You Under My Skin." "And you work out of a small studio in Jersey, right?" "Yes, Tom. Our studio is so small you have to go outside to change your mind." The conversation then turned to the fact that Floyd had begun to appear at The Bottom Line, which seemed to further mystify Snyder. And Vivino saw an opening: "We recently sold out two days, four shows at The Bottom Line. We broke Billy Joel's record for consumption of french fries on a Wednesday night in New York City." Snyder began to chuckle, and Vivino had him just where he wanted him. "Go ahead and laugh," said Floyd. "Do you know what the profit margin is on french fries?"

SCOTT GORDON: And so halfway through it, Tom brings up The Bottom Line. He says, "You've got a show at The Bottom Line coming up." Floyd said, "Yeah, interesting thing." And Floyd totally made this thing up, telling Snyder that we held the sales record for french fries at the club. And what happened was when Floyd came back to Jersey, we're taping the TV show, and he says, "Look, I did this on the Snyder show." We said, "Yeah, we know. We saw it." And he said, "Let's tell a couple of our followers that we did this and that we want to break the french fry record at The Bottom Line." Well, they sold out when we did the show two weeks later, and we sold more french fries than they did in an entire weekend in one show. By the intermission, by the break between the two shows, they were sending staff out to find and buy potatoes. And that's when Stanley came in and looked at us and said, "What the heck are you guys doing to us?"

ALLAN PEPPER: It was a big night at the club. Both Floyd shows were sold out, and we were expecting heavy standing room for each show as well. And sometime during the first show, Stanley and I were quickly summoned to the kitchen. Our chef, John Hargrove, was in a state of I guess you'd call it controlled panic. There was an enormous pile of orders that needed to be filled and an equally huge amount of orders that were cooked and ready to be picked up by the waitresses. Now John had been a cook in the navy and served thousands of sailors at one sitting as well as also having a lot of experience as a short-order cook, so he was never one to panic. But this one night he came about as close to panicking as I ever saw with him in all the years he was with us.

"What's up?" we asked. John never stopped what he was doing while he shouted to us over his shoulder. "Potatoes! We're running out of potatoes!" We looked around, and there were french fries orders everywhere—cut up, waiting to go in the fryer, in the fryer, and waiting to go out to customers. It became quickly apparent that pretty soon we would run out of a supply of potatoes that was supposed to last us four or five days. What in the world was happening? Our fries were good, but not that good. Stanley quickly rounded up three of our staffers and sent them to 9th Avenue and 38th Street where there were still wholesale produce stores open, and told them to buy any and all potatoes they could find. And between shows, when we had a minute to tell Floyd that we were going through a ridiculous amount of potatoes in one night, he let us in on why that was happening.

Uncle Floyd and Oogie appear at Vin Scelsa's "50/30 party" at The Bottom Line to wish Vin a happy fiftieth birthday and congratulate him on thirty years on the radio. Photo © Ebet Roberts.

UNCLE FLOYD: One night many years later I was doing an in-the-round comedians' show with Soupy Sales and Mickey Freeman at The Bottom Line. With no notice, comic Pat Cooper came up out of the audience and crashed the stage. He looks at Soupy and says, "Soupy, it's late. Go home. Have a glass of warm milk and some cookies and go to sleep." He looks at Mickey Freeman and says, "Mickey, it's 2000. Nobody cares about Sgt. Bilko anymore." Then he puts his arm around me and says, "Uncle Floyd. You never tried to get anywhere—and you never got anywhere. You, I like." Soupy made me a paid Friar at the great showbiz hangout, the Friar's Club. He said, "Floyd, you won't have to pay when you come here. We'll pay you—a nickel." He took me under his wing. People accused me of stealing his act, but that wasn't true, and he never felt that way.

You couldn't put a price tag on those shows we did at The Bottom Line. One time there I was on the marquee, underneath Hall & Oates, and then Prince. Imagine that. They knew how to sell a room out. Allan was a great showman operating in the modern world, and a total joy to work with—and you don't say that very often in this business. I could never get out of my mind how nice he was to my parents. He made them feel like they were very special and had those old-world values that I grew up with. Toward the end, my folks would come, and he'd sit them with Soupy at our shows. I never felt I was working there because we always had so much fun.

10 I GOT MY JOB THROUGH THE . . . VILLAGE VOICE? WORKING AT THE BOTTOM LINE

What was it like working at The Bottom Line, especially during its often dizzyingly paced and frantic first decade? A love of music certainly helped, as did (depending on the particular day's or night's events) a ready-for-just-about-anything attitude that could prove beneficial in dealing with temperamental artists, self-important industry executives, and difficult customers, as well as the motley assortment of co-workers and crew leaders—and, of course, owners Pepper and Snadowsky.

Here, then, are some employee perspectives—coming, respectively, from the kitchen to the "floor," and from the business office to the box office.

DEVON DICKER: I have intense memories from The Bottom Line. After I graduated high school in 1975, I moved from my folks' home in Montclair, New Jersey, to Manhattan to work at The Bottom Line. My brother-in-law worked with a guy at a record company, and he used to tell me about the club, and he said he knew the manager. I got in touch, and I think I just interviewed for a job and got hired as a dishwasher. And then from there I went from a dishwasher to second assistant cook to assistant chef under John [Hargrove], and then I started hosting as well. So I was all over the club. I worked there for about three and a half years before I moved on.

John was a pretty incredible guy. He had a shining personality. He was a deacon in his church. He'd always be in his whites, and he knew his profession. I mean, he would pick up hot things out of the fryer or up the grill with his hands, bare hands, and I was very impressed with that. I'm not saying John was a gourmet chef, but he was just right, definitely, for the kind of place The Bottom Line was. He was very personable, and loved flirting with the girls there. He also loved listening to the Temptations. He always had them on; I guess it was a cassette player, and then when they played the club he was just overwhelmed. I remember Melvin Franklin, was their bass singer, several times during their set, he made a reference to the pole that was on his side of the stage because it was in his way when they were trying to do their dance routines. I remember he kept saying, in his really low voice, "That damn pole." But John went crazy when the Temptations were there. And John really took pride in his work. I know when they had special nights where they had record companies come in and rent out the club for just their personnel, and he'd have to pre-make a whole huge thing of whatever, and it was pretty astounding. He always hit the nail on the head. And he could be pretty intense. I remember he told me a story once of someone, I forget who it was, but he actually ran out of the kitchen and came to a guy's rescue and punched someone in the face and knocked him down.

When I first started, Tony was the assistant manager slash bouncer, and then he went up to a manager after Michael left. Tony was one tough cookie, an intense guy. I think there was a mild rivalry between John and Tony because, well, you didn't tell John what to do in the kitchen or with any of his people. And Tony was the boss out on the floor. I always felt like there was a little bit of rivalry there because I thought Tony probably believed he should be in charge of the entire club, every square inch of it, and clearly John was in charge of the kitchen. And that was that. So there was a little bit of tension, but also respect, for sure.

Russell Wolinsky, the host, was also the lead singer of a punk rock band called The Sic F*cks, and one night we took John to CBGB's to see Russell with his group, and his eyes were like big saucers watching them. Back then I played guitar and I also had a group, the Eye Band, and some of the guys came down and watched me play, too. But it's funny: I know John was a deacon in his church, but when he went out with us, he used to dress up—how would I describe it?—total pimp style. It was the 1970s, and he had the long coat, like from *Superfly*, and he had all these turquoise rings on his fingers and stuff, and it totally was like, it just didn't fit who I thought he was, but that's how he dressed.

When I started at the club, John was the chef, his assistant was Larry, the second cook was Josh, and I was a dishwasher. Larry left, and then Josh became John's assistant, and then I became his second, like a prep cook. Then Josh left, and then I became John's assistant, and we hired another guy called Caesar, who was then the second. And I was looking for extra things to do because I wanted to get on the floor. So I became a host for about a year.

I vividly remember the bouncers. There was Jay Mason, a big guy who always wore a cowboy hat and this big *McLoud* jacket, like from the TV show, and he looked really big. But Jay was also a musician who played acoustic guitar and sang folk songs, and he even played at the club once, and one time when Mick Jagger was there, Jay went up to him and gave him a signed copy of *his* album because he'd covered a Rolling Stone song on it. There was Carlos Baez, who was a martial arts second-degree black belt. Carlos was great. And then there was the guy they called Big George, who also worked security at a lot of the Broadway theaters in town. Really nice guy. He would bring in these maraschino cherries soaked in brandy and pass them out to us. I always felt like they were these tough guys from Little Italy or something. Not gangsters or anything, but just kind of tough guys in the neighborhood.

The summer of 1977, NRBQ was performing, and halfway through the set, the power went out. It was the night of one of those big blackouts that sometimes hit the whole city, and it got dark and they kind of stopped playing, and one of the waitresses, Linda, who was a really perky girl with platinum blonde hair, she sat down on the side of the stage with an acoustic guitar and started singing and the whole audience was listening. That was really cool. And after Linda was done, this other waitress Dale started singing at a table where she'd sat down, ad-libbing the blues. Between all the guys working in the club and all the waitresses, there were a lot of boyfriends and girlfriends, and there was a lot of sex. A lot of them were aspiring, either dancers or actresses, and, I'm not sure if they were medical school or pre-med, but even an aspiring doctor. The waitresses were cool.

I remember seeing acts like Springsteen, Meat Loaf, and The Tubes. I remember they really stuck out, because they had this crazy stage show. When Santana played, I took the night off and I sat right next to the stage because I was a huge Santana fan. That was something else. When John McLaughlin played the club, he gave me some pointers on the guitar, and even gave me a set of guitar strings. That was great. One night Clive Davis was there for a private showcase, and one of the important a&r guys was with him at his table, and that guy had a girlfriend, and she had these micro hot pants on, and she kept getting up and walking the center aisle going off for different things, definitely strutting to show. She looked really good, but I remember she went to the bathroom and when she came out, she was strutting, and she had a long length of toilet paper stuck to her shoe. She was like prancing, showing how cool she was, and there she was dragging this long piece of toilet paper.

I started at The Bottom Line at eighteen and stayed three and a half years, and then for me it was just kind of time to move on. I ended up going over to Jimmy Day's in the West Village and becoming a cook and a bouncer there for another three or four years. I was always trying to be a musician besides everything else I was doing, and I did for a while. My band opened up for Yes at a few outdoor gigs, but we never fully made it. I got so close so many times. At one point, we were going to be signed by Atlantic Records, but it just didn't happen. We just never made it over the hump. After all that ended, I had an entertainment company called Dream Line that actually became pretty successful. Part of our business was distributing DVDs directly from the studios; we'd buy from Universal and Disney, and I'd go into Big Lots and stores like that. And by 2010 I saw the bulk of our money was coming from DVD distribution. Digital downloads were starting to come into their own, and I could just see the writing on the wall. That's when my uncle got in touch with me from Oregon. He'd started this company, Tara Labs, back in 1986 with a guy from Australia, and he asked me if I'd be interested in learning the business. I took over about twelve years ago, and I moved from LA up to Oregon. We make high-end audio cable, and we're actually known for the world's most award-winning high-end audio cable.

The Bottom Line was an important part of my life. I'd just graduated high school in New Jersey, and at age eighteen, I moved to New York and got a job at the premier nightclub on the East Coast. And many nights when I didn't work, I would still go down to the club just to be there to hear music. Which to me says a lot.

MATILDA PARENTE: It was funny because during the day I worked in the infectious disease department at Cornell on the Upper East Side, and then I would take the train downtown, put on my waitress apron, and work the Bottom Line shift till whatever ungodly hour. And sometimes we'd go out after that, of course, because we were young and stupid and didn't require a lot of sleep.

My hiring was crazy. When I saw an ad for the club in 1975, I was actually going on medical school interviews. I went on an interview down in Washington, DC, for the George Washington University Medical School. And at the time I was living in Manhattan, and again, young and stupid, I didn't really get that you dress up for a medical school interview conservatively. I thought if you dressed up, you went to a nightclub. So I went to my medical school interview in a mini-dress and platforms and all this other stuff. I can still picture the outfit. And since I had seen the ad for The Bottom Line, I took the train back to New York and went straight from the medical school interview to go interview for The Bottom Line. At least I think so. Either I went there on my way down to DC or on the way back from DC. But either way, it was ridiculous.

I think I interviewed only with Tony. I might have met Allan at the interview, but if I did, it was brief. Tony was very gruff, but he had a sweetness about him, too. Tony was the one who sort of slapped me around in a sense, in that there was a time while I worked at the club that I was thinking of not going to medical school. I had applied to five schools, and I did not get in, which was the shock of my life. I had always gotten in, and I didn't realize you don't just apply to five difficult medical schools. I had zero counseling. I was working at the club and planning to go on to medical school, and I was getting discouraged. I was thinking, "Wow, all these people are applying to twenty, thirty, even forty schools; how the hell am I going to do that?" Because every time you applied, it was a lot of money, every application. So I was getting discouraged.

Susan [Decreny], one of the other waitresses, was getting courted, or was courting, to work in the music industry, which she eventually did. I started thinking that maybe I would do that, too, and I told that to Tony, that I was thinking of just not even going forward with medical school and just going into the music business. And Tony was the one who was just adamant. He knocked his head and said to me, "Look. The music business is filthy—that was such an Italian word to use, filthy—and that's not for you. You are going to medical school, and you're going to be a doctor. Ok?" And I was like, "Ok." But he was adamant that the music business was just not for me, and he just painted this picture of it, that it was absolutely not for me. And it impressed me.

A lot of times after we finished up at two in the morning, or even later, we would just go out for food, because in those days in the Village, you could get breakfast at any hour of the morning. There was a place on, I can't remember the name of it now, but there was a place that had fantastic omelets, and you'd see a lot of the famous models at the time walking around the Village and going there at all hours for omelets, like that gap-toothed model who used to walk around barefoot, Lauren Hutton. When the club first opened in that section of the Village, there really wasn't much going on outside of the club in the immediate few blocks. For a while, I lived on Christopher Street, and we had these little blue jeans aprons that we wore, and so I would walk home with an apron full of cash. It wasn't a lot of money at the time. I mean, when you think about it now, sometimes I'd come home from working jazz acts where hardly anyone tipped, and you'd make almost nothing, like maybe $19, but sometimes you'd make quite a bit more, and I'd come home and I'd have a lot of loose change—and change rattles. I used to walk home at 2 a.m. or whenever it was, past the park and everything to get to the west part of the Village. Once I was past Washington Square Park and then Sixth Avenue, once I was past that, I felt safe. In those days, the thought of taking a cab or anything, that never even entered my mind. I was aware of not wanting to get mugged because it was kind of not a good time in New York then, and I never did, thank God, but the blocks around the club, there wasn't really anything happening.

We had one waitress, and I don't even know what her real name was, because Neil, the bartender, who was hilarious beyond belief, had nicknames for everybody, and this waitress was so dumb that Neil used to call her Gracie, like Gracie Allen. One day I come in and I'm wearing my Duke T-shirt—I went to Duke undergrad— and Gracie comes up to me and she goes, "Aw, that is so sweet." And I look at her, like "Sweet?" because she saw the "Duke," and she goes, "Yeah, that John Wayne shirt. That is so sweet." She would come out with lines like that, and she was totally serious. She had no idea Duke was a school. We also had some very smart women, like Susan. She had this posture thing going on where, even though she was petite, with a close-cropped haircut, she carried herself with tremendous grace. She just had presence, and she was very smart, very sharp, and very efficient. An excellent waitress. And then there was Jeanie, who was tall, like five nine-ish or so, with dark hair. And she was like a speed demon, also very smart, and so efficient. She used to get tipped out like crazy, and I'd be like, "How the hell does she get all these tips?" She wasn't particularly good-looking or sexy or anything like that, but she just had a way about her that, I'll tell you, she used to just rake in those tips. So I remember those two. And then John, the cook, he tried to keep it together, but he was always on high simmer, ready to boil over. But he worked and he worked, and he had all these expressions he'd always be throwing out at you and stuff, but he was terrific. He was one of those amazing people that every kitchen needs. He fed us dinner every night, too, which was nice. I loved his fried chicken.

Like I said before, Neil the bartender kept me, kept all of us sane. Some of the things he'd say to the customers! One night he had a rowdy group that were at the bar, and they were ordering single beers at a time, one after another. Back then the beers were very cheap, and their tab came to $19.90, and one of them gave Neil a twenty-dollar bill and told him to keep the change. Neil took the dime, gave it back to him, leaned over the bar, and said, "No, you take this, and go buy a condom, so there are no more people like you." He would get away with that stuff; he had this delivery that was hilarious. And then when we had really loud music, he had bushy curly hair, and he'd be like, "Oh my God, [*guitarist*] Les Dudek! The less Dudek, the better. This music is making my hair curl." And we had that bouncer, Big George. We used to have these little plastic coffee cups, and he liked coffee, and he was so gigantic when he would hold this little coffee cup, it would look like a thimble in his hand. But it was good having him around. I mean, I used to feel good about that because some of the crowd, I mean, it was almost always peaceful, but sometimes things could get a little rowdy.

I worked the Springsteen shows, and it changed my musical life. Up until then, I just didn't listen to any kind of rock music. I was like a jazz purist at the time. And past that, one night during their stay at the club, after the late show was over, Springsteen was still hanging around. He had some of his bandmates and roadies around him, and while I was cleaning the tables, one of his guys was cursing within earshot of me, and Springsteen got up and not only told him to watch his language, but he came over and apologized. "I'm sorry, Miss," he said. "We don't usually talk like that. I'm sorry that you heard what he said." I never forgot that.

There were so many memorable shows. As I said, I was a big jazz fan. I liked Oscar Peterson and that kind of stuff, and I got to see a lot of jazz at the club. I didn't like it for making money, working Charlie Mingus and some of these other shows, because we never made any money with the jazz crowd tips-wise. And even when the jazz artists came in as guests, like George Benson, he would order one or two bottles of the most expensive champagne and leave me a dollar. But I was there for great shows. Springsteen was phenomenal. I really liked the Ramones and Talking Heads, and every Henny Youngman show, I laughed at the same joke both shows every night. Flo and Eddie were fantastic. They were hilarious when they did their Joni Mitchell imitation. I mean, unbelievably funny. And Astrud Gilberto. I'm totally into that kind of music; it was like church for me. Seeing her was unbelievable. And Ashford and Simpson, I mean, their shows were rocking.

Billy Joel, I remember his performances. Billy Crystal was hilarious, and so was Elaine Boozler. And the acoustics were fantastic. There wasn't a bad seat in the house, and no smoking! That was fantastic. And if you liked fried chicken, you were in good shape because John's fried chicken was always good.

I think we had like nine stations that were divvied up among all the waitresses, and station number one had the artist, and when she played at the club, I had Dolly Parton. And of all the performers that I had at The Bottom Line, she was the sweetest of them all. There was nothing phony about that lady. She was a doll. On the other end of it, one night I had Sun Ra and his orchestra, playing crazy, crazy music, crazy, crazy jazz. At the end of the night I had to settle the tab, and I gave it to him and he looked at it and pointed near the bottom and said to me, "What's this?" I said, "That's the sales tax." And he says, "Oh, well, I don't pay the tax." I said, "You have to pay. Everybody pays the tax." He says, "No no. I am not of this universe. I don't pay that." I said, "You're not of...whatcha talking about?" And he said, "I'm from Saturn. I don't pay sales tax." I don't remember how I settled that.

I stopped working at the club in the spring or maybe the summer of 1978 after I got into medical school at San Francisco State. So after I got rejected from five medical schools, years later I got into the best medical school in the country—and as a New Yorker, as a non-California resident. So Tony gave me good advice. I ended up taking the longer, scenic route to pathology via orthopedics. I started in surgery for a few years, and that was not a good lifestyle for me, so I switched to pathology and practiced diagnostic medicine. A lot of people think it's like those TV shows like *House*, but of course, it's not. I haven't practiced hospital medicine in quite a long time now. I live in San Diego, and I've been doing consulting work in different biomed fields and medical communications.

I guess the best way I could describe what waitressing at The Bottom Line was like was that you were there to do a serious job, and you had to get it done efficiently, and with almost no room to maneuver between the tables, to not disturb people by learning to twist your whole body in all directions, often while carrying champagne.

LORRAINE REBIDAS DURYEA: I started my career in the music business when I went from working at Irving Trust Company on Madison Avenue to Capitol Records' promotion and publicity departments, and there I worked closely with Terry Knight, the manager of Grand Funk Railroad. He was an amazing person to work for. From there, I started working at a club in Brooklyn, Banana Fish Park, and they started hosting Don Kirshner's *In Concert* TV show tapings. It was kind of an interesting thing, but then my goal was completely different, and I had to work, so I went up to Boston. I got referred to Paul's Mall, the jazz workshop run by Freddie Taylor, and at that club I was chief cook and bottle washer, as was Fred. It was a club business, but it was different, and it was great. I got all the experience I needed. Miles Davis, Richard Pryor, Pointer Sisters. It was nonstop. But then my mother became ill, and it was important for me to be back in the New York area. Freddie knew that and said that he knew a club owner who was looking for somebody for him in New York, and that was Allan.

It was early in 1975 when I first met him, and it was a pretty interesting interview. I came down to the club, met Allan, and we went upstairs to this little office. We chatted for a little bit, and I didn't even know if Allan had looked at my resume, but he asked me to take a typing test. And I was like, "Is he kidding?" I really didn't think I was going to get the job because I wasn't sure if he thought I was over qualified—and now I'm taking a typing test? I forget how fast I could type, but I was a whiz and I could take stenography. All that old secretary art. Anyway, long story short, after the typing test, Stanley said he wanted to dictate a letter, and that I had to redo. Allan kept saying, "It's Allan, A-L-L-A-N," and I hadn't even written anything yet. He was very sensitive. I was like, "Oh my gosh." So I turned it in, and it was ok, and they hired me. But because of that, till this day, I have to stop whenever I spell Allan!

Anyway, here's what I observed: When I came in, though I was young, only twenty-seven, I already had a lot of business experience, and people were just coming in and out of the office all the time, interrupting both of them. And I was like, "Well, this is not going to work, ok?" My job was to work for them, and that was my priority. So that's how it started—and I took no prisoners. I was very strict and organized the office, and them. I worked in the day, I think my hours were something like ten to six. So every time I showed up at the club in the morning, the same as in Boston, it smelled like beer. And because of that dark little spiral staircase going up to the office, I usually didn't go upstairs until someone else was already at the club. I knew all the tech and stage crew; they'd come in in the morning because they had to get ready for the show that night. So they had a lot of demands. They had a lot of requests, or they had gotten the contract with all the X's crossed out and had to figure things out to get ready for shows. Rose the bookkeeper was in a little ante section outside the office. She also worked in the daytime. She was an Orthodox Jew, and she took off on Fridays. She called everyone "My Lorraine, my Pepperel, my Hindy"—and that was her daughter—and she did everything with a cigarette in her mouth and a pencil in her hand. And let me tell you, she didn't miss a nickel.

Tony and I shared a desk; well, basically, it was two small desks that were pushed together. His desk was very neat, and he had files of the waitress crew. He was very good that way. I came into work one day, and he had taken a window blind, and he said, "This way we can be separate." And when I pulled it down, there was a picture of him on my side of the blind. So he did have a sense of humor. Tony was as macho as they come, but since I was Italian and from Brooklyn, he wasn't a far reach for me. He was good at what he did, and he was given the right environment to do it. He wanted to do good business, and he didn't like a lot of the slipping and sliding.

A lot of people in the industry that I had worked for previously, knowing how crazed things could get at The Bottom Line, were like, "What are you doing there?" But I loved it. I knew what was required to get a booking done. Having worked in Boston, there was a lot of handling a lot of phone calls, a lot of managers and agents, and a lot of the same managers and agents that had crossed my path in Boston, the same crowd that came through my life at Capitol Records. So the same talent was developing, the same acts were getting booked, and new acts were coming in. So that was a part of what my job was: to keep that part of it organized for the two of them. Stanley taught me pretty much everything I was to learn about reading a contract. I always cherish that he felt that I had the brains to understand what he was talking about. So I got trained in contract reading from him, crossing out all those riders. All the managers and agents hated it, and then they would haggle over stupid things.

When I first came there, Allan was doing everything on those "You've got a message" little pink slips. And I was like, "What is this?" He'd say, "Well, where's my call?" and he'd be rifling through his desk, and I thought, "This isn't going to work." When I was at Capitol working for Terry, I had to have a daily call sheet for any number of reasons because of who would be calling and the timing of the call, and if it was Don Kirshner or Baskher Menon. I had to have everything documented. So I went to Allan and I said, "Where's your call sheet?" And he just looked at me and I said, "Ok, here we go," and I created a call sheet for him just like I did for Terry. And it worked. I think Allan really wanted a good assistant. I think he was tired of having to ferret through all his papers, and he was still a young father, and I had the skill to do that. Stanley, on the other hand, had the legalese, so he was able to appreciate it and also work with it. Allan became not only a mentor but a real friend. I started calling him Pop after my father passed away. I was a pretty serious person, and Allan taught me how to laugh. Stanley was a big man, and he was so gentle, though I did see him get mad a few times, and when he did, it was, *look out!*

One of the things that somebody said to me was, "You were the glue that held Allan and Stanley together." And I never saw myself that way, but I had certain criteria, and you couldn't cross it. For me, it was, "This is how it has to be run." They were used to chaos, and I couldn't work like that. My job was to keep it all organized. And I think with the crews—and there was the tech crew, the lighting crew, the cleaning crew, the kitchen crew—I got kind of a reputation. Riley had all kinds of nicknames for me, like "Dorothy," from *The Wizard of Oz*, and they used to call me "Godzilla" because I drew a line with them. And Tony never called me by my first name; it was always, "Hey, Rebidas." When I'd leave at six, he'd usually be on the floor and say, "What? You're leaving early?" There was Rose, there was Uncle Marvin; I mean, it was a cast of characters coming in and out every day. But it was a special time for me, too, because I was young and I had friends who would say, "Are you going to be there tonight? Can I get two tickets?" And I'm like, "I don't think so." But I would try and get them two tickets, or push 'em up a little bit in the standing room line. That is, if Tony was in a good mood.

I mostly didn't stay for shows—I didn't get paid for staying—unless it was someone I really wanted to see. I loved Peter Allen. Don't ask me why. And Elaine Boozler, Tom Waits, Patti Smith, Hall & Oates. Unless Riley told me I had to stay and see this, for someone like Emmylou Harris, or it was going to be a really big show like James Taylor and Carly Simon. When Dolly Parton played the club, I think it was Riley who said to me I had to see her. And he was right. Dolly came in and she did her show, and then they were having a party at the Top of the World restaurant at the World Trade Center. Now she was having buses for everybody at the club, so everybody was invited. But being Allan and Stanley's assistant, I figured I shouldn't go, that Allan would never approve. He was very strict with me. But the stage manager, Richard Joseph, told me to get on the bus. I said, "No, I'm not going." And he again said, "Look. Just get on the bus." So I got on, even though I thought I was going to get killed for it. So after we get on, Dolly comes in and she sits down in the seat right in front of me. She turns around, and I have never seen anybody with skin like she had; it really was peaches and cream. She had her long fingernails and her hair, and I said, "God, you look so pretty," and she said thanks and went on to tell me how she never went out without "all this," pointing to her wig and her makeup and her fake nails. And then we all went up to the Top of the World for the party. It was great fun.

A friend of mine was working at Rogers and Cowan, the publicity firm, and some people there were interested in seeing this comedian. So we went up to a comedy club and saw this guy who was really cute and funny, and it was Keenan Wayans. And Allan had said to me, "Let's let you get a chance to book something. What do you think of Keenan Wayans opening for Prince?" I said, "Yes. And Prince is brilliant." So of course when Prince played the club and came out wearing nothing but his underwear, Tony walked by the table I was sitting at and said to me, "I'm sure you had something to do with this."

One time Caroline Kennedy was outside the club waiting to get in. Allan said they were having some problems and I told him I knew her, and he looked right at me and said, "You don't know her." I said, "Yes, I've met her. I'm sure if I go up to her, we can get things squared away." So I went over and reintroduced myself to her, and she's like, "Oh, my gosh. How are you?" You see, there was a guy I worked with at Capitol who was friends with Peter Duchin, the pianist, and while I wasn't much of a photographer, I had a camera, and sometime I took pictures for him, and he had me go up to the recording studio when Duchin was recording. So I was there, and in came Jackie Kennedy, who was friends with Duchin. That was spectacular. She didn't say anything. She just looked beautiful. Of course. And then they came up and asked me not to take any pictures, so I got to hang out with Caroline and John Jr. And then she did remember me, thank goodness.

I didn't leave The Bottom Line on purpose. Allan and Stanley got the idea of starting a management company and a publishing company with songwriter Dan Daley. And because I was able to read contracts, because I had a good ear for music, and because I understood their business, they thought they could build in an ally, so I got to learn publishing lingo when they started developing Bottom Line Music. Then one day I got a phone call from the office of Salvador Chiante, who was the president of MCA Music, saying he wanted to meet with me. I was like, "Me?" So I went up and I met with him, and he made me a music publisher. Like they say, he made me an offer I couldn't refuse. I myself had mixed feelings about it. Allan and I had become very close. I had started calling him Pop after my father took ill and passed away. He was very supportive during that time, and his driver took me out to the hospital where my father was, because I didn't have a car and otherwise I really couldn't get there. So I developed a very deep relationship with Allan and Stanley, but they understood that I had to move on, and I took the shot. Not sure if it was the right one, but that's how I got into music publishing, which I did for quite a long time. That's a whole other story, working in music publishing. There was often the good and the bad. I was at Peer-Southern in LA from 1981 to '85, and while I was with them, I signed a songwriter named Liam Sternberg. He penned a little ditty called "Walk Like an Egyptian." I'm still waiting for my gold record on that one.

DONNA DIKEN: In the late 70s I was living in Orange County, New York, near Middletown in a place called New Vernon. My parents moved there from Ramsey, New Jersey, and that's where I spent most of my teenage years. I loved music, and I always went to concerts with my friends. We'd go into New York to see acts like Bowie and Aerosmith, all those types of bands and big arena shows. And when I was in the city, I'd go into record stores, and I found *Rock Scene*, *New York Rocker*, all those magazines, and *The Village Voice* weekly. I'd see the ads in the *Voice*, and look at all these great places to go, so I started going, well, trying to go to The Bottom Line, but I could never get into the early shows because it was always sold out. Like any band I wanted to see, the early show was a record company show, so I'd have to wait outside in line until the second show, but I'd be there since the beginning so I'd get in. The types of acts that I would go see at that time before I started working there were groups like the Cars and someone like Bryan Ferry. I missed Talking Heads because they were opening for him, but I had already seen them at CBGB's, so I was ok if I had missed them. So from the start I loved the club, and I wanted to work there.

In 1978, I was working at Pizza Hut in Middletown with my friend Tom, and one day he said, "Let's move to New York City. We got to get out of here." He was going to go to NYU anyway. So he said, "Come on, let's get an apartment together," and we found one on 12th Street between Avenues A and B for $150 a month, with the tub in the kitchen and all that kind of stuff. I wanted to work at The Bottom

Line, but I thought I should get some New York City experience before I applied there, so I wound up working at the Greene Street Diner on the corner, a block away from The Bottom Line. And then in 1979 there was a waitress walk out at The Bottom Line that got covered by *Soho Weekly News*, and the club was desperate for waitresses, so they had ads in the paper. So I was like, "Oh my God, this is my chance." I interviewed with Alison Korn, who was the head waitress at the time, and Tony didn't want to hire me, but Alison did, and she won out. And it's funny because then later Tony and I became really good friends.

A lot of times I waited on the tables straight back, where all the rock critics and music writers sat. I knew who they were because their names would be on the tabs that the record company would buy. I was a huge Lester Bangs fan, and the first time I waited on him, I said, "Mr. Bangs, I just have to tell you I'm a really big fan." And he's like, "Yeah, that's great. I'll have a Heineken." I was a little disappointed, but in a way, that's what I expected him to say. I expected him to dismiss me. But it was just like, "Oh, my God, Lester Bangs!" It was really exciting for me. So that's why when I became the industry liaison, I always tried to give the rock writers the best seats and all that, because I thought they had the coolest job besides being a musician.

Another good thing about the club was we would have a staff dinner. So even if you didn't make any money that night or whatever, at least you got fed, and even better, you could come in on a night when you weren't working and you could still eat. And I actually still have a paycheck from The Bottom Line that I always kept. It was for 5 cents. The reason is, on your nights off, you could go in and drink half price against your paycheck. So if you only worked two nights and you went to the club on other nights to have food and cheaper drinks, you'd basically spend your paycheck, so one week I actually received a paycheck for five cents.

I waited on Johnny Cash and June Carter when June's daughter Carlene played. That's when she said her famous, or infamous, "I put the cunt back in country" line, and I was like, "Oh my God. She's saying that in front of her mom?" And he was drinking white wine. I was just shocked that Johnny Cash drank white wine; he was trying to be good, I think. I did wait on Mick Jagger. He was there with Jerry Hall, and it's when he had a beard. So when I went up to them, they said, "We'll have a bottle of red wine with ice." And I'm thinking, "Ok, is that with ice? Do they want it in the glass? Do they want an ice bucket? What do I do?" So I put ice in the glasses, I put separate ice in glasses on the side, plus an ice bucket—all on that tiny little round table where the VIPs used to sit. And I forget exactly what it was, but all I got was like a 37-cent tip or something, whatever was left rounded off from the bill.

Another time, Ray Davies and Chrissie Hynde came to see a show, and they were barely watching the stage; they were making out the whole time. Then Nick Lowe, when he was dating Margot Kidder, they came to a show, and we didn't know they were dating, so it was like, "Oh my God, Nick Lowe and Lois Lane!" One time I waited on Mary Steenbergen and Malcolm McDowell, after they'd done that movie, *Time After Time*. It was maybe a table of six, and we were told not to write tabs for people. You had to charge them for every little drink. And I didn't do that unless I had to, because I'm not going to ask Mary Steenbergen and him for $4.92, because, of course, we had that tax on it, so it was never evened off. I ran a tab for them, but they wound up having a fight, and then they left without paying. I think someone might've ran after them and got them, but they let me off the hook. At least I didn't have to pay for their drinks.

One night Springsteen came to see Rachel Sweet, and when he left, there were at least six full Heinekens sitting on the table because everybody was sending over drinks. People wanted to say, "I bought Bruce Springsteen a drink!" Bruce was going to go backstage to say hi to her, but they didn't want him to walk through the throngs of people. So he came in the back, in the kitchen, and he went up over the bar into one of the dressing rooms. He kind of had to climb up to go over, and we were all just standing there, all us waitresses, just admiring Bruce's butt as he went over. That was nice. There was also the night when Billy Joel was first dating Christie Brinkley, and they came in. They came to a second set blues show, and there was hardly anybody there. One of the other waitresses and I, because it was kind of slow, we were in the ladies' room, which had a big long mirror in there. I was at one end, she was at the other, and we were touching up our makeup, and in walks Christie Brinkley. She comes in between us, and you could see she had absolutely no makeup on, and she looks in the mirror and just kind of flips her hair, and leaves. We both looked at each other and just put our makeup back in our bags and slunk away, because she was just so absolutely beautiful. I mean, why bother?

Allan would also have lots of magic shows and illusionists or those types of acts, like The Amazing Kreskin. And yes, we were always amazed by him. One time we were there early when they were setting up for the show, and there's no microphone. So we're like, I don't know how this guy does it, with his mind reading stuff. During the second show, there weren't that many people in the audience, and I was talking to the bartender at the back bar, and for some reason we were talking about Bo Donaldson and the Heywoods, I guess about that song "Billy Don't Be a Hero," and just for a minute. And then we walked back out to watch a little bit more of the show, and Kreskin looks in our general direction and says, "Over here, I'm getting Bonnie, Donald, Donaldson? Bonnie Donaldson?" Both me and the bartender were like, "We're not saying shit about this." And he's just really upset that nobody's owning up to Bonnie. But we were like, "There's no way. I don't want any part of this." So that was pretty funny that he actually read our minds.

Now famous or not, at The Bottom Line you had to do two shows. It didn't matter if you sold not one single ticket; you still did the two shows. And there were some notoriously great second shows with hardly any people there. One of the amazing ones for me was the Blasters. It must have been the first time they played New York, on a bill with the Plimsouls. There was nobody in the audience, except the members of the Go-Go's and their road crew who were also in town. They came down and just hung out because they were all LA bands, and they were sticking together when they first came to New York. And it was a great show, too. They played to the staff and maybe eight people in the audience. Maybe their record company made sure everybody was there for the first show, but now it was just for fun.

At The Bottom Line, you always got everybody on their way up, and then sometimes people on their way down. But the way up was the most fun. Like John Mellencamp, who was called John Cougar when he first started. He did two nights, and the first night Tracy Nelson was the headliner, and I love Tracy Nelson, but the second night she called in sick because they just blew her away. When Prince played, and I think it was his first New York show, he basically had a rock and roll band, and he came out wearing a leopard print bikini bottom and that was it. Almost all the people that came to see him were radio people from r&b stations, not rock and roll. They did not expect what they were seeing, and everybody was just like, "Holy shit, what was that?" It was just mind-blowing. They just did not expect it—not the music, not the bikini underpants, not nothing.

When I made the transition to be the record company liaison and be out front by the ticket office, for me it was an easy transition and exciting because I handled the guest list. I did some press releases, not a lot. They did have an ad agency that they used, but sometimes we did our own press releases and got some press for some of the artists there. I really loved all of it. I loved the music, I loved all the artists, I loved all the writers. I didn't make a lot of money, for sure. I definitely did not. Of course, what saved us is that New York was so cheap at the time that you could be poor and still have an apartment. You can't do that now. We were in the right place at the right time. We've all been frozen out of New York now.

One of the parts of my job, too, was when a record company might have a tab and I would be billing them and they would pay usually once a month. *Rolling Stone* magazine had a running tab, and Stanley had said, "Let's just keep it running, and we'll use it for an ad or something someday." And they were like, "Sure, no problem. We'll do that." So when the club's tenth anniversary came around, we had enough money to do a full-page ad in *Rolling Stone*, and *Rolling Stone* was not happy about it. It was a lot of money that they were expecting to get, but they had to let us have it. And if you went to a lot of record company shows, you'd see plenty of people there with coke spoons around their necks.

One of the saddest nights was when George the bouncer had a heart attack and died. He was six foot six so nobody would ever mess with him, but he was the sweetest, nicest man. He would make these cherries soaked in alcohol, and he would have the cherries in his pocket, and that's what he would eat. He didn't buy drinks; he would just suck on the cherries. And he'd always give us some. Another thing with George was that he would trade in twenty dollars and ask for crisp one-dollar bills so that he could tip people a nice crisp bill. He was a bodyguard for Raquel Welch when she was on Broadway, and he did that for Muhammad Ali and tons of other people. But he liked seeing shows at The Bottom Line, so he would work for Allan whenever he needed him, when they wanted extra security. And that night—I think it was a Lou Reed show—he was in the box office sitting there at one of the two desks, and he just slumped over. They laid him down on the ground on the carpet in the back, and they loosened his tie and his pants, and Tony was trying to give him CPR and stuff, and they called an ambulance, and he died when he got to the hospital. It was some type of aneurysm, and it was just heartbreaking because to see him, that was not what I was used to. He always dressed beautifully, so here was this really dapper, elegant man with his clothing all messed up. It was just really heartbreaking to see that.

Tony and I did clash a bit when I first got the liaison job because people would ask me for things instead of asking him, and I guess he got a little jealous that I got along well with people. So for a while, he was not nice to me. So finally I said, "Look, when you apologize, then I guess we'll talk again." When I was head waitress, I had been really good friends with his mother and father, especially his father after Tony's mother died, so I was the only person who waited on him. So when his father died, I, of course went to the funeral, and we made up, and after that everything was fine. I think it was one of those man things where they want to say something, but they can't. That was his generation, I guess.

I loved going to work every day. I became friends with everybody who worked there, and it was great. We would all go out after the club closed for the night. We'd usually go to Kenny's Castaways on Bleecker Street. I was more of a CBGB's, Mudd Club type of girl when I started working there. But this is where everybody went. I went, and that's how I met [my husband, drummer] Dennis. If I hadn't gone to Kenny's Castaways, I would never have met him. We'd probably get out of The Bottom Line somewhere between one and two, and Kenny's would stay open until four, and one Monday night the Smithereens were doing a late jam. Now usually I hated jams because it was usually just guitar noodling guys, and I steered clear of any type of anything with the word jam in it. But they were playing, and it was all the Beatles, the Who, and the Kinks, plus some originals that I thought were really great. After that, I went back every Monday, and one night I was at the bar and Jimmy [Smithereens guitarist Jim Babjak] came over and was standing next to me, and we both smoked the same type of cigarettes and drank Remy Martin, which was like three dollars at the time; so we were big spenders, instead of the 75-cent beers. We just hit it off and started talking, and then he introduced me to Dennis and the rest of the band, and it was a year and a half later, actually, when Dennis and I finally got together. We became good friends, and I went to Jimmy's wedding with Dennis as a date, and after a couple of gin and tonics, we were dancing, and he kissed me, and it was just an epiphany, like "Why did I not think of this before?" Before that I was trying to fix him up with one of my girlfriends because I thought he was just the nicest guy. That was 1983, and we've been together ever since.

Working at The Bottom Line and working closely with Allan, I really got a good musical education. There was some music that I didn't know that I liked until I worked there, or didn't even know existed until I worked there, like Richard and Linda Thompson. Seeing that show was just mind-blowing to me. I didn't know I liked jazz until I worked there. Even country music, because good music is good music. And so he really was a mentor to me. He was really an innovator doing so many different kinds of music shows, and also doing all the comedy shows that he did, shows about old black-and-white commercials, all that type of stuff. So I think he really was like a groundbreaker and a visionary.

I left The Bottom Line in 1995, after sixteen years. It was just time to go. I had to make money. If I'm married to a musician, I had to get a real job, you know what I mean? And for the last sixteen years I've worked as the manager of the interior design department of a design firm. We do the insides of corporate jets for all the billionaires out there. The job is interesting because working at The Bottom Line and dealing with some quote big shots there definitely helped me to be at ease with famous CEOs and their like. I mean, if I can deal with Lou Reed, I can deal with Elon Musk.

11 LEADER OF THE PACK

A VILLAGE SMASH, A BROADWAY BUST

Original holiday greeting cards sent out by Allan Pepper and Stanley Snadowsky were a part of The Bottom Line's early traditions, as the club's co-owners used the opportunity to poke fun at themselves, the music industry, and the times they were living through. In 1975, the card featured Pepper as the stooped-over, white-bearded Father Time '75, and Snadowsky as the diaper-clad '76 New Year's baby, and one year the card depicted the two promoters hawking tickets to the birth of Jesus. The last year they sent them out, in December 1980, their message was a bit different, though. "Season's Greetings," it proclaimed, "From the club with the chairs." In earnest, though, the bite that newer stand-up clubs were taking out of The Bottom Line's business was becoming more and more evident as the new decade unfolded, and Pepper knew he had to keep developing original productions to keep his club full.

In the fall of 1983, one idea in particular took shape in Pepper's head, and it led to one of the most remarkable, and complicated, stories in the entire history of The Bottom Line.

ALLAN PEPPER: I had received a book on girl groups of the 1960s by Alan Betrock, and I started to read it, and I got to thinking that there could be a show here. There was also a home video out at the same time on girl groups with interviews with some of those Brill Building songwriters who wrote all those great songs from that era. So I'd watched that, and I'm reading through the book, and the name of Ellie Greenwich keeps coming up.

Brooklyn-born Ellie Greenwich was one of the most successful songwriters of the 1960s. Among her many hits were such Phil Spector-produced classics as the Ronettes' "Be My Baby" and "Baby I Love You"; the Crystals' "Da Do Run Run" and "Then He Kissed Me"; Bob B. Soxx and the Blue Jeans' "Why Do Lovers Break Each Other's Heart"; Darlene Love's "Christmas (Baby, Please Come Home)"; and Ike and Tina Turner's "River Deep, Mountain High." Other Greenwich-penned hits included Manfred Mann's "Do Wah Diddy Diddy," Tommy James and the Shondells' "Hanky

Panky," the Dixie Cups' "Chapel of Love," Lesley Gore's "Maybe I Know," the Beach Boys' "I Can Hear Music," and the Shangri-Las' "Out in the Street" and "Leader of the Pack"—not to mention "The Kind of Boy You Can't Forget," recorded by Greenwich herself alongside her then co-composer and husband Jeff Barry for their studio group, the Raindrops, as well as their production (and often backup vocal) work on Neil Diamond's 1966-'68 Bang Records hits, including "Cherry, Cherry," "Thank the Lord for the Night Time," "Girl, You'll Be a Woman Soon," "Kentucky Woman," and "You Got to Me."

ALLAN PEPPER: I started thinking, "What if I do a show hosted by Ellie Greenwich, and maybe have some of the singers or groups from that era perform?" Now, keep in mind, I'd been doing the doo-wop shows with Bobby Jay, so I started to really think about how I might go about it. And the more I thought about it, I thought there might be a show in there more about Ellie Greenwich herself than the girl groups, because in the 1960s she was a successful woman making a good living in an industry dominated by men. There were a handful of these women, like Carole King, of course, and a theatrical show would allow us to examine the time.

Perhaps the biggest reason I kept thinking about Ellie is that I'd met her once before, at the club. In 1983 she'd come to see Darlene Love, who'd sung lead on a number of Ellie's hits back in the '60s. I got her a table for the show, and it gave us an opportunity to schmooze and talk a little bit. Meanwhile, I had a relationship with a director, Bill Partlan, who I first met when Eileen and I went away on a summer vacation and attended the Eugene O'Neill Playwrights Conference in Connecticut, and he was directing up there. Bill directed the first performances of a couple of August Wilson plays there, including *Ma Rainey's Black Bottom* and *Fences*, and while he didn't do musicals, I'd stayed in touch with him. I had Ellie's number, and I finally decided to call her and told her I had this idea of doing a show about her and around her, and asked if she'd have lunch with me. Now, Ellie was really kind of a recluse, but I convinced her to go to lunch with me. I pitched her the idea for a show, and she was kind of on the fence. She was listening, intrigued, but she also seemed, truthfully, kind of frightened by it. So I said, "Look, how about I bring Bobby Jay"—who I knew she knew—"and also my friend Bill, who's a director, and we just come to your house and we run a tape recorder and let Bobby interview you, just to maybe find the seeds of a show?" She said ok, and Bobby, Bill, and I went to her apartment. Bobby interviewed her, and he's wonderful and very knowledgeable, and so we got some tape, and it was really good stuff. But I could tell Ellie still had her doubts, and I couldn't get her to commit. She wanted to, then she didn't want to.

Now one of her best friends was a writer named Melanie Mintz, who was one of the people who came with Ellie to see Darlene Love at the club the year before.

So Ellie calls Melanie and tells her that we'd approached her, and Melanie relays to me that Ellie was interested, but was concerned that I might be full of crap, and she didn't want to put herself in a position where she could be embarrassed. Ellie asked Melanie to meet with me and make an assessment to see if it was worth moving ahead, and we set up a meeting at a coffee shop near The Bottom Line. So Bill and I are there sitting opposite Melanie, and I'm going to pitch, and as usual, I have no trouble pitching. I said, "Listen, I have this idea." I had read that Ellie loved The Shirelles, so I said, "How about this? The house is dark, and the first thing you hear is a tape, and it's me talking to Ellie, and I say, 'Ellie, I want to do a show about you at The Bottom Line. So, tell me, how did you get involved in songwriting in the music business?' And with that, it fades, the house music comes up and we hear The Shirelles singing 'Will You Love Me Tomorrow.'"

I keep pitching, and Melanie is sitting there stone-faced, and after a while I stop and say, "What do you think?" And she looks at me and she says, "Why would you start a show about Ellie Greenwich with a song that was one of Carole King's biggest hits?" And, of course, I said, "Good point." Anyway, we talked for a while, and she said she thought the idea was interesting, and she'd think about it. When we left the coffee shop, Bill turned to me and said, "Boy, she's opinionated." And I said, "Yeah, but she's right." Melanie went back to Ellie and told her basically that we didn't have it together yet, but that she thought my intentions were in the right place, and Melanie and I started to work on how to figure it out. And it was Melanie who did just that. She knew all of Ellie's work, and she selected the songs and put them in a certain order. She knew exactly what she was doing. At the start, it was only a three-night show, a tribute to Ellie Greenwich, and I was focused on doing a show to record to sell commercially as a home video. That was the original plan. But as it happened, it turned into something bigger. Much bigger.

MELANIE MINTZ: I had written a script at one point that was about a girl group from the 1960s. And while I was working on it, I was talking to people like Ronnie Spector and Jack Nitzsche, and Nitzsche said to me, "You know, you should talk to Ellie Greenwich." I wanted to talk to someone who was writing songs during that time, so Jack gave me her phone number. I called her, and she said she'd be delighted to meet me. What I didn't know at the time, was that she was a recluse; she never left her house. She put me off for about three months. And on the Sunday that I finished the draft I was working on, the phone rang, and it was her. I live in Lincoln Center, and she lives on 57th Street, so she's literally five minutes away from me, and she calls and says, "Mel, it's Ellie. Come over now." So even though I wrote the thing without her, I ran over there, and we just really hit it off. And then when she read it, she was impressed by what I did, so we became very good friends.

I always remember standing on a street corner with a gang in Brooklyn with a portable radio when I was twelve, maybe thirteen. You're noticing boys or whatever you notice at your age, and on the radio they're singing, "Will You Love Me Tomorrow?" Ellie and I bonded over that song. That was her favorite of all of Carole King's. When they say, "What song would you have liked to write?" for Ellie, that was the song. And I of course loved it; I was a huge Shirelles fan. But is there a better rock and roll song than "Be My Baby?" It's hard to say. It represented what we were all living through because those songwriters like Ellie, Carole King, and Cynthia Weil were only a couple of years older than us. So it's my street corner, and it's these songs that are telling our stories. "Will You Love Me Tomorrow?" "You've Lost That Lovin' Feeling." "He's Sure the Boy I Love." Those songs touched us, touched our generation in a very profound way. And I guess in ways they helped us form who we became. We all wanted, like the Ronettes, to go "Walking in the Rain." Why? Because it sounded so good on a record. Not because it made sense, but because it sounded true. So it was true. It helped us as adolescents to grow up. And that's a very, very tender, profound time in our lives.

After I met with Allan, I had some vague ideas about how to do it, and had done a little bit of putting together stuff before we even talked. Now I was really there to protect and defend Ellie, who really didn't trust anybody. But you could have just done a tribute to her by having some people just sing her songs, and that wouldn't have been the worst thing, either. But Allan, to his credit, really wanted to make it special. And when we met, what I saw instantly was Allan's sincerity and passion for wanting to do it. So I came up with how we were going to do it because he gave me the parameters of what we could and couldn't use. Bobby had to be the host and Bill had to be the director. And that was the beginning of it. We became very fast friends. We spoke the same language very quickly.

ALLAN PEPPER: We had to figure out who's going to be the musical director. I came up with Jimmy Vivino because I knew him from being Uncle Floyd's brother and leading the band when Floyd was at the club, and he had also been working with Phoebe Snow. I thought a lot about him, and I knew he did great arrangements. So I set up a meeting with Jimmy and Ellie and myself and Melanie at Ellie's apartment. Ellie didn't know him, and she was very funny and very fast. So she said, "So. Uncle Floyd's your brother—really? That guy with the silly hand puppets?" And Jimmy looked at her and said, "Yeah. And did you really write all those dumb songs?" And they bonded immediately. The other reason I picked Jimmy was because I thought he could do the arrangements and put the right band together, which was very important. Now Melanie had a very specific concept of how the things needed be done musically. Her notion was that these classic songs had to sound exactly the way people heard them when they were growing up, not some modern-day versions. They had to sound like the original recordings. So Jimmy put a band together for Ellie to come to The Bottom Line during the day to hear because she had to approve everything. Ellie heard the band, and she knew that Jimmy was capable of conducting it. But now we had to figure out how to really do it. As it turned out, Ellie knew Paul Shaffer and said she wanted him involved, so we got her to call him. And he said yes before she even finished the sentence.

Keyboardist Paul Shaffer first came to New York from his native Canada in 1974. He quickly found work in the orchestra pit for fellow Canadian Doug Henning's Magic Show, and the following year he joined the Saturday Night Live band for its fall '75 debut. He served as SNL's pianist and occasional sketch performer until 1983, when he left to become the bandleader for David Letterman's late night talk show—a post he held until Letterman's retirement in 2015.

PAUL SHAFFER: I think I remember meeting Ellie for the first time at Don Kirshner's office. Somehow when I first got to New York in 1974, I kind of gravitated toward Donnie Kirshner. I knew of him and his history with songwriters, like Neil Sedaka, Carole King, etc., and I wound up doing a TV pilot for him. It was going to be like a Monkees type of show, but updated to the '70s, and we made a pilot, which became a summer series several years later, but at the time it was unsuccessful. Nonetheless, I was able to hang out at Donny's office, and one day Ellie came up and I got to meet her and I don't know how, but our friendship flourished. We became friends, and then she asked Allan if she could get me involved in the thing they were going to do at The Bottom Line, and I of course said yes.

I played the role of Phil Spector in a few sketches and also supervised the music, which was beautifully conducted and arranged by Jimmy Vivino. And I played, too, under Jimmy's able baton. We came pretty close to reproducing that "Wall of Sound," for sure. And with Ellie being there, that made certain that all the vocals and background vocals were perfect, just like the records. That Phil Spector "Wall of Sound" was always sort of mysterious for musicians. How does he do it? It's magic. You can't hear everything clearly; you're not even sure what instruments are in there. Anyway, there was a lot of studying. And then eventually, getting to work with Spector himself in the studio, I learned a lot about his techniques, and we all applied them a little bit for the show.

JIMMY VIVINO: It was Floyd who first got me into The Bottom Line. Allan loved Floyd. He just loved everything about him. And after a while, I came in with Phoebe Snow, I came in with Al Kooper, I think I came in with David Johansen once as well, and I guess Allan started saying to himself, "Hey, this kid, he's got something going on; people are hiring him, and he's putting bands together for them." So that's where he approached me, and things just exploded from there. Allan mentioned the name Ellie Greenwich, and I kind of wet my pants a little bit because I said, "Well . . . ," and I started rattling off all the songs she wrote. And Allan said, "Ok. You've got to meet with Paul Shaffer," and since Paul was just starting with Letterman, Allan said we needed to get together quickly because he knew Paul was busy with the Letterman show. I, of course was already a big fan of Paul Shaffer's because I wanted to do what he did, to be a bandleader like him. So the next step was to go to the Gramercy Park Hotel and meet with Paul Shaffer.

They have me go there, and I'm thinking, "This guy lives in a hotel? Like Duke Ellington? I mean, who does that? Who lives in a hotel? Paul Shaffer lives in a hotel." So I go there, and I have my charts in a manila envelope. We had spoken on the phone, and Paul suggested we put some charts together for a few songs like "Be My Baby" and "Baby I Love You," so I put three charts together, and Paul looks at them and he just looks at me and says, "Well, this looks great." He says, "I'm a rhythm guy. I'll tell you what. I'll work with you on the rhythm section stuff and you can do all the sweetening, all that Jack Nitzsche stuff." And I'm like, "Oh yeah, man. This is going to be great." Then we started putting a band together, and auditions for drummers turned out to be the most memorable part, not being able to find the right guy. Ellie was like, she was used to Hal Blaine and Gary Chester and guys like that, so she was like, "No, no," to everyone we tried, and I'm like, to me, all these guys were ok. I mean, these other drummers, they were really good drummers. Then, finally, Leo Adamian comes in, and I hear the difference right away. So she loved Leo. He got up on the stage, sat down at the drums, and just killed us, man, all of us.

Paul taught me things about the band, about music, that I carried into all of my years of music direction. One was that if the bass drums are right, everything else will fall into place. Paul says to me, "You seem to hear music from the top down," and being a trumpet player before I was a guitar player, you hear stuff from the top down, and he says, "I hear from the bottom up. Somewhere in the middle, we're going to make something really great happen." And we did. It was fantastic. We really wanted to try and make this sound almost orchestral, but rock orchestral like on those original recordings. The way those songs sound, you can't just get on stage and start. You can't just get on stage and start doing "River Deep Mountain High." You have to kind of know what you're doing.

There were certain things; first of all, the way Paul plays piano. At the time, other piano players would come in at rehearsals, but it wouldn't be the same. The way Paul plays the whole record in his head; it's heavy. He's like a heavy metal guitar player down there on the bottom, and it's a rumble that he creates that is necessary because we would discuss this, like I think there's two or three pianos on this record. There'd be Phil Spector and Nitzsche playing a piano, or maybe Don Randi and Phil Spector would be playing one. And then Leon Russell would be on the high end playing all that stuff, like on "Not Too Young to Get Married." So we figured out how to do things, and to me, it was one of the greatest feelings when that whole band kicked in.

ALLAN PEPPER: Jimmy basically did all the arrangements, and Paul gave him little hints of what they could do musically to be like what people heard on those records and not make it sound like some oldies show. They were just subtle music changes, but it allowed people to hear it the way the records had sounded. But as the thing was progressing—and by now we had settled on the title, *Leader of the Pack [after the Shangri-Las' motorcycle-themed, doomed teen love affair classic]: An Evening of Songs by Elie Greenwich*—we realized that what we were doing was something a little different. And then Ellie said, "I want Darlene Love in it." And that was key.

The daughter of a Pentecostal minister, Darlene Love grew up singing in church choirs in the Los Angeles area. While still in her teens, she became the lead singer of the vocal group the Blossoms, who, beginning with their work on Sam Cooke's 1959 hit "Everybody Loves to Cha Cha Cha," quickly became pop music's most in-demand session singers. In addition to appearing on classic '60s hits ranging from Shelley Faberes' "Johnny Angel" and Frank Sinatra's "That's Life" to Bobby "Boris" Pickett's "Monster Mash," Love was hired in 1962 as a vocalist by Phil Spector. This led to her singing lead—uncredited—on the Crystals' "He's a Rebel," as part of the studio group Bob B. Soxx & the Blue Jeans' "Why Do Lovers Break Each Other's Hearts," as well as, under her own name, "Today I Met the Boy I'm Gonna Marry" and the holiday evergreen, "Christmas (Baby, Please Come Home)." Those last three, as well as several other songs featuring Love and/or the Blossoms, were all written by Ellie Greenwich, and having seen Love's thrilling Bottom Line performance in 1983, Greenwich knew she wanted Love in the show.

Darlene Love's path to her August 1983 Bottom Line debut was itself quite a story—one that actually started earlier that year in Los Angeles.

DARLENE LOVE: The Blossoms had done a lot of work going way back to when Lou Adler and Herb Alpert were just starting out. We worked a lot of hours in the recording studio, and they didn't have a lot of money, so we were working for them for little or nothing because we wanted to help them out. That was one great thing about The Blossoms. We did a lot of that. Once we got on top as one of the biggest backup groups, we wanted to help people who really were trying to succeed and were really trying. So we became great friends, and when I decided to become a solo artist in 1983, I needed a place to perform in LA. Now me and Lou were such good friends, I asked him if he could help me put on a show at his club, the Roxy. I had a band and singers to back me, and the next big thing was to get an audience that might know Darlene Love but didn't know her as a solo artist. Now it just so happened that the Grammys were coming up in LA, which meant that a lot of entertainers would be in town. So Lou said, "I'll get the audience for you. We'll put the show together, and I'll invite a lot of guests."

We did it, and I had a house full of stars that came to see me. Dionne [Warwick] came, and I figured she would because I'd worked for her for ten years, but I didn't think it was going to be people like Bruce Springsteen and Steven Van Zandt and all of those kinds of artists. I had never met Bruce Springsteen before, or Steven. And I just did the show that I do. But in that particular show, I was singing "Hungry Heart." I don't think Bruce knew I was singing it because a lot of people don't try to sing Bruce's songs, but there's some songs that are great songs for somebody else to sing. And I chose that song because my manager loved Bruce Springsteen. He said, "You got to do this song in your show. You got to." And I said, "Ok, let me learn it." So I did, and Bruce was so amazed at the arrangement that I did of that song, because I made it a Darlene Love song. It was great. And I kept that song in my show for years. I do mostly male songs. Very rarely do I pick a female song to sing. The reason I do that is because they don't have anybody to compare you to. They don't compare you to a male singer, but they will if it's another female. Like, "Oh, she doesn't sing it as good as so-and-so; she shouldn't have sung that song." But when I do a male song, they accept that better than they will a female song. And I didn't know that that's the reason why I was doing it, but later on, I felt that was the reason. It was meant to be. So Bruce and Steven came backstage and everything, and Steven told me I should come to New York. Actually, he said I should move to New York! I said, "You're kidding me, right?" And he said, "No, I'm serious."

STEVIE VAN ZANDT: We had released "Hungry Heart," and were in LA mixing the rest of the album. I run into Lou Adler on the street, and he says, "Man, I got a surprise for you. Darlene Love is playing the club tonight." And I said, "Darlene Love?" Because at that time, the greatest voice from the girl groups had like retired and disappeared, and Lou said, "Well, she's coming back tonight." I said to myself, "This is big news, man." I brought Bruce to the show, and she did "Hungry Heart," which was so cool for us, and we got to meet her. And I told her, I was, like, "If you're getting back into the business, you gotta get out of LA. You know, once you're over twenty-two, you're dead there. For us people of some experience, I think New York is the place to be. You gotta move to New York." I said, "We'll find a way to work together; we'll find something for you." So I talked her into coming, and she came. It was unbelievable. I thought, "Oh, man, I better figure this out now!" And it was tricky at first. People didnt know where she fit in, but I got her some gigs, and once people saw and heard her, everything started to happen for her.

DARLENE LOVE: I told Steven, "If you get me a couple of jobs, I don't know about moving to New York, but I'll come to New York and work." I needed to work to let people know I had this solo career going. The first two jobs I did in New York were because of him. I did the Peppermint Lounge and The Bottom Line, and that kind of started my solo career in New York. For me, a lot of times I'll just be going to places on faith and figuring this is going to happen, and I'm going to find a way. Now number one, you've got to have some money to get there, and then you have to find a place to stay. I'm not the kind of person who will go anywhere by myself, so I need to find somebody to go with me, someone that I'm going to have to try to pay their way there, and then we've got to find a place to stay. So my girlfriend Gloria Jones came along to be with me as my manager or my assistant or whatever, and she had a cousin who lived in New York, and we stayed with that cousin while we worked those first few shows, and then we headed back to LA.

Booking Darlene Love on Van Zandt's recommendation, Pepper somewhat knew who she was, but he wasn't sure about how much of a draw she'd be on her own, so he slotted her into a show as opening act for Joey Dee & The Starlighters. Dee, who'd ridden the Twist fad to brief stardom in the early '60s with his huge hit, "The Peppermint Twist," had gone on to carve out a serviceable career on the "oldies" circuit, so, in theory at least, the pairing made sense. After the first of the two evenings they appeared together, however, after Love dazzled everyone in attendance with her ever-powerful voice and spirit, Pepper reversed the billing, with Love now headlining, which a relieved Dee had no problem with.

While Pepper and Love would soon become great friends, their first meeting backstage at the club didn't go especially smoothly.

DARLENE LOVE: That first night, it was so funny. I hadn't met Allan yet, and I love cheesecake and coffee, so I ordered some cheesecake and coffee. And then they gave me a bill for it at the end of the show, and I went, "Who is this fool? They're going to charge me for a cup of coffee and cheesecake?" And Allan overheard me; he came into the room right as I was saying this.

ALLAN PEPPER: I walked in and introduced myself, told her I was the co-owner of the club, and she said, "Are you really going to charge me for the cheesecake?" and I said, "Why not? I have to pay for it." But we didn't charge her for the coffee.

DARLENE LOVE: I didn't stay in New York that long. We stayed for a week or so with the jobs that Steven had gotten me, and then we had nothing else. So we had to go back home, and I got a job singing on a cruise ship. Then Allan called me and told me that they had come up with this idea to do this show *Leader of the Pack*, and they wanted me to play Darlene Love in *Leader of the Pack*. I said, "Play myself? Hey, why not?" But it was a whole new show and there would be rehearsals, and if I came back East, I had no place to stay.

ALLAN PEPPER: As I was never known for paying very high salaries to people coming to play at the club, I offered—without asking Eileen—to let her stay at our house. She agreed, and, luckily, Eileen was good with it. And so was the whole family.

The other performer Ellie Greenwich insisted on playing her as a young woman in the 1960s was vocalist Ula Hedwig. Greenwich knew Hedwig from her lengthy body of work as an in-demand studio demo and backup vocalist—notably as one of Bette

Midler's Harlettes in the 1970s. And Hedwig already had her own interesting history with The Bottom Line.

ULA HEDWIG: David Lasley, who sang for many years with James Taylor, was the one who brought me into the backup singing world. He knew Bonnie Raitt from California, and one night she was playing The Bottom Line. So David took me, and we ended up going backstage to say hello. I'd never met her. And then she wanted us to sing on "Angel from Montgomery," so we kind of worked up the parts really quickly, right in the dressing room. And that was my first time on The Bottom Line stage, doing that song with Bonnie. I did *Hair* on Broadway, and then I did *Godspell* and a couple of other theatrical things, so I had one foot in theater and one foot in rock and roll backup singing. When Darlene came to New York, I was her first backup singer. We did the Peppermint Lounge, and then we did The Bottom Line when she was on the bill with Joey Dee. Joey was the headliner, and then the second night it got reversed because, well, she was amazing. She's still amazing.

I moved from New York to California in 1983. I was going to try to make it out there, and Allan started to call me every other day, saying "You've got to come back because we're doing this thing called *Leader of the Pack*, and Ellie Greenwich wants you to play her. By then I knew Ellie. I mean, we weren't best buddies or anything, but I knew her, and I was so flattered that Allan said Ellie wanted me to play her. At first I wasn't sure. I mean, I had just moved out to LA. But they really wanted me to do it, so, finally, I relented and came back to New York to work on it.

A third female singer—added, again, at Ellie's request—was Karla DeVito, as well as male vocalist Rory Dodd [probably best known as the "Turn around" male voice on Bonnie Tyler's "Total Eclipse of the Heart."]

KARLA DEVITO: I had just had a baby in August of '83. I came to New York that fall with my husband, [actor] Robbie Benson, who was running the New York City Marathon. We were staying at the Parker Meridien Hotel, and my manager, Winston Simone, who was pals with Ellie, brought her and a few others up to our room to see us and the baby. Ellie started telling us about what was going on with this show about her, and how she wasn't sure about it, and Winston is telling her, "Ellie, you've got to do this." And so she goes—and I loved Ellie so much—she goes, "Ok, I'll do it, but I want you"—pointing to me—"and you"—pointing to Rory—"to do it with me."

ALLAN PEPPER: Once we got everyone on board, we started to really work on the show during the day at the club. We put together a horn section, and because we had to have the wall of sound, we took some tables and chairs out and built an extension to the stage for the horns. We also brought in a very good choreographer, Ed Love. So now we had Bill, we had Ed, we had the singers, the musicians, and we had the concept of the show, and we had Ellie herself coming on at the end of the show's second act. Melanie had written some sketches between the songs as connective tissue, with Bobby Jay as the narrator framing the story, and also as our bass singer, too. We just were going to put it on for three days as a tribute to Ellie Greenwich, so we put the tickets up, and lo and behold, there's a roll and people were calling up and you could tell there was a buzz happening.

After I saw the last dress rehearsal, I was swamped by emotion. It was the culmination of so many things for me as someone who just loved to put on shows and give audiences something special. I was simply overcome by how the show had come together. I had to get out of there, so I walked across the street, ostensibly to give myself something to do, as if I were going to buy ice cream at Swenson's. I remember it was about four in the afternoon, and I just stood there, in front of an ice cream display case, and as I'm standing there, I realized tears were flowing. I wasn't sobbing, just weeping. I was so overjoyed by what we'd been able to accomplish. I had never, ever had that feeling with anything else that I was involved with. I've experienced shows at the club where there was an electricity in the air that you could actually feel it. It was so intense. Like when Bruce played, when Dolly played. And *Leader* had that same feeling of excitement.

On opening night it was freezing outside, and for the second show, the line was wrapped around the block; it was so cold that we brought out coffee to the people waiting in line. We start the show with Bobby onstage, in his role playing a disc jockey—we actually created a space for him on the side that resembled a radio station studio, and he says, "It's 1963, and wherever you were, whatever you were doing, the radio was playing this song." And then, with the whole band already onstage, Leo came in with that drumbeat, that "Boom, boom, boom" from "Be My Baby," the lights came up, and the three women, Darlene, Ula, and Karla, burst through the curtains, and the entire audience leaned forward in their chairs, screaming. And I mean screaming. They actually leaned forward; it was like you were on a ship and it was tilting. I'd never seen that kind of thing, where an audience was that physically moved, and the energy from everyone never stopped during the entire performance. *Leader* got such a great and immediate response that after the very first night, Lennie Petze from Epic Records made a deal with us to record the show for a live album, which they did the very next night. *[It remains unreleased.]*

RILEY: It was a shock and surprise how good the original show was. We were actually having regular shows, other regular acts at night and rehearsing *Leader* during the afternoons. So after the shows every night, the hosts would clear big areas of flooring for people to be choreographing in one area, dress fittings in another, and doing something else in another. But I was day manager at that point, and it was a total annoyance. I had no clue of what was in the works. I mean, I saw bits and pieces of it in rehearsal. Frankly, it just looked like a lot of oldies to me.

It was supposed to be Thursday, Friday, and Saturday, with two shows each night. Just a one-shot weekend, nothing more. But there was finally a dress rehearsal Thursday afternoon, and when they did the dress rehearsal, I went, "Ba Boom!" With everyone dressed in those '60s clothes, and the music and the singing and all of it being so great, I mean, I got it. And that Friday afternoon, Ellie, and I forget who else it might have been, maybe Paul Shaffer, went on the five o'clock news to get some PR done. I mean, we had already sold a ton of tickets. People were really interested in it. But as soon as that interview was over on TV, all five phones didn't stop ringing. I remember being in that little office with the box office person, and we couldn't keep up. And then I saw both shows, and the audiences went crazy. I showed up the next day and I see the remote CBS recording truck setting up cables and people going backstage, having people sign releases for an album. I mean, it was just overnight. And that was that. We were so proud for Allan, because he was the jazz fan who was thinking outside of the box into other areas.

KARLA DEVITO: I get the chills now thinking that Ellie Greenwich wanted me to sing "Be My Baby," "Baby I Love You," "Leader of the Pack," and then "River Deep Mountain High." I had done that on the road with Meat Loaf as a duet as one of our encores. I just felt so incredibly honored to do that. And Darlene—please! "He's a Rebel?" "Christmas (Baby, Please Come Home)?" And you just can go on and on about what she had done in her life. At the time I didn't even know that she had done a version of "River Deep Mountain High" for Phil Spector, and then he gave it to Tina Turner instead. And I'm like, "Oh my God." And then I got to sing it in the original version of *Leader of the Pack* at The Bottom Line. I don't know if I would've been able to do it had I known that.

PAUL SHAFFER: Darlene was a revelation. Performing with her every night, I felt like she carried the whole show on her shoulders when she sang. Everybody knew that you had to try to rise to her level.

The day after the performances, The New York Times *published a rave review by arts critic Stephen Holden, who had attended the debut show. "A cast of six and an excellent band led by Jimmy Vivino captured both the innocent optimism of Miss Greenwich's songs and the essentials of Phil Spector's 'Wall of Sound,' he wrote. "Darlene Love, the pop-gospel singer who sang on some of the original Spector records, joined Ula Hedwig (playing young Greenwich) and Karla DeVito to form an archetypal 'Girl Group' of the period. Miss Love, who seems hardly to have aged in twenty years, belted out songs like 'Wait 'Til My Bobby Gets Home' with a raw intensity that most contemporary pop-soul singers would be hard put to match . . .* Leader of the Pack *is now more a rock concert than the full-scale musical it wants to be . . . But in its performances and in songs that capture the essence of teenage joy and longing, it's a powerhouse."*

ALLAN PEPPER: So we do the thing, and lo and behold, Stephen Holden writes this great review in *The New York Times*. There were a lot of uptown people who had come down to see the show, including the theater producers Liz McCann and Nelle Nugent, who I'd previously had some dealing with. Their walls were full of Tonys. I had invited Liz to the debut the first night, and she loved it, and then Nelle came the second night, and they saw the reaction of the crowd, and they basically thought it was wonderful and that it should go to Broadway. We made a deal with Liz and Nelle to become co-producers, and they in turn struck a deal with the Schubert organization to put up 90 grand for a six-week workshop run at the club to really develop the show. So now we're really excited. I absolutely thought they were the right people to help us transfer.

Pepper had good reason to think Liz McCann and Nelle Nugent would be able to successfully bring Leader of the Pack from The Bottom Line uptown to The Great White Way. The two began working together as theater producers in 1976, and by 1984 they'd run up a remarkably successful string of Broadway hits, garnering Tony Awards every year from 1978 through 1982 with such critically acclaimed winners as Dracula, The Elephant Man, Mornings at Seven, Amadeus, and The Life and Times of Nicholas Nickleby.

Stanley had only seen moments of the show while it was in rehearsal, which led him to say, "I don't really get it. It seems like an oldies show." But once he saw the whole show, he was blown away. He became one of its biggest fans and got completely behind it. We expanded the cast, and at the end of April of '84 we began new performances and really started refining it. And we were selling out and getting standing ovations every night. Melanie had by now really shaped the show so that Act One is Ellie's life story told through her songs, coupled with a series of humorous vignettes, and Act Two is a concert where Ellie now joins and sings with the cast. The notion was, "You've heard about the woman. Now you're going to meet her."

We were doing business and word of mouth was spreading. And one of the phenomena we saw, which I didn't understand at that point, was that we were doing a lot of repeat business during the week when the tickets were cheaper. And the audience, when Paul Shaffer would come out right at the end of Act One, and he'd put his hand up to his head and he'd do an imitation of Phil Spector, and he'd say, "I'm hearing in my head, I want it to be a symphony, a rock and roll symphony," and the audience up front would be saying the line with him. It was almost like *The Rocky Horror Picture Show*. And I was kind of taken aback and a little thrown by it, not realizing at that moment what it meant: That you were getting people coming to see it more than once and that they were embracing it and loving it. Because what Melanie did was find a real way of threading people's lives through the music.

Before we started the second run, Darlene had returned to California, but she came back to stay with the show, and she again stayed with us at our house in Jersey. And she really became a member of the household: When she came, her luggage was lost by the airline, and for the first two weeks until the suitcases showed up, she wore Eileen's clothes.

DARLENE LOVE: Living with them, it was amazing because it was just so natural. It was like people I knew all my life. I mean, I moved in lock, stock, and barrel. I was there for the long run, rehearsing the show and trying to get it together and staying with Allan, and I just loved that whole family. I fell in love with everybody, all the kids. I was one of their buddies. They would come in my room, I'd be in there sleeping, and Allan and Eileen would have to run them out. They'd tell them, "She needs to sleep. Don't be caught running in there," because it was one of their rooms that they gave me. I was a smoker then, and the twins, they did everything they could to keep me from smoking. They'd go, "Darlene, it's not good for you! You don't need to smoke cigarettes." They even started putting signs up in my room: No Smoking! And I just told them one day, I said, "Listen, I'm a smoker and I can't stop smoking right now, so now y'all are starting to get on my nerves." But I really loved my time living with all of them.

ULA HEDWIG: We took a break, and they reworked it and added three backup singers because the first iteration, the three of us sang all the songs and all the backups, and it was like a hundred songs. So they decided to put extra backup singers into it the second time around to take the weight off us a little bit. Karla had other commitments, so [former Shirts lead singer] Annie Golden replaced her. Paul still played Phil Spector, with Jimmy leading the band, and it was the wall of sound up there on the stage, and it was incredible.

JIMMY VIVINO: It was fun every night. We were so tight on stage. At the end of "Christmas, Baby, Please Come Home," with Darlene, I would turn, and I knew when this vein popped out of her neck while she was singing that she was in it, man. And meeting her—I mean, when I walked into the club to meet Darlene for the first time, I didn't recognize her. There was a woman with glasses sort of halfway down her nose reading the Bible, sitting at one of the little round VIP tables in the afternoon. And I met her, and she was so sweet and smart and just beautiful. I mean, I'm thinking now, she was maybe forty years old then, and in her prime singing better than ever, even better than she'd done on those originals.

BOBBY JAY: Paul was just great as Phil Spector. He is a ham. And he's such a great, great keyboard player, great piano player. He would play so intensely and so hard. He would play until his fingers would bleed.

ULA HEDWIG: And the crowds, I mean, after a while, they were just ridiculous. I remember Liza Minnelli came with Chita Rivera—they were appearing on Broadway together—and Liza was standing on her chair. She was like, "Wow!"

And by the time we did "River Deep Mountain High," she was just hooting and hollering. People were very, very responsive to that.

BOBBY JAY: Our show attracted so much attention when we remounted it. And so many people came. Danny Aiello came to see the show. Robert De Niro came. Bette Midler came. Chita Rivera and Liza Minelli had such a good time they invited our cast to be their guests at their show, *The Rink*.

JUDY JACKSINA: A friend took me to see one of the late shows and I'm watching this thing, and I'm like, "Oh, this is fabulous. Really. It's a whole new way of putting on a show." You heard the music, and you started to remember where you were in life when it came out, and they're up there and it's sounding like when you heard the song on the radio, and it just took me back to those times. And you know, I'm a theater person and we all just think we're such big shots on our big Broadway stages, and here you had all these stars and they're up there delivering this emotional bomb from this little Post-it size stage. Darlene Love! I mean, oh, my goodness. I knew she had sung those songs in the '60s, and I think the thing that struck me most was twenty years removed from when she sang some of these songs, she was still belting them out as if she had recorded them the day before. And Bobby Jay! Just the whole vibe was, you could see it in Bobby Jay's eyes. They're just up people, and they're madly in love with the music. Even if they had an abscessed tooth, we didn't know it. They just took us to heaven.

I asked Allan, "So what are you guys going to do with this?" Now at the time I was very close with Tommy Tune, who was doing *My One and Only* on Broadway with Twiggy. And they said, "Will you bring Tommy to see it?" I said, "Absolutely." So I called Tommy and told him he had to come with me to The Bottom Line to see a show. He started to ask me about it, and I said, "Tommy, I don't want to talk about it. I just want you to sit at this table. This is exactly where I was sitting last night. Just watch it." Well, the curtain goes up, and whoa! Tommy is blown away. He's having more of a religious experience than I had. I thought it was brilliant because it was raw. It was emotional. And all of it without it being a "big" production. I mean, they just had a few lights. And isn't that the way it's supposed to be? So Allan comes over to the table, and Tommy says, "I would love to get involved." And then he looked at me because we sort of did things together. He looked and said, "You in?" I said, "I'm in." So they had both of us. Tommy says, "Keep working. But do not fire the choreographer. Do not fire the director. You keep those guys. I'm just going to come and help them. We're just going to lift this thing up, and we're going to walk it up to Broadway. And then we're going to put this show onstage. The exact thing is happening on the stage on Broadway that is happening here. I don't want a custom stage. I want nothing changed. Nothing. Just the sound will be better because we'll be in a bigger theater." Tommy looked at me, and I said, "Works for me." I'm already in my head thinking, Oh, I can sell it this way. I can sell it lots of ways. We're going to do records. We'll have all the rock press in on it. So I'm already in my head working. So Tommy was talking to them about helping out with the directing, and while there was nothing formal, because that wouldn't happen until after they finished at The Bottom Line and started the process to get to Broadway, we thought we had a deal.

MELANIE MINTZ: Liz and Nelle made a decision, without really discussing it with Ellie or Allan, that the director they wanted would be Michael Peters. He was a protege of Michael Bennett, who'd done *A Chorus Line*, and Peters had helped choreograph *Dreamgirls* and did the same for Michael Jackson's "Beat It" and "Thriller" videos. I guess they thought if they hired Michael Peters, they could get Michael Bennett to maybe oversee everything. So unbeknownst to almost everyone, they got rid of Tommy. Liz calls me up and says, "Listen, I want you to meet with Michael Peters," because the one thing Liz knew was that I was the only one who understood the show and knew how to put it together inside and out. She said, "I want you to have a meeting. I want you to come out of the meeting and tell me if you think he's really the right guy for this." Now, I already thought Tommy was, so I didn't even understand why I was meeting with him. A meeting is arranged, I go to his apartment and he ate his lunch during the entire meeting while we're talking, that's how this meeting was. He said, "Let me say one thing right off the bat. This show is no longer about music. It's about dancing." He actually said that to me. So I said, "Isn't that odd for a show that's about rock and roll songs?" And he said, "Well, that's the way I'm going to do it." And then he says, "And I don't want anybody ugly in my show," and he starts ripping apart everyone that I guess didn't fit his image of what he wanted—including Ellie, who was overweight.

I'm stunned by this, truly stunned by this. I finished the meeting, and in those days we had phone booths, not cell phones. I literally walked to the corner and I call Allan at the office and he patches in Liz. And they say, "How'd the meeting go?" I said, "I'm speechless. Let me start with this. He wants it to be all about dancing. I even said to him, 'So you're telling me you don't like the songs?' And he said, 'Look. I grew up dancing to that stuff. I know what to do.'" I said, "He thinks Ellie is a pig. He doesn't like how almost everyone looks." And Liz says, "Ok, but do you think you can work with him?" And I said, "Why would I want to work with him?" And that was the beginning of the end, because we didn't know they'd actually already hired him. He thought I was auditioning for him, and I thought he was auditioning for me, and shortly thereafter, I walked off. I wasn't going to have any part of it. And then everything changed. If Tommy Tune had done what he wanted to do, it would've been great. I think it would've really been terrific.

JUDY JACKSINA: One night, we're in Tommy's dressing room for *My One and Only*, and there's a knock at the door and it's [British] choreographer Arlene Phillips [*best known at the time for her work on music videos by, among others, the Bee Gees, Tina Tuner, Cliff Richard, Elton John, and Donna Summer*]. Yikes! Visiting royalty. She'd come to say hello to Twiggy and then stopped by to see Tommy and me. We start to talk, and she goes, "I just want to say right now. . ." and I say, "Oh, we're going to dinner. Why don't you come with us?" And she says, "Well, I'd love to come to dinner, but let me just say right now, I'm really sorry about you two being let go." And we're like, "Excuse me? What do you mean let go?" She says, "Oh, gosh. You don't know? You two are off *Leader of the Pack*. Oh, my gosh. I'm so sorry I'm the one to tell you this." Apparently, over in London she'd heard about what was going on with the show, and she knew about the producers going with Michael Peters before we did. Soon as she said it, she knew she'd stepped in it. She was so uncomfortable. And then the rest, I don't know what happened. Everything just went haywire from there.

ULA HEDWIG: One day after The Bottom Line show ended its run, Michael Peters called us all; we thought, just to meet the cast. So we all went down to a rehearsal space, and then one by one, he asked us each to get up and sing. It felt like an audition. After it was all done, we went downstairs and were standing outside, and we were all kind of in shock, like "What the heck was that?" And as it turned out, it really was an audition, and I guess they picked who they wanted, and they got mostly outside people to do the show. They wanted name people for the Broadway elites, I think, which is why I didn't get hired. I mean, I could have gotten hired at least as a chorus member, for God's sake. I think for everybody involved, that was a sore subject for all of us for a while. It was just a weird thing because I did remember seeing Michael in the audience for some of The Bottom Line shows, and you could see he was just sitting in the back and he was lit a little bit, and when everybody else was hooting and hollering, he sat there, stone-faced, like he was dissecting the show, and I think he just thought in his mind, "Well, I'm going to change this thing." And he certainly did.

BOBBY JAY: The path up to Broadway got very complicated for everybody when Allan and Stanley, who always had a dream of doing a Broadway show, got hooked up with those ladies, and they lost the essence of our show. Our show was done onstage with the band onstage. The band was a part of the cast. We couldn't have done it without Leo Adamian on the drums. I mean, we couldn't have done it without any of those guys. And then when it was decided that the show looked like it was going to have an afterlife, and they shut down for weeks, and that's when we found out they were recasting. The only ones who made it were Darlene and Annie Golden, and they replaced the rest of us. I went to what I thought was going to be a rehearsal, but it was an audition. And those auditions, they don't care who you are or what you are, they just talk freely in front of you. Somebody said, "What do we need him for? There were no bass singers in the sixties." I knew then I was gone. I wanted to yell at them, "No bass singers? Then who the hell is *[Temptations vocalist]* Melvin Franklin? You idiots." And they wound up replacing me with an offstage baritone singing the parts. Please.

ALLAN PEPPER: Liz and Nelle had these creative meetings. It was Melanie, myself, Stanley, Liz and the ad exec and the director, and they were saying these crazy things. At one meeting, Nelle got up and announced, "Don't be fooled into thinking you have a hit. This show is not ready to go to Broadway." There was stunned silence, and then Stanley said—very calmly, as he usually was in these types of situations—"I don't understand what you're talking about. Every night people are yelling and screaming, and every night we have trouble getting them out of the club. If it ain't broke, don't fix it. People are loving it. I can't understand what you're doing and why you're trying to do it." We realized Liz and Nelle were trying to rewrite this entire thing. They decided that they wanted to emphasize the drama of Ellie's personal life after she and Jeff Barry split up. Melanie said, "What, are you crazy? Nobody's coming to the show to learn about Ellie Greenwich's nervous breakdown. They want to come to hear and see "Be My Baby" and "Da Do Run Run" and "Leader of the Pack," and "Then He Kissed Me" and "River Deep, Mountain High."

Maybe I should have had an inkling of what was to come when, on the opening night of the second run, one of the heads of the Schubert organization, Jerry Schoenfeld, came down and saw the show at the club. And while his wife was standing on her chair and singing along, obviously having a great time, he just sat there and stared; he just didn't get it. Afterward I asked him what he thought of the show going to Broadway, and he looked at me and said, seriously, "Nothing that six jokes won't fix." And soon as we finished the second run and they started taking the show uptown, everything went downhill. Melanie and I found out that there were meetings going on behind our backs to hire new people and change the show. When Melanie found out they were basically completely rewriting the script, she walked off the show, and that changed everything for me about the whole production. We wanted to take it out of the club and move it to a theater, but we didn't envision it as a Broadway book musical. And Tommy Tune totally got that. He didn't want to change anything. He said to us, "You guys created your own genre with this," because it really was somewhere between a concert and a theater piece. But Liz and Nelle wanted to make it into a legitimate book musical, even though Melanie kept telling them it wasn't that kind of thing. It was like Liz and Nelle were trying to put a square peg in a round hole.

I would be coming back to the club from the production meetings, and I'd be very upset. It was taking a toll on me, and Stanley could see it. One day he just looked at me and said, "This is really upsetting you. Is it worth it? Maybe we could get somebody to buy our rights." As it happened, Francine Lefrak, who was one of the other producers who had invested, was game to buy our rights. Stanley said, "Look, it ain't ever going to be what you guys created, and it's tearing you apart. If we sell, at least we can walk away and make some money, because we've spent a lot of money on it. So at least we can not only maybe break even, we can make some money on it." One of my favorite things that he did happened when we went to Francine's lawyer when we sold our interest in the show. He said, straight-faced, "Counselor, I just want to go on record, saying that I think your client is paying an awful lot of money for a piece of shit. Now where do I sign?" We had something quite beautiful, but it was gone. So we sold our rights.

There was a point where I thought I was going to call Jimmy and ask him not to do it. And I thought long and hard, and I didn't think it was fair to him because I thought this could be a shot for him, so I just backed off. I just did not think it would be fair to him. And I didn't want to hurt him. I didn't feel it was right. I was hurting for Ula. I cared about Ula a lot. It is very hard to say just how much this thing meant to me, and just how much the people in it meant to me. And then Melanie and I were at arm's length because she was very hurt. She left the show, and not only that, she lost her best friend because Ellie kept listening to everyone from the outside. Melanie understood this project better than anyone who came to the table, because she understood the woman. Nobody understood how to put this together and breathe life into it more than she did. And, look, Ellie was a victim, too. She wasn't strong enough to say, "I'll stay with the ones who brought me." Melanie and I, mostly Melanie, did everything we could to keep Ellie from getting in her own way. But she just wanted Broadway so badly she let too many other people get into her head.

In taking Leader of the Pack *to Broadway, McCann, Nugent, and director Peters completely revamped the show. Of the cast from* The Bottom Line *performances, the only ones to move uptown with the show were Darlene Love (who became the narrator as well as chief vocalist), Annie Golden, and in small parts, backup vocalist Pattie Darcy and Peter Neptune, who had played Jeff Barry at The Bottom Line. Ula Hedwig was replaced by Dinah Manoff to play Greenwich as a young woman, and Patrick Cassidy, younger brother of David and Shaun, was chosen to play Barry. Even Paul Shaffer, who had nimbly balanced his duties on the Letterman show and his work on* Leader, *was also replaced.*

PAUL SHAFFER: I was going to be in it, but I needed, during the rehearsals, some time off. I said, "Look, I've just got to have those two hours off from the rehearsal in the afternoons to go and tape the Letterman show." And Michael Peters said, "No, it won't work. You have to be at all the rehearsals." I wasn't able to do it for that one reason. I'd done all the Bottom Line shows without a problem, but Peters wouldn't let me miss rehearsals. He wouldn't budge, and that was that.

On April 8, 1985, after nearly a year of changes, revisions, and over fifty preview performances, Leader of the Pack *finally debuted on Broadway. It received uniformly negative reviews from the critics, most notably from* The New York Times' *Frank*

Rich. To say Rich's takedown was scathing would be a gross understatement; on virtually all levels, Rich eviscerated the production.

"Of all the Broadway musicals that had come along this season," Rich wrote, "this show does lead the pack in such key areas as incoherence (total), vulgarity (boundless), and decibel level (stratospheric, with piercing electronic feedback) . . . What makes Leader of the Pack *a particularly impressive fiasco, however, is that it, unlike its competitors, didn't have the advantage of starting off with a humdrum score. There are some fun songs in this show, and one can only wonder at the ingenuity and strenuous effort required to stamp the life out of nearly all of them . . . They're delivered by mostly charmless performers whose primary responsibility is to model an extravagant assortment of hideous costumes and grotesquely campy beehive wigs. . . A lengthy prom sequence is so sparsely decorated that the prom might well be taking place in a reform school. In the title song, motorcycles are represented by prancing chorus men holding bicycle handlebars—and even so, they soon disappear into a smoke effect that leaves the closest spectators gasping for breath. . . Unlike the dancing, the script at least has the good grace to call it quits twenty minutes before the show does—with an abrupt, post-divorce nervous breakdown for a heroine who had previously seemed to possess a nervous system somewhat less developed than that of a Barbie doll."

ALLAN PEPPER: Liz and Nelle invited us to the opening, but I could not go to see it. It would have been too painful. Eileen went with Melanie, and they came back and said that it was pretty terrible.

Mintz went a second time as the show was floundering, and only because an interested party insisted. By the time Leader of the Pack *was previewing on Broadway, Pepper and Mintz were working on a new musical featuring the music of Greenwich's fellow songwriters Barry Mann and Cynthia Weil.*

MELANIE MINTZ: Cynthia came to New York and said, "Mel, I want to see *Leader*." I didn't want to see it, but she said, "You are taking me to see *Leader*." I called Liz McCann, the producer whom I sued and hated, and I called her office, and she gave us fifth-row seats. It was excruciating for me to sit through. But the interesting thing was it bore no resemblance to our show. There was only one similarity between the Broadway show and the Bottom Line Show, and it was the title. I'm not kidding. All the music arrangements were entirely different. They became muzak, which is what I fought against in the original. So they were no longer like the records. They were these cutesy versions. They wrote a book that was horrible, including Ellie's nervous breakdown onstage, which I would not put in the play before I walked off of it.

RILEY: Allan and Stanley's assistant Christie and I were told we could see *Leader* anytime we wanted. So we put it off because we heard bad things. We were upset that they said Ula was not stage-worthy. She had been the soul of the show, and she was great. She's such a striking figure—a tall, mysterious, loud presence. Finally, when we heard it was going to close, Christie and I went. The first song was "Be My Baby," and instead of having three women come onstage and belt it out, they had the three women with horrible wigs enter dressed, actually dressed, as forty-five records. That was the first thing we saw. And we cried. The two of us actually broke into tears. It was such a degradation of Allan's creation. The next day, Allan asked, and I just said it was horrible. I didn't even want to give him any details.

DARLENE LOVE: I can't tell you all the heartache that I went through on Broadway doing that show. It was horrible. They made my life miserable. I said I'd never do another Broadway show. That's how miserable I was from working with Mr. Peters and all the crazy people. I thought, "If this is Broadway, y'all got this crap. This is not how I want my career to go." If you watched *The David Letterman Show* while we were down at The Bottom Line, almost every night David would say to Paul, "Hey, are you still doing that show down there?" And then Dave would say, "Are you sure they don't have a part for me?" And Paul would say, "No, Dave, it's not your kind of show." I thought that was fantastic, that we were getting all this free advertisement. So how can you tell Paul Shaffer he has to quit his daytime job to do the show? Are you kidding me? Did they not understand the advertising we could have been getting for a Broadway show, for free, every night?

Between the bad reviews and lack of audience interest, the Broadway version of Leader of the Pack *closed after less than four months at the Ambassador Theater. While he had a successful career as a choreographer and director on television, Michael Peters, once dubbed the "Balanchine of MTV," never directed another Broadway show.*

MELANIE MINTZ: Liz and Nelle were sued by the investors who came down to The Bottom Line and said "I'm in" and gave them checks. *[The group included Clive Davis.]* The suit said that "That's not the show we invested in; it's a completely different show." And while they didn't win, they were correct. Their money was taken. Except on Broadway, that's the way you do things.

In reporting on Leader's demise, the Times *critic Rich couldn't help noting that "The show's producers engaged each other in litigation that entertained Broadway for far longer than their show had."*

BOBBY JAY: Liz McCann and Nelle Nugent, their names will live in infamy. As it turned out, they had infamy. But it'll remain, as long as I live, one of my happiest, happiest experiences as a performer. Doing that show, I mean, it was grueling. We were tired, but once the overture kicked in, you got a new life—every night. And isn't that what it's all about?

Ula Hedwig emerged from the Leader experience maintaining her status as an A-list background vocalist. Over the years, she has toured and graced stages with stars ranging from Paul Simon and Peter Allen to Robert Plant and Donald Fagen's Rock and Soul Revue. A frequent presence on the Letterman show, where she worked with old friend Shaffer, she sang background over the years for the likes of B. B. King, Tom Jones, Aaron Neville, and Rosanne Cash. And she was a go-to vocalist for numerous Bottom Line productions over the years.

Alongside his stint in Leader at The Bottom Line, Bobby Jay continued his career as one of the metropolitan area's most popular radio DJs with long stints at both r&b station WWRL (1970–1985) and New York's reigning oldies station, WCBS-FM (from 1985 to 2005). In addition to his work with his first vocal group, the Laddins, Jay spent decades serving as the bass singer in numerous New York-centric vocal groups—most notably with various incarnations of his beloved teen band, the Teenagers.

If there was one true silver lining to the entire Leader of the Pack *saga, it was the effect that Darlene Love's nightly show-stopping performances in the show, both at The Bottom Line and on Broadway, had on her then fledgling solo career. Love, who was such a force of nature that in 1963 she sang lead on so many national hit records (both under her own name and, at times, anonymously) that she was, literally, competing with herself on the AM charts, at last began to be rightfully recognized for her prodigious talents. A decade after Leader, she triumphantly returned to The Bottom Line for what turned into a year-and-a-half near-weekly residency with the Melanie Mintz-scripted "Portrait of a Singer" whose popularity led to a cover story in* The New York Times Sunday Magazine. *She also became known for her post-Leader stage and screen work—most notably her recurring role as Danny Glover's wife in all four Lethal Weapon movies. And then, of course, there were her close-to-thirty-years annual yuletide appearances on the Letterman show performing Greenwich's "Christmas (Baby, Please Come Home)."*

PAUL SHAFFER: I was doing the *Leader* show and doing Letterman at the same time, and the show was just a killer. The people stood up and screamed every night, and I was having a great time, and I was talking it up every day at the Letterman show, and Dave said, "I'd love to come down." So I arranged for it, and he just fell over. It was so great, and he especially reacted to Darlene. He loved her "Christmas (Baby, Please Come Home)," which was interesting because David constitutionally hated holiday and novelty songs. It's part of his DNA. Every Halloween, all I wanted to do was play "Monster Mash," but he hated it. His tastes were a little bit divergent from mine, but the one place where we agreed was, "Christmas (Baby, Please Come Home)." I loved it. He loved it. He had Darlene come on that year, and the first time she did it was just with the four-piece band that I had at the time, the four of us playing for her and singing the backgrounds ourselves. And then David said, "Let's have her again," and that became again and again, and it turned into a real holiday tradition for us. And the band became bigger and bigger every year. I would listen to the original recording and hear new things, and I said, "Well, we've got to do that. I think there's an extra trombone. Let's get an extra trombone." So every year we got closer to the actual record, and we did it all different ways, even with big choirs—one time with the Naval Choir from Annapolis. And Darlene got better and better every year. I recently looked up her first appearance with just the four of us, and I swear it was just as good. When she opens her mouth, she doesn't need any background. She rocked it with the four of us, the same as she did when we had twenty-one pieces behind her. We taped a version [in 2023] for Dave's YouTube channel, just very informally. We did it just with me on piano and her singers. And again, it just took us all back—and she just rocked the house.

Liz McCann and Nelle Nugent dissolved their partnership in the latter part of the 1980s. Ultimately producing some sixty theatrical shows, McCann would take home four more Tony Awards over the course of the rest of her long career, as well as winning several Emmy Awards for producing the annual Tony Awards ceremony for television in the early 2000s. Meanwhile, Nugent went on to co-found the East Coast chapter of the Producers Guild of America in 2001. Significantly, neither of their bios tends to mention Leader of the Pack.

ALLAN PEPPER: In the end of the whole *Leader* affair, the best analysis came from Stanley. He said to me, "You know, Allan, Liz and Nelle had a hundred decisions to make. The law of averages are that if you make a hundred decisions, you get 50 percent right and 50 percent wrong. They got a 100 percent wrong."

12 FAST FOLKS

FROM THE COOL, COOL, COOL TO THE HOT, HOT, HOT

The late 1970s and early '80s gave rise to a new generation of singer-songwriters arriving on the scene in New York. While they were primarily acoustic guitar-toting musicians, their sensibilities as artists tended toward modernism rather than tradition, and in so doing, they represented a fresh outlook on the always dubiously labeled genre known as "folk." With the music industry—and in particular the recording industry—increasingly running with the marketplace demands imposed on it by the unavoidable influence of MTV and the music videos it began broadcasting 24/7 in the summer of 1981, these young artists seemed less like fish out of water than outright endangered species. Within their own circles, however, a work ethic borne of respect for the craft of songwriting kept them afloat, at least creatively if not commercially, with downtown coffeehouses comprising their almost completely closed circuit for performing.

A key to their survival during this time was the loose-knit Fast Folk cooperative founded by downtown denizen Jack Hardy. A composer and performer himself, Hardy presided over weekly songwriting workshops at his rent-controlled West Houston Street apartment where budding young artists were required to keep presenting new and often fragmentary in-progress works for others to listen and respond to (hence the name "fast" folk). Hardy also guided lo-fi recording sessions where songwriters could record their material, which was then released together as albums accompanying the co-op's bulletin board-styled magazine. As one of mentor Hardy's charges, Jeff Gold, later put it, "Jack didn't give a hoot about the music business, just about the business of writing a great song."

Allan Pepper became aware of Jack Hardy and the Fast Folk crowd primarily through singer-songwriter Christine Lavin. Known for such gentle-humored tunes as "Sensitive New Age Guys" and "Prisoner of Their Own Hairdos," Peekskill native Lavin began her long career in the mid 1970s in Saratoga Springs, New York, at the fabled Caffe Lena, where she began to write songs while working as the club's bread baker and waitress.

CHRISTINE LAVIN: In 1975, I drove the club's owner, Lena Spencer, up to Cape Cod to see Bob Dylan's Rolling Thunder revue—Dylan had famously played for Lena right when he started in 1961—and I wrote a song about Ramblin' Jack Elliott, who was on early in the show. It seemed like he had to go early in the show because he sounds so much like Bob Dylan, or rather that Bob Dylan sounds like him. So I wrote this song, though I never said his name in the song, and it's kind of vague what it's about, but I can tell people now because it's such a long time ago. So I wrote that song, and one night Dave Van Ronk showed up on the way back from Montreal with his wife, Terri Thal, and he was sitting at the executive bar downstairs from the cafe and Lena asked me to play it for him. It was a noisy bar with the TV on and everything, and I played the song, and Van Ronk closed his eyes in the middle of it, and I thought, "Oh, great. I've put him to sleep." But at the end he opened his eyes, and he said, "You should come to New York." I said, "Oh, I will, but I think I have to learn how to play guitar better." And he said, "That's ok, I'm a teacher." So a week later I moved to New York. I had an old college roommate who had an empty room and free rent for three weeks, and I signed up as a temp, and I worked during the day for eight years before I was able to quit it all and just start doing music. I got to know Jack Hardy and I was appearing in Fast Folk shows and also working as a volunteer helping produce the Fast Folk recordings and getting them mastered.

Before I knew Allan, I was opening a lot of shows at the Bitter End. Owner Paul Colby was a real hothead. He was always screaming and yelling. One time I opened for comedian Henny Youngman, and he actually got a gig that he could do in between the two shows if he could go on first. He was on the phone in the dressing room, and he turned to me and said, "Hey honey, do you mind if I open for you tonight because I'm going to do my stockbroker's birthday party?" I thought he was kidding, but I said ok. So he went out on stage first, and Paul came backstage screaming and yelling, and the fur was flying; he was so angry.

What happened to me was that after a while playing there, Paul told me he wanted to be my manager, and he threatened me. It was in his office on the second floor, and he started running around his desk saying, "Where's my gun? Where's my gun? If you don't sign with me, I'm going to shoot myself." I didn't know what to do, so I ran down the stairs and started running toward Sixth Avenue without stopping. Paul was behind me, and I don't know if he was actually waving a gun because there was no way I was going to find out, and I could just hear him screaming, "Slow down! I want to talk to you." I jumped into a cab, got on the bottom of the floor of the cab and said, "Please take me to the Upper West Side," where I was living. And I never set foot in The Bitter End again until many, many years later. And I think I would have never gone to The Bottom Line looking for work if that hadn't happened.

ALLAN PEPPER: You can't do what I did for so long without being a fan. In booking the club, there was a part of me that needed to be excited by what we were presenting and therefore what I was booking. It's the excitement of sharing the aspect of discovery with an audience that gives me joy in what I do. So, in the mid-'80s I found myself with a real dilemma. I was bored.

A lot of the music released by the major record companies being played on the radio no longer sounded fresh to me. It was no longer as eclectic and exciting as it had been in the 1970s. It was predictable. I wanted more.

Now there were a handful of people I always trusted for musical recommendations. Eileen's ears were number one on that list, but there were others as well, like disc jockeys Vin Scelsa, Pete Fornatale, and Meg Griffin. Their musical tastes always appealed to me, as did their radio shows on WNEW-FM and later on KROCK. And whenever someone like Christine Lavin told me about someone, I always made time to listen to them. It was Christine who first told me about Suzanne Vega, Shawn Colvin, and Dar Williams. So, in late '83, when Christine came and told me about a scene at places in the neighborhood like Folk City, Speakeasy, and the Cornelia Street Café, and about Jack Hardy, I took it very seriously.

Christine told me that Jack had an idea of doing a benefit concert for the magazine, which would be recorded and then included in a future copy of Fast Folk, and he believed a concert would a great opportunity to raise some money as well as a vehicle to recruit new subscribers. Christine thought The Bottom Line would be the ideal place for it and suggested that Jack and I have a meeting. As a result, in late January 1984, with Jack and Christine co-hosting, we presented the live version of The Fast Folk Magazine at The Bottom Line, with mini sets by Jack and Christine, along with Lucy Kaplansky, Frank Christian, Rod MacDonald, and David Massengill. I didn't have any high expectations of doing any real business, but I loved the notion of what Jack was trying to do and thought it should be supported. What happened next amazed me: We presented a bill with a lot of artists nobody ever heard of, but we did a little more than half a house on the first show and almost half a house on the second one. And then a year later when we did a second Fast Folk show, with Christine and Jack and a new round of artists that included Suzanne Vega, John Gorka, and Shawn Colvin, we did even better business.

Something was happening and yet the record industry at that time wasn't interested. If you identified yourself as a folk artist, trying to get a major record company to sign you was the kiss of death. And as I said before, mainstream radio was changing, and not for the good. Stations like WNEW that had offered a diversity of different types of music, everything from Billie Holiday to Phil Ochs to Led Zeppelin, sometimes back-to-back, were now being programmed by high-priced consultants creating playlists that tended to mirror MTV, in pursuit of a younger audience and higher ratings. And the collateral damage was that singer-songwriter folk artists no longer had a home at most mainstream radio. Stations that used to play singer-songwriters as part of what they did had now kind of abandoned these people. But Fast Folk showed me there was an audience for what Jack was doing. The Fast Folk artists were finding airplay with either self-produced albums or tapes that were starting to get played around the country on radio stations with more open formats, like college stations, public radio stations, and specialty shows on mainstream radio like Vin Scelsa's "Idiot's Delight" or Pete Fornatale's "Mixed Bag." Both Vin and Pete had their own devoted following who took them very seriously, especially Vin, who was considered a tastemaker by a lot of people in the music business who listened to his show, and he started to play many of the artists that were emerging from Fast Folk. At the same time, I began to book many of them as opening acts for national recording acts in an attempt to increase their profile nationally. So once again I felt inspired, and Eileen and I started listening to college radio. All in all, I think we helped legitimize these new singer-songwriters by putting them on our stage.

RON OLESKO (Radio host, WFDU): During the 1980s, there was a new folk revival happening. For me personally, it gave me the spark to start doing a folk radio show, which I continue to host to this day—and I hold The Bottom Line responsible! Singer-songwriters were once again populating the Village, but it wasn't nearly as popular as it was a few decades before. Jack Hardy, Richard Meyer, and the Fast Folk artists put on shows at Speakeasy, which was actually the back room of a falafel restaurant on MacDougal Street, a few blocks away from The Bottom Line, but miles away in terms of recognition and audience awareness. While it probably would have been easy to look at the Fast Folk/Speakeasy crowd as competition, Allan recognized what was blossoming and embraced many of the artists. While people like Shawn Colvin and Suzanne Vega surely benefited from the exposure of the Bottom Line shows, it also was important for the careers of many other singer-songwriters who might not have been fortunate enough to be given a record label contract, but it helped establish them and grow an audience for their music, and many of them are still performing and creating to this day. I credit The Bottom Line as a key part of their career development and for helping to perpetuate the folk scene.

I was also privileged to see a number of artists who blazed trails during the '60s Folk Revival return to a Village stage at The Bottom Line. I remember a weekend when Mimi Farina led a group of artists from the 1960s in a sort of reunion show, including names like Odetta and Ed McCurdy, many of whom got their career start at the old Folk City which was located just around the corner from The Bottom Line before they moved in 1970. The Bottom Line was instrumental in keeping the folk traditions of the Village alive and perpetuating new artists who carry on to this day.

One of the young singer-songwriters who, in many ways came to represent the Fast Folk collective as she achieved notable critical and commercial success in the mid-to-late '80s, was New Yorker Suzanne Vega. As evidenced by such keenly crafted songs as "Small Blue Thing," "Marlene on the Wall," "Tom's Diner," as well as her surprising (given the subject matter of child abuse) 1987 hit "Luka," Vega demonstrated an almost journalistic eye for character detail and a distinctive knack for quick-cutting, evocative imagery. Those qualities as a songwriter, coupled with her clear-voiced, straightforward singing style, helped make her not only a popular but also a quietly influential figure on New York's alternative music scene of the era.

SUZANNE VEGA: The first time I heard about The Bottom Line, I guess, was probably in the 1970s. I was a student at the High School of the Performing Arts, and I was a dance major, but I had also written all these songs on the side, and I had just started. I made friends with one of the musicians who used to play for the classes; he was a songwriter who just played for the classes for money. One day we got into a long discussion, and he gave me this advice, which was not to go into the music business because he said the music business was horrible. And anyway, he said, they're running out of vinyl. So that was in 1976. His advice to me was to pick up *The Village Voice* and look for coffee houses and go just play in coffeehouses because, he said, those people just want to be pleased. And then he also gave me advice about the local venues down in the Village. He told me to try and get a gig at The Bitter End. He said, "Try going there, and then you can work your way up after that. You should try and get a gig at The Bitter End, and once you've got that under your belt, you go to Folk City. And if you're really good, you get to play The Bottom Line."

I was sixteen then, and so I got stuck for two years trying to get a gig at The Bitter End. I would go down there and get rejected, and I had this hierarchy in my mind: How could I get a gig at Folk City if I couldn't even get a gig at The Bitter End? So finally, after two years, I gave up on The Bitter End, and I went to Folk City—and I was embraced immediately. Everyone was, "Wow, you're great. You have all these great songs."

The Cornelia Street Cafe didn't fit into the hierarchy as such a venue. It was more like a coffee shop that was a genuine cafe, and we would meet there for the songwriters exchange. So, as a venue, it was more like where a person would go on Monday nights, and you would sing a new song, and Jack Hardy was running the Songwriters Exchange out of his place on Houston Street back then. But once they did open the venue at Cornelia Street downstairs, it became a really beloved place that I returned to until the actual day it closed [in January 2019].

Fast Folk was supportive, and it was also competitive in the best of ways. Jack would be kind and supportive; he could also rip you to shreds if he felt like it. But I have to say, I loved being part of it. I loved the people I met and the conversations we had, the discussions about songwriting and poetry and politics and all of that. I really felt as though I found my crowd. The idea of being seen as a folk singer didn't matter to me one bit because I was born in 1959, so in the '60s I was a baby. I had very young parents, but they never went to the Village, or if they did, they didn't take us. We lived in East Harlem and the Upper West Side. So the idea that we were trying to recreate from the '60s, that was not exciting to me. This idea that we could take folk music and add other elements to it, like punk or new wave, the idea of moving folk music along and making it modern, that was more exciting to me than, say, continuing anything that had been before. And that must've been cool for the people back then, and it must've been fun. I know my youngest brother became sort of infatuated with the Beats and that whole era, and that was a very vibrant scene down in the Village in the '50s and '60s.

By the time I got to The Bottom Line, I guess it was probably 1984, and I had done a few of the *Fast Folk* magazine shows. So finally getting there, that I felt was big time.

Suzanne Vega made her Bottom Line debut in June of 1984 opening for the iconic British folksinger Ralph McTell (of "Streets of London" fame), and then appeared again two months later on a Meg Griffin-hosted edition of the Local Heroes series on a bill with the Fleshtones and Richard Hell and The Voidoids. Here, her smart, self-aware, folk-adjacent style worked well complementing Hell's edgy, literate punk rock and Peter Zeremba's garage-stomping Fleshtones.

SUZANNE VEGA: I don't remember the Ralph McTell show, but the one I really do remember is the Local Heroes one because my hair was cut really short back then. I think I performed in this huge oversized, olive-colored T-shirt sort of dress. I mean, I must've looked really weird, but I got a good response, and I still meet people who saw me at that show, and it was, somehow, a memorable occasion.

Another Fast Folk-associated songwriter who by the end of the 1980s would make their mark was pianist Julie Gold, best known for penning the anthemic international hit, "From a Distance." The Bottom Line holds special meaning for Gold for a variety of reasons.

JULIE GOLD: My first manager was Milt Kramer, who also managed Loudon Wainwright for a number of years. He called me one time and I was out, and he said, "Where were you when I tried to call?" I told him I was swimming. "Where do you swim?" he asked. I said, "I swim at the Y." "Oh," he says, "Well, you're going to have your own pool." When he first handed me his business card, he said to call him collect, so I called him collect from Philadelphia where I lived then, and a woman answered and said, "Well, this is an answering service and we're unable to accept collect calls." Welcome to the music business.

But Milt got me my first gig at The Bottom Line. I had not been there before because I didn't live in New York yet. The first time I played there, in 1979, I opened for Tom Rush, and Milt said he was going to invite a whole bunch of industry bigwigs, and I would get signed to a major record deal. That was the goal. And everyone was there—Walter Yetnikoff, Tommy Mottola, probably Clive Davis—anyone you could name that was really a player in those days came. When I got to the club in the late afternoon, there was a big bouquet of flowers sitting on the bar, and I thought, "Oh look, everything's going my way. I have a manager, I have a job, I have an apartment, I have a car—and here are flowers for me." So I nonchalantly tear the envelope the flowers came with open. I can't wait to see what it says. And it says, "Dear Tom Rush: I love your music." I put it back together as best I could. And within a month, I lost my job, my car, my manager, my gig, everything. That's show biz.

In 1985, Gold wrote the peace-seeking anthem, "From a Distance," which was first recorded by Texas singer-songwriter Nanci Griffith in 1987. It would go on to become a huge hit for Bette Midler in 1990, leading to composer Gold winning that year's Grammy for Song of the Year, and over the years "From a Distance" has been recorded by scores of other artists ranging from Judy Collins and Sinead O'Connor to Donna Summer and Kathie Lee Gifford. Here, Christine Lavin again played a significant role behind the scenes, leading to the song's recognition and success.

JULIE GOLD: I sent my demo of "From a Distance" to many, many people, and it was always rejected. Now Christine Lavin and I had been friends since the 1970s when I was first coming up to New York from Philly to do Fast Folk songwriting workshops. So I brought her ten cassettes that she offered to send out to people for me, and within two weeks, a guy named Dick Pleasant in Boston played it, and Vin Scelsa played it on K-Rock. And then I got this phone call: "Hey Julie, my name is Nanci Griffith. Christine Lavin sent me your song 'From a Distance,' and I think it's the most beautiful song I've ever heard, and I'm making a record for MCA called *Lone Star State of Mind*, and I'd like to put it on that record." And that's how it started. When the album came out, I was a secretary at HBO, and everybody knew not to send me anything big at my house on West Fourth Street because the mailbox was like six inches by eight inches. So the record came to me at HBO and I left it on my desk. Now all my bosses had turntables in their offices, and they respected me. They knew what I was doing in my dreams. So I took the album out. There was my name on it, which was really the dream. I got my dream. So we put the record on one of my boss's turntables. I shed tears, and then I went back to my desk, and that is really true. And it was the beginning of this miracle, and it became this bond between me and Nanci, and we had a great relationship. I owe her so much. She was like the big top coming to town, man. Whenever she came here, she'd play every venue in New York and either shouted out to me in the audience or brought me up to perform the song with her. When she sang it for the first time at The Bottom Line in March of 1987, she gave a shout out to me, and Bill Murray was in the audience and after the show I was introduced to him backstage and he said, "Keep writing those great songs!" And the next time Nanci played the club, she sang it again, and as I looked around the audience, I saw people singing along with it, and I knew my life had changed forever. She presented me with a plaque that night, and I walked with it back up Fourth Street to my apartment. It was really a life-changing moment.

Christine was also involved with Bette Midler recording the song. She sent it to critic Stephen Holden from *The New York Times*, and Marc Shaiman, who was working as Midler's musical director, had gotten in touch with Stephen looking for songs for her to record. Holden asked if he'd heard "From a Distance," which he hadn't, so Stephen sent my original demo to him, and then Bette recorded it and it became a huge hit, and I won a Grammy for it. Oh, and how many record companies had I pitched it to? At that time, they only wanted blonde waifs. It was after Suzanne [Vega]'s success, and they only wanted blonde waifs with guitars. No pianos. I saw Suzanne in all the bars and played Folk City with her, and at all those clubs, I had to rely on their house pianos, and they were all shitty. I still tell the story about the Folk City owner, Mike Porco. I'd say to him, "Mike, can't you do anything about the piano?" And he'd say, "What's the matter? We just painted it."

* * *

Between her first Bottom Line performance in the fall of 1981 and her last in December of 2003, Christine Lavin appeared at the club well over fifty times, on shows ranging from numerous solo sets to her many turns cohosting annual Fast Folk shows and anchoring the recurring series of performances by her side group, Four Bitchin' Babes, of which Gold was a semi-regular.

CHRISTINE LAVIN: Originally, it was going to be Megan McDonough, Sally Fingeret, and me, and we talked to Allan about playing his room, and he said, "Christine, you should add a fourth person, and give it a real snappy title." He always liked those snappy titles. So Sally came up with "Buy Me, Bring Me, Take Me, Don't Mess My Hair." Which means nothing except that. It's just sort of fun, and it's got a good alliteration, as they say. And I couldn't believe it when the Babes were celebrating their thirtieth anniversary a few years ago, because it all came about because Allan Pepper said, "If you have four names and a snappy title, I will book it. And that will open up doors for you around the country." And he was right. He always knew what he was doing, and it was a really great thing because we thought it would just be the three of us, and then Patty Larkin came on board, and she was such a great guitar player.

Ever the prankster, Christine Lavin also still holds memories of a November 1985 Bottom Line show in which she opened for Donovan—though not precisely because of the concert itself.

CHRISTINE LAVIN: The night before I was scheduled to open for Donovan at The Bottom Line, I did two shows on my own at Club Passim in Cambridge, Massachusetts. The next day, I flew the shuttle from Boston to New York, and by coincidence, Donovan was on the same plane. Now, in real life I am shy, so it took about half the flight to get my courage up to the point where I felt bold enough to introduce myself. I made my way up to his seat, stuck out my hand, and said, "Excuse me, are you Donovan?" He took my hand, smiled, and said, "Yes, I am." So I said, "Hi, I'm your opening act tonight." He looked confused. "You're my opening act? What are you doing up here?" Now, to this day I don't know why I said what I said, but it went something like this: "Oh, it's a Bottom Line tradition that when you open for one of your musical heroes, you find out what city they're performing in the night before, you go to that city, then the day of the concert you go to the airport to see what flight they buy a ticket for, then you buy a ticket for the same flight, wait until you're exactly midway between the two cities, then introduce yourself and shake their hand just to make sure his concert goes really well that night." Donovan's eyes grew wider and wider as I spoke, and when I finished, he said, "You've got to be kidding, right?" And I whispered, "Yes, I am. But you are going to put on a phenomenal show tonight." And he did, twice!

* * *

Had he first emerged in the late 1970s instead of the latter part of the previous decade, it's likely that singer-songwriter Loudon Wainwright would have fallen in with the artists of the Fast Folk collective. A masterful, open-book-living storyteller and thoroughly idiosyncratic live performer, the suburban New York-raised Wainwright enjoyed—though perhaps "survived" might be the better word—his lone hit single, 1973s novelty number, "Dead Skunk," to fashion a windingly varied and successful career, both as a tunesmith whose works have been covered by artists ranging from Johnny Cash to Mose Allison, as well as an occasional actor, in films directed by the likes of Martin Scorsese, Tim Burton, and Judd Apotow, and on Broadway (Pump Boys and Dinettes).

Wainwright's connections to Allan Pepper and Stanley Snadowsky preceded The Bottom Line, and as both a performer and a patron, he became one of the club's most dependable "regulars," from its earliest days right through to its final ones.

LOUDON WAINWRIGHT: I first met Allan and Stanley [in the early 1970s] when they were booking Gerde's Folk City, and they wanted me to play there, but my manager at the time, Milt Kramer, advised against it. After they opened The Bottom Line and that became the kind of happening new venue, then Milt gave us the green light to work together. But they had pursued me; I guess that might be the proper word, though I don't know why they did. I remember the first show they had at the club, with Dr. John, in 1974, and I was in that audience with Kate McGarrigle, who I was then married to. I made a record in 1975 called *Unrequited* for Columbia Records, and half of it's live, and that was recorded at The Bottom Line, and I think that might've been the first live album that was recorded at the club. I had two records prior to that I'd made for the label: The first had the single "Dead Skunk," and then I made another record in Nashville in five days, which was not successful. So *Unrequited* was kind of my last shot with Columbia. And I just was kind of in a general career confusion. I'd been fiddling around with rock and roll bands, and I just guess Milt and I thought that maybe we should just record a show at The Bottom Line because for me, being a live performer, it could be argued that my songs are best presented in a live setting. So I think you make decisions as you go along, and we got a truck in there, probably from The Record Plant or something like that, some big studio, and recorded it, and certainly used it, and I think it made for an interesting record.

We were just a group of young, mostly male, although we had Kate and Anna who were there early on, and the Roches were coming soon. There were just a bunch of young people who missed the big folk boom that had already happened in the Village with Van Ronk and Dylan and Phil Ochs and all that jazz. But this was kind of the second wave of that, I'd say. We were just full of beans, drinking too much, sleeping with each other, and running around having fun. And after The Bottom Line opened and we all started playing there, it was always fun being at the club. When you walked in, to the left, there was a long bar, and Allan and Stanley gave us the welcome to just drop by the club and hang out at the bar and to see whoever we wanted to see. I don't remember them ever asking to pay for walking into the room. The focus was on the music, and the sound system was good. I mean, they really worked to make that good, which is very important, and they got the best people. So it was a great place to play, and because New York was my hometown, I could just drop by and see whoever whenever I wanted, it was just always one of my favorite places. There were great nights there for me personally, not just my own shows, but seeing other people. And when the Roches were doing their Christmas shows there in the '90s, that was always a very big event, and for me specifically, it was a family affair.

Maybe the one night that I remember the most, though, or that comes to mind right away, is a night [October 4, 1986] when the Fairport Convention played there. Those guys are contemporaries of mine, and because I spent a lot of time in England in the '70s and early '80s, I know pretty much all those players—Simon Nichol and Dave Pegg and Dave Mattacks and Richard Thompson. I didn't know Richard when he played with the band, but I know all those guys. They were playing at The Bottom Line, and I had a night off, and I went down there and was excited about seeing the show and went back and said hello beforehand. Now that's a band that was famous for working. They were one of those bands that worked 250 nights a year. I mean, there was never a night off. They just were real workhorses. I should say at the outset of the story that they were tired and they were probably at the end of their tour or whatever it was, and probably desperate to get back home. So they were backstage, and there was some drinking going on, and Dave Pegg, who was acting as, I don't think they even had a manager, I think Dave was kind of the baseball player/manager of the group, and he wanted to negotiate with Allan. He wanted to film the show for a video, and Allan had some policies that he stuck to. I mean, you had the Hershey Kisses, the Oreos, and the apples in the dressing room. Allan did things the way he wanted to do them, and I think that's commendable—he didn't waffle around—but he had a policy about people filming shows. So he told Dave, "Hey, that's great, you can do that," but that he was going to need to get whatever it was, $250, $500, I don't know what the exact figure was. Dave and Allan argued about it, and Allan finally said, "No, you can't do it unless you agree to our policy." So anyway, I remember sitting at that table that's kind of directly in front of the stage where friends and guests would sit, and the group came out and took the stage, and they started to play, and all of a sudden Dave stopped the band, and I don't do accents, so I'm not going to try to do a Northern English accent, but he said basically, "Allan Pepper is a cheap"—I think he used the C word—"because he's a tight one." And he just went off on Allan. Now, Allan was in the back of the room by the front door standing with one of those big bouncers with the cowboy hats. And I was thinking, "Wow, this is intense." And even the other guys in the band were looking at Dave like, "Oh, Jesus, here he goes." So anyway, Dave threw out his insults, basically, and then they started to play another song, and they finished the second one, and Dave started in again. And I was thinking "This isn't good," and eventually it made me so uncomfortable because I was friends with Allan and I was friends with those guys that I just got up and left. I couldn't handle the tension in the room. I mean, Dave was clearly out of line and had had too much to drink. But anyway, the story finishes when I come back to The Bottom Line, I don't know, the next week or somehow I see Allan and I mention the Fairport show and I ask him how the other night ended up, and he said, "Oh, it was ok. They finished the show anyway." He didn't do what a lot of people would've done, which would've been "That asshole, man. Those guys are never coming back to this club." And, sure enough, they came back and played just six or so months later [July 3, 1987]. Allan did not take it personally, which I felt was remarkable considering that it was, I mean, I thought those bouncers were just going to come up and storm the stage. But that to me is an example of Allan's character. It's a quality about him that I really appreciate.

* * *

The legendary Bronx-born singer-songwriter Laura Nyro, composer of such classic '60s hits as "Eli's Coming," "Stone Soul Picnic," "And When I Die," and "Wedding Bell Blues," made her first appearance at The Bottom Line in mid-July of 1978, performing four sold-out solo sets over two nights. Julie Gold, who was in the audience for one of the shows, marveled at her songwriting idol Nyro, then eight months pregnant, as she sat at the club's piano wearing a strapless red gown, telling her rapt audience that "We're both really happy to be here." Precisely a decade later, after taking time off to raise her son, Nyro returned to live performing, and in July of 1988, she began her "comeback" tour (dedicated to the animal rights movement) at The Bottom Line, where she was accompanied by a small backing group put together by guitarist/arranger Jimmy Vivino.

JIMMY VIVINO: I'll say this, I think that Laura Nyro was the only artist, if you will, and with all due respect to everyone else I've ever worked with, who lived in an artist kind of space that John Coltrane or Nina Simone would live in. The real world, as we call it, was not her world. She was beyond it already. I know Jimmy Webb is a great songwriter, but he wrote to a means, to an end; it was like, someone's going to pick this up and record it. But Laura was like, she wrote stuff, and she just put it out. If someone picked it up, she had nothing to do with it. Didn't even care if anyone covered her. So all of a sudden, the money started coming in, and when I met her, she had a recording studio in her house, a giant estate in Connecticut. But she actually lived in a little Japanese hut up on the top of the hill on her property. She didn't even want the house. Her accountant told her, "Buy this." So she did.

I got to be really good friends with John Sebastian and then Felix Cavaliere at the same time, and they both knew Laura really well. Through them, I met engineer/producer Roscoe Herring, and he brought Laura to see me playing with Ben E. King at the Lone Star. She was there kind of incognito, looking a bit like the Unabomber, wearing shades and a hoodie. And then I got a call to go visit her. Roscoe brought me up to her place, and we didn't go in the big house. We went up the hill and there was this little Japanese hut, made from some sort of bamboo, with what looked like rice paper walls, and it had just a tatami mat with a brick that she put her head on. And one chair. So I sat in the chair, and she handed me a paper plate, and on the paper plate, written from the inside and spiraling out to the edges, was her idea for the band we were going to put together and the music we'd do. And she's got me spinning this plate, reading it, and my head's twisted—and she's got me. I don't care. I want to do this because I never been around anybody like this in my life. And her ideas were about harmony, and using equal amounts of men and women. Like the perfect band would have three women and three men, with she being one of the women. So me, and Dave Wofford, a bass player who I knew from Spyro Gyra, and drummer Frank Pagano, who I went to grammar school and high school with, would be the men. And then she and Diane Wilson, who was a great harmony singer, and Nydia Mata, a percussionist who was in Isis, would be the women. And I'll tell you, every night onstage with Laura Nyro had that kind of feeling, like, "We have nothing to prove here."

ALLAN PEPPER: Laura Nyro was shy, but determined. She knew exactly what she wanted. One year she was doing a Christmas show, and because she had these harmony singers in her show, she wanted them onstage physically in a configuration around her, and she thought she couldn't get it sitting with the piano sideways. So instead of playing the piano sideways, across the stage where everyone could see her, she wanted to point the nose of the piano toward the audience. Now this meant that the people sitting at the front tables, right under the stage, wouldn't be able to see her. And we'd sold out, so we knew people would wind up sitting there. When I told her that, she said, "All right. So how about I give those people who want to sit there a tape of one of my albums?" And I'm thinking to myself, "But they still won't see anything. They'll just hear her." But she said, "Why don't you try it, and we'll see what happens." So that afternoon, she gave me a couple of boxes of cassettes, and she said, "Let's make it their choice," and when people came in for the show, that's what we did. We said, "Look, you can sit anywhere you want, but those seats under the piano in the center, up close, you won't be able to see anything. You'll just be able to hear. But if you do decide to sit there, Laura wanted you to have this as a gift. It's your choice." And wouldn't you know it, those seats filled up faster than any other place. No one complained. And when she came back in before the show and I told her about it, she just smiled. That's where she wanted to be that night. It was where she felt the most comfortable, and it went off fine. She knew her audience, and they loved her and felt she could do no wrong.

Laura Nyro would continue to appear at The Bottom Line regularly over the next seven years, including a series of holiday-themed shows in the early 1990s. Her final Bottom Line performance, on Christmas Eve of 1994, would be among the final live concerts of her career. She retired from performing in early 1995, and after being diagnosed the following year with ovarian cancer (which had also taken her mother), she passed away in the spring of 1997 at age forty-nine. She'd written "And When I Die" when she was seventeen.

* **

In early November 1988, the Texas-based folk-rock group Edie Brickell and the New Bohemians came to New York to appear on Saturday Night Live to perform their breakout hit, "What I Am." Paul Simon attended the broadcast, and as he was standing next to the camera when the group performed, Simon caught Brickell's attention. (As she later recalled, "Even though I'd performed the song hundreds of times in clubs, he made me forget how the song went when I looked at him.") They met for the first time after the show and continued to talk at the SNL after party, and before the night was over, Simon asked if she was going to play in New York again, and Brickell told him she'd be back in the city soon to play The Bottom Line. Two weeks later, on November 18, Brickell appeared at The Bottom Line with Simon in attendance—and as he told Sirius Radio's Howard Stern many years later, the club played an important role in the beginning of their romance and eventual marriage.

PAUL SIMON: She was going to do two shows that night, and after the first set, I went backstage to her dressing room, but it was packed with record company people, so I just was able to say hi again. I said, "Well, you're so busy, I'll see you." So I left, and I was driving away and I thought, "Why am I driving away? I came down here to see her." So I called the club and got through to her and I said, "How much time do you have before the next set?" And she said, "Oh, maybe an hour or something." I said, "Well, I know a good Japanese restaurant right in the neighborhood. You want to go and have dinner?" So that was our first date. And things progressed pretty quickly. I went down to Texas to see her and she picked me up. It was hilarious. She had this 1972 mustard yellow pickup truck, and we went to the parking lot and she said, "Well, here it is." I said, "That's your car?" I mean, being from New York, I really was not into the world of pickups, which is a great world, but was foreign to me at the time. And I got in the pickup, and she drove us back to her place. And we've been together really ever since.

* * *

As previously noted, the first time that David Johansen played The Bottom Line was with the New York Dolls shortly after the club opened in early 1974 and, certainly from Allan Pepper's perspective, it was not a pleasant experience. Between a bomb scare that necessitated the club being cleared for nearly a half hour and the brand-new dressing room mirror that was smashed to pieces by bass player Arthur Kane's errant toss of a bottle aimed at lead singer David Johansen's head, Pepper vowed to never let the band, and in particular Johansen, back into the club again. Four years later though, well after the Dolls had broken up and Johansen was about to release his self-titled debut album on Blue Sky Records, Pepper agreed, mainly as a favor to his old friend, Blue Sky owner and now Johansen's manager, Steve Paul, to let David once again perform on his stage. Thankfully, those late July 1978 weekend shows, highlighted by frisky performances of such enduring new Johansen tunes as "Funky but Chic" and "Frenchette," went off without a hitch. And in the process, it brought the rousing Staten Islander rocker not only back into Pepper's good graces but helped begin a whole new chapter in their relationship. It blossomed into a full-fledged friendship in the mid-1980s, when Johansen first brought his pompadoured, lounge lizard alter ego Buster Poindexter to The Bottom Line stage for what soon *turned into a full-fledged star turn residency that would last for several years—especially after Johansen and his Banshees of Blue recorded their raucous reworking of Montserrat soca/calypso singer Alphonsus "Arrow" Cassell's 1982 tune "Hot Hot Hot" that became America's number one party song in 1987.*

DAVID JOHANSEN: I started doing the Buster thing at [the downtown east side club] Tramps because they were dark on Mondays. I'd been on the road and I was playing all these shows opening for Pat Benatar, and it was really like a fucking drudgery. But I used to listen to all these blues records and stuff like that on my Walkman, and Tramps was two blocks from where I lived, my neighborhood joint, so I decided I'm going to do this little show where I sing these songs. I did it for four Mondays, but by the fourth week, because I didn't want to have people still screaming at me to sing "Funky but Chic" or some other old song, we just put Buster Poindexter in the ad in the *Voice*. And it just kind of blew up.

In the beginning, there was, I don't know, maybe thirty people there. But by the fourth weekend, the place was overflowing, and we were doing two shows, and then I started playing Thursday, Friday, and Saturday at that place. And I was like, "Why am I killing myself on the road traveling in vans in the middle of nowhere? Maybe I could make a living just walking to work." There were no plans to make it into a career or anything. The band grew naturally; I would look up and there'd be a horn player up there, and I didn't even know who the guy was. But after a while, it was like, I dunno, fifteen or sixteen people in the band in the little room in the back, and eventually, the band got too big for the stage at Tramp's, and we got an album out and moved things over to The Bottom Line. And it was really fun. Of course, after a while, you start thinking, "This guy is taking over my life." But then you realize, "Oh, this is actually who I am now." So it got confusing. But eventually, after a lot of therapy and a stint at Betty Ford, I was pretty much back to normal.

Over the course of his many subsequent years performing at The Bottom Line, Johansen explored a variety of his musical interests, such as Latin dance music with his Spanish Rocket Ship band and pre-World War II American roots music with his Harry Smiths—all with the blessing, and encouragement, of Pepper.

DAVID JOHANSEN: I love Allan, and if it weren't for that club, I don't know what would've happened to me. I mean, good or bad. So I'm very kind of thankful that that nightclub was there and I had a chance to do all the things I like to do. I was working on this project with Brian, my band leader, and we were making this *Buster's Spanish Rocketship* record that we just did kind of at our leisure for about a year. So we had all the different kinds of Latin beats on that record. I have always liked Latin music. I liked a lot of salsa records and stuff, but I never really kind of understood where the one was, and so I just kind of devoted myself to educating myself about that kind of music. I called it Spanish Rocketship because I read somewhere that Spain took Timothy Leary's ashes and sent them into space. I didn't even know there was a Spanish rocketship. So we named it after that. But the reason I made that record is because we would play a lot of dances, parties and stuff, and every time we would do a boogaloo or something, everybody would get up and dance, and then we would do a jump blues thing, and people would mostly just sit and watch. So we decided, let's make a record of all these Latin beats that you can keep dancing to. And then it just kind of took over as an obsession, and for a while I didn't want to hear anything but Latin music.

But then when we finished that record, finally I started listening to other stuff, a lot of old blues records, and I realized, "Oh my God, there was a time before that I would think if I ever hear another blues record, it'll be too soon." But I started listening to all my old records—stuff I used to sing at the JCC before the Dolls even started—and they just sounded really new and different to me, I guess because I had cleared my head through the Latin music thing. I was approaching them from a new direction. So at that time, Allan called me and he said that he was having some anniversary at the club. I don't know how many years it had been. I think it was maybe the twentieth anniversary, and he said to me, "I want to do a group of shows with the people who are working here all the time, but not doing what they normally do," which I thought was a pretty interesting concept, and instantly I knew what I wanted to do. So he was kind of responsible for me putting the Harry Smith band together and putting that show together. We were just going to do one show, but then we got a good write-up, and we just started doing regular shows there, and then we started actually traveling around and we did a couple of records and stuff like that.

Allan had pretty much a guaranteed clientele: People knew that if he was doing something it would probably be good, so you could call him sight unseen with an idea and he'd go for it. I love that guy. He was a really good influence on me, and I appreciate the hell out of him. He's been there for me in all of my debaucheries.

13 FROM THE BLUEBIRD TO THE BIG APPLE

A BUNCH OF SONGWRITERS SITTIN' AROUND SINGING

A significant event at The Bottom Line that few people outside the club ever found out about happened in March 1989, on a "dark" night when there were no scheduled shows.

RILEY: The Bottom Line box office would be open, whether we had a show or not, seven days a week, and on dark nights someone would come in at 9 a.m. and work till 6, and someone would then start at 6 and work till 11 p.m. Whether we sold a single ticket or not, Allan wanted it ingrained in the public's mind that tickets were available seven days a week, so I was working one of those nights. Now because of New York City's fire codes, putting locks on doors in clubs is very complicated, so the doors leading from that little lobby where the box office was into the club could not have locks on them on either side. People could walk in and sometimes on a dark night, there's no one else inside, while you were selling a ticket and someone else might walk in behind them waiting in line and wander into the club. There was nothing to stop them. So that was something everyone was used to.

This one night, though, a tall figure in a long coat with a scarf around the bottom of his face just walked right in off the street, and without stopping in front of me as I was sitting in the box office, he walked in through the lobby doors and went toward the inside of the club. I got up out of the box office and turned around, and he was right in the doorway, and I said, "Out, out, out, you can't come in here." And then he pulled a sawed-off shotgun out of his coat and aimed it at me, I mean directly at me, and fired. And if I hadn't at the last minute kind of jumped to the side, the bullet would've gone straight into my heart and not my side. I was pretty loud telling him to get out. Which probably made it very easy for him to get pissed off if he was high or something. I was immediately freaked out, and he just walked into the box office, opened the drawer, took whatever cash was in there, which was like a couple hundred dollars, and left.

I was in sort of a semi-state of shock. After work, I was supposed to go from the box office over to hang out with this actor friend who was a bartender at the club and lived in the neighborhood. Somehow in my mind, I didn't want to call 911, and I called him and asked him to call 911, which was pretty freaky for him. Then I was in and out of consciousness, and before I knew it, there were firemen around me bringing me back. They carried me out of the office and put me on the floor in front of the cigarette machine, taking off my sneakers and loosening my shirt, and then they took me to St. Vincent's Hospital not too far away. The lucky thing was the head surgeon of thoracic surgery was on his way to a dinner party, and he just wanted to stop in and look in on someone who he operated on the night before, and he got pulled in and took the bullet out of me.

I was in the hospital about a week, which I was told was an extremely speedy recovery, but the psychological thing lasted quite a while. I was constantly trying to act like it never happened, anything I could do to erase it, including having all these people who cared about me, this nation of people at the club who cared about me, I made it clear that I felt like, "Let's never talk about this again," which was a mistake, even after I had a second surgery to finish the job. Then, three months after that, when I went back to the club to work, it was my way of saying nothing happened. The only difference was I wouldn't work on a dark night again. Allan and Stanley were caring and supportive. They just kept me on the payroll, and even after the final surgery, when I was in good physical shape to go back to work, they let me take off three more months with pay, and then that was it.

I worked for a year, and I knew something was still wrong inside me. And finally the girl I was dating, who worked at a big design firm in the West Village, convinced me to leave the club and come and work in her firm, which I did. And it ended up being a good gig for several years. While I was there, my father convinced me to go to therapy, trauma therapy. And it was there that I found out that the big thing that was hanging deep inside of me and confusing me was that someone I never met in my life, never did anything wrong to, actually tried to kill me. So that came out during sessions and then it became very obvious that I was finally on the way to healing. And one more thing that came out of the trauma was I was stabbed once during a fight with a girl at an after-hours club. And I had been at St. Vincent's then, too, though just overnight. And the therapist told me to write it all down. So what was the difference, other than the fact that one was almost a death and one was just a bad wound. And I wrote in my journal that while a knife can be used to cut bread and a knife can be used to carve wood—not only to stab people—a gun only has one purpose—to hurt and kill.

* * *

By the latter part of the 1980s, a significant shift had occurred in country music. With most large-market contemporary rock radio stations continuing to bend toward young audiences with playlists filled with metal, early grunge, and hip hop, a growing group of older listeners not particularly interested in feeling the noise began to find in contemporary country songs the kind of listener-friendly melodies and narrative styles they'd grown up with throughout the 1960s and '70s. Since, from its very beginnings, country music has been an adult medium, with an adult tone and addressing adult concerns, a significant number of radio stations in major cities across the United States (and not just in the South or Southwest) began to successfully attract older audiences through country formats. While at first it was helped along by the surprise 1980 hit film Urban Cowboy, the trend turned sharply over the course of the decade, as many performers falling outside of the older country stereotypes found receptive new audiences for their music.

Dating back to its earliest years, The Bottom Line had regularly showcased mainstream country performers, including the aforementioned Tanya Tucker, Dolly Parton, and George Jones, as well as the likes of Waylon Jennings, Kris Kristofferson, Emmylou Harris, Jerry Reed, Johnny Paycheck, and Hank Williams Jr. Starting in the late 1980s, a batch of singer-songwriters dubbed "Adult Alternative," "Roots Music," or, ultimately, "Americana" artists, including country-based and/or country-adjacent performers such as Marshall Chapman, Delbert McClinton, Kathy Mattea, Guy Clark, Suzy Bogguss, Lyle Lovett, Townes Van Zandt, Alison Krauss, Joe Ely, Nanci Griffith, and Mary Chapin Carpenter, began to appear regularly at The Bottom Line—especially after the closing in 1988 of New York's only truly country-oriented club, the original Lone Star Cafe on Fifth Avenue and 13th Street.

ALLAN PEPPER: Eileen discovered a couple of local college radio stations that were playing country music a few hours a day, and she began to look forward to listening to those shows. Music is an important part of who Eileen is. She plays piano, guitar, and sings and she taught music for over thirty years. As a child in middle school, she was asked to run for student government, and because she stuttered, she didn't want to do it—until her father suggested that she sing her campaign speech. He told her that when you sing, you don't stutter. So she wrote her speech, and then, to the tune of "Getting to Know You" from *The King and I*, she sang it and won the election. So you really could say music changed her life.

What appealed to her about the country music she was hearing was that notion of the singer-songwriter and the subject matter they were dealing with and the way things were structured. So she liked that so many of the songs were like little short stories in three verses. When she first heard K. T. Oslin's "Eighties Ladies" in 1987, it really caught her, and she started to listen to the country station WHN, and when it became a sports talk station later that year, we started listening to WYNY, which was also a country station. And so when we were driving in the car, she started to tell me that I should start listening to this stuff and be aware of it. She was pointing out different artists to me, like Gary Morris, who was a pretty big country star but was appearing on Broadway in *Les Miserables*, and Kathy Mattea, who had a huge hit with "Where've You Been," a song co-written by her husband Jon Vezner based on a real-life incident with his grandparents. So I started listening to the country station she had on in the car, and I found that what I was hearing there was interesting me much more as a fan than anything I was hearing on mainstream rock radio.

Now around the same time that I was having these conversations with Eileen, I got a call from Amy Kurland, who owned The Bluebird Cafe in Nashville. After some small talk, she got to the reason for her call. She said that in 1985, strictly by happenstance, the club booker booked what was advertised as a songwriter's night featuring Thom Schuyler, Fred Knobloch, Don Schlitz, and Paul Overstreet. The songwriters decided it would be a more intimate experience if instead of performing on the stage, one after the other, they'd place their chairs in a circle in the middle of the room and sit facing one another taking turns playing each other their songs, and that night was so successful that it became a regular feature of the club's weekly schedule, and it was christened "Writers in the Round." She told me that the format was so popular that many well-known writers and artists were taking part, and that several promising singer-songwriters were signed to record deals as a result of being seen at one of the writer's nights. So she wanted to do a version of "Writers in the Round" at The Bottom Line with writers who performed regularly at The Bluebird and wondered if I would consider working with her on it. The idea intrigued me, especially since I was now, thanks to Eileen, more familiar with many of the songwriters who had done her shows. But I told her that while the idea appealed to me personally, I didn't think there was enough of an audience up here that would support it, especially since The Bottom Line was much larger than The Bluebird and we did two shows a night. On top of that, I didn't think the artist fee I would guarantee would even cover the airfare and overnight hotel cost for the four writers. So, after a long conversation, we agreed to put the idea on hold and perhaps revisit it if things changed.

Now when something's in the air sometimes you just can't get away from it, and country music was now in the air. This really started to become clear to me when I got a phone call from Carl Griffin, a record producer who had been hired as a consultant by the ad agency that handled Marlboro cigarettes. Seeing there was a new popular interest in country, the agency wanted to create an association between Marlboro cigarettes and country music by launching a "Marlboro Country Music" campaign. Part of the rollout involved finding the best unsigned country band in the metropolitan area. There would be competitive showcases in local clubs where bands would perform before a panel of judges, and the judges would pare things down until they arrived at a group of finalists. Carl wanted to know if they could hold the finals at The Bottom Line, with us making it open to the public and selling tickets. We said ok, and on May 11, 1988, we hosted the first "Marlboro Country Music Talent Round-Up" Finals, and it did pretty well business-wise.

So now I'm listening to country music at home and in my car. I'm booking more country or country-leaning shows that are starting to draw more people, and I'm getting the same feeling I had with the Fast Folk shows that there's a growing audience willing to support this music. During the next year, the buzz on country grew even more, and I'm now starting to integrate more country artists into our format, either as opening acts or headliners. So, in the period of a year, I either introduced or featured or headlined, among others, Nanci Griffith, Rosanne Cash, Mary Chapin Carpenter, Kathy Mattea, Rodney Crowell, Tammy Wynette, Foster and Lloyd, New Grass Revival, the Seldom Scene, and Kris Kristofferson. Not only had my commitment to country increased during that year, but so had Marlboro's. They planned to repeat the talent search competition in 1989, and they also had a concept for a show featuring four country music songwriters that they wanted to present at our club. The idea was to have two shows—one in the late afternoon with free admission on a first-come first-serve basis, and one at night with a paid admission. The shows would focus on the craft of songwriting, with the Vice President of the Country Music Hall of Fame in Nashville leading a discussion between songs by singer-songwriters Joe Ely, Lyle Lovett, Guy Clark, and John Hiatt. And both shows filled the club to capacity.

Well before terms like Americana and roots music came into vogue, Indiana native John Hiatt arrived in Nashville in 1970 at age eighteen and began writing wide-angled songs that were hard to classify stylistically, leading to recordings of his own which, beginning in the mid-'70s, consistently garnered critical acclaim but meager sales commercially. Significantly, however, his compositions over the years—songs such as "The Thing Called Love," "Have a Little Faith in Me," "Ridin' with the King," and "Drive South"—worked their way into the repertoires of country, blues, pop, and rock performers ranging from Three Dog Night, Jeff Healey, Rosanne Cash, and Rodney Crowell to Bob Dylan, Bonnie Raitt, Eric Clapton, Suzy Bogguss, and Odetta. And as "roots" music as a genre took hold during the latter part of the 1980s, Hiatt, who'd debuted at The Bottom Line in 1979, became a regular and popular performer at the club.

JOHN HIATT: The first show I did at The Bottom Line, I opened for *[teenage new wave princess]* Rachel Sweet, who was all that and a loaf of sliced bread. We had just come out with the *Slug Line* record when I was in my angry young man phase, and we got the opening slot. I'll never forget her dad was managing her. She was from Akron, and he was a tire salesman, as he told me. He came into my dressing room between sound check and the show, and he was a big guy and very upstanding as I recall, and he said, "John, Dick Sweet." Long silence. "John,

Dick Sweet. I manage my daughter Lisa." So he'd gone into the music management business right then and there. He was a proud papa. Very nice guy. And as I recall, the place was packed. She was part of that Stiff Records crew, and I don't know what happened to Rachel, but she was hot at the time. I was just trying to get going. I was very inspired by these English kids—well, first the Ramones, but then these English kids, all wanting to play rock and roll again as I remembered it. And that's what got me. Of course, I was very young, twenty-seven, twenty-eight.

When I started playing New York pretty regularly, I had a good friend, Jack Williams, who'd moved from Nashville to New York. He'd been trained in opera, but he was doing a lot of Broadway and stage work—he'd had a big role in the original *Sweeney Todd*, and he'd put me up when I came to New York because, for a while I wasn't making any money anywhere. He had a beautiful freaking voice. He could scare the shit out of you or sing a baby to sleep. It was just amazing, his voice, the range. I asked him, "Should I take voice lessons?" He said, "No. You should never take voice lessons. It'll just fuck you up." I said, "But Jack, I don't know how to sing." He said, "Yeah, I know. But it'll just screw up whatever that little weird thing is that you have." Good advice, I guess.

I'm always flattered when somebody sings my songs. That's my number one feeling. It's like it's one of your kids and somebody says something nice about them. You just say, "Well, thanks. I love 'em too." You just kind of let them go. And I've loved all the odd covers. I mean, from Paula Abdul to Iggy Pop? I love that. I'm proud. I think the reason is that a lot of my songs are malleable. You can bend them a lot of different ways.

Over the years, Hiatt shared Bottom Line shows with the likes of Robert Cray, Syd Straw, Marti Jones, and Don Dixon, and a Bluebird show in 1987 with fellow Nashvillians Matraca Berg, Trisha Yearwood, Raul Malo, Gillian Welch, and David Rawlings. There was also the 1989 Marlboro show that saw Hiatt alongside three Texas-bred tunesmiths.

JOHN HIATT: I think we called that one the "Four Horsemen" show. It was Lyle Lovett, Guy Clark, Joe Ely, and myself. Those shows were just amazing. I mean, most of the time you're listening, and just to hear Guy Clark so close up was something. I was the gratuitous Hoosier, or Yankee, as the case might be, but they accepted me, God bless 'em. And subsequently, Ely and I started going out on tour together, and not too long ago, Lyle and I toured as a two-man show. But I loved those Bottom Line shows.

As the decade turned, the Four Horsemen show proved to be a pivotal moment for Pepper and The Bottom Line.

ALLAN PEPPER: One of the more attractive things about the Marlboro songwriters show was the interplay between the songwriters and how they reacted to each other's songs, which sometimes had them playing along with each other. I thought about that show long after it was over, and I also thought about the conversation that I had with Amy Kurland about "Writers in the Round." I wondered if there was a way that we could take elements of what they were doing at The Bluebird along with elements from the Marlboro shows and add our own twist to it. What was missing for me in both of these formats was more variety, and I started to think that since a good song is a good song, and if it's a show about songwriting, then it shouldn't matter if it's an r&b writer onstage next to a country writer and then I knew how we could make it our own. We would keep the idea of a host asking questions from the Marlboro show, and encourage the interaction between performers that The Bluebird did, and we'd also keep the notion of presenting the songs from each writer in rounds. I also liked the idea of the last round having each songwriter play a song that they didn't write but wished that they had written, which was how the Marlboro shows ended. But for us, we would choose songwriters who were known for songs from different genres, giving us the variety that for me was missing from the other presentations.

I knew such a series would gain momentum quickly if we could get two things right from the beginning—the right mix of songwriters and the right host. As far as mixing and matching the songwriters, I'd just have to get lucky, but as far as the host, there was only one choice, and that was Vin Scelsa. I knew instinctively that Vin could make this his own and, in doing that, because of his skills as an interviewer and his high regard among his fans and his peers, he could make the series really special.

I approached Vin about it, and we had a meeting at Swenson's, which I used to use as my off-premises office. I laid it all out to him, and I had prepared a whole set of questions, maybe twenty or so I'd thought of, just to give him an idea of the kinds of the things I thought we could ask. I'd spent a lot of time doing this, and while I'm telling him about it, he's just looking at me, and he says he likes the idea and the concept, but he doesn't like the questions being so thought out in advance. He wants to do it spontaneously. Now I know that Vin's a terrific interviewer, so I figure I should trust him if that's how he wants to approach it, and we'll just see where it goes. I told him I'd try to put together a group of songwriters, and he gave me a list of about a dozen or so people that he liked or was interested in, and I started to get in touch with them.

I knew we had to sell tickets, so how would we do that? We had to have songwriters who had copyrights *[songs that were very well known]* because Vin would have to get on the air and say, "Oh man, you know who we're going to have? We're going to have so-and-so, you're not going to believe some of the songs they've written," and he could play some of their music, and that was the way of promoting the show. So I went out of my way to have writers that you'd say, "Holy shit, they wrote *that*?" So one of my tasks was I had to get at least three people who had real copyrights, and I always also reserved the last choice for myself. What I wanted to do there was get people who wrote killer songs that nobody knew, people who were starting to break through, and some of these great story song composers who were very funny or very clever. Like Don Henry, who co-wrote Kathy Mattea's big country hit, "Where've You Been?" So that after the show they'd say, "I came for so-and-so, but I was knocked out by" whomever. I didn't want to do what the Marlboro thing did, and I didn't want to do what Amy was doing just for country people. That was one genre, and that truthfully didn't interest me as much as really mixing it up. And it all became real fun for me.

With Vin Scelsa hosting, The Bottom Line's In Their Own Words series debuted on May 24, 1990, with a lineup featuring Mary Chapin Carpenter, Don Dixon, Ellen Shipley, and Fred Koller. Before the semi-regular series ended in 2003, more than 250 songwriters, from mostly unknown (to the general public, anyway) hit tunesmiths such as Dan Penn and Spooner Oldham, Gary Burr, William Bell, Arthur Alexander, Sonny Curtis, Pat Alger, and Gary Nicholson, to major stars including Ric Ocasek, Al Kooper, Felix Cavaliere, David Byrne, Kris Kristofferson, Lou Reed, Joey Ramone, Lucinda Williams, Jimmy Webb, and Tom Paxton, all swapped songs and stories from their well-traveled careers.

A typical show was an April '92 edition with alt-country hero Jimmie Dale Gilmore, Australian rocker Paul Kelly, folkster Michelle Shocked, and New Orleans icon Allen Toussaint. A highlight of the series was a 1997 edition featuring this disparate trio: Country storyteller Tom T. Hall ("That's How I Got to Memphis," "Old Dogs, Children, and Watermelon Wine," "I Love") recalling going to a bar in Nashville and having a conversation with country singer and guitarist Billy J. Walker, who was trying to sell a guitar. Hall, thinking of buying it, picked it up, strummed it, and said, "You sure you want to sell it? There are still some good songs in it," and the first tune Hall composed on it was "Harper Valley, PTA"; popster Toni Wine ("Groovy Kind of Love," "Black Pearl") relating trying to get paid double union scale as a session singer for providing the voices of both Betty and Veronica on the Archies' "Sugar Sugar"; and Motown's Barrett Strong ("I Heard It Through the Grapevine," "War") remembering how the inspiration for writing the Temptations classic "Just My Imagination" came after he looked out the window of his home and watched a pretty girl walking down the street.

Rosanne Cash, who took part in several ITOW shows, as well as several Bluebird-sponsored Writers in the Round shows, made her first Bottom Line appearance in 1981, just as her third album, Seven Year Ache, was about to help launch her to major country stardom. Like Hiatt, she would return to the club later in the decade as she moved into the next phase of her career away from Nashville's glitz as a thoughtful and forthright singer-songwriter, and from then on she would appear at the Bottom Line periodically for the remainder of the club's existence.

ROSANNE CASH: I remember the first time I played the club I felt very intimidated. The Bottom Line had such a reputation, such a prestigious reputation; if you played The Bottom Line, that was a big deal. And I remember being nervous, and I think that was also the time that Jill Krementz came backstage and photographed me. I opened for *[former Eagles bassist]* Randy Meisner, who had a tough time. I don't know if he wasn't happy with the gig or he wasn't happy with things that were going on, but I remember he wasn't happy with the monitors, and he kind of had a little bit of a meltdown about that onstage. It actually relieved some of the tension for me. I just thought, "Well, I don't get thrown that easily." *[Meisner memorably attempted to take apart his dressing room bathroom after his show, which recalled Bruce DeForeest's carefully considered constructions of the dressing room walls backstage so they'd be strong enough to handle just such tantrums.]*

I have a lot of memories of being at The Bottom Line, and some of them have been really important touchstones in my life—not just my career, but my life. I went to see Leo Kottke in 1991, and I had just moved to New York, and I was kind of, well, my head was spinning. I didn't know what was going to happen in my life. My marriage *[to fellow country star Rodney Crowell]* had fallen apart. I had my eye on John Leventhal, but I didn't see how that was possibly going to work out. I was lonely, and I felt kind of despairing, and I was sitting at a table, and I think I was by myself, waiting for Leo to come out, and I wrote the lyrics to "Seventh Avenue" on a napkin sitting at that table. I ended up giving the lyrics to John and saying, "Do you want to write the music to these lyrics?" and that was the first song we wrote together. So I owe The Bottom Line for that. Thank goodness they had the napkin sitting there. I remember the first time that I played with my husband John [Leventhal] when *The Wheel* came out; we played there. John says that that's where we met for the very first time in the '80s when I was doing a show, and I vaguely remember it. I remember passing this tall guy in the tiny space where you went backstage and saying hello, but I don't have as clear memory of it as he does. I remember doing a songwriter show with Mary Chapin and Nanci Griffith, and one with Lou Reed, David Byrne, and Luka Bloom. I remember Luka Bloom, so clearly, played LL Cool J's "I Want Love," and it just killed me. I remember how impressed I was with that, and Lou was sitting next to me, and he was a little irascible, but still nice to me. I remember he was doing vocal exercises in the dressing room, and he showed me this exercise about how to open your throat with your tongue, and I thought, "Uh, ok."

A February 1994 installment of the In Their Own Words series found Reed alongside Kris Kristofferson, Victoria Williams, and Suzanne Vega.

SUZANNE VEGA: The show with Lou Reed, Victoria Williams, and Kris Kristofferson was really interesting. I was pregnant with my daughter, so I remember being backstage and posing, and there are some photos you can see with Vin, and Lou is being really mischievous. He keeps trying to touch my shoulder or something. He has his arm around Vin, but he's kind of trying to put his arm on me or touch me. And at one point I realized what he's doing, and I start laughing, and he starts laughing, and you can see it develop through the photos. I think that's one of the shows where he had just started dating Laurie Anderson, so she was in the audience, and there was this really funny kind of thing going on backstage. Because he was still being managed by his former wife, Sylvia, and he was yelling at her backstage, so that was weird. I was pregnant and kind of all involved in that, so I was just trying to stay out of everybody's way. But I really enjoyed the opportunity, not only to do the show with Lou, and I didn't really know Kris Kristofferson's work that well, but I knew Lou and I knew Victoria a little bit, and I enjoyed the banter between everybody on stage. I also loved that Vin Scelsa always asked everyone on those shows to do a cover, and I chose Bob Dylan's "It's Alright, Ma, I'm Only Bleeding," and I'm like, "It's eight minutes long. You don't want me to cut this back?" And he said, "No. Do the whole thing." And I did the whole thing, which was a thrill.

It was great to have that venue to talk about songwriting and just to be in that company. Lou was very friendly back then. I mean, he had Sylvia call me up one day and invited me out to dinner. She said it was a dinner to honor Victoria Williams. So I had imagined that there was going to be all these people, and when I got there, it was basically Lou, Sylvia, Victoria Williams, and me. I had asked if I could bring Mitchell Froom, who I was dating at the time, and I guess he reluctantly said yes. It was a very weird evening, but Lou was very friendly.

Not long after that show in 1994 came a May edition of In Their Own Words that found Roger McGuinn, erstwhile leader of the legendary '60s rock group the Byrds, alongside folk giant Pete Seeger, whose "Turn Turn Turn" the Byrds had turned into a Number One pop chart hit nearly thirty years earlier, in late 1965.

ALLAN PEPPER: It was very exciting for me but even more for Eileen because she was a huge folk music fan. I tried to get Pete to perform at the club a number of times, and I wanted him for an In Their Own Words show, but every time I tried to call him, I would get Toshi, his wife, and she would very politely turn me down and say he wasn't available. I wanted to put together a show with Roger McGuinn, and Roger's wife Camilla asked who else was on the show, and I said I didn't have anybody yet, and she said, "Well, if you get Pete Seeger, Roger will be there." So I called the Seeger house figuring I would get Toshi, and who answers the phone but Pete. I tell him about the show and that Roger McGuinn will be on it and he says,

"Sounds great. I'll be there." I said, "Really?" and he said, "Yes." I quickly called Camilla back, and she said Roger would do it, and that's how we got the show.

For McGuinn, who performed at The Bottom Line from 1974 until the winter of 2002, and who along the way shared the club's stage with the likes of former Byrdsmates Chris Hillman and Gene Clark, as well as a 1977 date with his then up-and-coming semi-doppelganger, Tom Petty, the show with Seeger—one of his boyhood idols—has remained perhaps the most cherished of all his many appearances at the club.

ROGER McGUINN: I guess it was the very early 1950s that I heard "On Top of Old Smoky" and "Kisses Sweeter Than Wine" by The Weavers on a big old wooden radio. I used to go to Chicago's Orchestra Hall and I saw the Weavers there a few times, and after Pete split from the group and went solo, I went to see him, but I was a little skeptical. I thought, "The Weavers are so great, how's he going to pull it off?" But he did. He had four instruments onstage with him, and he got the audience singing a three-part harmony. And I said to myself, "Man, this is what I want to do when I grow up." One time I went to see him and I took my banjo to one of his concerts. I never took it out of the case, but I had it with me. I don't know why, maybe in case we could have a jam session, but that was a concert that got canceled at the Navy Pier. And Pete being the great guy he was, didn't want anybody to go away disappointed, so he did an impromptu concert on the loading dock in the back of the venue, and I was one of about twenty kids standing around and I got to talk to him. I said, "Hey, Pete, you're really popular now. How do you account for that?" He said, "Well, I think it's because I got people singing along. They hear themselves singing, and then they like me." That was his personality. He was inclusive. He just wanted community. I mean, I think that's what it always was about for him. One time I was at the Old Town School of Folk Music in Chicago and Pete visited and he didn't bring an instrument with him, and I had a Vega longneck five-string banjo like Pete had at one time. It was kind of an expensive instrument, and he said, "Does anybody have a banjo?" and I raised my hand, but he didn't pick my banjo. He picked the lousiest banjo in the whole place, and he made it sound great.

I don't think people are aware that the show at The Bottom Line was the first time we ever performed together onstage. I guess Allan called my agent and said, "We're having this In Their Own Words series. Would Roger be interested?" And my wife got involved and she said, "Well, if you can get Pete Seeger, Roger will do it." So Allan called up Pete's house, and fortunately Toshi was out because she would've vetoed the whole thing, and Pete picked up the phone, and he said, "Oh, Roger McGuinn. He's a nice guy. Sure, I'll do it." And that's how it happened. The day of the show, we had a break time between the rehearsal and the show, and we went over to the Minetta Tavern in the West Village and had dinner together. It rained, so we bought an umbrella for ten bucks on the street. We still have it. We call it the Pete Seeger Memorial Umbrella. So we bought Pete dinner and then went back to the club and did the show along with Ted Hawkins, who was great. It was an amazing night.

It was really the first time that I'd actually spent that much time with Pete. I mean, just to talk and just shoot the breeze and talk about stuff. I told him about how I grew up in Chicago and went to the Old Town School of Folk Music, and I was taught by Frank Hamilton, who was a friend of Pete's and was the guy who helped popularize "We Shall Overcome" along with Guy Carawan, who was also an old friend of Pete's. At the show, I performed "Bells of Rhymney," and afterwards, Pete came backstage and told me it was the best version he had ever heard. He even sent me a postcard later saying it again. That was quite an honor. Later, I got to go up to his house in Beacon, New York, and play with him, and we recorded together for my *Treasures From the Folk Den* collection, and it got nominated for a Grammy.

* * *

Like Roger McGuinn, Al Kooper appeared at the Bottom Line from the club's beginnings almost right up until its closing days, including several editions of In Their Own Words. The multi-instrumentalist's storied career began with his tenure as a guitarist with the Royal Teens (of "Short Shorts" fame) while still in high school in the late 1950s, and would over the ensuing decades find him writing hits (Gary Lewis and the Playboys' "This Diamond Ring"), playing organ on such legendary recording sessions as those for Bob Dylan's "Like a Rolling Stone" and the Blonde on Blonde album as well as the Who's "Real" and Jimi Hendrix's Electric Ladyland LP, and, additionally, playing French horn on the Rolling Stones' "You Can't Always Get What You Want." Kooper also discovered Lynyrd Skynyrd, whose classic debut album he produced. His own works included being a member of New York's pioneering mid-'60s band the Blues Project, founding the jazz-rocking Blood, Sweat and Tears, and helming the surprise million-selling late '60s Super Session live jam album alongside guitarist Mike Bloomfield.

In February 1994, Kooper celebrated himself with a three-day fiftieth birthday party at The Bottom Line that featured reunions by both the entire original Blues Project and members of BS&T, as well as one evening with the Rekooperators, his band with Jimmy Vivino. Much of it is captured by one of the finest live albums recorded at The Bottom Line, 1995's Soul of a Man: Al Kooper Live.

DANNY KAPILIAN (Concert promoter): I'd gotten to be good friends with Al, and he brought me aboard to help produce those shows. I coordinated everything, cut the deals with everybody in the band, like trumpeters Lou Soloff and Randy Brecker. And we got Stephen King [*who, along with authors Dave Barry, Amy Tan, and Matt Groening, as well as Kooper, performed for a while as the writers-rockers band, the "Rock Bottom Remainders"*].

Unbelievably, Allan, God bless him, so famous for the Oreos and the apples in the dressing room, actually sprang for a trailer parked on Fourth Street for the shows so that there'd be enough dressing room space for everyone. We were all like, "Holy shit! Pepper's spending a little money, and in the sweetest way." For the shows, Al created these long-sleeved polo shirts with sixteen different portraits of himself at all different ages in his career. But of course, he wasn't self-centered or anything. It was like, "Hey, I may not be a legend, but I'm a lot more than a fucking footnote." He was making such a big deal out of turning fifty that, besides a birthday cake, I came out onstage one of the nights with my birthday present to him—a walker, to which I taped a box of condoms, so he wouldn't feel so old. Al is rock's reigning curmudgeon. You need good curmudgeons in this business.

JIMMY VIVINO: We did the *Soul of a Man* shows, which was amazing, with The Blues Project and the Rekooperators, and the *Child is Father to the Man* Blood, Sweat and Tears album, and we had John Simon, who produced the record, play auxiliary piano. I just played guitar on that. And John also led the string quartet overture from the album that goes into "I Love You More Than You'll Ever Know." So we went full out on it, and we just had a good time. The Bottom Line was a place that allowed you to do those kinds of things. Allan would never say, "What are you going to play?" or "What are you going to do? What's your set list?" Some places, they want to know. And so it was always a surprise. Always different. Through Al, I got to know Bob Dylan. I've never been in Bob's band. So we're still friends, and I say that with all due respect. I like it. There's nothing like when you're in a room and Bob Dylan comes over to you because he recognizes *you*. I mean, that's it. You don't need anything else. I don't need to know anything else, and because of Al, I could wind up playing with [*Chuck Berry's original pianist*] Johnnie Johnson, or Joe Walsh, whoever. Al hates when I say this, but he was kind of like a rock and roll Zelig. Anytime anything was happening, there was Al. It's true. And he kept moving. All through his career, he kept changing and doing things in and out of this and that. It's amazing.

Al KOOPER: When I signed with Columbia after Blood, Sweat and Tears, I didn't have enough stuff to put out a solo album, and I didn't want to do it prematurely. I had become knowledgeable about Mike [Bloomfield] from playing with him on the Dylan record, and we became friends, so I thought, "Why don't we just do a jam record?" And he said, "Sounds good," and we picked the musicians, and then I think Mike did one night and then he disappeared. We were recording it in LA, so I said, "Fuck, who do I know in LA?" I said, "I wonder if it would work with Steven Stills." So I called him up on one day's notice, and he came down and boy, wasn't that wonderful? It was really just a serendipitous kind of thing that happened. I guess I've had a lot of those over the years.

* * *

ALLAN PEPPER: One of the other things Vin Scelsa and I did with In Their Own Words was that we'd have these pre-production meetings, and we'd explain how the thing worked. And Vin would say, "Look, it's about having fun for us onstage as well as the audience. So if you feel moved and you want to play a different song than you'd originally planned, or sing along to someone else's song with a harmony part, or sing on the chorus, that will make it fun for us, too. And if you don't want to, you don't have to." And that worked. Also, Vin, because he hated doing two shows, in many cases he'd ask the same questions, but he also tried to come up with different questions, which made it more interesting for everybody. So between us, over a period of time, we perfected it. Vin also wanted a theme song for the show. I asked him if he had any particular one in mind, and he said he thought we should play Sinatra's "Without a Song" right before every show. And after a few of the shows, the audience came to know it because we'd put it on the PA five minutes before the show, and when they heard that, they started to applaud. Soon as the series got going, I figured, "I'm going to have fun with this. I'm going to introduce people to somebody they've never heard of, and I'm going to have fun mixing up the genres." And a lot of times I came to Vin with people he didn't know, and it was just such an interesting combination of people that sometimes would meet each other for the first time and later write a song as a result.

Now Vin had tremendous stage fright, which was very weird, since he was so well known and so comfortable on the radio. We had a tradition that before a show, I would take Vin and his wife, Freddie, and myself and Eileen out to eat near the club. We'd all order, and before the food came Vin would be all white. He'd say, "You've got to excuse me, I can't eat," and he'd leave and spend the whole time walking around the block just trying to calm himself. Now, if you saw him at the shows, you would never know it. The other thing about Vin, why he was such a perfect host, is that he had wonderful chemistry with the artists. He would ask the artists questions that you could see people hadn't asked them before. But the next day, when I'd call him bright-eyed and bushy-tailed to discuss the next show, he'd say, "I'm sorry, Allan, I can't keep doing this. I really can't." And I'd say, "Yes, you can," and I'd give him all the reasons why we were doing it. And I held him in place for about four or five years, until it was becoming more and more of a problem for him and, as a friend, I let him stop hosting the shows. I couldn't keep putting him through this. *[Other hosts for the series were Philadelphia's World Cafe host David Dye and FUV's Pete Fornatale and Rita Houston.]*

A very creative agent, Marty Diamond, who at the time was working for Wayne Forte, asked if I would be interested in taking *In Their Own Words* on the road and put together a tour of clubs around the country. Marty then got concert promoter Danny Kapilian to produce and tour-manage the show. Since we needed a host, Danny proposed that in every city we went into, we'd either hook up with the local radio station that was playing music associated with the artists on the tour or else a journalist who would normally cover those artists. Marty and Danny booked the tours and selected the writers for the tour because they knew which artists would sell tickets in which markets. And I had them stick to the formula I had come up with for putting the shows together, combining writers with copyrights with a writer who was probably unknown to most of the audience but was a killer songwriter. Danny has an intuitive gift for spotting talent, and Marty has great taste, so between them, they put together terrific packages that were always produced as *"The Bottom Line Presents: In Their Own Words."*

As a result of the success I had with Marlboro Country and the response we got from the start with In Their Own Words, I called Amy back and said, "Amy, things have changed. You want to try some of your shows at our club?" So we started doing regular "Bluebird Style" country shows, and for these it was she, not me, who picked the songwriters. I trusted her implicitly the same way I trusted Vin, the same way I trusted Christine Lavin and Danny Kapilian. So Amy would send me these writers, some of whom were starting to break through on country radio, and I started to integrate those writers into In Their Own Words, and then maybe book them for regular full-set slots at the club as well. So working with Amy turned out really well. It was fun that I was not having to book a lot of stuff that was very much in the mainstream because, like with Fast Folk, the thing that turned me on was that we were ahead of the curve. It maybe hadn't turned the corner yet, but it was in the air. You felt like this is going to happen. And that's thrilling. I didn't just do it to make money selling tickets. If that's what I was most interested in, I would've done more things in concert halls.

Take Cheryl Wheeler. I booked her as a folk artist, and she was writing all these songs that were becoming country hits by other artists. But if the country audience in Nashville back then had only seen her performing "Aces," which Suzy Bogguss had a big country hit with, they might've all done triple takes. So I put her on a show opening up for Kristofferson. I discovered Gary Nicholson *[writer of such country hits as Lee Roy Purnell's "Givin' Water to a Drowning Man" and Don Williams' "That's the Thing About Love"]* through Amy and the Bluebird shows, and I brought him back to do In Their Own Words a couple of times, and he was the perfect example of "Wow, who *is* this guy?" Another thing for me was that, as joyous as those shows were, and they were for me, very joyous, they were some of my all-time favorite shows because I looked forward to just sitting down and listening to the music and the stories. Most shows, I'd be all over the club making sure things were ok, but for In Their Own Words and the Bluebird shows I just sat with Eileen and watched them from the audience. For us, it felt like a date.

I have many great memories of the In Their Own Words shows, including one that has to do with something that didn't happen. Kris Kristofferson and Willie Nelson were handled by the same manager-slash-agent, Mark Rothbaum. Kris was booked to do an ITOW show with Lou Reed, Suzanne Vega, and Dave Alvin, and

Mark called to confirm the date, and he said, You know, Allan, Willie will be in town and off that day, and Willie just doesn't like to sit in a hotel room. So I'm thinking maybe he can come and do that show with you." I got so excited I just about jumped out of my chair. And so within that enthusiasm, I started saying, "Ok, well if he's going to do it, he's got to be here at four o'clock." I start to lay out for him all the ground rules for the show—"We have a little bit of prep with the four writers and the show host. And we do it in four rounds . . . "—and there's a silence on the other end of the phone. And after a few seconds, Mark says to me, "Allan . . . " And I said, "What?" And he says, "Willie doesn't do too good with rules."

But there is one very sad memory as well, and that was when our beloved "Big George" Roberson, who did security for us on some big shows and was really well known on Broadway as the "Bodyguard of the Superstars," collapsed from an aneurysm right at the club. It happened on February 18, 1993, at the ITOW show we did with Lou, Rosanne, David Byrne, and Luka Bloom. Inside the club was a little office that was behind the box office, separated only by a thin wall, and while Tony DiGiovanni and George were just sitting around talking, Big George, all six-foot-five of him, collapsed and fell down across the whole length of the small office. Tony tried to give him CPR, and tears were in his eyes because he knew just how serious it looked, and meanwhile, on the other side of the wall, Donna was out front at the box office handling tickets when she heard somebody yelling, "Get on the fucking phone and get an ambulance here," and when she realized what was happening, she started crying, too. We could tell it was life and death.

So here was the public coming in all charged up to see the show, and at the same time, behind closed doors, there we were trying to keep someone from dying. So Stanley and I had to make some immediate and clear-headed decisions. We couldn't just stop everything and clear the club while we waited for EMTs and the ambulance, the only thing we could really do was to try and proceed with the show as best we could. When the ambulances came and pulled up, we tried to do it as quietly and quickly as we could, even though we had to take the door of the office off its hinges to get George out of there. And somehow we were able to do it with only a few people really knowing what was happening. While we got him to the hospital as fast as we could, they couldn't revive him, and he passed away. It was about the most unsettling example of the old slogan "The Show Must Go On" that I've ever experienced.

*　*　*

Betty Buckley's stunning, Tony Award-winning performance of "Memory" in the role of Grizabella in the New York production of Cats *in 1982 was, at the time, and still remains, the stuff of which legends are made. Yet the Texas native has, across multiple decades, distinguished herself not only on stage (*Sunset Boulevard, Triumph of

Love), *screen* (Carrie, Tender Mercies), *and television* (Eight Is Enough, Law and Order: SVU), *but also as one of America's most compelling interpretive vocalists. As such, The Bottom Line's sizable but still intimate atmosphere made it one of Buckley's favorite places to perform from the 1990s through the club's final years in the early 2000s.*

BETTY BUCKLEY: I think I did my first New York concert after I left *Cats* in 1984 at St. Bart's Church, and it was recorded and released on Rizzoli Records, which was a new record company. While I was still doing theater, I started getting more requests to do concerts, and somehow Allan reached out to me. I did my first Bottom Line concert in 1990. All my favorite bands, rock and roll, and great singing artists and musicians played there. And along with being a Broadway actress-singer, I wanted to be a concert artist. I have this big theatrical voice, so The Bottom Line with its resonant acoustic space seemed to be the place for me to be. I had put together this band of incredible jazz musicians. My band included Kenny Werner, a very renowned jazz pianist, as my pianist and arranger, Jamie Haddad, a drummer who later played for Paul Simon, saxophonist Billy Drewes, and bass player Tony Marino. And at times I had different synthesizer players, depending on what body of music we were doing. And so, following that, Allan kept bringing us back every year at least twice a year, and I would put together new groupings of songs. Allan invited a Columbia Records attorney, Mort Drosnes, who was starting his own record label, Sterling Records, to come and see us, and because of that, I was offered my first real record deal, per se, and we did five studio albums for Sterling of the various collections of music that I'd put together for The Bottom Line.

For me, every time I do anything, even in the smallest room, it's a concert. In fact, when I first started doing concerts, a couple of pretentious critics would say things like, "Well, this is not cabaret." And I'm like, "I'm not trying to do 'cabaret.'" It used to annoy the hell out of me. "Cabaret" isn't a style of presentation of music. It's not a form. Cabaret is a place, a small place where people can have food and drinks while they're listening to music. But the thing about The Bottom Line was there was a real sense of space. My voice is a resonant instrument that was made for an acoustic space. Singing in The Bottom Line, because of the resonance, was a very gratifying experience, like singing in a cathedral. You could sing, you could do anything you wanted. I mean, I just like a lot of different kinds of music. I'm a storyteller, and I choose good songs, whether it's a standard from the Broadway Songbook or one by a singer-songwriter, from the sixties or contemporary, it's the song itself that strikes me. And then, what I can do with it with my brilliant collaborators, how we interpret that song—I like to think of it as painting with music—of a situation, place, experience, or relationship.

I was one of the first Broadway artists who did Broadway music in concert, interpreting it differently than it was done on the cast album. The diehard Broadway enthusiasts who were really old school, thinking all Broadway material should be done as it was in the show, were a bit perturbed and said so in some of my early reviews. And my pianist/arranger Kenny used to say, "Until this stuff is recorded, nobody's going to really get it." So I was the central storytelling voice in this incredible band of jazz musicians, and then, when the same people could sit with the recording, they started to get what we were doing. And if it hadn't been for Allan, probably that would've never happened, any of it. You could really present music beautifully at The Bottom Line, and have a beautiful intimacy with the audience. From those concerts, we began to have a very eclectic audience. I had a collegiate following, and my age group, and, back then, older than my age group, which was nice. And whenever Allan would present us, the lines would literally go around the block. It was a blast!

In 1982, they had already recorded the original London cast album of *Cats*, and everybody in musical theater knew about that and had it. But the show itself was kind of a mystery unless you'd flown to England to see it. They were holding auditions for the Broadway company, and my agent submitted me for the role of Grizabella, and I was like, "Well, who is she?" I'd only seen this very small little color photograph on the album. And my agent said, "Well, she's the older cat. She's the one who sings 'Memory.' It's the big song in the show." I learned the song for the audition, and yeah, it's a beautiful song, but what it took to learn how to stop the show with it was quite a journey. And I'm grateful for that journey to this day because it taught me how to bring myself to a song and bring my understanding and how to make a soul connection with an audience through a song. So learning how to do "Memory," and working with Trevor Nunn and Andrew Lloyd Webber, Gillian Lynne, and all those wonderful original people that did the original Broadway company was an amazing kind of odyssey for me.

Learning how to do "Memory" was deceptively difficult. It sounds like just a song, but it's so much more than that. It allowed me to go through the doorway of my potential as an interpreter. I learned not just dynamics, but what the principles are that allow me to best serve a song and connect with the audience. Even though I'd been a singer since I was eleven years old, and a professional since I was fifteen, I had been studying for all those years. And after the *Cats* experience, I felt that I finally knew what I was doing. Then, I was able to form our music ensemble— and Allan Pepper gave us a platform with which to start creating more and more music. Over the years, I have recorded nineteen albums, and that all began with Allan and his patronage. I used to call him one of my patrons. And Stanley, who was tough, taught me just how to negotiate. I love those guys!

* * *

Bill Scheft spent twenty-four years (1991–2015) as a staff writer for the David Letterman *show, during which he was nominated for fourteen Emmys—"without winning a single one," he cheerfully notes. A onetime humor columnist for that bastion of mirth,* Sports Illustrated, *Scheft's bachelor's degree from Harvard may not have helped him much during his decade-plus career as a stand-up comic, but it did look good on the resume. Whether that helped him initially get to The Bottom Line stage in 1990 remains a mystery, but his love of music did make his recurring engagements at the club a lot of fun for him—and, at times, for the audience as well.*

BILL SCHEFT: The Bottom Line didn't have a giant stage. So if Allan was booking a comic, you didn't want a guy who moved around a lot if you had a lot of pieces behind you. I was dying to play there, but I never pursued it because it looked like he had a stable of guys. But then I got a call about opening for Tower of Power. Now unbeknownst to Allan, they were my favorite band growing up when I was in high school. I was so excited because I'd been to the club, I'd seen some other people there, and it was a great room, with great sound. So I was a huge fan of Tower of Power, and now they didn't know this. So I went up, and I did really, really well. I came backstage and they're big comedy fans, and they said, "We've had a lot of big acts open for us, and they don't do well. Why did you do well?" I said, "Because they know I'm one of them. The audience knows that I just want to get off stage as quickly as I can so you guys can come out. I made that clear." They wanted me back the next time they came in, and that night they pulled out all the stops. I think Huey Lewis came onstage and sang, "You're Still a Young Man," which was huge, and then Saturday Night Live's bandleader [saxophonist] Lenny Pickett, who used to be in the group, came over, and right after that they got a record deal and they hadn't had one in maybe ten years. So I kind of became their good luck charm. I kept opening for them when they would play the club, and I made friends with them, which was great.

I opened for a lot of people at The Bottom Line, and the thing about Allan was I had to get there earlier and earlier so we could trade jokes. And that was another great thing about playing the club. I certainly gave him a couple that he hadn't heard, and he gave me a couple that I hadn't heard. I played there the night before I got married. That was June 3, 1990. I remember my father saying, "Who opens for Leon Redbone the night before he gets married?" I said, "Comics do." My wife Adrianne was also a comic, and she worked The Bottom Line a couple of times, too. She opened for Tower once, but she also opened for a reconfiguration of The Mamas and Papas in 1992. It was Denny Doherty, Scott McKenzie, Mackenzie Phillips, and Spanky McFarlane, and in the middle of the set, we're in the audience, and Adrianne turns to me and says, "Hey, it's a new thing. It's called a rehearsal. It's going to be very big because only Denny Doherty knew how badly things were whacked up."

I think just about every comic of my generation has a deep abiding respect and love for Lenny Bruce. And anytime you could approximate where he might've been or what he might've done, for me, it was just a thrill. I remember the first time I ever worked The Bitter End or any of those clubs in the Village, I felt a responsibility to be different and, as Lenny would say, to not be as fucking charming because it was New York and you wanted to do the material that you couldn't do anywhere else. And for me, The Bottom Line, it was definitely a step up for me, first of all, because it was literally a step up since the stage was raised so nicely, and second, because it always felt so comfortable. It wasn't a room for comics necessarily, but comics loved that room. Richie Belzer told me that the only choice for his first special was The Bottom Line, and that was in 1986. And we talked about just how comfortable it was there, and I don't know why I think that people understood what it meant for a comic to come out before some jazz artist or some maybe avant-garde musician or some act with a solid following. They understood what that meant.

Back in those days, there were two guys that we were all worried about if they'd ever work. We knew they were brilliant, but we weren't sure if they'd ever be able to make a living. Gilbert Gottfried was one of them, and Larry David was the other. We knew they were two loose cannons you never thought would really make it. But then I opened for Gilbert one time, and Adrianne came with me, and he did an hour, and this is when he had started to hit with *Aladdin*, and now he gets a standing ovation. I remember Adrianne saying to me, "He's going to be all right." And of course, he was more than all right.

I've been friends with Larry for over forty years, and people, straight people, go out and something will happen, and they'll say, "This is just like an episode of Seinfeld." But the thing is, when you're with Larry, the stuff really does break out. One night we were at a dinner, and the end of it, I say to him, "Dessert?" and he says, "No dessert for me. Ted Danson and I have a bet. No dessert for a year." And I figure, "Wow, it's Larry David. It's Ted Danson. They're both billionaires. The bet is no dessert for a year. I bet you the bet's like $50,000. I bet you the bet's maybe like a million dollars." So I say to him, "Wow. No dessert for a whole year? How much is the bet?" And he says, "$200." I said, "Honest to God, Larry. Really? Have a piece of fucking cake."

14 'TIS THE SEASON

CAROLING CAROLERS, HALLELUJAH CHORUSES, AND NEW YEAR'S HI-JINX

Maggie and Terre Roche first made their presence known in New York in the late 1960s when, as teenagers, they came to town from their home in Park Ridge, New Jersey, to sing Christmas carols for passersby on the streets of Greenwich Village. So it's no surprise that many a Yuletide season at The Bottom Line, especially in the late 1980s and early '90s, found Maggie, Terre, younger sister Suzzy, and numerous members of their extended families (including Loudon Wainwright and his and Suzzy's daughter Lucy) at the club to help celebrate the holidays. The trio's unique blend of sparkling three-part harmonies and wink-smart songs such as "The Married Men" and "Nurds" had already made them neighborhood favorites on the Village's club circuit before they made their Bottom Line debut in 1979, and they became a regular and ever-welcomed presence at the club over the ensuing decades—even though Terre Roche's first encounter with Allan Pepper and Stanley Snadowsky was anything but cordial.

TERRE ROCHE: My older sister Maggie and I had a duo going back to the late '60s. In the early 1970s, we went down to Louisiana and spent time in this town called Hammond, where someone we had met on the coffee house circuit had started a kung fu temple in an abandoned telephone company building. So there were all these people kind of squatting there. It was a very rural town at the time, and I understand now that Hammond is kind of a little more upscale; there's a Starbucks there, a Gap maybe. But at the time, there was none of that. We came back to New York after about a year of being down there, and we went to Folk City where Mike Porco gave us both jobs. We were bartenders and waitresses. With Folk City, you'd have one bartender and one waitress each night, and he gave us the jobs. There were hardly any customers in there at the time, so you didn't make much money, but it was definitely a scene. And at that point, then, our younger sister, Suzzy, she was in college, and she used to come in on the weekends and sit at the bar and hang with us and stuff. And that's when we started to sing as a trio.

Now somewhere along the line, all of a sudden Allan and Stanley were the people at the door. We didn't know them, and of course, I felt like Folk City was my living room. I didn't respect someone telling me I had to pay, or even ask me who I was. So immediately I took a dislike to these two guys. I don't remember this incident, but Allan remembers me saying something like "Fuck you" to him when he was working the door, and just walking past him and going in. Folk City was very different from The Bottom Line. Anyone could play at the hoots. I mean, you could wander in off the street and you just put your name down, and you're going to be onstage, maybe not until near four in the morning when the place closes, but you'll get up there. And Mike Porco, that was his way. He was a real character. And of course, Maggie and I, and Suzzy, I think at this point too, we were in there every night. So I was used to thinking, oh, I can just saunter into the place. And there's these two guys, nobody says who they are, and they're asking you who you are. I didn't know they had started booking the place for Mike. Allan always brings it up to me that I told him to fuck off. Anyway, we would play Folk City, and then two weeks later, we'd play Kenny's Castaways, and Pat Kenny, who owned Kenny's Castaways, at first he didn't want to hire us because he thought we were too low-key for his club. His room was a little rowdier. So they were the two places we were playing.

It was at Folk City that Linda Ronstadt and Phoebe Snow caught a show by The Roches, which led to the two of them talking about the group and performing Maggie's "The Married Men" on Saturday Night Live. *And as the sisters began to attract increasing attention, Pepper, at this point more than anything just bemused by his first impression of Terre, booked the trio for The Bottom Line for the first time in April 1978.*

SUZZY ROCHE: John Rockwell, who used to write for *The New York Times*, was a fan of ours. We had just gotten signed to Warner Brothers, and at the same time [ex-King Crimson guitarist] Robert Fripp got signed to Warners as a producer. Fripp asked John Rockwell, "Who should I see in New York?" and John told him to come to see us at The Bottom Line. I remember that night because he was standing at the bar and I walked by, and he said something to me, which I can't really remember, but that was the very first time I ever met and heard of Robert Fripp. I didn't know who he was. I was just like a little snotty kid from New Jersey. I didn't know anything.

TERRE ROCHE: I didn't know who he was, and a friend who'd been at the show said he was in King Crimson. And I said, "Wait, is that the album cover with the guy with the big mouth and the ears screaming?" That's all I knew. And then when we met and we were sitting in the room together to talk, I still hadn't thought to go look up his music. I just thought, we'll see who this guy is. And something about that meeting, I think we all felt like this is a really interesting collaboration, whoever this guy is. I think when you don't know the person's work, it plants you in the present moment. And he did a great job producing us.

SUZZY ROCHE: We had so much fun. He was a real character and he had kind of a public persona of being prim and proper and everything like that, but he really wasn't like that. And there were a lot of laughs—a lot of laughs.

It was Suzzy Roche who, in 1987, got the group involved with a holiday show at The Bottom Line.

SUZZY ROCHE: Well, it's probably hard to imagine now, but way back then there weren't really any special Christmas-themed shows at the clubs, so I had an idea that I wanted to do a benefit show. I wanted to do a Christmas show and donate the money to Mother Teresa's operations. Maggie and Terre both did not want to be involved officially. They didn't want to have to do it as The Roches. We were going to do it, but they didn't want our name to be doing it. Everyone knew we sang Christmas carols and stuff like that; it was a big part of our history. It's really how we started singing together. And since 1982 we'd been doing some December shows at The Bottom Line as The Caroling Carolers. So I went to Allan and I asked him if I could do it with just my name, and he said yes, so it was billed as me hosting with and starring The Caroling Carolers, as well as some others we invited to take part. And it was a huge success. And then of course it became the Roches Christmas show and it was our idea that each person who was a guest would write a Christmas song, and then we would also do the traditional songs. And we had the Caroling Carolers vocal group, and we also had a band to do our versions of the traditional carols.

TERRE ROCHE: Once we made our Christmas album [1990s *We Three Kings*], it became this natural thing for us to do a show every year, because we had started out as street-singing Christmas carolers. But one of my most vivid memories that I love is a performance that Lucy and I did together. This was for a show that Allan put together for an all-acapella night. The [mixed vocal group] Accidentals were in there, and there was a bunch of really, really good heavy-hitting acapella people, like [ex-Rockapella Sean Altman's] Groove Barbers. Somehow, Lucy and I, just the two of us, got drafted into this thing, and we did my song, "Star of Wonder," which is a very tricky song to sing acapella. We practiced it and stuff, and she was pretty young; I think this was the first time she was performing as not just being the little kid in the carolers. So we get up there, we get halfway through the song, and something happened and it broke down. So we started again, and the same thing happened, and then a third time it happened again where we couldn't get through it. I looked at Lucy and I said, "One more." And she said, "No, I don't think so." And I said, "No, one more," and we got through the song, and Allan told me afterward that he loved that performance because it was so real. My feeling was that I didn't want her to have a failure experience for her first time not being part of this big group. *[Lucy Wainwright Roche, of course, has gone on to a highly regarded career as a solo artist as well as a duet performer alongside her mother Suzzy.]*

Another familiar face on The Bottom Line stage during many Christmas seasons was Ronnie Spector. In 1988, working off an idea of Pepper's and scripted by Melanie Mintz, the club presented a reimagining of the recording sessions for Ronnie's ex-husband, producer Phil Spector's legendary 1963 album A Christmas Gift for You. *The show featured ex-Ronette Ronnie and Darlene Love recreating their roles from the original album, with Ronnie singing "Sleigh Bells" and "Frosty the Snowman" and Darlene doing "White Christmas," "Winter Wonderland" and her signature song, "Christmas (Baby, Please Come Home)." There were also contributions from many of the original cast of* Leader of the Pack, *including Ula Hedwig, Bobby Jay, and Pattie Darcy, along with members of Pack's instrumental band led by musical director Jimmy Vivino. And, as an extra bonus, Pepper got Sonny Bono who, as part of Spector's Wall of Sound orchestra had played percussion on the album, to appear in the show as Spector.*

Ronnie Spector presented her own Bottom Line Christmas shows in 1992, '93, '95, and '96, and on that last date her opening act was singer-songwriter David Forman. As he did in over a dozen shows at The Bottom Line throughout the 1990s, Forman performed in the guise of his alter ego Little Isidore, a World War II Eurasian war orphan who became a 1950s doo-wop child star and disappeared just as the British Invasion was happening, but was now, as an adult, making a triumphant return to the concert stage. It was a return that bore benefits for Forman, too, as he—make that Isidore—scored a hit with his falsetto classic "Christmas of Love," used in the film How The Grinch Stole Christmas. *(Besides David Johansen, Forman seems to be the only person who ever performed at The Bottom Line as two completely different people, though Forman is probably the only one to do so at a single show—a feat he accomplished in 1998 as part of the all-star cast of a presentation of the concept album* Largo, *in which both Forman and Isidore appeared separately onstage.)*

DAVID FORMAN: I had a great time with Ronnie, and even got to sing with her. We did a fantastic "ABCs of Love," with me and the boys from my band the Inquisitors doing the Teenagers to her Frankie Lymon. The only mistake I made with Ronnie was that when I went out there, I kind of embraced her, and I endangered the security of her wig. I was asked, "Please don't do that. Don't touch her hair. It's very precarious." And I said, "Ok, sure. I got it, man." I just totally wasn't thinking.

Little Isidore also did a solo holiday Bottom Line show on Christmas 1999.

DAVID FORMAN: I remember that one. The shows were long, and I guess because it was Christmas Day itself, they hadn't sold many tickets to the late show, and Allan said he'd give people a refund and we didn't have to do the second one. But we had people who were at the early show who wanted to stay, and we were having such a good time that I told Allan, "No no no. My peeps are staying for the late show, and even if it's just a dozen people out there, I want to do it. Happily." And we did.

* * *

Of all the holiday season shows at The Bottom Line, the one that certainly proved the most personally rewarding to Allan Pepper was "The Downtown Messiah," a reimagined version of Handel's famous work that was presented for the first time in December 1998 and would continue every year until just weeks before the club's closing in early 2004. Its origins came about through Pepper's work with New Jersey-based show producer Jeanne Stahlman, which began in 1994.

JEANNE STAHLMAN: My whole history with The Bottom Line starts with the fact that I was a Willie Nile fan. After I saw him at the club, I went backstage and introduced myself, and we talked for a while and then he said, "A bunch of us are going over to the Corner Bistro after the show. Why don't you come?" And I did. That led to so many musical friendships, and one of them was that I met Tom [Goodkind] and Lauren [Agnelli] from the Washington Squares. It was not long after their guitarist Bruce Jay Pankow had passed away, and they wanted to do a show in his honor and they were like, "You'd be really good at this. Can you help us?" God knows why they thought so, but Allan agreed to present the show because they had played the club often, and he liked them. When I first met with him, this is what Allan said to me: "I don't know you, but I see your name on so many guest lists at my club, and I don't know how it is that so many people know you." So that was the beginning of our relationship. Nobody knew me for anything in terms of producing a show, but every person I called, including David Johansen, Marshall Crenshaw, Richard Barone, John S. Hall, and Lenny Kaye, they all said yes. I had no idea what I was doing, but Dave Steck, the Bottom Line stage manager, said, "I can tell you haven't done this before. I will teach you." And it just started from that. Every single thing I did with every other club started from that single one-off in 1994.

The Downtown Messiah came about because after a while I was working a lot of Christmas shows at The Bottom Line. For years, I helped [songwriter and keyboardist] Glen Burtnik with his Christmas benefit shows, which we brought to The Bottom Line in 1994 and continued through 2001. I also worked on a holiday show with Sean Altman from the group Rockapella. Allan would bring me in to help line up talent for these multiple-performer shows because he wanted somebody back there who could corral all these people.

ALLAN PEPPER: One night backstage during the holiday season in 1997, Jeanne said, "I love doing this with you. It's exciting. The only drag for me is I miss seeing the Messiah, which I see every Christmas at Carnegie Hall." And, in a very flip way, I said, "Well, maybe next year *we* should do a version of the Messiah," not having the vaguest clue of what that would entail. And she said, right off the top of her head, "Yeah, and we could call it 'The Downtown Messiah.'" And that was that. Then in the middle of the year, I started to think about it, and I spoke to her, and we began to talk seriously about doing it—and keep in mind, all I knew was the Hallelujah Chorus and maybe one other thing from it. So I knew I needed to put together a music team, and one of the things that we talked about was trying to make it our own. I went to Richard Barone, who I had been doing some other projects with at the club, and asked if he would be the music director, and he got what I was talking about. To make it our own meant that we'd keep the choruses exactly the way Handel had composed them but take the musical arias that were sung between the choruses—the recitatives—and present each one in a different style that would sort of reflect the kind of music you might hear on any given night in the Village. So musically it would be folk or jazz or whatever, and we wouldn't change the lyric content, but we'd let people take liberties.

Richard Barone first played The Bottom Line in 1982 as leader of Hoboken's poppy new wave band The Bongos as part of the Prisoners of Rock and Roll series. Since then, he'd been involved in numerous Bottom Line presentations over the years, including recording his 1987 Cool Blue Halo *album live at the club, as well as cohosting, alongside fellow singer-songwriter Jules Shear, the Writers in the Round Bluebird Style series throughout the 1990s.*

RICHARD BARONE: I was at The Bottom Line every year for Glen Burtnik's holiday shows, where I got to sing Darlene Love's "Christmas (Baby, Please Come Home)." One year at the club, Allan grabbed me by the arm and took me over to the bar and said, "I have to talk to you about something." I said, "Ok, what's up?" And he goes, "I want to do a version of the Messiah here at the club." I said, "You mean Handel's Messiah?" and he said, "Yes." And I said, "That's crazy. How can we do the Messiah here? It's like a church piece or something, right? How do we do that here?" And he says, "I dunno, but do you want to be kind of the musical director?"

ALLAN PEPPER: Now Richard at the time was also working on an off-Broadway musical called *Bright Lights, Big City*, and I knew he was very busy with that and couldn't make the full commitment that I needed. So I reached out to Margaret Dorn [leader of the hip vocal octet The Accidentals] about leading the choir, and I also wanted to find someone to work on the musical arrangements. And then my secretary at that time, Jill Davis, casually said to me, "What about Peter Kiesewalter?" Now we knew Peter because he was [singer-songwriter] Jane Siberry's accompanist and had also done arrangements for her. I liked Peter, and I reached out to him and I said, "Does this interest you?" And he got it in a nanosecond. He got everything about it. So I went to Richard and I said, "I've got this guy, Peter Kiesewalter. You guys can have a conversation. He'll work on the arrangements, and you can be the director." Choosing Peter to be the arranger was one of the luckiest things I did because his arrangements, more than anything else in the whole production, made the music sound contemporary while also preserving the right classical sensibility. Richard loved the notion of directing something that big that was theatrical, so he said yes, and then we had a meeting with myself, Peter, Margaret, Jeanne, and Richard. Jeannie knew the Messiah intimately, inside out, and we knew we couldn't do the whole thing. It was way too long. So we understood it'd have to be a shortened version, and we'd have to figure out how to do that.

So we went to the Apple restaurant up the block where I held a lot of meetings, and we're sitting around and I'm listening to them talk about it, and I'm thinking, "Whoa, wait a minute. They want to hold auditions, they want a chorus of like twenty people, and they're talking about the band and maybe some strings," and at one point, Jeanne says to me, "So how familiar are you with it?" And I said, "Not that familiar, other than the 'Hallelujah Chorus.'" And Jeanne says, "Go over to Tower [Records]. You'll be able to get a copy of it." So I go over to Tower, which was right down the block from the club at Fourth and Broadway, and I'm overwhelmed by how many versions there are, like thirty or forty versions of this thing. I buy two or three versions, and I listen to it, and I realize that perhaps I've bitten off more than I can chew. And so for the first time in my life, in terms of getting an idea and moving forward, I'm actually thinking of calling the whole thing off. So I called Margaret and I said, "Look, Maggie, I'm in a weird position because I had no idea it was this big, and I hate to do this, but I think I'm going to bail." And she said to me—and I trusted her—she said, "I'll get you through it. I'll audition the singers. I'll conduct the choir. You won't have to worry. And Richard and Peter will get you through the musical end." And I trusted them as well. So I took a deep breath and then I spoke to Jeanne, and she said the same as Margaret: "I'll get you through it." So they started to put it together, and they made a list of what there was to do.

RICHARD BARONE: I kind of knew the Messiah, but I wasn't that familiar with it, nor had I really gone to performances of it. So I started researching it, and I found that it was not a church piece. It was done in music halls originally, and it was actually done as a charity piece. They raised money by doing the Messiah as a story, and I liked that it had a lot of Old Testament and New Testament, so it was not just a New Testament thing, if you know what I mean. It covered a wider range originally. And I thought, "Ok, I can get into this." And I thought I had the idea about having the artists doing the arias in their own style, whatever that style might be. If it's folk, then super folk; if it's blues, I mean, do a really deep and dirty blues. And if it was a rock or a pop rock piece, let's try that. So we'd have to get a choir, and we'd need at least maybe twenty people in it to give that sound of a choir. But then every other part was a solo done in a different genre, like what would be played in the clubs of Greenwich Village. So that really tied it to The Bottom Line and the music that came out of there, and Allan loved the idea, so I started working on it.

ALLAN PEPPER: The other thing was Richard and Peter came up with the notion that they would audition the people they wanted in the morning, and do the rehearsals during the week in the mornings and afternoons when the club was dark, and Margaret said she would do the rehearsals with the choir separately every Sunday for four weeks before the thing debuted. And then a week before the show we took time off from our nighttime shows and I actually kept the club dark for a week, which was a big expense, and we started to blend everything together. So the first day, let's say, would be a Monday, and we did Act One. Tuesday, we did Act Two. Wednesday, we solved any problems. Then came Thursday; we did the two acts together with the soloists. And Friday, we performed it.

JEANNE STAHLMAN: I had the idea that we should have a reader, because I said, "We can connect all these pieces; something that would take ten minutes to sing we can do in a minute." So we put together a narration, and Vin [Scelsa] agreed to do it. That sort of became the structure, and Peter Kiesewalter did the arrangements, Margaret Dorn ran the chorus, and Richard directed—and that's where it went.

RICHARD BARONE: The chorus served as our anchors to make sure we had some people singing in tune, and we had a good choir. Then we filled it in with other people. So we had a large choir, a string section, two violins, a viola, and a cello, and Peter led the rhythm section and conducted the strings. We somehow pulled it all together, and it was, I think, a very big hit for Allan.

The Bottom Line's Downtown Messiah proved to be one of the most popular original productions in the club's entire history. After its debut in 1998, the show was presented every year right through the 2003 holiday season, garnering critical acclaim and sold-out performances each and every year. Moreover, each year found new artists coming aboard to participate, including Dan Bern, Susan Werner, Don Byron, the Accidentals, Tony Trischka, Dar Williams, Syd Straw, Hubert Sumlin, and Soozy Tyrell.

RICHARD BARONE: The Downtown Messiah had a lot of people from the Bottom Line community, like Jane Siberry, Terre Roche, David Johansen, and Pete and Maura Kennedy—just a lot of people who had played the club many times over the years. So it felt very homey. It was a really nice way to have a holiday show that was a little different because it had an experimental edge to it, as well as being one of the most well-known holiday oratorios. It was also great because of the different styles of the artists that we had in it.

ALLAN PEPPER: Each year it was really interesting bringing in different artists, and so until the end, it was in a constant state of evolution. That was because Margaret, Peter, Richard, and Jeannie would come back every year wanting to include material that wasn't in the last one and wanting to make it better. That creative department never said it was finished. They were always adding something to it. And look at who we brought to it. Once again, if you look at the artists, a lot of those artists a) were people within the Village community or b) were people that I had relationships with over the years, like Terre Roche, Randy Brecker, Marshall Crenshaw, Vernon Reid, Gary Lucas, and Pete and Maura Kennedy. And David Johansen took part, God bless him, and he was the only one that, even though we'd say, "You got to stay with the lyrics," he'd try to change the lyrics because, well, that's David.

JEANNE STAHLMAN: I had told everybody, "I don't care what you do with the music, obviously we're not trying to do a classical piece, but you can't change the lyrics . . . And I'm there at a rehearsal and I hear David, and he's got the devil with the red dress in his song. And I'm like, David, "There's no devil in the red dress in the Messiah."

MEG GRIFFIN: The Downtown Messiah is something that, and I know I'm not alone in this, I miss every year at Christmas time. The first couple of times it was done, I attended as an audience member, and I was very supportive. I talked about it on the air a lot. Vin was the narrator and he did a beautiful job. And Vin, like me, had stage fright. I know people don't really expect this from radio people, but it's true. Once we're up there, we're ok, but for weeks leading up to any of these things, he and I both could be just sick to our stomachs. And with the Messiah, Vin was finally like, "I can't do it anymore." And I'm telling him, "But you're Vin. You're so good." But when you feel like it doesn't matter if people tell you you're good, you're like, "I don't care. I can't take the nausea anymore." So Allan asked me, and really hesitatingly, I agreed, because I never liked to say no to him. And I did like to sort of push myself toward my fears.

When I took over the narrating position, some of the artists were consistent, and then there would be rotating new artists every year. So it was a way to really discover how great certain people were. One of the ones who struck me, and I had only seen her to that point at The Bottom Line as a backup singer for Buster Poindexter, was the incredible singer who really has a good jazz career going now, Catherine Russell. Catherine would always sing at The Downtown Messiah. She would do, I believe, "I Know That My Redeemer Liveth," and I mean, she would just take the house down. It was such an honor to be part of it because, after all, it was Handel. And Allan found a way to find these incredible downtown hipster musicians who were classically trained, so as much as they were a bunch of downtown beatnik types, it was high quality.

I took my father and mother to it one time, and my dad knew something that the audience didn't know, and I didn't know, and Allan didn't know. When it got to the point in the show where the "Hallelujah Chorus" is performed, I'm on stage looking across the room and I'm seeing my father standing up. He was tall, and he had beautiful white Irish hair at that point, and you couldn't miss him. And he's standing and I'm like, "What is Dad doing?" And he's turning around and he's looking at everybody in the room who's seated, and he's signaling to them with his hands to get up. And what he taught all of us that night was that it was a tradition going back in history to Ireland to the earliest performances of this, that when the "Hallelujah Chorus" is played, the audience should stand. And Allan recognized that. In future years after my father had passed, he would put out a sort of program guide, and on one of them, he put, "Dedicated to Jim Griffin, who showed us the way." I really loved being involved in it because it would be packed with people who really loved the music. People from all different kinds of backgrounds would go to it. It was a holiday thing that everybody could share and love. And it had that spirit of community, and very much a New York thing.

ALLAN PEPPER: Now, there was one big reason that the Downtown Messiah was very, very special to me. I noticed over the years, Eileen would come and see the shows, and I would see she always wondered what it might be like to be on that stage, not from an ego standpoint, but to play, to perform, to be creative, right? And so I came to her when we were putting this thing together, and I said, "Eileen, I have something I want to talk to you about. I have a gift for you." So she said, "What's that?" And I said, "You know the way you always talk about what it would be like to be on that stage, how important that stage is." She said, "Yeah." So I said, "Well, we're going to do a version of Handel's Messiah," and she knew what it was, and I said, "I've talked to Margaret Dorn about it, and I want you to be in the choir." And she looked at me and said, "Really?" And I said, "Yeah, I really want you to be in the choir. You're going to have an opportunity to perform onstage at The Bottom Line." She was very touched.

So she leaves the room, and after a while, she comes back in and says, "I'm not going to do it." I said, "What? Why not?" And she looked at me and said, "Because everybody is going to think I'm only in it because I'm your wife. And I'm very uncomfortable with that." I said, "Eileen, you sing great, and you read music," because the chorus had to sight-read while Margaret was conducting it, and the singers had to be great. We only had four weeks to pull it together. And I said, "Eileen, all I'm doing is opening a door. You'll walk through it. But here's what you have to understand. I would not compromise myself or put you in that position if I didn't in my heart feel you could do this. I wouldn't embarrass you, and I certainly wouldn't compromise my integrity, that's for sure." So that made some sense to her, and I think that made her feel good. Well, nobody treated her like she was my wife. She was treated instantly as one of the singers. Not everybody in the chorus knew each other going in. So basically, when they started, and I was kind of watching, she fell right in. Immediately Margaret would say, "Ok, let's go to this aria or this chorus," and she'd count off and they'd do it, and Eileen would fit right in.

The other reason that this was so important to me was that this production, more than anything I ever did, became a real family affair. Besides Eileen, my son Gordon, who also can sing and has perfect pitch, was the section leader for the tenors. Margaret would say, "Gordon, we need—what's that note?" and he would sing it. So it was Gordon and Eileen." And then in the second year of the Messiah, I thought we needed a little bit more from the standpoint of exits, entrances, and stage traffic. When I talked about it with Richard, he brought up my daughter Stacey, who was a choreographer, and had worked with Richard before. She was an assistant to Lynne Taylor-Corbett, who did the movie *Footloose* and was a Tony nominee, and Stacey had worked on a couple of Broadway shows. Richard and Stacey had their own relationship, and at the same time I felt a bit protective as a dad, as he was asking for her to be on the production and I was concerned about how that would come across. I talked about it with Stacey, and she told me that I taught her to hold her own, and she did. The irony was that some of the biggest creative conflicts were between the two of us, and we would work them out late at night over milk and cookies when we got home from rehearsal. It was one of the most rewarding experiences of both of our lives.

Every year we presented The Downtown Messiah, from 1998 to 2003, and I got it broadcast live on WFUV. It was actually taped at a performance ahead of time because we generally did the show at the club about a week before actual Christmas, and it was then aired on Christmas Eve. After the success of the first one, the Metro Channel cable station produced a half-hour documentary about the making of the show, coupled with a half-hour of taped highlights of the 1999 performance. The following year, the Metro Channel returned and taped the whole show live to be broadcast on Christmas, and in 2002, with the assistance of FUV, The Downtown Messiah was broadcast to 120 public radio stations around the country. It meant a great deal to me that my family was involved artistically in the production, as well as the fact that it all started with a flip remark that I made to Jeanne Stahlman at a Glen Burtnik Christmas show. To this day, it reminds me that you're only limited by your own imagination as to what you can achieve.

* * *

Mark Volman and Howard Kaylan are known to multiple generations of fans as the singing frontmen of mid-1960s folk-rocking hitmakers the Turtles ("Happy Together," "Let Me Be") as well as their alter agos Flo (the Phlorescent Leech) and Eddie, whose early 1970s stint with Frank Zappa set them down a path of musical mischief from which, for their devoted followers, they gleefully never recovered. As a foreshadowing of just how wide the duo could wander with their musical shenanigans in just the blink of a winking eye, their history with The Bottom Line began with shows in 1975 that included such surprise guests as Lou Reed, John Belushi, Gene Simmons, and former boss Zappa. In 1980, the two appeared on backing vocals on Bruce Springsteen's first bona fide hit single, "Hungry Heart"—the genesis of which came after Stevie Van Zandt caught one of their Bottom Line performances and suggested to Springsteen, who was looking for some Beach Boys-styled harmonies, that he use them on the track.

HOWARD KAYLAN: At the time, we really had very little idea how big Bruce was. The first time we met him we were coming back from some European tour. We were at an airport and bumped into this guy who unveiled himself to be a roadie. He said his name was "Natty Dreadlock." Sure, pal. And he lived it, and he wanted to be it, but he was a roadie. So we're in Columbus, Ohio, and we're changing planes, and we meet this guy and he says, "You ought to come to the Springsteen show tonight. I'm helping out." We had the day off and didn't have anything to do. So we said, ok, and went with this guy, whose name I still don't know to this day. We got to the venue and stood in the very back of the auditorium, and we listened to Bruce do one of his legendary three-hour sound checks. We'd never really heard the guy at all before, and after one of the run-throughs, he brought Ronnie Spector up onstage to sing with the band, and she sounded wonderful with them. And then Bruce goes up to the mic and he goes, "Yo, Flo and Eddie out there. Why don't you come up here and sing with us?" So we said, "Yes, sir," and we came up and sang with Ronnie for "Baby, I Love You" and "Be My Baby," and one or two other Ronette songs, which were easy to know and to remember and to do, and it sounded just beautiful. And Bruce said, "Ok, tonight." And so we said, "Sure thing, man." So we hung out and watched the show, and then he called us up onstage when Ronnie came up and we ran up and sang with them, and we really didn't think much of it. It was just a fun night, and that was about it. But then Steve came to see us at The Bottom Line, and I think that's when the idea of us singing on the song came to him.

So we got a call from the studio when they were recording the next album, *The River*, and they said Bruce had a song that he wanted us to do. We went down and heard the rest of the album, and it sounded like Bruce, all right. Then he played us "Hungry Heart," and Mark and I looked at each other and it was kind of like, "God, this doesn't sound like a Bruce Springsteen record at all. Where's Sandy? Where's the motorcycle in the night? We're not getting Jersey vibes from this, at all." It was so different for him, really, that we questioned his sanity. We kept asking, even as the tape was rolling, "Are you sure, man, you want to do this song that way?" And Bruce says, "Yeah, this is what I want." And we said, "Ok, we'll do anything you want, man." We just went, "Wow, that doesn't sound like Bruce at all, but we get it. It's a very interesting record, and what a strange way to take it, but we'll do anything he wants." So he laid out what he wanted, and it was simple, and it only took an hour, maybe two hours to do. And we left there never thinking it was going to be as big as it was—at all. But as an album cut, we just figured, "Sure, that'll be wonderful." And then we had spies, Steve among them, and Steve was the guy who called us and said, "Ok, you're not going to believe this, but it's the single. You're going to be hearing a lot of yourself soon." And then sure enough, the record took off, and I'm still sort of surprised it was as big as it was, but it was wonderful.

In 1981, Allan asked us to do a New Year's show, and people came and we did well. We always delivered for him, and he was always looking for that. It didn't matter what genre of music you did, if you were an acapella group or a magician, if you could deliver the people, Allan wanted you back. The regulars were coming to all our shows, people who had seen us before, and who wanted particular songs—like "Hey, play 'Nikki Hoy,' play 'Where's the Hippo.'" Stuff like that. And we're basically whores when it comes to that kind of thing. We'll do anything to please an audience. Actually, we're like a USO show coming through town. And once we started doing the New Year's Eve shows, it just kept going, year after year.

All told, Flo and Eddie played The Bottom Line either on or around New Year's Eve from 1981 to 1994. Their band throughout that entire time was anchored by Meat Loaf's ex-touring drummer Joe Stefko, who had helped get the duo back on the road after they'd taken a break from performing live and were concentrating on their rock and roll radio talk show and film/TV work. Stefko's initial introduction to them had nothing to do with music, however.

JOE STEFKO: Flo and Eddie were producing my friend's band The Good Rats on Long Island. One day in the middle of a blizzard, their drummer Joey Franco calls me up and he says, "Joe, you really got to help." I said, "What do you need? What's up?" He says, "Well, we're in the studio with Flo and Eddie. We really can't get out of here. We're snowed in, and they're out of weed. Really, it's bad." I said, "What do you want?" He says, "Two ounces. Can you get here with two ounces?" I said, "Yeah, I can." So I go down to the studio and I sell Mark and Howard two ounces of weed. And that's how I first met them.

I got the guys from the Meat Loaf band to go out with them, and they started touring again. Now The Bottom Line, that wasn't the only thing we did. We got a deal with Harrah's in Vegas and Tahoe and Reno every year, so we were just working more and more, and we got hooked up with this big sports agent who wanted to get into music. We were the first band he was an agent for, and he had this idea to get four or five bands like us and put out a tour, and they ended up calling it The Happy Together Tour. This was right at the start of the 1980s. It was like Gary Puckett and the Union Gap and the Grass Roots; every year it was different people, but it was always the Turtles, and we closed the show. On the tours, every band just did their hits. You go up, you do six songs. So we were touring and doing very big venues, doing Jones Beach with 10,000 seaters with these four bands, having a great time with all these guys.

We'd be out there for months at a clip in our tour bus, and whatever we were into that year of touring, it could have been Elvis movies, it could have been John Carpenter films; whatever it was, we took notes, and that's what we did for the end-of-the-year shows at The Bottom Line. The Bottom Line, to us was a way to just do whatever we wanted to do, and it was like giving a monkey a gun. And we had some great openers: We had some great comedians open for us: Richard Belzer, Chris Rush, Chris Rock. One year, it was "Weird Al" Yankovic.

"WEIRD AL" YANKOVIC: My manager, Jay Levey, was New York-based, and he was very well aware of the club and, of course, had a relationship with Allan Pepper, and he kind of got me up to speed. He let me know how cool it was that I was playing The Bottom Line. It was an amazing thing doing that show with Flo and Eddie. As a Californian, I remember it was very cold since it was the middle of winter in New York. But just the vibe of it was amazing, certainly, especially starting out very early on in my career; it was very cool that I got to play there. When I started out, it was just me and the accordion, with perhaps my drummer banging on the accordion case. But by the time we played The Bottom Line, we had really just formed as a full band, and it's the same band that I've had to this very day. So that was probably 1983, and I know that year I also played The Bottom Line, where they had a Rocky Road ice cream eating contest, which I was doing then to promote my single, "I Love Rocky Road." And I just remember that up until that point, I liked Rocky Road ice cream pretty well, but after that, I had eaten so much of it that it turned me off to that flavor for a few decades.

HOWARD KAYLAN: Of course, sometimes the New Year's audience just didn't understand what the hell we were doing. I think the show that really got everybody on edge was one we did with the Monster Killer Guy in the hockey mask in the audience who terrified everyone—even Allan Pepper. We had programs printed for it, and we put them on every table. It was called *Welcome to Hell, Man*. We learned some new songs for the show, along with at least twenty minutes at least of John Carpenter instrumental stuff from *Halloween*, *The Fog*, *The Thing*, all of his stuff, and we played it very seriously.

Some people in the audience kind of got freaked out, especially when the monster Steven started roaming through the audience—he was a huge man, like a 300-pound man in a hockey mask— and he's holding a machete and going from table to table, threatening these people, sitting on girls' laps and just being rude. And actually, he was a real asshole of a guy. He was a friend of the crew, and he was one of those guys who just would keep asking, "Can I be in your band?" And we would always just go, "Er, no, man, you can't be in our band. That's not really how things work." But that one year, we told him we had a place in this particular show if he wanted to be the monster. And he of course says, "Oh, hell yeah! That'd be great." So he was the monster and he scared everybody, including the staff. I think some of the waitresses did go up to Allan's office maybe and say, "This is not what we signed up for. We signed up for, like, an evening with Leo Kottke, and now it's New Year's Eve and we get these morons and they're jumping around, and the guy's got a hockey mask and people are screaming and he's got a bloody machete." Well, he took it very seriously, our monster guy.

The second night we did kind of soften it up a little bit. We had to. Allan just said, "Uh, uh boys. Uh,uh." And we said, "But this is the only show we know now, Allan. We've learned it. We've rehearsed it. Everybody knows everything. We've got girl singers, we have horn players. I mean, we can't just tell them no." So the next best thing we could do was instead of Steven the Monster, we changed him to Shakey Greene, the Monster from the Catskills. It made things much easier, and Pepper felt much better about it. After all, he is a Catskills guy. So instead of threatening the audience, this guy would stand up on stage and scream terrible jokes, terrible Henny Youngman one-liners that were just, "Oh God, no." But for us that was way more hideous than a machete, because the horrible jokes never stopped.

We did an Elvis-themed show one year, and it was magnificent. We looked for the worst songs from Elvis' movies we could find—and we sure found them. We had Stefko sing "Go East Young Man" from *Harum Scarum* wearing a sheik outfit while sitting on a tasseled lounge chair with harem girls dancing around him. The audience had no idea what we were doing, and this was maybe even more difficult to explain than the monster—like, "Why are you doing these songs, and what are the girls doing onstage in harem outfits?" Well, yes. We did have two girl singers in sparkling harem outfits, with long, glittery, see-through pants and stuff. And they weren't very good because, well, if they were good that would've defeated the purpose.

We did one show that was yacht rock pretty much, and that was difficult because the songs that were available to do were just pathetic. They still are, but unless you've got a sense of humor, no one wants to be Rick-rolled. We were always ok as long as we could please ourselves. It really wasn't a matter so much of pleasing the crowd, because they were always along for the ride no matter what it was. Sometimes we demanded a lot of them. I know we did, but our attitude was, "Fuck 'em if they can't take a joke." I mean, that's been our attitude for a long time. I think it holds up rather well. I mean, we weren't charging $150 a ticket. This wasn't Broadway. This was a cabaret show we were doing there for people at tables. Every single Christmas holiday we were there doing about six or eight nights wrapped around New Year's. So it got to be wonderful for us, and it was good for the club too. I mean, I think it kept them on their feet through that tough Christmas vacation period when a lot of groups just don't want to work anyway. The Bottom Line was a wonderful place to kind of have as a home base in New York. Being from California, I think there was that juxtaposition that people actually got. I mean, there we are on stage in Hawaiian shirts and stuff, and we were definitely not of the East, though we were on the radio in the East. We had sort of a foundation, doing our rock and talk show on WLIR out on Long Island.

JOE STEFKO: That Bottom Line New Year's crowd, we owe them everything. They allowed us to do whatever we wanted, and they loved it. Every year we would talk to the fans, and it was like, "We couldn't wait to see what you were going to do, what the theme would be each year." We did so many different things. We did a Jerry Lewis show, and we did "I Lost My Heart in a Drive-In Movie," from *The Patsy*, and Mark sang it like Jerry, and that was hilarious. One year we opened with a warm-up that was the band doing our version of *Wheel of Fortune*. I came out in a fur coat, dressed as Vanna White, and the guys in the band would say, "Ok, Vanna, I want to buy a vowel." And a couple of letters would be showing, and they'd say, "I think I got it—Ike Turner!" And the buzzer went off to signal it was wrong and of course it ended up "The Turtles." And then Mark and Howard came onstage. I mean, we did all this before we actually did a song. Where else could you do something like this? It didn't matter what we did, no matter how stupid it was. The audiences loved it.

Mark and Howard were the greatest. And after John Cale and after Meat Loaf, and then I played with Edgar Winter, and I like him, too, but with these two guys, even though I know that I'm not going to make a fortune and I'm probably shooting my career in the foot, I thought, "I'm staying here." I mean, I'm playing, playing my ass off. They're used to drummers who are out to lunch and play like crazy, like Johnny Barbata and Ainsley Dunbar. And I would do the craziest things, and they never ever complained to me, and I'd play the craziest things, and one of them would turn around and smile, like "I know where that came from," or "Where did you pull that out of?" And I just thought, "This is where I want to be." And I wound up being with them for forty years.

A special highlight of the Flo and Eddie Bottom Line shows was their send-up of Springsteen, in which Volman launched into a monologue, playing Bruce in his young scuffling days at the Jersey shore, telling his old man that "I don't want to be a bus driver. I want a guitar," and determining that all he really needed to make it big was a Fender Stratocaster and "a big Black guy playing saxophone." As the band vamped, Kaylan would take over, mimicking The Boss for a spot-on melodramatic rendition of Crispian St. Peter's left field 1965 hit, "The Pied Piper" that came complete with a bridge consisting of the theme song from the early 1960s sitcom Car 54 Where Are You? *As Stefko would say four decades later: "To this day, I cannot hear the theme from Car 54 without losing it."*

***

Besides Flo and Eddie's long run, New Year's Eve shows at The Bottom Line over the years featured a truly wide range of performers including Barry Manilow (1974), LaBelle's Nona Hendryx (1977), Ula Hedwig and the Harlettes (1978), Garland Jeffreys (1979), NRBQ (1994), Buster Poindexter (1995, 1997), Dan Bern (1998), Billy Bragg (2000)—and, during the club's final three years (2001–2003), Buddy and Julie Miller.

One of the true MVP's of American roots music, Ohio-born, New Jersey-bred Buddy Miller's winding career has seen him recording and/or touring with the likes of Emmylou Harris, John Fogerty, Steve Earle, Lucinda Williams, Robert Plant, and Alison Krauss, Solomon Burke, and Jim Lauderdale. Meanwhile, his and songwriter wife Julie's songs about life, love, and faith have been recorded by numerous artists including Lee Anne Womack, the (Dixie) Chicks, Brooks and Dunn, Garth Brooks, and Jimmy Scott. He also spent several years as the music producer for the TV series Nashville, where the Millers have lived since the early 1990s. Still, his connections to the New York music scene, and to Allan Pepper and Stanley Snadowsky, have their own deep roots.

BUDDY MILLER: It's a funny thing. When I was just starting out in the early 1970s, I was in a band in upstate New York, outside of Woodstock, called St. Elmo's Fire, but way before the movie came out. We had a—I want to put quotes around this—"producer," Richie Drew, and his attorney was Stanley. I think it was probably due to Stanley talking to Allan that maybe Allan put up with us, and we played Folk City. It was a strange pairing because we had two banjo players and a fiddle player, and I played guitar and pedal steel at that point. We did two nights with a jazz band, the Brecker Brothers, and then we did another show there with Phoebe Snow before her first record came out. So anyway, that was the first and earliest connection. We'd come in, and when we'd stay overnight, we didn't have any money, so we'd sleep in our school bus on the street, and if it was wintertime, then we'd come in and sleep on the—they weren't really sofas, whatever you'd call them—in Folk City during the day as we were freezing and didn't have any place to hang.

I was still in that band when The Bottom Line first got going, and I remember I saw an ad that said that Waylon Jennings and Linda Hargrove *[a singer-songwriter known as the "Blue Jean Country Queen"]* were playing at the club [August 1974]. We were flat broke and didn't have money for tickets for anything—it was like one of those communal things where everybody puts their money in the pot, and that's what we used to eat on—but I talked them into driving down to New York, and that was my first Bottom Line show. I was almost as big of a Linda Hargrove fan as I was of Waylon. It was a great pairing. It was like what Bill Graham had been doing at the Fillmore East, a very eclectic, great, thoughtful pairing, and I loved it. And I don't remember if it was the Hells Angels or what biker gang was there for the late Waylon show that we were at, but it was wild.

I moved to Austin right after that show, and then after Julie and I got together, we moved from Austin to the New York area. We didn't move into the city. I was just a little too nervous that my van with all our gear in it would get broken into, so we moved to Union City. And then we got broken into two nights in a row out there anyway. But that's where I met people like [guitarist] Larry Campbell and [jazz musician] Lincoln Schleifer, all dear lifelong friends. That was a really special time. While Julie and I were up there, and it was just a short time, we were working six or seven nights a week, but there were two shows that I didn't want to miss at The Bottom Line. The first was The Wild Tchoupitoulas, and seeing them there [June 1979] was insane. I'd seen the Neville Brothers in Austin, but I hadn't seen them do the Wild Tchoupitoulas thing, and The Bottom Line was such an intimate space with the raised stage, and almost anywhere you're sitting in there, you're kind of pretty close up unless you have one of the pillars in front of you. But we were pretty close up, and seeing those amazing Mardi Gras costumes was something. And, interestingly enough, young [bassist] Daryl Johnson was in the Nevilles at that point, and here's a guy who would later be playing with Emmylou. So that was one of two shows that I took a night off from gigging and splurged for tickets for.

The other one that Julie and I went to together was the George Jones show where Linda [Ronstadt] and Bonnie [Raitt] showed up [in August 1980]. As a matter of fact, I was living up there during one of his No-Shows, and I think I could be wrong about this, but I was driving into New York before one that I think was broadcast on whatever the country station was in the city that he was supposed to be playing, and they were saying, "Well, he's not here." But that George show we went to I remember because his and the band's buses were parked right there by the club, and as Julie and I were walking to get in line, we saw George looking out of the bus, shaking his head like, "No, I can't sing anymore," and pointing at his throat and just going, "I can't sing." But that night he did show up, and it was a typical and spectacular George Jones show that ended with Linda and Bonnie sitting in. It was just insane.

I went to high school up in Jersey, and I went to a lot of shows at the Fillmore East before The Bottom Line was around, and it was very cool and there were great pairings. But it was a big venue, and The Bottom Line was just such a perfect size venue for that kind of thing. The Bottom Line was unique, and later on, when we got to play there, it was always a big deal to us. It's funny; we were so unaware of knowing anything. This was even before we played there, but when those DeLorean cars went under, I think it was *Time* magazine's cover that week that had a picture [of John DeLorean] that said "The Bottom Line. . . Busted," and Julie, who didn't know anything about DeLorean cars, just saw it and thought it was about the club.

After we played there a few times, we got an offer to play New Year's Eve, and I thought, "Bottom Line on New Year's Eve? Why not?" So we played there three years in a row, I guess [2001–2003]. It was a big deal to us. Maybe it was just sold out because it was New Year's Eve at The Bottom Line, but they were great shows. The crowds for us were always so appreciative. That was the place we wanted to play, and we'd always have friends join us there too, like Larry [Campbell] and his wife Theresa [Williams], and Steve Earle. Chip Taylor [composer of "Wild Thing" and "Angel of the Morning"] came out and sat in with us at one of those New Year's Eve shows, and he's a friend and a hero, and [singer-songwriter] Kim Richey was on one of those dates with us too. And Allan also booked me when Julie stopped going out on the road for a solo show with me and J. J. Cale [composer of "After Midnight"], and that was incredible, even with just the little basket of Oreos in the dressing rooms—and if it was two nights, you couldn't count on the Oreo basket being refreshed. All the Bottom Line shows were such special gigs for me, but that's the one that really stands out—being able to play, listen to, and hang with J. J. Cale. Oh, man, I just loved it.

David Johansen performs "The People That Walked in Darkness" accompanied by guitarist Gary Lucas (left) and vocalist Catherine Russell in the original production of *The Downtown Messiah*, 1998. Photo © Ebet Roberts.

Richard Barone, the director of *The Downtown Messiah*, gestures toward jazz trumpeter Randy Brecker as they perform the aria "The Trumpet Shall Sound," joined by the full choir, 2002. Photo by Chuck Pulin / Courtesy Barry Skolnick.

Musical arranger and conductor Peter Kiesewalter leads the orchestra from the piano as they accompany the choir singing "Behold the Lamb of God" in the 2001 production of *The Downtown Messiah*. Behind him is cellist Lisa Haney. Courtesy Richard Barone.

Surrounded by fellow choir members, Eileen Pepper (lower right) and Gordon Pepper (upper right) sing "Lift Up Your Heads, O Ye Gates," in *The Downtown Messiah*, 2001. Courtesy Richard Barone.

Choral director Margaret Dorn conducts the choir—and the audience, in singing the "Hallelujah" chorus, the finale of the original 1998 production of *The Downtown Messiah*. On the left is beloved radio personality Vin Scelsa, who read the recitative. Photo © Ebet Roberts.

15 STANLEY

ALLAN PEPPER: Riley once told me he overheard a conversation between two agents where one of them referred to me and Stanley as the Cocker Spaniel and the Doberman. I found that amusing because Stanley was anything but a Doberman. To those people who really knew him, he was kind and very caring. He was generous, providing free legal advice to members of the staff as well as loans to close friends. He was a great listener who often could cut right to the heart of a problem with an obvious solution that others would miss. One of the reasons Stanley was such a fine lawyer was his ability to close a deal. He firmly believed that a deal was not a good deal unless both parties walked away feeling they got something. But to those he negotiated with, he could be intimidating, not so much by his size (he was a big guy) or his demeanor, as much as his intellect, because he was a very, very smart man. Stanley always listened carefully while others spoke, and no matter how emotional the other side got, he was always calm, and when he finally did speak, he was measured, and what he said was well thought out, precise, and to the point. As someone who knew Stanley since we were ten years old, I learned early on that when arguing with him, I should never accept his first premise, because if you did, the argument was over whether you realized it or not. I was ruled by emotion and gut instinct based on first impressions, while Stanley was practical, analytical, and governed by facts. It all helped him be very successful at gambling and helped pay his way through college with a weekly poker game.

As disciplined as he was about business, the one area of his life that was his Achilles heel was his weight. It was the one area he was very sensitive about. So when on a limo ride back from Atlantic City, a well-meaning but abrasive gambling buddy bet him $10,000 that he couldn't lose a hundred pounds in a year, it just wasn't in Stanley's nature to turn down the challenge. And with $10,000 at stake, he wasn't about to be casual about it. He stopped ordering desserts and began eating smaller portions of everything. Water became his drink of choice and there was no eating after dinner. Every afternoon he'd put on his new sweat suit and walk around the perimeter of Washington Square Park for an hour. He did this, rain or shine, seven days a week, and by the end of the first month, you could start to notice a real difference. He'd started to drop off pounds, and by the end of the fourth month, he'd made real progress toward claiming that $10,000.

There's a Yiddish expression my mother would use which, in its wisdom, declares, "Man makes plans, and God laughs." Stanley was religiously maintaining his diet and exercise agenda, and then two things happened that made everything he had achieved go sideways. His father, Jack Snadowsky, was diagnosed with terminal cancer and wound up in Brookdale Hospital in East New York, and shortly after that, his wife Michelle, who was pregnant with Stanley's second daughter, Daria, developed a serious complication with her pregnancy, which was treated by extended bed rest at Northshore Hospital in Manhasset out on Long Island. Stanley would now start every day spending his mornings with his dad in Brooklyn, followed by afternoons with Michelle on the Island. Trying to maintain this brutal schedule, the only thing that brought him any comfort was food. And so, all the weight that Stanley had worked so hard to lose quickly came back on, and as his weight increased, his chance to claim the $10,000 rapidly receded. Even though there were still several months to go before the bet came due, Stanley, being Stanley, knew circumstances were so against him that he wasn't going to be able to lose the weight. And the thought of having to pay this guy $10,000 was making him crazy. "What are you going to do?" I asked. "I don't know yet," he answered, "But I'll think of something." By the next trip to Atlantic City, Stanley was prepared to deal with it. As soon as I saw him the next day, I asked, "Did you admit you lost the bet?" "Sort of," he chuckled. "Well, what did you say?" I asked. Stanley smiled. "I settled it for $6,000."

Stanley was a complex guy. There were many sides to him, and as serious as he often appeared to those he did business with, he had a terrific sense of humor that could be very mischievous. One Friday afternoon, I was working at my desk when the intercom buzzed. The box office was asking if I could come down because they were having a problem with a customer. "What's the problem? I asked." "Did you and Stanley present Herbie Mann at the Loew's King's in Brooklyn twenty years ago," she said. "Does that have something to do with the problem?" "Well," she said, "we have a gentleman in front of us who has two tickets for that show who couldn't make it because of the torrential rain that day and would like a refund." A few minutes later, I was standing in front of a polite young man who explained that his father had made plans to take him to the concert, but because of the weather, they never got there. He had been looking forward to the concert and had been so disappointed that he had carried the tickets in his wallet for years. When he passed by the club and saw Herbie Mann advertised as an upcoming attraction, he thought it was an opportunity to at least get a refund. He then produced the two tickets.

I was stunned. I pointed out that the concert was twenty years ago and that would have been the proper time to get a refund. I also attempted to patiently explain that the concert at the Loew's King's was put on by Alstan Productions, and that the current Herbie Mann concert was being put on by The Bottom Line—a completely different entity. He countered with, "But you and Stanley were Alstan, and you and Stanley are the Bottom Line." I was speechless. He became more animated with my silence and continued, "My father not only bought advance tickets, he got me flyers and posters to hang in my room. "Then," he said, "wait here," and before I knew it, he was gone and back, carrying a stack of flyers and posters that were twenty years old. It was at that moment that I looked around, like this can't be real, and said, "Ok, what's going on?" I heard a muffled guffaw from the bar area. Stanley, who had orchestrated this charade, was watching this whole thing play out and was now beside himself; he could no longer contain his laughter. It had all been a joke—on me.

What had happened was that earlier in the week, Stanley had been cleaning out his closet and found several boxes of unused tickets and flyers for our disastrous concert. That gave him an idea: He got to the club early, hoping to find someone coming up to the box office to buy advance tickets for the upcoming Herbie Mann show, and he found a young guy wanting to buy two tickets for that show. Stanley asked him if he would like to see the show for free and then told him what he had to do, gave him the two unsold tickets, and instructed him that no matter what I said to insist that he was due a refund. He then found a place in the bar area that he thought would give him cover, told the box office to call me, and anxiously looked forward to my reaction. It was like we were back in elementary school.

Stanley was a huge fan of Harry Chapin, a fact that was not lost on Ed Micone and Mike Piranian, the two ICM agents who booked Harry. Piranian felt that while Stanley was a very tough negotiator, even he would be vulnerable negotiating a deal when it came to someone he admired. Micone, who was more experienced and had done a lot more business with Stanley over the years, was skeptical, believing that when push came to shove, business would win over pleasure. Piranian disagreed, so they made a bet over it when they called in late 1980 to offer us Chapin's 2,000th career performance. I knew nothing about the bet when Mike called, and I also didn't know that Ed was secretly listening in on an extension. "I think I have a real winner for you and Stanley," he said. "Harry Chapin is looking for just the right place to celebrate his 2,000th concert, and he is leaning toward doing it at The Bottom Line. And to make the deal even sweeter, the guarantee for the three days won't be excessive."

As Mike was talking, I was thinking: "Harry's 2,000th performance. Lots of press, probably a sellout for all six shows, a reasonable fee for Harry, so we stand a chance to make money. What's the catch?" Sure enough, Mike shifted his spiel and went into pressure mode. He told me that Ron Delsner had already said he'd take it, but because Harry had a relationship with me and Stanley that predated The Bottom Line, Chapin would prefer to do it at our club. He also said that he knew that Stanley was a huge fan of Harry's, so the date would be personally important to him as well. Only one small detail had to be settled. Now, as I suspected, came the catch. "Harry's manager is willing to take a small guarantee versus 85 percent of the gross box office receipts, whichever is greater," he said. That meant that if Harry sold out, we'd have the glory of hosting him, but we'd get only 15 percent of the box office receipts as opposed to our usual 50 percent. And that would turn a sure winner into a loser for us business-wise. I started to say "pass," but I caught myself. It would be unfair of me to make a unilateral decision knowing how much Stanley loved Harry and how important Chapin's music was to him. I put Piranian on hold and turned to Stanley at his desk near mine. "Stanley," I said, "Good news-bad news. Mike Piranian's on the phone. He's offering three nights on Harry Chapin." Stanley's entire body language changed. He was beaming. "There's just one problem. They want 85 percent of the ticket sales if that turns out to be greater than the guarantee." With that, Stanley's smile disappeared.

From our first days in the music business, Stanley always said to me, "Remember those are two separate words—music and business. Without one you can't have the other. When art and commerce are at cross purposes, you can never forget the second word." I could tell he was totally conflicted weighing the pros and cons, and after about fifteen seconds came his one-word answer: "Pass." "Really?" I said. "Are you sure? I know how much you love Chapin. How will you feel seeing this go to Delsner and knowing it could have been here?" I got back on with Mike and told him that I was talking to Stanley and we needed another minute, but as I was telling him this, Stanley said, "No. I'm positive. Tell him it's a pass." Before I could say anything, there was a burst of laughter from two people on the other end. They'd heard Stanley in the background, and suddenly I heard Micone's voice screaming in my ear, "I won! I won the bet! I knew it!" I was dumbfounded. Luckily, the two agents were only horsing around to see who was right about Stanley, and fortunately for everyone, we were able to book the dates—and on our usual terms.

When Harry played those January '81 shows, Stanley was there for all of them; it meant a lot to him. And it would mean even more when, just six months later, Ed Micone called again, but this time bearing the sad news that Harry Chapin had died in a car accident.

Here's one of my favorite Stanley stories: In the fall of 1979, I got a call from Ted Kurland, Sonny Rollins' booking agent, wanting to know if we wanted to play Sonny for a weekend in November. My immediate reaction was, "No Fuckin' Way." I was still pissed off and hadn't forgiven Sonny for how he played me at the Town Hall show with the last-minute addition of The Bass Violin Choir, which cost us a lot of money. Stanley, never more than four feet away from me (our desks were right next to each other), was thinking about the future, not the past, and knew if he could just get me to look beyond my anger, we could make back the money we had lost on that concert. He quickly picked up the phone and joined the conversation, and after some small talk, Stanley filled Ted in on our history with Sonny. Given that history, he said the only deal he would offer was one without a percentage because he felt Sonny was too much of a wild card. Basically, he was telling Ted he didn't trust Sonny. On the other hand, Stanley continued, if Sonny accepted a flat fee, provided I was ok with it, we would do a deal, and Kurland said he would take Stanley's offer to Sonny, which he accepted, and Sonny did four sold-out shows.

After that, he began to appear twice a year on a regular basis, and we all got to know each other better, and his were some of my favorite shows. I always looked forward to them. One night at the end of a very successful engagement, Sonny came to the upstairs office to get paid. He always started the conversation by telling Stanley how concerned he was about Stanley's weight and the impact it was having on his health. Sonny and Stanley found they had things in common. They both owned homes in the Catskill Mountains, near Margaretville. They spent the next ten minutes in deep conversation about living in that area and the common experiences they shared. After more time went by, the intercom rang, reminding us that the band was waiting downstairs to get paid. After all, it was close to 3 a.m. Sonny's fee was bundled on Stanley's desk in individual stacks of a thousand dollars. Sonny picked up the first pack and began to count. Stanley said, "Sonny, you don't need to count it, It's all there." Sonny stopped counting and looked over at Stanley. "What if it's short?" he asked. "It won't be," Stanley answered. "I just counted it. If it's short, call me and I'll send you whatever is missing." Sonny, just a little bit skeptical, said, "Suppose I called you and told you it was short $100?" "Then I'd send you the $100," Stanley said. "Just like that?" Sonny asked. "Just like that," Stanley answered. "It won't be short. I guarantee it." "Ok, Stanley," Sonny finally said, "Your word is good enough for me." And with that, he picked up the stacks of bills, placed them in his sport jacket, and left the office.

The following year, Stanley, Sonny, and I find ourselves once more at 3 a.m. in our office. Once again, Sonny's fee is laying on Stanley's desk in individual stacks of a thousand dollars each, and once again, the intercom buzzes reminding us that the band would like to get paid so they can go home. So Sonny picks up the first bundle to start to count it, but this time he asks Stanley if he still guarantees it, and Stanley says he will. "So if I called you and said it was short $500, you'd send it to me, no questions asked?" Sonny asked. "Yes, I would," Stanley said, "because, as always, I've already counted it, and it's all there." "Ok, that's good enough for me," said Sonny, and with that, he gets up, distributes the stacks in his sports jacket, and starts to walk out—only he stops halfway across the room, turns around, and walks back to Stanley and throws a $20 bill on his desk. "Stanley," he says. "You were $20 over last time." And without saying another word, he turns around and leaves.

Anyone who knew Stanley, knew the thing he cherished most was his family. He was devoted to Michelle and their daughters, Leslie and Daria. He was fiercely proud of every one of their accomplishments. Simply put, his family was his life's greatest joy. Nothing gave him greater pleasure than when he could bring both worlds together so that the family could fully enjoy what he helped to create at The Bottom Line. So it made perfect sense to Stanley to have Leslie's Sweet Sixteen party at the club. At Leslie's request, we booked one of her favorite party bands, Buster Poindexter and his Banshees of Blue. It was shortly after that that, to my amazement, Stanley started to become Bill Graham. One afternoon a few weeks after I booked Buster, Stanley casually asked me, "Where do you think we should put the dance floor?" "What dance floor?" I asked. "The one for Leslie's Sweet Sixteen," he answered. "You can't have a disc jockey without a dance floor. And by the way, do you know a good disc jockey?" This was Leslie's night to shine, and Stanley was determined to make it memorable. "I'm on it," I said. Then a week later, he asked me, "Do you think we need a comic?" On and on it went until the big night arrived, and by that time everyone knew that Stanley had a shot at pulling off the perfect party. To everyone who was there, it lived up to those expectations. For Stanley, though, it wasn't that the food was great, or Buster was great, or that the DJ had everybody up dancing that made it a perfect evening. It was the smile that never left Leslie's face the whole night.

*　*　*

In 1993, Stanley decided to move to Las Vegas with his family. This is how it happened: Stanley had a boyhood friend, Mel Schrager, who he knew since junior high school, and they had kept in touch over the years. Mel lived in Vegas, and I think Stanley was kind of restless. I know for a while he and Michelle had looked at houses to buy outside the city; they looked in Connecticut, they looked on Long Island, and there was nothing he was feeling right about. And this friend Mel said, "Stanley, you'd love it out here," and he talked about the gambling and about the lifestyle. So I guess Stanley was starting to think about it, and then he was invited to a wedding out West or some kind of family affair, and he went out there and he told me that, for part of his trip, as long as he was going to be out there, he was going to spend a week with Mel. And he did. He'd never been to Vegas before, and I think he just fell in love with the place. He came back to New York and he convinced Michelle. I don't think she was up for it at first. But it had everything that would appeal to Stanley. It had the constant gambling, and it had all these perks that you'd get if you were a regular, plus the fact that they had these buffets, which went on forever, so they treated you well, and he knew he could work the system. So for Stanley, from the mindset of who he was, if you really think about it, it was Nirvana.

It took a while for his family to get on board with it, but he ultimately moved out there with all of them in '93. Stanley had come to me and basically said, "Look, I want to make this change. We'll do anything you want." He was always like that with me. He said, "You can buy out my share of the club. Or we can still be partners.

I'll do whatever you want." Now I was committed to what I was doing, but I was also committed to him. And he said, "I can continue to do what I do from out there. I can still help with the negotiations. I can still help with the deals." Because one of the things that Stanley did that he was a master at was he'd negotiate unbelievable deals with record companies or anybody who wanted to rent out the place. So he said to me, "I'll still do all that. I'll still negotiate the contracts. I'll still deal with the business aspect of it." He asked me to think about it. So I did, and I told him that I wanted to keep everything intact, and he said, "Then that's what we'll do." And so we did, right up to the end of the club's existence.

* * *

DAN DALEY: I saw Stanley more in Vegas in later years. He introduced me to video poker. It was my first time in Vegas, covering a trade show for a magazine. There wasn't a hotel room to be had. I called Stanley, and he said, "Stand by. I'll give you a call back in ten minutes." So he calls back in less than ten and says, "Ok, you're all set. You've got the Gotti suite at Caesars." I said, "Stanley, I don't think the magazine will pay for that." He said, "Don't worry. There are things you can get in Las Vegas that no amount of money can buy." And he was right. My flight was late getting in, and I met him at the Caesars casino. He was sitting there playing video poker, and he said, "I'm looking forward to showing you the room." So we went up to see it, and it's a four-bedroom suite with a sunken living room. That was my intro to Las Vegas. So every time I'd go, I'd call him. Sometimes he could meet me, sometimes not. There were four or five casinos he'd frequent, and we'd go out to dinner and never paid. He was comped for everything.

STEVE MARTIN (Talent agent): After Stanley moved to Vegas, when I had to go out there usually once or twice a year for other things, I would always spend a day or a night or an evening with Stanley. He loved people from New York coming out to visit; he really enjoyed it. I always liked hanging out with Stanley because I'm a big guy, too, but I wasn't as big as Stanley was. I used to tease him. I told him I felt small and petite hanging out next to him, and he'd laugh. He'd have on the trucker jeans, the big poker belt buckle, and the flannel shirt. He looked like he had just parked his semi-truck in front of the place to come in and gamble. But as soon as he walked into the casinos, well, walking around the casinos with him was like walking around with Moses. The pit bosses would always come right over. "Oh, Mr. Snadowsky, how are you? So good to see you." He was comped at every five-star restaurant in Vegas he walked into. It was quite remarkable. He got me comped at the Luxor and the Desert Inn. I think all I paid for was telephone calls and tips.

He clearly had juice in the town, and it was fun to watch him play blackjack. He'd switched to blackjack more than poker, and he was an incredible blackjack player to the point where he was banned from the Steve Wynn casinos. If we would go into a Steve Wynn casino, somebody would come up to him within the first ten minutes and say, "Mr. Snadowsky, you're welcome here, of course to do anything you want. Play any game you want—except blackjack." And he didn't count cards. He just had a betting system, and he stuck to it. He was a very disciplined player.

One night, actually, I was going to leave to take a red-eye back to New York, and we'd had a great time. I remember we were at the Luxor. Now, I always looked at gambling as entertainment until I hung out with Stanley, and I'm not a gambler. I mean, I've never gone to Atlantic City to gamble. But if I'm at a resort or something that has a casino, I'll play some blackjack or poker slots or something, but I'm just not that guy that's going to Vegas to gamble. I would set aside 300 bucks, maybe 500 bucks that I figured I'm going to lose and that's ok. Well, Stanley turned that right around to me. He goes, "No, no, no, no. If you gamble, you should play to win—and *you* don't play to win." He taught me his little simple system for it, so I think it was the second time I was out there, and he and I had played a couple of evenings, and we were having dinner, and he goes, "How'd you do?" I said, "I'm down 60 bucks, but I still have 440 out of the 500 bucks I could blow. So the fact that I'm only down sixty, to me, it's a win." So as we finish dinner Stanley says, "Let me see if I can get you your 60 bucks back." I said, "No, it's ok. I have to go back to the Hilton to get my stuff before I head out." He goes, "No, no, just give me a couple of minutes." And he always preferred to play at a private table. He didn't like other people playing at the tables because they'd fuck up the game. So a pit boss gets him a private table, and he takes out a thousand in cash—he always carried a big wad of money—and he gets a thousand dollars in markers. Now I'm not playing. I'm sitting there looking at my watch. Stanley blows the thousand in about five minutes, gets a $5,000 marker. He goes through about $3,500 in another couple of minutes. So now I am freaking the fuck out. And he says, "Relax. It's totally fine." Now he's down like $4,500, and I'm like, "Really?" And I have to get to the hotel and then to the airport. He goes, "Give me another minute." And then it was like out of a movie: The cards turned, he plays how he plays, and within two minutes, three minutes, he had paid off the marker. He's up $1,500, and he gives me 60 bucks in chips and says, "Ok, let's go." It was just fantastic, and he enjoyed it so much.

He had a very strict routine. He would do his New York work during the day—and he talked to Allan five times a day, at least, and then about when The Bottom Lone would be opening, it would be about four o'clock in Vegas, and that's when he'd call for a car, and some casino would send him a car. He was a very, very serious gambler, but he was good at it. One time we were walking through a casino, and there's this big slot machine, just a random slot machine to me, and he goes, "Oh wait, this is a good machine." So he gets out a hundred dollar bill, puts in the machine, and I'm like, "Who takes out a hundred for a slot machine?" And the fucking thing pays off two grand.

16 THE "BOTTOM LINE" SINKS THE BOTTOM LINE

ALLAN PEPPER: After Stanley moved to Vegas, while we talked multiple times a day, and he continued to be involved in all our business dealings, things were different without him there in person. And then in early 2000, our bookkeeper Rose left because her husband had retired, and she wanted to spend more time with him. Her retirement was very difficult for me. She came to work for us three and a half months after we opened and had been with us ever since. She had extraordinary skills, and I depended on her a great deal. With her background, when she came to work for us she came into a world that was totally alien to her, but at the same time, it fascinated her. She was very loyal and extremely protective, and treated Stanley and me as if we were her own kids. Before you got into our office, there was a little outer office where Rose sat and worked, always with a pencil in one hand and a cigarette in the other. Melanie Mintz said that Rose was always friendly and always nice, but she would not trust you unless, in her own way, she made a judgment that you were not there to exploit Stanley or me, and then she was more relaxed with you.

Early on after Rose started, she showed me an invoice from a beer company that had undercharged us for several cases of beer. I said, "Ok, we'll add that amount to the check, right?" and she said, "Pepperel"—she always affectionately called me "Pepperel." It's not our job to do their bookkeeping." Then there was the time she called James, who worked in the box office. "James," she said, "did you work in the box office last Wednesday night?" James said, "Yes, why?" "Well," she said, "I was just going over our latest phone bill, and we were charged thirty dollars for a call made to Jamaica last Wednesday night, which was a dark night, which meant that the club was closed except for the box office." And before he could confess, she cheerfully said, "It's ok. We'll just deduct it from your next paycheck."

Of all the times Rose surprised me, the one I remember most fondly happened at the end of the 1990s when almost every day was tough. I opened a piece of mail from Con Ed that said that unless we paid what we owed immediately, they would be shutting off our electricity. I couldn't even speak. I just went to Rose's desk and handed her the bill. She read it and, without saying anything, picked up the phone and called Con Ed's customer service. Once she got the representative on the line, she started whispering into the phone. "Can you hear me?" she asked. "My name is Rose Singer, and I'm the bookkeeper at The Bottom Line. We received a notice that our electricity was going to be turned off. I need to tell you that I had the payment ready to be mailed along with some other bills, but I was about to go on vacation and was rushing to leave, and though I thought I mailed them, they got stuck in the back of my desk drawer and I just found them. Can you please give us a few days to get the payment in? If my bosses find out, I could lose my job." She sounded so sincere that they said ok and gave us another week. She'd made the whole thing up on the spot just to give us some breathing room.

After she left, I had to reach out to try and replace her, and keep in mind, finances were very tough, and so money was very tight, so bringing in a new bookkeeper at that point, you couldn't even offer them a market rate. And Rose had been with us from the beginning. So with Stanley in Vegas and Rose gone, I started having to do things that I absolutely did not want to do. I had to be much more involved with the business and less involved with coming up with concepts and being creative, and that was such a drain on me that it really made things much harder. Not long before Rose left, I hired a new assistant, Jessica Weitz, and that helped—a lot. She had real skills, so I started to teach her, and I got to a certain point where she would do some of the booking herself, and in a sense, she became the young Allan Pepper. I found myself in a place where Mike Porco and Art D'Lugoff had found me. There was too much happening to keep the club going that needed attention, and I couldn't do the booking and everything else, too.

JESSICA WEITZ: I had moved to the city; I guess it was in late 1999 or early 2000. I was an actress at the time, or trying to be, which meant I felt I needed to have a waitressing job. I had been living in London, so they thought I was foreign, even though I definitely didn't sound like I was, so nobody would hire me. But when I was in college, I worked for a TV station and wound up interviewing a lot of celebrities and musicians who came through, and a lot of them wound up playing The Bottom Line. I figured if I was going to be a waitress anywhere, it should be somewhere where I love the music, so I went down there looking for a job. They didn't have anything posted. I had no experience. I was living in Queens, with literally, I think, $23 left in my bank account, and I got to the club, and this guy Gene, who was sitting in the box office, was like, "Well, I think we might have one job for you." And I'm like, "Whatever it is, I can do it." And he's like, "Well, it's a secretary. We need somebody with chutzpah." And he was a big Black guy, so for him to say that, it was very funny. I met Allan, and we hit it off right away. We had a second interview where I'm like, "Just so you know, I'm moving back to London in six months, but I'll give you six months." And he's like, "Well, we'll talk about that."

But then I had my final interview, a conversation with Stanley who was living in Vegas at that point, and he made me do a typing test, and that still brings back terrible memories. I had to listen to him on the phone, and he had a gravelly kind of voice, and I had to type as he was speaking. It was a legal document, and I had done that kind of work before, so I was feeling pretty good. I finished, and he's like, "Ok. Read it back." So I read it back to him, and he's like, "Do you think you did it right?" And I said, "Yes, I think I did it right." And he's like, "Really? Because this one word is not what I said." I've shut it out, but it was a legal term. It was like "Where within" or wear something; it was like three words put together that I made into one. And he's like, "Well, that's not a word." And I'm like, "I'm so sorry. That's what I heard." And Stanley said, "Well, if that's what you heard, then you're wrong." And I didnt get the job.

I thought I had built this rapport with Allan, and that this was a perfect job, but then I didn't get it. I remember going home to see my family in New Jersey that weekend, and I thought I had something going. My dad was like, "You should just send a thank-you note anyway. Don't disregard the connection you think you had." So I did that. I wrote a thank-you note, and Allan called me, and evidently, it was all a big test. I mean, not from Stanley's perspective, but from Allan's. And I found out later that they'd had a fight about it afterward because Allan felt like I was an honest person. Stanley didn't, because I lied about the word, even though I didn't lie about the word. And he's like, "I said to Stanley, if you wrote me a thank-you note or reached back out to me after what happened, then you were the right person for the job. And now I want to hire her." But now I was so angry that I felt like they were playing around with me that I'm like, "Well, I don't know if I want this job anymore. We need to meet again."

So we met again, and my one requirement to take the job was that we never talk about this again. I told him, "I don't want it brought up if I do something wrong; I don't want it used against me. We start from scratch." And he agreed. It still makes me so upset. For a word, one word. But thank God it all worked out because literally it was—I mean, it was a career that I didn't know I wanted or didn't know existed, and it changed my entire life. Every single thing that has happened to me since, that I've accomplished, the people I've worked with, it all goes back to Allan and The Bottom Line. It's crazy.

I started on May 1, 2000. I worked in the daytime, from eleven a.m. until seven, but I would also work the shows sometimes to make extra money. I would sell merch or other times just because I was there, and I was the first one in, and I didn't mind being the last one out. I loved it. I was so happy, and I made no money, and obviously, since I worked for Allan and I wasn't part of the club's nighttime staff, I had to pay for everything to eat or drink at the club during show hours, so sometimes my dinner was the cherries, the olives, and the orange slices from the bar. But it was fine. I mean, I guess it kept me from getting scurvy. And then as I progressed, he let me book shows at The Bottom Line, so then I would stay for those.

Allan was always the same. I mean, twenty years later, he still wears the same outfit, the light blue button-down shirt with the pencils and pens in the shirt pocket. There's a great joke about Richard Belzer, who played the club a lot over the years, and at one show Allan was standing where he always did, between the bar and backstage, and Belzer, out of nowhere, points and says, "Ladies and gentlemen, lets' hear it for the best dressed man in show business—Allan Pepper."

It's funny, though. Stanley wasn't there, but he remained a very large presence, even though I think I only ended up meeting him one time in person. Allan and Stanley spoke all day long, back and forth, all day long. And again, this was before cell phones, so it wasn't like they were texting, and Allan didn't email, so it was like phone calls all day. What they had was beyond special. I've never seen anything like that before or since. It's similar to what Allan has with Eileen. There's this connection that goes beyond anything I've ever witnessed in my life that goes from professional to personal.

I went from being the secretary, and then I got a promotion to be the assistant, and that was considered a jump. I started learning who the different players were. Going back to everything I've done since, it's how I learned how the business worked. I was interacting with agents who were begging to get a shot, and agents who were doing their job well, or sometimes not well, for their clients or the record labels, which was frankly the thing that would save us when we would get a call when Clive or somebody from his J Records would call, and then we knew it was a rental, and the stars aligned. It was, as Allan always put it, the dance, and we quickly fell into this groove where I could anticipate what he would want when he came in in terms of, like, I'm going to need this person on the phone, and then I want to talk to this person. And have we figured out the rider for this person, which the rider was always just, you cross the whole thing out and you just wrote 'Oreos and fruit basket.' So it was like just flowing with him like that. Allan trusted me to be a part of everything, and to be able to witness things with a 360 view; I think it allowed me to understand the different parts of the business in a different way.

I certainly didn't go into this thinking I would stay in the music business. I didn't grow up like so many people dying to be in the music business. I learned so much that way and the path of the job from secretary to assistant to finally when he let me book some shows and I got to be an assistant producer or associate producer, whatever the title he gave me for any of those things. I booked the opener for a show that we produced at the Beacon with Dar Williams, and I got [Canadian singer-songwriter] Ron Sexsmith, and I'll never forget that day. I will also never forget the negotiation that I did with his agent, who maybe is still his agent, and afterward, Allan took me out. We probably got a tuna fish sandwich, and he bought me a book, *The Commitments*, and he's like, "This is where you are right now." And it was amazing. And I still have the book.

And flash forward after the club closed and because I didn't know what I didn't know, I opened up my own management company. The first call I got was from a band I had helped while at The Bottom Line, and then the second call was helping produce talent for, I think it was a Planned Parenthood event. And eventually I opened up two companies, one of them for working with nonprofits, and the management stuff wound up working really well until I stopped to concentrate on the work I was doing with the ACLU. I'm in-house there now, leading all of their artists and entertainment work. None of this would have happened without my relationship with Allan and those I developed through my time at The Bottom Line.

* * *

As the twenty-first century began, The Bottom Line continued to attract showcase performances by up-and-coming acts, including several spring and summer performances in 2001 by the budding country singer-guitarist superstar Keith Urban and another of Clive Davis' discoveries, pianist-composer Alicia Keys. But stiff competition for club dates arose again when, in 2000, a franchise of B. B. King's opened right in Times Square on 42nd Street just west of Eighth Avenue. As Jessica Weitz noted: "They had corporate money, which we never had to play with. So we lost a lot of acts to that room at that point. The feeling was 'They'll come back around. They might get this paycheck now, but they're going to miss what this room brings, and who wants to go to Times Square to see a show? We want to be in the Village.'" But then 9/11 happened, casting a dark shadow over the nation's psyche, and an even darker one over downtown Manhattan within the perimeter of Ground Zero—the fallen Twin Towers of the World Trade Center.

ALLAN PEPPER: Right after 9/11, all the shows that I had booked were canceled. We couldn't even get to the club for three days after. On Tuesday, we were part of the frozen zone. First time somebody could get in was Friday. Alright. Right after it happened, and I guess along with a lot of other people, for whatever reason, I could not listen to music. I don't know why. Since music means so much to me, I could not listen to music. And that weekend, I think it was Saturday morning, and I walked into the kitchen, and Eileen had the radio on and she was listening to Jerry Treacy on WFDU and his show, Crash on the Levee. She could listen to music because it brought her solace And I sat down at the table while she was making breakfast, I heard the music, and once again, it touched me the way music can touch you. And I said, "How many other people out there are feeling like me?" I wasn't afraid to go into New York, but I was so overwhelmed by what had happened and what we were finding out on TV and in the newspapers.

I said to Eileen, "I'm going to try and do a show where it's going to be free, and I'm going to try to put together as many acts as I can, just to get people to come out and come to see the show." And so I did that, but I wanted it to have a feeling of community. So I got people from various radio stations to co-host it. And I reached out and got a whole lot of artists to take part. And we weren't going to do two shows. We were just going to do one long show, and people could stay for as long as they wanted to. And the key was, it was free. So it was kind of my gift back to try and be helpful in getting people to start to come out again, and not be afraid. We called it *"A Gift of Music,"* but we could have called it "Don't Be Afraid." So I got these forty acts, and WFUV broadcast it live, and I think it ended at one-thirty in the morning.

On October 1, less than three weeks after 9/11, The Bottom Line presented A Gift of Music: A Gathering of Friends. Among the performers at the free six-and-a-half-hour show were Christine Lavin, Julie Gold, Willie Nile, Richard Barone, Terre Roche, Jill Sobule, the Bacon Brothers, Tom and Jen Chapin, Martha Wainwright, Lucy Kaplansky, The Kennedys, Jules Shear, John Sebastian, Phoebe Snow, Jennie Muldaur, Freedy Johnston, David Massengil, and the Fab Faux, and the hosts included Jerry Treacy, Neil Lifton, Bill Ayers, Doug Tuckman, Darren DeVivo, Claudia Marshall, John Platt, Vin Scelsa, Meg Griffin, Dennis Elsas, Delphine Blue, Corny O'Connell, and Mai Pang.

ALLAN PEPPER: Some amazing people performed, and everybody performed really well. Phoebe Snow, with Jimmy Vivino on guitar, did an amazing version of "I Shall Be Released" and then "America" that brought the show to a complete stop. It was very emotional. There was a firefighter in the audience who got up and talked about what it was like at Ground Zero. People in the audience stood up and talked about what their experience was like. It really felt like a piece of history taking place. So I did it from a standpoint of community, and the fact that I think nothing brings people together more than music, and it was something that everybody could get behind. But even though it was a free show, we couldn't even fill the house. We couldn't get 400 people. Over the course of the whole show, we had a maximum of maybe 275 to 300.

The impact that the attacks on the Twin Towers had on bordering neighborhoods such as Greenwich Village, both psychologically and economically, as well as both immediate and more long-term, deeply affected local businesses like The Bottom Line.

ALLAN PEPPER: It was devastating to us because we were not that far from the site, and for months after, you couldn't stand outside the club because you would smell the smell of smoke and burnt plastic and your throat would tighten up. There were a lot of people who came to New York to want to support New York, but they went to Ground Zero, took pictures, and then went to see a Broadway show or ate in Midtown. They didn't support any of the restaurants downtown that were just barely hanging on. And the other thing was that a lot of people were afraid to come into the Village. People who lived in New Jersey and Long Island were even afraid to come into New York. So I had one particular show, I don't remember who was an act on Atlantic Records, I think, that had a very big local following in New Jersey. And they were going to rent a couple of buses and bring people over. And then there was one of those shifting of the warning, remember there was a color-coded thing and yellow or whatever it is, had gone to dark red or whatever, and it canceled the buses. They wouldn't come over. So it was hellacious for anybody trying to run a business.

I mean, we never fully got back to speed. We spent a year or a year and change just trying, but people just didn't want to go out. They didn't want to go to downtown New York. They wanted to go places where they felt they were safe. And here's the other thing: There were a lot of people who weren't touring for a while, who just didn't want to fly, and if they were, they didn't want to come to New York, plus there were other people from Europe who had tours, and for a while, they couldn't even get into the country. So it was devastating. It affected the whole economy of New York, but the Village was really hit hard. It would've been so much better if people had come in, took their pictures, and then supported the local businesses. So they were helping the economy of New York, but they weren't helping the local community.

We had business interruption insurance, which means that we could be paid by the insurance company for all the revenue lost because of the days we'd been closed. We had an evaluator who spent a week at the club watching the kind of business we did. They wanted to see the bar tabs and everything else, and just my luck—or so I thought—we had Tower of Power there that week, so we did really good business. And because they used that to evaluate the claims of how much we'd lost, the number they came up with, and I'm just making this number up from memory, between the bar, admissions, and everything else, it was something around $125,000. So the claim got processed, and we got a call from the adjuster that we'd been cleared, and that they'd give us $35,000. We said, "But your own guy said it was over a hundred thousand." They said, "Well, you can always protest this, but that'll mean that I can't write a check for $35,000 that you can have tomorrow. If not, I can put this on the bottom of the pile and we'll get to it when we start getting to all the disputed claims." So Stanley figured we'd better settle, and we did. So that's the kind of stuff. So you pay for business interruption insurance or whatever, only to find out that it was worth a quarter of what you should have gotten. So those are the kind of things that we were dealing with.

* * *

Throughout the two-plus years following 9/11, The Bottom Line continued its eclectic mix of local, national, and international performers from across the musical spectrum. In addition to the stable of club regulars such as Loudon Wainwright, Uncle Floyd, Betty Buckley, David Johansen, The Roches, Willie Nile, Richard Barone, and Christine Lavin, such artists as Dave Edmunds, Nancy Sinatra, Ralph Stanley, Doc Watson, Leon Russell, Pam Tillis, Lisa Loeb, and Brad Paisley appeared on the Bottom Line stage. And in 2003 alone, the club saw appearances by the likes of Tony Levin, Dan Hicks, Solas, the McGarrigles, Levon Helm, Eric Andersen, Jill Sobule, Dave Alvin, Lenny White, Procol Harum, Savoy Brown, Sonny Landreth, Tony Trischka, Mark Lindsay, Billy J. Kramer, Gary Lewis & The Playboys, Roomful of Blues, Ute Lemper, Citizen Cope, John Hammond, Tom Russell, Marty Stuart, Jerry Jeff Walker, Bruce Cockburn, Jimmy Webb, Rodney Crowell, Chocolate Genius, Tommy Castro, Duke Robillard, Sophie B. Hawkins, Fairport Convention, Laura Cantrell, Don Dixon, Rhonda Vincent, Leslie West, Cheryl Wheeler, Suzy Bogguss, Brave Combo, Tom Wopat, Todd Snider, Marshall Crenshaw, The Kennedys, Nellie McKay, David Amram, Odetta, Chris Hillman, Maria Muldaur, the Dixie Hummingbirds, Paul Brady, Chris Smither, Susan McKeown & The Chanting House, Robyn Hitchcock, NRBQ, Pierce Turner, John Gorka, the Strawbs, Mary Lee's Corvette, Peter Rowan, Mick Taylor, and Ramblin' Jack Elliott.

Continuing at the club from their origins in the late 1990s were also two ongoing series co-produced by Jeanne Stahlman: Nightbirds, which was named in honor of groundbreaking late night WNEW radio host Alison Steele and showcased both new and known women artists, including (well before the 2002 release of her smash debut album Come Away With Me) Norah Jones and (in 2001, between her star turns in Rent and Wicked) Broadway's Idina Menzel; and the popular "The Beat Goes On" shows, co-curated by singer-songwriter Ed Rogers, which celebrated music from decades past with thematic, multi-artist extravaganzas ranging from "Singers, Swingers and Crooners" and "Music of the Brill Building" to "The British Invasion Revisited" and "From the Ronettes to The Ramones."

* * *

In March 2003, Pepper scored a major coup when Ringo Starr and his band The Roundheads played a semi-surprise late-night set. For Sean Altman, founding member of the acapella vocal group Rockapella (creators of the theme for PBS's Where in the World is Carmen Sandiego?), and a Bottom Line regular throughout the 1990s and early 2000s, Ringo's show was a particularly memorable event among several he experienced in his years at the club.

SEAN ALTMAN: There was one Bottom Line night that I'm particularly proud of when Rockapella was headlining. The show was packed and the kitchen was out of commission, so on our own dime, we ordered pizza for the entire audience and had it delivered. That was a lot of fun. And we did two double bills with the Bacon Brothers, and [actress] Kyra Sedgwick, Kevin Bacon's wife, said to me backstage, "You have a voice I could fall in love with," and I just sort of gasped because she was so beautiful. But my favorite story was when Ringo came to the club for a warm-up show for his tour. I'm a huge Beatle fan, and I have all this memorabilia and I really wanted Ringo's autograph on something. So I asked Allan, "Is there any way you could get me backstage to see Ringo so I could have him sign this little plastic bass drum that's on this Ringo figurine that I have?" And he said, "Sean, I can't let you go backstage, but here's how it's going to go. Everybody thinks Ringo's going to leave after the show through the front door, but I know he's going to leave through the side door on"—I think it was Greene Street—"so when the show is over, you go wait at that side door, you'll be all alone. Ringo will come out and you'll be able to get the autograph." So the show is over, and I'm waiting there in the dark next to that side door on the street with my Sharpie and my little plastic Ringo drum while this throng of people is waiting for him at the front of the club. And I was thinking, "Wow, this is so nice of Allan. He's totally set me up to get the autograph." But then the door creaks open really quickly, And it's Allan, and he says, "Change of plans. He's going out the front." So I sprint over to the front, where me and about a hundred people then are literally chasing Ringo down the street all trying to get a photo or something. And Ringo gets into this vehicle and speeds away. But Allan tried. I'll always remember him running back to tell me, "Change of plans."

* * *

ALLAN PEPPER: During those years in the early 2000s, especially after 9/11, we got behind on the rent and we could never recover. And there were elements, there were elements that were working against us, whether it was the economy, whether people were putting their money other places, whether it was the competition; there were just elements that we couldn't overcome. We were trying to cut down on our expenses, and to that end, Stanley said to me, "I'll defer my salary," and then ultimately I did as well, especially because we didn't want to lay anybody off. So often for weeks at a time, we both worked for no salaries.

STEVE LEEDS (Music executive): Allan could not compete financially with what some of these other clubs were offering. It was crazy. That's the one thing with Allan and Stanley. They had their way of doing things, and no matter what happened, including things changing in society and the industry around them, they changed their formats, but they never changed how they ran the club. The parameters of the club were what they were. Their fees were set, and the two shows were set. People were throwing a lot more money than Allan and Stanley could ever possibly make with their club. That didn't help them, but they stuck to their guns.

While the club continued functioning, storm clouds were gathering around its relationship with its landlord, New York University. The school, which in the mid-1970s began using images of The Bottom Line in its promotional literature to help entice prospective students as a campus-adjacent cultural attraction and had always had a good relationship with Pepper and Snadowsky, abruptly shifted gears as the latest lease was ending at the close of 2003.

ALLAN PEPPER: We kept renewing the lease—in the beginning it was every ten years—and then it got to a point where it was every five years. So now we'd fall behind in our rent and then come back and we're able to pay it off. Stanley had developed a relationship with the bank. So when he needed to, we would just get a loan to get us by and then pay our bills. But at the end of the 1990s, the market got very weird. By 2003, we were falling more and more behind in the rent, and so we'd pay a partial amount, then we'd skip a month and we'd kind of catch up, and we were getting behind the eight ball to a point where I think we were in arrears something like $180,000.

JESSICA WEITZ: One of my jobs every month was to deliver the check to NYU. It wasn't NYU; it was like a realtor for NYU. And so I'd have to do that, walk with the check, and sometimes it was the full check and sometimes it wasn't. And I'd have to explain what was happening. And it was horrible.

ALLAN PEPPER: I got a call from NYU that they wanted to see me. It was their real estate people. I went over there for a meeting and there were these two guys who said that unless I gave them a check for the $180,000 by the end of the week, they were going to start eviction proceedings. Now, the interesting thing is that we had gotten behind in the rent before, and nobody ever bothered us because the president of NYU, whose name was Jay Oliva, was a musician himself, and he was very partial to the arts. He understood that having the club on campus was more than just real estate; it provided something for the university. It provided a quality of life element for people in the neighborhood. I can't tell you how many people, including young people who worked for us as students while they attended NYU, told me that The Bottom Line was one of the reasons they wanted to come to the school.

So we found ourselves in a place with NYU saying we weren't paying market value. At that point, I think our rent was $11,250 a month. Now, keep in mind, the rents in the Village were already sky-high. Everything in this city was changing, real estate was going up, and apartment buildings were going up with ridiculous rents. And that affected the situation in the Village. And the guy who became the president when Oliva left had been the dean of the law school, and he didn't see any real value in The Bottom Line. He came at it a different way for him. His thing was pure real estate. And the value to him was the money the university could make that they weren't getting. So rather than try and work something out with us from the standpoint of the value of what we offered, they said, "Nothing doing. You either pay up or you're out of there."

The first person I called for help was Clive Davis because I start to think, "Who do I know that would have any pull with NYU?" And he had founded the Clive Davis Institute of Recorded Music there. So I called him, and he was very generous. I mean, he listened to me and he was a little taken aback by what I told him. He said he would make a call for me in the morning and plead my case. And I thanked him. And he called me at home the next morning and he said he had had a long conversation with the president, and he said they assured him they would try and work something out. And I thanked him. And then, a week later, I was served with eviction papers.

I then went to their PR people and I said, "Look, I'm a very private person, and the fact of this being in all the newspapers and everything like that is a very painful thing. Could we try and see if there's some kind of way we could work this out or mediate it? Because, frankly, a lot of people from the press come here and they view us as valuable. And I think a lot of people will take our side in this dispute." And her attitude was, "NYU can take care of itself. You shouldn't worry about us getting bad publicity," which later on they indeed resented. Then, with Meg Griffin's help, Sirius Satellite Radio [now Sirius XM], which launched in 2002 and had been broadcasting live shows from The Bottom Line with increasing regularity throughout 2003, stepped up and said they would cover the rent.

MEG GRIFFIN: Allan called me one day in my office at Sirius and told me that the club was in danger of losing its lease. Maybe he didn't reach out and specifically ask me for help, but maybe he had an instinct to think that I could. And given that I am an eternal optimist, I thought, "I know I'm not some big powerful mogul or whatever, but I'm going to do something here." I asked him, "Allan, how much do you owe?" And he says, "$180,000." So I went to the head honchos at Sirius, even though I had only worked there for a short time at this point. We were new, but I suggested to them that if they could put this money up, if they could save this beloved New York City music institution, this nightclub, it would also put a big shiny star on Sirius. It would be good for them. And we're new at this point. We need the press. And it did. It got a whole lot of press in all the New York City papers. It kind of played out in the papers as it was playing out in court.

ALLAN PEPPER: But Sirius had a caveat. They weren't going to cover the total back rent unless NYU granted us a new ten-year lease because their attitude, which was correct, was they could put up the $180,000 and NYU could still kick us out. So Sirius went to court with us, and they got up and they said they were prepared to help us pay up, but in order to do this, we had to work out a new lease. The judge ruled that we should postpone for a month, and that I and NYU should try and come to some kind of an agreement. We got together with them, and that's when they said they wanted "fair market value," and said they would double our rent up to close to $23,000, which was horrifying. If you are running a business like ours, unless you're doing great business night after night after night, you're working on small margins, and everything is tight. We tried to explain this to them. We offered to do an internship program with them, where people from the Clive Davis School could intern at the club to get practical skills, including mixing sound. We put forth all kinds of different programs. But to make a long story short, they didn't want to settle with us. It was clear they wanted us out.

Eileen was wonderful. She came to court with me every single day, as did Jessica and Meg, and Eileen started a journal, writing down everything that was happening. Meanwhile, NYU started to get emails from people, and I think all told they got close to 2,000 letters and emails from people. Now, this was in 2003 before blogs and all the big social media. Can you imagine what it would've been like today? I remember one email saying, "I'm an NYU student, and I'm ashamed to walk through the Village and see your (NYU's) banners everywhere. It's like this has become your fiefdom."

After the month came and went, the court ordered the eviction, but at the last minute, somebody stepped forward who knew about the club and had a relationship with NYU, and they said they would try to broker an agreement for us. We went and we had a series of meetings, and we actually had an agreement ready to go. Sirius said they would put up the money for the $180,000 covering the back rent in escrow. Bruce Springsteen wanted to help. His people said, "What do you need? How's fifty grand?" And I said, "Can you make it a hundred? You don't even have to give it. Just make it a loan and we'll pay you back." And they said ok.

As the negotiations with NYU continued, word got out that The Bottom Line was in serious danger of closing. Throughout December, there were a series of "Play to Stay" shows at the club, featuring artists such as The Indigo Girls, Keb Mo', Christine Lavin, Jane Siberry, and David Johansen, as well as a Sirius-sponsored "Lease Party to Save The Bottom Line" show on December 4 with Dar Williams, Suzanne Vega, and John Hiatt.

JOHN HIATT: The closing seemed kind of imminent. It was in the air. I remember there was a snowstorm, and I was worried about getting out of town. While I knew things were getting very difficult for him, after I saw the little basket of cookies and fruit in the dressing room, I told him I was glad to see that he still hadn't skimped on the opulent backstage spread. But there was a certain weight to the show, and reverence was being upheld by the three of us. I felt like, and maybe everybody who came in that night felt the same way—what a wonderful place, an amazing venue for so many years, and we might be reaching the end of it.

On December 12–14, 2003, The Bottom Line held what would be the final presentation of The Downtown Messiah.

RICHARD BARONE: We were one of the last big shows that was at the club. It was still iffy if it was going to stay open or not. Allan always closed the club for a week to do the Downtown Messiah, so we could rehearse it every day before we did the shows. And he did warn the choir that we could at any moment get closed down, maybe even during the rehearsal days, so we were kind of on pins and needles. It was very tense and sad because I loved Allan and the club, and to be even thinking about that, like federal marshals could come in and close us down, was really sad.

ALLAN PEPPER: Besides Sirius, a couple of other people stepped forward, including a personal commitment from Sirius' Mel Karmazin, and all told, we had pledges of $750,000, including the back rent. And we did come to an agreement with NYU. We were going to sign it and get the new lease the next day, the twenty-second of January 2004, which was my twin daughters Stacey and Bonnie's thirtieth birthdays. And that year, I think, it was Martin Luther King Day. But what vetoed the whole thing was that, at the last minute, NYU wanted us to commit to a sum of money to make improvements, not only on the inside of the club to bring it up to current code, but also to the outside of the building to conform with the look of the rest of the block. They even wanted us to take down the awning and the marquee. I said, "If we take down the marquee, how do we let people know who's playing?" And they said, "Put a sign in the window."

Now while this was all happening, Stanley was, of course being kept informed. And the night before, we had a conversation and he said to me, as he always did, "Look, Allan, I'll do whatever you want to do—but I'm going to give you my two cents. We have $750,000 committed to us. But they're making it impossible between the increase in rent and the improvements they want made." And this was even though an engineer they hired came in and thought we'd be grandfathered in for a lot of what they wanted done. So Stanley said, "We'll be able to run for a couple of months, and if we get lucky and get some good shows, we'll be able to run it for a few more than that."

"But," he said, "there's no way that we can run this place the way we've run it. Within five to six months, we will have gone through all the money that people have put up in good faith to help us. And then people are going to say, 'Well, these guys, they just didn't know how to handle the money, and they took people's money.' I can't see a good way out of it. Even if we take the money, ultimately in six months, we're going to be exactly in the same place. We won't be able to pay the rent. We're going to have bills." And I told Stanley, "Let me think about it." I got off the phone with Stanley and sat down with a yellow pad. I drew a line down the middle, and on one part I put "Pro" and the other "Con." And when I finished I saw that I had written down four things under pro and twenty things under con. So I'm looking at it, and I'm saying to myself, "Well, this tells the story."

I told NYU, "We're not going to sign it. You can arrange to pick up the keys." So the club closed, and it closed on my twin daughters Bonnie and Stacey's birthdays. They'd been born just a few weeks before we opened, and now we were closing almost exactly thirty years later, just a few weeks before what would have been the thirtieth anniversary of The Bottom Line opening. As I was leaving that day, the locksmith NYU sent was on his knees changing the locks on the front door and the vestibule. I handed in the keys, and as I walked out, he looked up at me and said, "I never thought they would fucking do this to you." And that was *their* locksmith.

For the record, the last show at The Bottom Line took place on January 10, 2004. Produced by Jimmy LaFave and narrated by Bob Childers, it was entitled, "Ribbon of Highway, Endless Skyway: A Concert in the Spirit of Woody Guthrie," and featured performances by LaFave, Childers, The Burns Sisters, Slaid Cleaves, and Eliza Gilkyson, as well as Guthrie's granddaughter (and Arlo Guthrie's daughter) Sarah Lee Guthrie and her partner Johnny Irion. Fittingly, it was a concert that would have been perfectly at home forty years earlier right across the street on the south side of Fourth and Mercer, where the original Folk City had once stood. Like that club, where Bob Dylan had made such an indelible mark in 1961, The Bottom Line, where Bruce Springsteen had done the same in 1975, would soon become another lost piece of New York musical and cultural history.

* * *

ALLAN PEPPER: At first, after they took possession, NYU was going to put a business in there. I think ShopRite had made them a huge offer, but there was so much pushback from the community that they backed off. Then they were going to try and put I think a CVS in there. In the end, they just made it a lecture space. Their rationale was, we need the space—and yet they were going to put a supermarket or drugstore in there.

Shortly after The Bottom Line closed, a friend, John Dillon, introduced me to a terrific guy named Andy Breslin, whose family were first-class operators of a lot of pubs, clubs, and restaurants in the area. Andy said he wanted to help me reopen The Bottom Line. We made a deal that we were going to be partners in it, and his family had committed to put up a lot of money—I think it was as much as 2 million. They were going to take care of everything else, including food and drinks, which would then free me to just take care of bookings and talent. But in order to do it, I needed to raise another 8 million, because we had to start from scratch. So I looked around and looked around, and the Village had outpriced itself. I wasn't going to go back to the days of Folk City. I knew from all my experience that the only way you could make money and compete was to have capacity, because you can't compete with, say, 200 seats. Over the course of several years, Andy and I looked at a lot of places in Brooklyn before Brooklyn became too expensive, and at one point I found a wonderful place within walking distance to the Barclays Center with, I think, 22,000 square feet, with no poles and high ceilings. Andy and I met with the landlord, but it was going to take a whole lot of money. Whereas when we started in 1974, and Marvin had thought he was going to be in for about $75,000, when all said and done it took about $150,000 to get the whole club up and running from scratch. And now here, to do it right, we were talking about a multi-million dollar investment, and that just wasn't doable. So even though Andy was enormously supportive, that was about it for me.

I got an offer from several club owners to do things like monthly "Bottom Line Nights," but I turned them down. All it meant was that I would be booking their clubs once a month, using my goodwill and relationships in a place where I had no control over the environment. Because that's what it always boiled down to. For me, The Bottom Line was a concept. It was an idea. It was a way to present music. I wasn't just a booker; I was a producer. I was a curator and a creator. And that had to do not just with the music. It was the music and the way it was presented, along with everything that came with it; it was a total package. So by offering me a Bottom Line Night, they only showed that they didn't get it. They just didn't get it.

MEG GRIFFIN: In the end, Allan just couldn't do what NYU wanted. And so in good conscience, he would not take the $180,000 from Sirius and all the other money that might have been committed. It was one of the biggest heartbreaks ever. And when I think of it, it still hurts. But I have to remember that places of legend, like The Bottom Line, and also CBGB, do not last forever. And aren't we lucky to have been part of their heyday to sow benefit from it? And to have experienced what we saw and heard there?

I remember one night at The Bottom Line. At this point, I'm working at WFUV, so it's late nineties [May 1999], and June Carter Cash had made a new record, and June was going to be showcased at The Bottom Line as any important artist with a new record would be. We were so excited to have had her up at FUV that afternoon. There was a song on that album; I think, because her granddaughter was dating Quentin Tarantino at the time, June wrote a song called "Quentin Tarantino Makes the Strangest Movies I Have Ever Seen." She was just such a card. But anyway, I got to the club early, and I'm sitting there, and remember, at The Bottom Line you had to walk in through the front door like anybody else and around the tables to get backstage. You really couldn't have total privacy entering; everybody was going to see you. I see June and her people going in, and among the people who are with her is Johnny. And I'm like, "Oh my God, Johnny Cash is here."

Now when he walked in, you could see it. It was like, "Oh, God love him. He's really weak." So June comes out and she's doing her show and then, all of a sudden, she invites Johnny up onstage. And in that time period while he walked on and the mic was put in his hand and he performed with her, his whole body took on great strength. You watched this amazing transition because he was doing what he loved with the woman that he loved, and he became really strong. And then as soon as the song was done, he kind of shrunk down again and had to be kind of helped out as he walked off the stage. But it was that time in there, specifically with Johnny and June, I was like, "Did I just witness a miracle?" And of course it was The Bottom Line. Because stuff like that just always happened there.

* * *

It was sometime after The Bottom Line closed its doors that Allan Pepper received an email from Loudon Wainwright, who had just done a show at B. B. King's the night before. "I was backstage, Allan, and I realized something was very, very wrong," he wrote. "There were no Oreos."

EPILOGUE

ALLAN PEPPER: Looking back over the thirty years that The Bottom Line was in business, I'm still amazed that Stanley and I never compromised our vision and always stayed true to being proactive for the artists as well as the fans. Although we took our share of grief for how tight we were on talent fees and food and drinks for performers and their crew, we were generous in many other ways which, in the long run, benefited both the artists and the fans economically. We made choices that served the artists even before the club opened, like doing away with options *[the practice to be able to re-book an act for a future performance at a predetermined rate]*. The practice of asking for options allowed a club owner to take advantage of an artist who would go into a place for very little money because they needed exposure and, as part of the deal, would agree to two additional engagements at a predetermined rate, giving up the ability to take advantage of any career progress they might have achieved between engagements. To Stanley and me, the practice of options was equivalent to "indentured servitude."

In the late 1980s and early '90s, when lots of artists who were signed to independent record companies made deals to buy their product from the companies at cost and then turn it around and sell it at their shows, usually the club owner would want a percentage of those sales. We never took a percentage of sales. We knew that money was tight for a lot of those acts, and selling their product at shows could, in some cases, be the difference between them making a profit from a tour or losing on it. The only time we asked for anything was if they wanted one of our people to sell their merchandise at the show. And we wanted that person on our staff to get a dollar per item sold to compensate for their time.

We never renegotiated a deal. It was common in those days if an agent pushed a club owner to offer more money than an act was worth, and the act didn't do the business, a lot of club owners would say, "Look, we didn't make it tonight, so you have to take less money. "We would never do that. We fought hard for a guarantee we could live with, but once a deal was struck, that was it. Another thing very current at a certain time was what was referred to as "pay to play." Simply put, it meant that if an unknown local act wanted to open for a national recording act, they were asked to pay the club for the privilege of being on the show. Certainly, with a club that was as prestigious as The Bottom Line, I could have easily said, "You can open this show, but we're not going to pay you; in fact you have to pay us. We're giving you great exposure, and that's worth something." But we would never ask a band to pay us or to work for free. Our guarantees may have been smaller than other venues, but every band that worked at The Bottom Line got paid a guarantee that was agreed upon whether they did the business or not. And one thing we always did for all our artists, which most clubs didn't do: For every new engagement, we had a piano tuner come in, and they were also on call, because there might be a performer who was there for a few days, and if played really hard, the piano had to be tuned every day—sometimes, even between shows.

Like decisions having to do with talent that were made before the club opened, there were also choices we made regarding the public. From the word go, the club never had a minimum. The same admission price got everyone in, and if that's all you wanted to spend or could afford, so be it. One reason I fought so hard with agents for lower talent fees was it helped to be able to maintain a no-minimum policy. It would've been very easy for somebody in my position doing the booking to get a lot of acts that you knew would sell out by just giving the agent whatever they asked for and then pass the price on to your customer. Under those circumstances, all of a sudden, the seat that you were selling to the public that you would normally charge 15 or 20 dollars for you're now charging 30 or 40 dollars plus a ten dollar minimum.

In negotiating deals with agents, I always identified with the customer. I always had a sense of excitement at hearing the name of an act that wanted to play the club in the same way a fan might feel on seeing the advertisement of an upcoming appearance in our ads. But I especially kept the customer in mind when it came to arriving at a fee for the talent because your guarantee usually determined what the ticket price would be. Eileen and I have four kids who were young during a lot of the time we had the club. So, I knew that when I took the family out, even in Jersey, to a movie, by the time I got done with tickets and the concession stand and maybe a trip to a restaurant before or after the movie, it cost a lot of money. So my own personal experiences with my family finances played a role in setting ticket prices at a Bottom Line show.

I never wanted the experience at The Bottom Line to be an elitist one and mainly for people who had the money and could afford high ticket prices and minimums. That's why we kept our admissions so reasonable. When some of the later clubs opened up and had corporate money behind them, they could make high offers for talent, and then they'd just jack up the admission price to make the money back. That stuff really always bothered me, and at The Bottom Line I fought long and hard not to pass on the talent costs to our customers. Stanley and I wanted all types of people to have access to the club and whatever it was we were presenting on any given night. Plus, neither he nor I drank, and it seemed crazy to us to have a minimum. To us it was just a tax put on the customer. If you weren't a drinker and you weren't hungry when you came to the club, why should you be charged for something you didn't need or want? That offended both of us.

In the later years when we were fighting to keep the business going, we had to reduce our expenses because every day we were digging ourselves into a deeper hole. So, Stanley said to me, "I think we have to have a really serious conversation about what we are going to do." He put some suggestions on the table, and all of them went counter to what our original vision was. I wrote down all of Stanley's ideas, and these were hard decisions that we had to make. One of the things on that list was closing the kitchen and discontinuing our food service. This was a painful thing to discuss because we had had the same chef, John Hargrove, since the day we opened. Stanley, as always, was sympathetic to how I felt, so I finally prevailed upon him, and the compromise we arrived at about the kitchen once again showed Stanley's instincts to look at things in a different way and figure out a solution that might not be obvious. At first, he said, "Alright, we've got to close the kitchen," but then he said, "but if we still want to serve food, let's see if we can rent out the kitchen to another operator so we'll be able to maintain food service." And that's what we did. We lost the salary of the chef, plus whoever was assisting him, and we no longer had to pay for the produce and all the food coming in, so that was a big savings. And then we got a monthly rental from the outside operator as well as some money toward the waitresses' salaries. So we not only cut our costs, but we also turned it around and made some money out of it. And, most important of all, we didn't disrupt the notion of people being able to eat something at the club if they wanted to. We always tried to make the experience as pleasurable as we could for anyone coming in, and I think we were able to do it, right up to the very last day we were in business.

When I first said to Stanley, "It'll be great. We'll go into the music business," his immediate reaction was, "I don't want to be in the music business." It was the furthest thing from his mind. When I think back in retrospect to the fact that he put up the $250 when he had worked hard to make that money, I realize how naive I was. I didn't realize at that time what that moment must have meant for him. Stanley was always an independent thinker and always his own man. I'll never know why he made that decision, but I think he was intrigued by me, because I guess I was so different from anyone in his circle of friends. And in turn, he was very different from anyone that I hung out with. He was unique in that he was the only one I knew who aspired to be a lawyer and also had any interest in business. So it made perfect sense for me to ask him to go with me to that first meeting with Dudley Gaffin. Stanley was always very confident and clear-thinking, and his confidence gave me a level of comfort I lacked without him. If he wasn't at that meeting, I would have been a fish out of water, and his mere presence allowed me to relax.

"Uncle" Marvin became our third partner by putting up the money for The Bottom Line because he loved Eileen, and she was his favorite niece. But make no mistake about it, the one person who gave him comfort was Stanley. Stanley understood numbers in a way that most people didn't, and Marvin was a businessman before he was anything else. He would not have put up the money if it was just Eileen's husband spinning a fantasy.

Stanley struggled with his weight since we were kids. As we got older and started to raise our families, it became harder for him to maintain any kind of control over it. He tried multiple diets, having luck with some and little success with others, but he could never get himself to practice moderation when it came to food. For Stanley, eating was more than a diet. One night, when we were alone in our upstairs office, I tried once again to discuss the need for him to lose weight. He listened to me without pushing back, and when I was done, he said, "Allan, I'm addicted. Just like somebody's addicted to drugs or cigarettes or whatever, I'm addicted to food. And it's very difficult for me; food is different for me." At that moment I realized we were talking about something much more significant than just a diet.

Stanley's weight was his undoing. Eventually, he developed diabetes, which he just ignored until it was too late. It got so bad that out in Vegas he had to get one of his legs amputated. And it wasn't all that long after that he passed away from complications from the diabetes, surrounded by his family, on February 25, 2013. His funeral was held in Vegas, and it was followed four months later by a memorial in New York at The Cutting Room, where more than 500 people showed up to pay tribute and celebrate him. I booked the memorial as I had booked Leslie's Sweet Sixteen, but this time instead of Stanley working out every detail wanting to make sure everything was perfect, it was Leslie trying to give her dad the perfect send-off. In her program notes, she provided something that probably gave a smile to everyone who was present. She pointed out that "Snadowsky was a champion poker player, winning the Rolling Stone fortieth anniversary celebrity poker tournament at the Hard Rock Hotel in Las Vegas in 2007—with a hand consisting of three deuces."

After the club closed, Eileen and I would watch *Jeopardy* together every night, not in a competitive way. We would do it as a team. But apparently, Michelle and Stanley, when they watched it, became competitive, especially when it came down to final Jeopardy and she was beating him. She was getting it more than he was. So one day a lightbulb went on in Stanley's head. He realized that *Jeopardy* aired three hours earlier on the East Coast than out West. So he called me one day—and keep in mind, we still spoke all the time—and he said, "Did you watch *Jeopardy* tonight?" I said, "Yeah." And he said, "Do you remember what the final *Jeopardy* answer was?" I said, "Yeah," and he said, "Ok. What was it? And do you remember the question?" I said, "Yeah," and I told him the answer and the question. And that night he got it right and Michelle didn't, so he started calling me every day to get the final *Jeopardy* information from me. Now Michelle's no dummy. And after a while, she said to him, Stanley, how are you doing this? Where's this coming from?" And he looked at her and said, "I don't know. It just comes to me." And she never found out. I think I may have mentioned it to Leslie at the memorial, and then she told Michelle.

The memorial started with a nod to the traditional notion of the New Orleans "Second Line," with The Red Hook Ramblers Dixieland Band entering the room from the back of the house and parading through the audience. The Ramblers were followed by Meg Griffin, who served as host, and then there was a succession of speakers and performers. The speakers included Ira Mayer, Vin Scelsa, Carol Klenfner, John Scher, and Elaine Curran, the managing director of the American Diabetes Association's Research Foundation, as well as Leslie speaking for the Snadowsky family. The performers included a cross-section of people that Stanley and I had known throughout our entire careers going back as far as the Village Gate: David Bromberg, Al Kooper, Suzzy Roche, and Lucy Wainwright Roche, David Johansen, and The Stan-tasticks (a doo-wop acapella group put together by Rockapella's Sean Altman). There was also a video message sent by Artie Butler. And finally, it was my turn to speak. I told Leslie I didn't know if I was going to be able to do it, and I would make my decision during the course of the afternoon.

Stanley and I loved each other, and we enjoyed each other's company. We also laughed a lot. I would come up with these wacky ideas and he'd figure out a way to make them happen. But that doesn't mean he wouldn't give me his honest opinion as to why he didn't think something was a good idea. He was always there whenever I needed him, and in turn, I was there for him, too. When he went to find out if he'd passed the bar exam, he was so nervous, and I was the one he asked to go with him. I never forget that. Our friendship and business relationship became like a lifelong dance. As I listened to everyone remember how smart and kind he was, and how skilled he was in business, I thought about how funny he was and how silly we could be together. I finally told Leslie I would speak. At that moment, I knew what I would share about my best friend.

A couple of years after the club closed, Artie Butler came to New York from LA for a couple of days and had lunch with Eileen and me. During lunch, Eileen and I told him how we first met in the library of Brooklyn College, how she had given me a review of Terry Gibbs after she saw him open for Miles Davis at Birdland, and how that led to a cup of coffee at the diner near campus. Two weeks later, out of nowhere, we got this signed picture from Terry Gibbs, who probably was the actual reason that we wound up at The Sugar Bowl. It was inscribed, "To Eileen, Artie Butler and I are your biggest fans. Best wishes, Terry Gibbs."

Eileen has always been a teacher at heart, and when the kids were growing up, she had a knack for framing things for them so they would learn from their thoughts and actions. When Gordon was about ten years old, he and Eileen were having a conversation about what he might do with his life, and he said that when he grew up, he wanted to take over The Bottom Line. He'd own it, and he'd sell tickets in the box office. And she said to him, "No, you're not going to own The Bottom Line. That was your father's dream. You'll need to find your own dream."

All of our children used to come to The Bottom Line all the time when they were growing up. And when Gordon, Stacey, and Bonnie were in college, Eileen often brought our youngest, Jessie, to the club as well. She'd sit in the front box office with her schoolbooks and do her homework with the music muffled in the background. On breaks she'd sit at our table for a song or two, then head back out to finish her studies, and on the ride back to Jersey, they'd discuss the music Jessie'd heard—letting Eileen use the club as a classroom to help give her an essential music education.

As Eileen got older, her MS progressed. In 2014, she suffered multiple seizures as a side effect of the medication she had been taking to help improve her walking. Because of the seizures, she lost her ability to fully use her legs. Up until that point, we were living at home independently, with me doing the cooking, shopping, and helping her in and out of the shower, and she was still able to move around, but only with the use of a walker. But now that she was no longer mobile, I really could no longer take care of her, and we had to think about a nursing home. It was at that time that my daughter Bonnie, a licensed psychologist, became aware of The Actors Fund Home, a multi-residential care facility in Englewood, New Jersey, that included skilled nursing home care, assisted living, sub-acute for short-term rehab, memory care, and an accredited dementia care unit, which was in walking distance from our home. So on the last weekend of August in 2014, Eileen moved into the nursing home at the AFH, which would now become her new permanent home. I began to visit every day from noon to eight, usually leaving a half hour after *Jeopardy* ended, right before she would go to bed. This continued every day for a year and a half until I had an opportunity to move into the assisted living facility of the complex in order to be closer to her. Now we watch *Jeopardy* together in her room every weeknight, and when she's ready to go to sleep, I take an elevator to another part of the building to my room.

Music has always meant so much to me. Whether it was rock and roll or jazz or wherever it took me, it always added something to my life that made living more enjoyable. And it's always meant so much to Eileen. So when we met, it was like two perfect pieces fitting together—even though we listen to music differently. Eileen listens like a musician, and I listen like a fan. Throughout our married life, I have always teased her about having the "best ears" I've ever come across. In fact, on one of her birthdays, as a gag, I tried to get her ears insured for the day from Lloyd's of London, but they were not amused. For my part, a wonderful part of owning The Bottom Line has been sharing every day of it with her. At the AFH, we still listen to music every day—and on her nightstand right next to her bed is that framed and signed picture from Terry Gibbs.

When all is said and done, I was able to make a living doing something that I loved and would have paid someone to let me do. My passion since I was a kid was to share music that I loved with others, and not only was I able to do it, but I did it with the two people that I loved. What could be better than that? My dream came true.

ACKNOWLEDGMENTS

Our sincerest thanks to all those who were gracious enough to take the time to talk about the intersections of The Bottom Line and their lives and careers: Sean Altman, Mike Appel, Richard Barone, Randy Brecker, David Bromberg, Betty Buckley, Artie Butler, Rosanne Cash, Patrick Clifford, Andy Cohen, Janet Coleman, Yolanda Cuomo, Dan Daley, Clive Davis, Devon Dicker, Karla DeVito, Donna Diken, Rick Dobbis, Lorraine Rebidas Duryea, Sam Ellis, Dennis Elsas, Helen (Hindy) Finkel, David Finkle, Marty Fogel, David Forman, Wayne Forte, Terry Gabbis, Julie Gold, Larry Gooberman, Scott Gordon, Meg Griffin, Paul Guzzone, Susan Haskins-Doloff, Ula Hedwig, Carolyn Hester, John Hiatt, Bob Iozzia, Judy Jacksina, Bobby Jay, David Johansen, Danny Kapilian, Lenny Kaye, Howard Kaylan, Carol Klenfner, Al Kooper, Jon Landau, Christine Lavin, Jack Leitenberg, Mimi Lieber, Darlene Love, Alan "Riley" Luzinski, Jude Lyons, Steve Martin, Ira Mayer, Ann McDermott, Roger McGuinn, Sam McKeith, Buddy Miller, Melanie Mintz, Budd Mishkin, Richard Neer, Ron Olesko, Matilda Parente, Fritz Postlewaite, Bonnie Raitt, Steve Rosenblum, Suzzy Roche, Terre Roche, Sonny Rollins, Bill Scheft, John Scher, Bobby Score, Paul Shaffer, Susan Decreny Siering, Marc Silag, Michael Simmons, Winston Simone, Bruce Springsteen, Jeanne Stahlman, Joe Stefko, David Vanderheyden, Suzanne Vega, Floyd Vivino, Jimmy Vivino, Loudon Wainwright, Max Weinberg, Lenny White, Russell Wolinsky, Stevie Van Zandt, Jessica Weitz, and "Weird" Al Yankovic.

Thanks as well to these additional people who volunteered to share their memories: Pam Cherico, Lynne Taylor Corbet, Michael Eidman, Annie Golden, Marsha Garelick, Nick and Sherri Greco, David Hirsch, Sharon Jochimsen, Steve Jordan, Lenny Kalikow, Paul Kowal, Lynette Kral, Barbara Krinitz, Sue Leventhal, Ken Levitan, Larry Lieberman, Lyle Lovett, Linda Jean Maier, Rhonda Markowitz, Elizabeth Marsden, Rod Marsden, Pat Mazzucca, Marcella Moran, Holly Near, Tracey Nieporent, Ricky Orbach, Tom Paxton, John Platt, Doug Riecken, Vin Scelsa, Jane Siberry, Lauren Stitch, George Szarmach, Jerry Treacy, and Cheryl Wheeler.

Additional thanks also to those who in a variety of ways helped make this book a reality: Deborah Aiges, Gregg Bendian, Greta Boghdasarian, Mariela Bradford, Cathy Brighenti, Jeff Calhoun, Dana Cardali, Anthony DeCurtis, Dave Goldberg, Diana Guthey, Mara Hennessey, Terri Hinte, Danny Kahn, Susan Monosso Kooper, Marilyn Laverty, Mark Lesly, Jay Levey, Lew Linet, Tammy Logan, Camilla McGuinn, Eileen Millan, Olivia Mayo, Camilla McGuinn, Ali Oscar, Carla Parisi, Karla Rice, Ebet Roberts, Neal Shulman, Saul Singer, Barry Skolnick, Mark Spector, Walter Weintz, and Kathi Whitley.

From Allan Pepper: Thanks to those people that always believed that there was a second act: Lise Avery, Gregg Bendian, Andy Breslin, Lori Cheatle, Michael Eidman, Tom Fontana, Ron Fierstein, Bob Frank, Nick Grillo, Don Duggan, Marty Herman, Lenny Kalikow, Steve Leeds, Julie Lokin, Eric Overmeyer, Don Scardino, Rob Thompson, and Jessica Weitz.

To friends we lost along the way: In Memoriam: Richard Belzer, Marvin Bernstein, David Blume, Paul Colby, Lynne Taylor Corbert, "Banjo Jim" Croce, John Curtin, Pattie Darcy, Bruce DeForeest, Art D'Lugoff, Margaret Dorn, Pete Fornatale, "Futz," John Geier, John Garcia Gensel, Bill Graham, Jack Hardy, John "the Chef" Hargrove, Linda Jacobs, David Johansen, Sharon Jochimson, Richard Joseph, Jack Leitenberg, Teak Lewis, Neil "Shecky" Lifton, Hank Medress, Chuck Nanry, Joe Newman, Gladys Oderman, Steve Paul, Mike Porco, Fritz Postelwait, "Big George" Roberson, Maggie Roche, Mike Rosa, Steve Rosenblum, Freddie Scelsa, Rose Singer, Michael Snadowsky, Michelle Snadowsky, Stanley Snadowsky, and Mark Volman.

Special thanks to Tony DiGiovanni, there from day one, who loves my children as if they were his own and always had my back. He was as much a part of The Bottom Line as the acts that graced the stage.

To Phil Kurnit, whose considerable legal skills and Talmudic wisdom are only exceed by his extraordinary humanity.

To Melanie Mintz: If you hadn't fallen in love with Shirley, Tina, Ronnie, and Darlene, all of our lives might have been different. Who would have thought forty years later, after that first meeting, we'd still be collaborating on projects, and you'd still be showing me the way to figure it out.

To Leslie and Daria Snadowsky: To me, your dad is only gone physically. He is with me every day in memories that I cherish. I hope this book has some stories about your dad that you've not heard, and they will be added to your own stories about how special he was.

To Cynthia Sesso, the administrator of the Raymond Ross Archive: Ray spent a lifetime documenting the jazz community and during our long friendship, gave me many of his photos, some of which have been included in this book, thanks to Cynthia's generous consent.

To our agent, Anne Devlin, of the Max Gartenberg Literary Agency: Thank you for always being a mensch and making this whole process easy when, clearly, it's not.

To our original editor John Cerullo, who saw what this book could be long before anyone else. To editor Christopher Chappell, as well as Bloomsbury/Backbeat Books assistant editors Barbara Claire and Emily Burr: Your responses to questions that were vexing helped make life less stressful in an often-mysterious process.

To a rare group of friends who have become family: Ann Fleisher, Bobby and Cynthia Jeffers, Lisa Kerbaugh, Jackie Nanry, Amy and Ali Saperstein, Nitza Shamah, and Gerry and Laraine Whitcomb. And gratitude to our loving family, especially Eileen's sister Cindy and her brother Ronnie, as well as their spouses, Paul and Rose, and their children Heather, David, Michael, and Sharon.

Special thanks to Jordan Strohl, Executive Director of the Actors Fund Home. There is no way to capture in a few sentences how grateful I am to Jordan for the excellent care that Eileen and I have received at The Actors Fund Home. Jordan is the rare executive who will never say no if he can figure out how to say yes! Thanks as well to Annmarie DeFeis Lisa, administrative manager of The Actors Fund Home. From the first day I walked into her office her support and assistance has been invaluable. I am so thankful for her, "no problem," response to any request that I made. And to nurse Lisa Kerbaugh, who will always be Eileen's Lisala.

To my children Gordon, Stacey, Bonnie, and Jessie: You are everything in my life I'm most proud of. From the day each of you was born, you have enriched the lives of your mother and me. And now, with the presence of our four grandchildren, Owen, Samantha (Sammi), Elaina, and Lyla, along with the addition of our sons-in-law Aaron, Mark, and Carlos, we have been doubly blessed.

There were many people who contributed to what ultimately became The Bottom Line, but none more consequential than Stanley Snadowsky, Eileen Pepper, and Marvin Bernstein. Without them, it never would have turned out quite the way it did.

From Billy Altman: No journey such as the one taken to write this book with Allan would have been accomplished without the faith and support of my many friends in the various circles I continue to waywardly travel in. Thanks to my faculty colleagues at the School of Visual Arts, including Humanities & Sciences Department Chair Kyoko Miyabe and SVA president David Rhodes, who respectively endorsed and approved my request for a sabbatical to work on this project. Thanks as well to the SVA-related gang at Molly's Shebeen, who kept me supplied in Black & Tans, onion rings, and good cheer throughout the process, including Louis Phillips, Carl Adams, Zoran Amar, Jeff Beardsley, Mac Bica, Mark Curley, Tom Gorrell, Peter Kloehn, Richard Wilde, and our dear departed pal Joe

Karoly. Many thanks also to the motley "Out to Lunch" baseball crew at Luke's: Marty Appel, Rich Goldstein, Tony Guida, Steve Jacobson, Dave Kaplan, Lee Lowenfish, Jerry Rosenthal, Brian Silverman, George Vecsey, Willie Weinbaum, and our group denmother, Ernestine Miller.

Special thanks to Richard Lally, Lee Lowenfish, Ken Shuldman, Woody Graber, Gary Bridges, Bruce Gordon, Scurvy B., Eileen Hecht, Marilyn Altman, and Jeff Nesin, for being there for me, always.

To my cherished wife Joyce, whose accomplished skills as a professional copy editor continue to make my sentences read far better than how they start out, and to our beloved daughter Emma, who loyally continues to indulge in my endless war stories from a lifetime of elbow-rubbing inside the twin universes of music and sports.

And, finally and fittingly, thanks to all my fellow journalists and rockcrit scribes who night after night crammed alongside me into the designated "guest list" back tables at The Bottom Line, and to the many record company publicists, booking agents, and artist managers who throughout the club's thirty year existence put us—and put up with us—there. Two free drinks, an order of french fries, great company, and great music: We really did just about live on it back then, didn't we?